Behind the old sea wall at Kirra on the Gold Coast
— taken on our first trip to Queenland.
From the left, Midget in Lee's Twin Spinner Ford
with a girl, Les Mulray sitting on the bonnet, me
looking cool, Lee with another local girl, someone
I don't know, Rodney Sumpter clowning around,
Willy Overton and Mick Dooley.

Nat's Nat and that's that

an autobiography

NYMBOIDA PRESS

Foreword

*A*LONG WITH MY YOUNGER BROTHERS *and a few enthusiastic mates who loved to bodysurf, I would often frequent the breaks at North Narrabeen, one of Sydney's premier surfing beaches through the seventies and eighties, and in the course of snatching the odd lefthander, especially when there was a sizable swell, enjoy a "dolphin's eyeview" of the best surfers of the era.*

Some were well known figures, professionals, who often graced the pages of surfing magazines. Others were "locals", part time surfers who knew their break and how to get the best out of it. But when Nat Young paddled onto a wave something quite special happened. For Nat's surfing was a thing of beauty to watch and mostly everyone did watch, whether from water or land. Somehow he combined grace and power with an unerring ability to get the best out of the wave that marks out the artist from the pedestrian.

Nat Young it seems, was born to surf.

Blessed by huge stretches of surfable coastline and temperate weather, Australia has produced a string of outstanding surfers and often led the world in surfboard design and related surfing paraphernalia: clothes, wetsuits and the like. For since Duke Kahanamoku rode a 9/10 foot plank of timber on the gentle swell of a Sydney beach called Freshwater in 1915, here, "Downunder", we have embraced, with an almost religious fervour, the surfing experience. Amongst the many champions and legendary watermen and women this country has produced, Nat Young, along with a handful of others like Tom Carroll and Mark Richards, stands out.

This is partly due to the fact that not only has Nat been on the victory dais many times and thus stamped himself into the history of competitive surfing, but also because his entire life so far can be read as a giant surf adventure, a fantastic tale of all that might come upon someone who takes the ideal of surfing and by attempting to live from the ideal, turns it into a lifetime's experience.

This autobiography reveals Nat Young to be a man of many parts:

This photo of Peter Garrett and me was taken by the talented Gerald Jenkins for Australian Style magazine.

teenage world champion, rebel, film maker, author, board designer, businessman, drop-out and champion again. Nat has a remarkable story to tell. From hell-raiser to spokesperson for a generation, in jail, almost in Parliament and always carving one kind of face of nature – be it snow, air or water – Nat, as befits most people who excel in their chosen field, always went for it. His is the quixotic life of a professional surfer who somehow manages to marry his love and knowledge of surfing with making a living at the same time, whilst continuing apace a relentless quest for new thrills and experiences.

Inevitably this frenetic activity takes its toll and despite a remarkable renaissance period when he returns to the graceful and vintage execution of surfing on the longer Malibu board, and once again achieves the status of world champion, there is a strand within this yarn of a man facing down his mortality which gives this book an unexpected depth and belies the public image of the author.

Far more than a recital of competitions won and lost, or waves at exotic locations conquered, Nat has chosen the honourable route of telling his story. He bares all. And in doing so reveals his all too human frailties and imperfections that are a part of every one of us as well. It is probably a good thing he waited till now to write his story, for I doubt whether a younger man would be so candid. Perhaps wisdom and honesty are partners of a kind and the unexpected climax which concludes the story provides a striking contrast to the "action man" career that won Nat great renown.

As befits a surfer's memoir, this is also a reflection of the hedonistic elements that are typical of the surfing lifestyle, and yet there is more to these reflections than raucous tales of single minded excess. It is true that surfers often show an almost contemptuous disregard for the opinions and aspirations of others. This testing of muscle, character and fibreglass against nature is an individual's pursuit of the ultimate experience in the blue cathedral, the perfect wave, and social obligations outside the tribe are often ignored.

This can even be the case where the marine environment that surfers inhabit and profess to respect is concerned. There's always a lot of talk about taking care of Mother Ocean, but until recently, little collective action. Many surfers have witnessed the deterioration and privatisation of the coastline over the past decade, and despite the best efforts of a small number of individuals and the establishment of organisations like the Surfrider Foundation, the assault on the world's coasts continues without any mass checking of this insanity by the surfing community.

It is to Nat Young's great credit that he saw fit to take a stand and speak out and campaign on matters of coastal protection, to the extent of running for political office. And it is testimony to his plain speaking and the high regard that many of his neighbours held him in, that he nearly won a seat in the New South Wales Parliament; and probably would have if he had been prepared to put in the long hours gladhanding and smooching through the electorate which is the typical fare of most politicians. But Nat was true to form, he said his bit and went surfing instead!

The crazed and sometimes erratic Nat Young existence, it seems to me, has been anchored, not only by his own prodigious talent and self confidence, but also by the enduring support he has received from the significant women in his life. Here is a wild man who would long ago have fallen hard and not easily risen were it not for the presence of his Mum, as he took on the world as a grommet with a mission, and later on, wife Ti, who was always there to pick him up after another spectacular wipeout on land or water in any part of the globe he happened to come unstuck. Nat's free acknowledgement of this fact leads me to hope the role of women might be increasingly valued in the surfing community and in our world!

This candid reflection will delight those who have followed Nat Young's career from gangly meteoric surfer to respected elder statesman of the tribe. He has told his story well so that we might share the highs and lows, victories and defeats and the coming of age of one of surfing's greats. Nat's accomplishments are many, but the most memorable so far is that he has chosen to share his story with everyone. So read on...you won't be disappointed.

Peter Garrett
Sydney, 1998
International Year of the Sea

Contents

The first surfing photo ever taken of me. I'm
riding the nose on the same board as in the shot
below.

That's me looking as brown as a berry with my new
balsa board with Pixie Mouse painted on the front.
My next door neighbour Kenno on my right hand
side. The late Ron Perrott took the shot at the
first Malibu surfing contest at Narrabeen in 1960.

1

Henry and me with the Grunter

I HONESTLY CAN'T REMEMBER the first time I rode a wave. I suppose it was while playing in the shore break and I must have come to it so gradually that the memory has faded. It was probably inevitable that I'd learn to surf, for the ocean was my backyard. It was where I played every day from one season to the next and riding waves was a part of it. I'm sure it's the same for anyone who grows up in close proximity to the sea – it becomes your home, your mother, the very essence of life. The Hawaiians have an expression for it: Piliwai He'e Nalu. I do know that I rode my first real wave on a Surfoplane, an ancestor of today's boogie board. About a metre long, the "surfo" was like a small air mattress made of tough, thick rubber reinforced by elongated ridges and with handles at the front. Together with the "igloo" – a sort of beach umbrella-come-windbreak that looked like its namesake in cross-section and protected against both the wind and the fearsome Australian sun – they were an institution on Sydney's beaches in the late 1950s and were available for hire at every beach.

At Collaroy beach, I got to use the surfos for nothing by look-ing after the owner's interests when he took a break. I still get a real tingle when I remember what it was like to take off on a big close-out dumper; kicking and paddling into it, rushing straight down the face of the wave and skating way out in front before being engulfed by tonnes of white water, desperately fighting to keep my grip on the handles till I was washed up on the sand, grin-ning and ready to go again. The surfo rental stand was about 6 metres from the Collaroy Surf Life Saving Club, right beside the steps leading down to the beach.

When I think about it, it isn't surprising that I ended up hanging around the club in awe of the big, strong lifesavers. This was the heyday of the Surf Life Saving Clubs, coasting along as they were on the tight camaraderie formed during the Second World War. The clubs were the meeting places for many of the "Old Mates" and the centres for their activities, from patrol duty to getting pissed on

Sunday afternoons. The latter was a regular occurrence at Collaroy and I'm sure it was a ritual repeated at thousands of surf clubs all over Australia. For a youngster, hanging around the club could be a bit trying at times, especially on Sunday afternoons when it was the custom to put on a keg of beer for the older "Clubbies". They'd get stuck into it with gay abandon and, naturally, some would wind up pissed as newts. The most hilarious Sunday-afternoon act I ever witnessed involved a character known as "Legs" Lane and the bus belonging to a local church group who held regular Sunday School picnics on the beach. One Sunday Legs decided he'd take the bus for a bit of a spin and my mates and I craned over the edge of the Surf Club roof while Legs ambled over and climbed into the driver's seat. Firing up the engine, he roared around all the picnickers, out of the park and on up the hill towards Long Reef. We thought that it was a really funny stunt, but for the most part the younger members like myself bore the brunt of the Clubbies' sadistic revelry.

There was one particular activity that kept me away from the club on more than one weekend. The old boys often liked to engage in some activity while they were lowering the level in the keg, and digging a deep hole was a good thing to do – it got up a bit of a sweat and you could always pass the shovel to someone else while you had a breather. When the hole was 2 metres-or-so deep, they'd round up all us kids and throw us in. To any casual observer it would've looked really bizarre – distraught kids trying to avoid the odd piss or chunder that rained down on them as they scrambled to climb on one another's shoulders to get out. Sometimes it was a water hose at full pressure; all quite inventive and funny as long as you weren't one of the ones in the hole.

* * * * * * *

I was born on November 14th, 1947, in downtown Sydney, not long before my family – my parents Greta and Harold, and my two older sisters, Pam and June – moved from Auburn, in the heart of the sprawling, landlocked western suburbs of Sydney, to Collaroy, a beachside suburb on the Northern Peninsula. Mum often told me stories of her life in Auburn; of the semi-detached weatherboard duplex with the cake shop out the front. She ran that shop for years, with the help of one of my Aunties, baking the cakes in the house. Then they turned the cake shop into a corner store and with even longer hours of hard work managed to get ahead, in spite of the hardships associated with finding direction after the war.

The house we moved to in Collaroy – where my younger brother Chris was born – was called "Westward Ho" and was once a doctor's

Going on holidays in 1949 in our Willys Overlander.
From the left, that's me holding hands with my Mum,
eldest sister Pam, cousin Barry, Aunty Edna, Dad,
sister June in the tartan suit she made herself
and Trixy our dog. Uncle Doug took the shot.

home. All the big houses seemed to have names in those days; I'm not sure if it was the fashion or because the owners took such pride in their accomplishments. My earliest memory is of lying in my pram beneath the big palm tree that grew in our garden, crying as I was divebombed by an aggressive maggie. My next is of myself screaming with delight as Grandpop lifted his legs to tease me as I came tearing along the cement path on my dinky, trying to run over his toes. Two of Westward Ho's distinguishing features were the huge gable facing Pittwater Road and a profusion of massive hydrangeas growing on the Stuart Street boundary. However, the most impressive thing about the house was its location – right on the beach. Just over the back fence, literally, were golden sands and the Pacific Ocean, putting me in a perfect position to become a surfer.

In those days, Pittwater Road was the main route to the northern beaches from the city. It had only one traffic lane in each direction and a tramline that ended at the Narrabeen Terminus, about 3 kilometres north of Collaroy. As a suburb, Collaroy was well-positioned in relation to Sydney, not being too far out of the city. Growing up in that environment was real *Alice in Wonderland* stuff. The sand and waves right in the backyard made an incredible kids' playground and we could play act at anything we dreamed up. From my front door, the local infants school was 800 metres north and across the road from it was the primary school. The same distance to the south were the Collaroy shopping centre, the park at the beach, and the infamous Collaroy Surf Life Saving Club.

Looking back, it was probably lucky that the family moved to Collaroy a few years before the rivalry between the "Surfies" and "Rockers" – or "Westies" as we called them at our beach, with all the ugly connotations the name carries – had erupted into all-out war. Strictly speaking, I suppose someone bent on testing my loyalty could've called me a Westie too. I recall Mum once warning me to come straight home after I'd finished surfing as it'd been reported in the Friday evening newspaper that the Rockers were going to be swarming all over the northern beaches that weekend, looking to have a final punch-up with the Surfies.

Buying Westward Ho put my parents under tremendous financial strain; making the payments on such a grand house was really difficult for Harold and Greta Young as they had only one income at the time. To make it all possible we always had boarders living with us – I never kept the same bedroom for too long – and in 1962 Mum decided to open a kindergarten in one end of the house. Harold did the renovations and the kindy was a success right from the word go. The idea for Collaroy Kindergarten was all Mum's and was a real stroke of brilliance. Coming from such a humble background and being able to live in style right on the beach was a definite step up for Mum and Dad. They were now a typical two-income, hard working Aussie couple with bright prospects for the future.

When we first moved to Collaroy, Dad started a business called Collaroy Taxi Truck. I can remember standing on the Stuart Street side of the house – together with all our family and neighbours – watching in stunned silence as Harold drove his pride and joy into our driveway. He dearly loved that vehicle, his first brand-new truck; I suppose he viewed it as a symbol of his success. I've never forgotten that ute; a gleaming, bright-red, 1950 single-spinner Ford. It really was a beauty. I never did know much about Dad's taxi truck business other than that he had a contract to deliver *The Sun* newspaper to the northern beaches. Every afternoon he'd line up with other trucks at the newspaper's office in the heart of Sydney to load the bundles of papers for the run from Manly to Palm Beach. Whenever I was allowed, I'd sit up in the front seat and accompany him on the run. This was right at the beginning of the television era and afternoon newspapers were still the most important source of information. People would be waiting at some places along the run, anxious to find out what was going on in the world – and my Dad had the goods.

It seems to me that Sydneysiders today aren't too different from the Sydneysiders back then; they still pour down to the sea on weekends to enjoy the beach and have a picnic. For me as a kid, the biggest bonus brought by this influx of visitors was the fact that they left soft drink and milk bottles behind them when they departed. All bottles had a refundable deposit in those days and it was quite substantial, even by today's standards. A big soft drink bottle was worth threepence and a milk bottle sixpence, with a purchasing power of about 20c and 40c today, but we didn't scavenge many milk bottles, as people didn't drink much milk at the beach. At our beach it was a fight to see who would get to the bottles first. Competition was fierce among the local kids and the sight of my little brother Chris suspended over the rim of a 44-gallon garbage drum, legs and bum in the air and teetering on the verge of falling in is another childhood memory I'll never forget. My brother and I picked up bottles all the time, in the afternoons after school and at weekends. The redeemed deposits financed an incredible collection of Matchbox toys – small metal replicas of buses, trucks and cars. I really wish I still had them for my kids to play with today, for unlike plastic they were virtually indestructible. Sadly, my collection is long gone. When, much later, I asked Greta about them, she said she'd given them to some Christian charity.

Slowly the fascination with collecting bottles began to wane;

My best friend from kindergarten to high school was the late Winston, Henry, Verkroost. All our old mates had to dig pretty deep to find a pic of Henry surfing. Kenno took this shot of him stalling his board on a clean little right behind Westward Ho in Collaroy.

perhaps the return on milk bottles took a dive or perhaps we were just getting older. Collaroy Beach had a picture theatre which was a ready source of entertainment and sometimes the cash from the bottles would be used to buy a ticket to "the pictures". No one feature film of the period sticks in my mind, but the weekly serials kept me coming back every Saturday afternoon for years. One, in particular, seemed to be all about "goodies" and "baddies" waving swords and guns while chasing each other around on horseback. Each episode inspired a mob of us to go to the bamboo patch near the local pool where we'd break off bamboo "swords" and fight each other all the way home along Collaroy Beach.

Lots of monumental things happened around or near that sea-fed swimming pool where the bamboo grew in such profusion. It was, for instance, the first place I ever watched two people have sex. And the pool itself was where I was forced to learn to swim. A friend and I were wrestling on the wall that separated the shallow kids' pool from the "big people's" pool when my mate got the better of me and threw me into deep water. My choice being sink or swim, I swam back to the wall, where I sat for a while thinking about what had just happened: I'd just swum. It wasn't that hard and I'd survived. In retrospect, I suppose I survived because I'd imitated what I saw other people doing and the idea of sinking didn't appeal to me. Either way, from that moment on, I could swim, and a whole new world opened up to me, although being self-taught, my swimming style remains rough to this day. The transition from the calm waters of the pool to the open sea and its waves came perfectly naturally to me.

Right beside the pool, on the rocks that made up the point, were lots of tidal pools where thousands of small fish and sea creatures hid from small boys like me. I can't remember if somebody showed me how to do it or if I stumbled upon it myself but I learnt to corner an octopus, grab it, and when I felt its tentacles wrap around my arms and the pressure of its suckers on my flesh, quickly stick my finger into its body, turning the poor creature inside out before dropping it into the bucket that held all the other treasures I'd collected.

I think it was through these collecting trips that I became close to Winston Verkroost, alias "Henry". He'd got his nickname the same way I'd got mine; lumbered with it by some wag at Collaroy Surf Life Saving Club. The wag reckoned the little kid with the snow-white crew cut looked like Henry, a popular cartoon character of the time. Henry was my best friend, a funny little Netherlands-born kid of my own age. We'd been in the same class at school from the time his mum and dad had set up house above a block of shops between Collaroy and Long Reef after emigrating to Australia in 1950, and we were inseparable. We even fell in love with the same teacher, Miss

White, and from our seats in the front row we'd watch her every move. One day she slipped her shoe off to wiggle her toes, so I reached under the desk with my foot and slid the shoe back to Henry who picked it up and put it under his desk. When Miss White went to get up and couldn't find her shoe, she looked right at us, knowing who'd taken it but not wanting to lose face with the rest of the class. We just sat there, smiling, aware of her discomfort but thinking that this was the only way we could let her know how much we cared. When the other kids left the classroom, the shoe miraculously reappeared, right there by her foot.

We cared enough to take in everything she did and said and during recess one day as the little bottles of milk were handed out – milk that had often been sitting in the sun for hours – she invited us to go to Queenscliff beach with her on the following Saturday. We were stoked! We both got the okay from our Mums on the strength that we'd be with our teacher and on the day took the bus from Collaroy. Miss White met us and we walked to her house. We didn't go inside but said hello to her mother before heading off down the hill to the beach. Our teacher wore a white one-piece costume with a full bra cup and swung a brightly coloured cotton towel – she looked fantastic and prattled on about what a beautiful beach Queenscliff was and what a great day we were going to have together. We frolicked in the shore break and dug a big hole that filled with water every time a wave came; things were going just fine and then a big lifesaver blocked out the sun and Miss White introduced him as her boyfriend. Our bubble burst. I saw the look on Henry's face and can imagine what mine must've looked like; I was devastated. Our Miss White had someone else; we weren't as special to her as she was to us, but we kept our cool. This was the first major experience shared by Henry and me, but it definitely wasn't to be our last.

During our first year in Narrabeen High School, Henry and I were again together in the front row. Our attentiveness varied depending on teacher and subject. To put it simply, we found school boring and more often than not would sneak out through the back of the playground, through the reedy marsh, then catch the bus or hitchhike down to Collaroy and our boards stashed at the Surf Club. This was a pretty standard drill and we had it down to a science, waiting until we'd been marked as present on the roll and then be gone. But one particular day was a total disaster. We'd begun hitching along Pittwater Road and almost immediately a car pulled up. We ran up the road to where it had stopped and Henry got there first, peering through the passenger-side window and leaping in. At that instant it must have hit him and he turned to look at me just getting comfy in the back seat – the driver was Mr Ashford, our English teacher, and we were supposed to be in his class that morning. We were trapped; caught red-handed wagging it. He flew off the handle for a minute then turned the car around and headed back to school. He finished his rave by telling us what a fortuitous thing it was that he had a dental appointment in Narrabeen and that he was sure the headmaster was going to love to get his hands on two little truants. He marched us directly up to the headmaster's office and Mr Burke promptly reached for his cane. We didn't get a word in but there was really nothing to say; it was an open-and-shut case.

The cane hurt. Henry went first and bravely stood there while Old Burkey let loose with six of the best, three on each hand, making them bright red and swollen. Then it was my turn. Mr Burke flexed his cane and told me what a disgrace I was, how disappointed he was and that he'd inform both our parents. I stood there and took it – six of the best, just like Henry – but all the while I was thinking about how great it would be to turn the tables like the new kid had on our music teacher, Mr Duffy. Duffy had been about to administer justice to the big Yugoslav-born student but as he swung the cane down for the first strike, the new kid grabbed it and turned on the teacher, beating him around the body until he ran screaming from the classroom. I loved the thought but knew I could never do it. That afternoon, Henry and I talked about our situation. We decided to get much more creative with our excuses for not going to school, perfect the forgery of our parents' signatures and make sure we never got caught again – and we didn't.

* * * * * * *

Hanging around the Surf Club with Henry and a few other kids was never boring. We were called "gofers", because we were constantly being told to "go for this and go for that". Basically what we did was go to the shop for the big blokes while they were on beach patrol or too busy – or too lazy – to go themselves. Most times you were rewarded with a drink or something to eat but the real bonus was in getting to hang around close to your heroes and do some close-up perving on their voluptuous girlfriends. Lying in the warm sand ogling the super-sexy older girls while listening to a tune called *Bim Bom Bay* on the transistor radio is a memory that'll stay forever etched on my mind. One of these girls was called Suzy – and she had the biggest, most beautiful breasts on the beach, the white bra-top bikini she wore lifting and separating them and making them stand out like a couple of giant headlights. We'd all lie around Suzy in a semi-circle, listening to the radio and watching her tits as she rolled over to sun each side of herself in turn. There's no doubt she knew what we were doing but she never sent any of us packing and obviously enjoyed the adulation.

Besides being called gofers we were also referred to as "gremlins" or "gremmies". The origins of this word for an imp or goblin are unknown, but it was widely used by Second World War aircrews who blamed them for mechanical problems that couldn't otherwise be explained. I can see the link, and I think Peter Clare was the first to call me a gremmy. Apart from the crew at Collaroy, he was the first person I met who rode a surfboard. He was also a member of the Long Reef Surf Life Saving Club but wasn't really a "Clubbie" by my standards. Peter was smooth and suave and talked a bit like an American, or perhaps his accent was just a bit more posh than the average Collaroy Clubbie. He only came to our beach when the waves were big and the wind was from the south. On his orange board, with his girlfriend beside him riding one identical, he was graceful to watch. Robyn Proctor was his girlfriend's name and she seemed to be Peter's constant companion.

I recall going down to Collaroy Point on one sparkling morning to watch Robyn, Peter and my next-door neighbour, Robert "Kenno" Kennerson, put on such a dazzling display it made me green with envy and confirmed my future direction. Kenno was four years older than me and in lots of ways he was my big brother. I remember the smell of varnish as he re-coated his sixteen-foot, hollow "toothpick". Sitting up on a drum in his backyard shed while he diligently sanded the board back and built up the coats was a good thing to do, but having a go on his board never really crossed my mind. Those old boards were so big and heavy, Kenno could only just carry his to the water where he would leap on and, kneeling, paddle off into the distance, down to Collaroy and back again. Mum always gave me a call when, from the kitchen window, she could see Kenno sitting out the back waiting for a wave to come in on, usually the first wave of a set. Kneeling, he'd position himself so carefully, it had to be just right, then paddle as fast as possible until the wave was just about to break. Then, in a manoeuvre called "broaching", he'd slide over a side rail and spin the board sideways, going over with the curl. Once at the bottom of the breaking wave with foam crashing all around, he'd straighten the board back up and, standing straight and tall in the turmoil of white water, ride in to the beach. It was so dramatic, my brother and I would scream and clap every time he made it and my Mum always had her heart in her mouth. Kenno would sometimes cop some savage wipeouts and perhaps this was why I had no desire to ride a toothpick – but when he got his first solid-balsa Malibu board, it was a completely

RON PERROTT

Looking down Alexander Street into the heart of Collaroy. That's the infamous surf club right on the beach with the fabled break called The Kick behind the pool. It's a big south swell and White Rock is breaking on the northern side of Long Reef.

different story. Watching Kenno cruise across the green face of a wave looked such fun that my mind was made up. I really wanted a go on his Malibu.

Collaroy Surf Club always had a strong contingent of boardmen and two of the older guys, Pat Boyle and George Reid, were the standouts. They both had real guts and tonnes of talent. When I was just getting into surfing, Henry and I pedalled our pushies up to Long Reef and watched George and Pat ride the Second Bombora, a big-wave location more than a kilometre out to sea. Watching Pat and George ride five 10-foot waves in an hour and a half was an incredible spectacle which Henry, myself and the occupants of ten parked cars were lucky enough to witness. It was too far out to see who was actually on which wave, but the display was so awesome that it put George and Pat up there as my all-time idols.

Right around this time, I was really working on Mum to help me get a board. She kept saying I should continue my paper run, save my pocket money and we'd see what would happen on my tenth birthday. The only person my age who rode a surfboard at Collaroy at the time was a kid named Tony "Trapper" Raper. He was a really nice boy who went to a private school and came from the posher end of Collaroy, up near Long Reef. His mother was very approachable so Greta called her to get some advice on how to go about buying a Malibu board. I've never been sure if it was due to Trapper's mum or Kenno, but it all came together on the 14th of November 1957. Pat Boyle was getting a new "sausage" board from Bill Clymer and I became the proud owner of his old Mal. It was 10-foot 6-inches long, quite narrow in the bow and made of solid balsa wood with three redwood stringers spaced evenly across its width. For me, looking into the grain of the balsa, highlighted by its coating of fibreglass-reinforced resin, was like entering another world. The colour of the balsa was like sand or golden wheat, contrasting with the deep burgundy of the redwood – it was so beautiful. An accomplished local surfer, an older guy named Lionel Bray, delivered the board to my house. I've no idea how he got involved. He was the local chemist, a quiet studious type who, though classed as a Clubbie, was more of a surfer who just happened to be in the Surf Club.

From the minute I got the board, I went surfing behind our house, only coming in for food and drink. Sometimes Kenno would come out with me if the waves were better down our end of the beach than at Collaroy itself. I surfed everything in the shore break behind Westward Ho, come rain, hail or shine. For some reason the boys in our family seem to stay small in stature until they reach fourteen or fifteen, then they shoot up like weeds, growing up to 30 centimetres in a year – I've watched this in my own boys. I was really small at ten. I couldn't even carry my new board over the sand and used to hassle Dad to do it for me. In time, the fascination with riding the shore break behind our house began to wear a bit thin. By the end of that first summer the swells were starting to get consistently bigger and I couldn't get out the back on lots of occasions, and I was missing the close contact with Henry and all the other Collaroy gremlins who'd also taken up board riding that summer. Kenno advised me to build a board trolley, he had a fancy one with two pushbike wheels and a metal frame that was hitched behind the seat of his bike. He showed me how to take the two little wheels off an old pram, shorten the axle and nail it to a piece of "four-by-two" supporting two more pieces of wood wide enough to hold the board turned on its side. I'd jam the board in tight with old carpet and secure it across the top with a bit of inner tube. Within a few minutes I was off on my trusty old pushy with one hand to do the steering and the other holding the fin. The set-up worked well until I tried to cross the gutter around the carpark at Collaroy. The trolley's wheels were just too small and caught in the ditch. I was unable to do anything and the board was reefed right out of the trolley and dragged along the road for a good 6 metres.

It was a real mess, the balsa was poking through in several places and my world was absolutely shattered; sitting there in front of the chemist shop, I cried my eyes out. Lionel Bray came to my rescue, picking up my board and consoling me, then, after storing my pushie and board around the back of the shop, he drove me home. Lionel said for five shillings he'd fix my board by the following weekend so I used the time to modify my trolley. Next Saturday morning I met Lionel at the chemist shop to pay him and pick up the board. It was perfect, you could hardly see the repair and I spent all that day surfing at Collaroy and everything was sweet in my life again. All through that winter I transported my board, towing the trolley behind my pushie, between home and Collaroy Point and even over the hill to Long Reef on occasions. As the days grew longer and the summer patrol duties started again, I found my enthusiasm for the Surf Club fading. The first day I was rostered on, the waves in my backyard were fantastic. I just couldn't tear myself away from them and I never really went back to the Surf Club.

The two best things I got out of my years hanging around the Collaroy Surf Life Saving Club were the knowledge of how to save someone in difficulty in the ocean, and the nickname that's still with me. My balsa Bill Clymer board was called the "Queen Mary" even before I got her from Pat Boyle – she'd been his big-wave board. The real *Queen Mary* was supposedly the largest ship then afloat and the Clubbies all reckoned the board and I were totally out of proportion,

The winter of '62. I can tell it's winter, we are all wearing
our bear suits, which were really ex-flying suits from the
Air Force surplus store. From the left, Dennis Tenfoot
Anderson, Hans, Westie, Henry, Belly, me, Kenno and
Wally. You can see that Henry and I have the same
design on our boards. I think both these photographs
were taken on the same day at Long Reef.

saying I looked like a gnat on the end of the *Queen Mary*. Over time "The Gnat" became "Nat" and that, as they say, is that.

It wasn't long before I wanted a sausage board like everyone else had; the Queen Mary was no good for nose riding and too big and heavy for hot-dogging. I had a long talk with Mum and she talked to a friend of a friend of hers, a man named Grantham who lived at Warriewood. A cabinetmaker by trade, Mr Grantham had built the odd board under his house, more for the love of wood than anything else as he wasn't a surfer. We talked about what I wanted and he went to have a look at a few sausage boards, then agreed to make one for me in two months. That two months gave me time to save the £35 – worth nearly $600 today – for my new, hand-made board so I worked diligently at my paper run and odd jobs, continually hassling Greta to call Mr Grantham for progress reports.

One day Mum said Mr Grantham had agreed to let me go up to his house after school. I took Henry. Getting no response when we knocked on the front door, we followed the sound of work in progress to the garage, where we found Mr Grantham hard at it. Balsa shavings were knee deep all over the floor and he was standing over my new board with a bottle of what the label identified as hydrogen peroxide. After greetings were exchanged, I was told that it was all coming along fine. He'd managed to get some lighter balsa from a new shipment that the timber merchant, Arthur Milner, had brought in from Brazil and was just about to bleach it. He asked if I'd help while he cleaned up a bit. I was completely stoked! It was all furry, as shaped balsa wood is; a perfect 9-foot 4-inch sausage board, just like everyone else's down at Collaroy. Henry and I carefully carried it out into the yard and waited while the sunshine and peroxide did their thing, bleaching the balsa white as a sheet. A few weeks later my board was ready and I was off on a completely new adventure. In order to give it that personal touch, Kenno let me use his garden shed as a workshop and I painted a portrait of Pixie the mouse on the top front of the deck. Pixie, Dixie and Mr Jinks were my favourite cartoon characters at the time and I felt really comfortable having Pixie on board with me. I found I could turn quicker and nose ride longer with my new board and found it much more suited to the typical small beach break of Collaroy than the narrower and longer old Clymer.

Henry and I were as thick as thieves during this time, partly because we were in all the same classes at Narrabeen High School, but mostly because of our mutual love of surfing. In woodwork classes we carved miniature sausage boards and in art we painted them with the designs we wanted on our next boards. We made up elaborate colour schemes and passed them around the class for approval. We all wore desert boots, white jeans, white shirts with the obligatory school tie and were the coolest kids in first year – or so we reckoned. My only problem was my hair – I hated it. It was so curly and frizzy and impossible to keep neat and flat like everyone else's. I tried plastering it down with soap and combing it straight until the soap dried but it itched and the soap came out in little flakes if I ran my fingers through my hair. One day after school, Henry and I attempted to bleach my hair as white as his was, first using lemon juice then, the next day, hydrogen peroxide. Now I had a snow-white fuzz ball that looked even sillier than before.

About this time, Kenno and another older surfer named Wally, pooled their resources and bought an old Morris Cowley bread-delivery van. First they gave it a coat of royal-blue paint and then Dennis "Tenfoot" Anderson, the artist in our group, painted "Murphy the Surfie" in various poses all over it. Murphy became our role model; actually with his blond mop he looked a bit like Henry. We'd just seen the first American *Surfer* magazine with Murphy featuring in it and Tenfoot's painting made our new surf wagon absolutely king! Every weekend or on days when Kenno didn't have to go to work, we'd all arrive at his place before dawn and chip in for petrol money. Kenno was working for Scott Dillon Surfboards at that time and we all desperately wanted Dillon boards.

The use of blown foam for surfboards was in its infancy back then and it was lighter than balsa and a bit more "corky" in the water. Dillon's foamies were slightly more parallel in plan than most, but the best thing about them was that you could get them customised, all the way down to the colour of the pin-line around the design you were having on the deck. My new board was going to be a soft powder-blue on both top and bottom with an orangey arrowhead, pin-lined in white, covering the deck and pointing to the nose. Henry worked out a red-and-white design that was just as elaborate, and then we were off to Brookvale to put in our custom orders at Dillon's factory. Board factories were exciting places where anything could happen. We once saw a bloke working with acetone set himself on fire with a cigarette, while another time a mouse was cornered in the finish-coat room, caught and dropped into hot resin, immortalising him.

Within a few months all our crew had Dillons. The fibreglass mat he used was twenty or thirty ounces, as thick as a doormat, but we didn't care, we were only concerned with the colour. Everyone's board was a full-colour pigment and hatchet-shaped fins were 12 inches deep. Thanks to Kenno and Wally's van we were surfing all over the northern beaches, from Manly to Palm Beach, wherever the surf was best. It was in this way we came to know of the existence of other groups from other beaches and little did we realise that our sport was about to become the most fashionable thing a young person could be doing in 1963, helped along no doubt by the Beach Boys on the radio and Frankie Avalon and Annette Funicello in suggestive poses in the movies. Who could forget *Muscle Beach Party* and *Gidget?* Our gang had a great life at Collaroy; it seemed as though Huey the surf god always smiled on us, with great waves at our home beach or on the other side of the headland at Long Reef. Long Reef's bomboras – "bombies" as we affectionately called them – only worked when the wind was straight offshore, blowing from the northeast. This was the dominant wind during the six weeks of the Christmas holidays so we spent most of our time hanging out over there.

By now, girls were starting to figure in our surf program. Sex was, in fact, the main thing on our minds beside boards and waves. I remember well the first day we spied a prissy looking girl getting off the bus in Collaroy. Dressed in the dark-green uniform of a girls private school, she was plump in a nice, schoolgirlish kind of way and Henry, Westie, Belly and I all started to chat her up. It was common knowledge that Westie was the best-looking guy in our group – and the best talker. After about half an hour of sweet talk, Westie got her into the casualty room of the Collaroy surf club, then he came back and told Belly to wait a few minutes before coming to take over. Westie had strategically positioned the girl so that she was lying on her back with her head facing away from the youthful group of lechers and so was able to give the nod over her shoulder. As he slipped out, Belly slipped in, then Henry and I had our turn in the same manner.

As all the girls at our beach were very chaste, "The Grunter", as Westie called her, changed our whole perception of girls. The most any of us had managed up till then was a tongue kiss or rare feel of a girlfriend's breast. The Grunter was really into group sex and we all greeted her with open flies every time we saw her getting off her school bus. This began happening a few times a week on a regular basis, then every weekend when all the crew at Collaroy would join the queue. The scene was starting to get a bit out of hand, the line getting longer and longer as friends and acquaintances from other beaches joined in. The Grunter was becoming famous – apparently our local football club had her grace one of their victory parties – and groups from other beaches followed her home, picking her up just down the road from her house on the Collaroy Plateau. Other girls from our beach started to get a bit jealous of all the attention The Grunter was getting and some decided it was better to join her if they couldn't beat her. The competition was terrific. "Brenda the

Bender", "Sally Apple Bowels", the list got longer and longer and we had plenty of activity down at the beach in between riding waves.

Back in the days when The Grunter was ours alone, Henry decided that he and I were going to have sex with her off the point at Collaroy. He picked the day carefully: no wind, smooth and calm, in the dead of winter with a high tide after school. The three of us paddled out on two surfboards and then began rolling around together, almost drowning in our attempts to get her cossie off and manoeuvre between her legs. Henry ended up getting it together somehow, with me holding the nose of the board to keep it stable. So The Grunter had her first screw on a board, a feat that I'm sure won't have been tried, let alone perfected, by many to this day.

One day we were all sitting around the back of the surf club in the sun when a fawn Holden ute with "Gordon Woods Surfboards" written on the side pulled up. It turned out that this was the famous surfboard maker Gordon Woods himself. At Bob Evans' suggestion – Bob was already an influential figure in the surf scene and you'll read more about him later – he'd come to Collaroy to watch me surf. I couldn't believe it at first, but he didn't have to ask me twice. I grabbed my board and headed out to ride a little left that was peeling into the corner. A mate named Blackie was already out there ripping the tiny curls to bits and I remember thinking as I walked down the beach that Blackie might get a Gordon Woods sponsorship because he always surfed on lefts so much better than me. However, later that day, Woodsie called my Mum and offered to sponsor me with a new board to replace my Dillon. So Henry – who, of course, just had to have one too – and I went to work to design the colour scheme for our new boards. Mine was to be strawberry malt and his chocolate. What Woodsie did was have "Stork", the finish-coat man, mix the resin with tons of white pigment. The mixture was then spread on the surface to be coated and another colour, red in my case, to simulate strawberries, was then dribbled into it. The whole thing was then brushed to create a mottled effect that looked fantastic. I had the first one, Henry the second and after Kenno left Dillon's to work at Woodsies, all our group had them! In this way I got my first sponsor. After riding Gordon's boards for a few months he told me he was going to pay me £5 for every board order I took. I was a bit dubious at the time but decided not to look a gift horse in the mouth and see what happened.

2

Midget's my hero

I RECKON MOST PEOPLE experience changes in their circle of friends as they go through life and it's particularly true of kids. As they progress through the years at school, friendships come and go and bonds are formed and broken. In my class that first year at Narrabeen High School was a kid called Rodney "Gopher" Sumpter – Gopher because of his rather prominent front teeth. Henry and I talked surf with him all the time and were curious to see how good he really was. Gopher lived at North Avalon, some 20 kilometres north of Collaroy, and we decided to check it out when we were next up that way with Kenno on one of our weekend "surfaris".

North Avalon looks a real picture on a summer's day when it all comes together. The small bay is open to the southern swells but an enormous rocky headland at its northern end blocks the winds from that direction. Rocks line the northernmost point and all these features combine to create the consistently high-quality waves that make "North Av" so attractive to surfers. Most of the time, a little right-hander is running into the rip in the corner but it tends to close-out when the swell is too big.

When we pulled into the carpark that first morning, I remember having had to climb over my mates in the rear of our wagon to get a glimpse of the waves. I had a quick geek at someone tearing up one of the rights before I was yanked back into the mass of arms and legs in the van just as everyone who could see yelled, "Didja see that? Who is it? Wow! King!" The decision was instant and unanimous – we'd all be surfing North Avalon. As we watched the surfer who'd impressed us all walk up the beach, it hit Henry and me at the same time – it was our schoolmate Gopher. As I watched him ambling along with his board tucked under his arm, stopping momentarily to chat to an obvious fan, then weaving his way in our direction through the congested carpark, it occurred to me that he had a definite aristocratic, English look about him. I suppose it was understandable, since his family had come to Australia from England only a few years before – and it's a fact that all the

Kenno and Wally jointly owned our surf wagon.
Other than walking to Long Reef it was our only
way of getting away from Collaroy when the
wind was on-shore and the waves were hopeless.
Our crew out the back of "Westward Ho". From
the left, my brother Chris, Doug Parkinson, Mark
Dawson, don't know, Warwick Twigg, Richard
Cush, Barry Stark, Kemo with his dog Trigger,
Tenfoot, Yubo Krilich and Marty Vaggs.

photos of the time show this "aristocratic" element in his surfing style.

I started to spend a lot of time with Gopher. He'd stay at my house or I'd stay at his, depending on what we thought the surf was doing that weekend. Gopher's room at *Sphinx*, his parents' house on Harley Road, North Avalon, was basically a closed-in veranda. I thought the beds were the best... they were curved like hammocks. In retrospect they must have done terrible things to our spines, but it really didn't matter because after surfing for six hours straight at North Av you'd sleep anywhere.

Gopher and I definitely got into some strife together. Very early one morning, we went creeping down the garden path in a neighbour's front yard, intent on stealing the milk money. As we tried to remove the coins from under a bottle, it fell over, the noise instantly bringing the house's owner out the door. Held by the scruff of the neck, we were marched up to the Sumpters' house. Meryon Sumpter, Gopher's dad, ordered us to his son's room and told us not to come out for the rest of the day. Meryon was the consummate English diplomat. Hardly pausing to draw breath, he smoothed the neighbour's ruffled feathers, then phoned Harold and Greta. Finally, right on dusk, we were summoned to the lounge room for a meeting with our parents. We had no defence, there was nothing to say. Meryon stood up and told us they'd decided not to get the police involved – this time – but if we were ever caught doing anything like it again, the police would be informed and we'd never see each other again. Our life of crime came to a sudden end.

Around 1960 or 1961, living down by North Avalon carpark, in a 1938 Dodge half-buried in sand, was a bloke by the name of Lee Cross. I suppose Gopher had come to know Lee out in the surf and, because I was spending a fair bit of time at North Av, we all started to hang out together. Although Lee was some six years older than Gopher and me, he seemed to enjoy being with us. Handsome and street-wise, he came from Bronte, an inner-city beach in southern Sydney and I think he'd worked in advertising before throwing in his job to go surfing. When the council eventually evicted him from the carpark Lee moved back to his parents' place but would still come to the northern beaches whenever he could. A bit later on, he bought a big black twin-spinner Ford and every Friday afternoon he'd be waiting outside the high school to take Gopher and me away for the weekend.

We usually drove to the Wollongong area, a couple of hours to the south. This was partly because we were constantly fantasising about riding waves through the piles of the fabled Bellambi Pier (that looked so similar to the structure in the "pier-shooting" pictures shot at Huntington Beach, California) but mostly for the comradeship and the adventure. Lee was a totally dedicated surfer and it seemed to us he had girlfriends everywhere. Most of them were his age and they found Gopher and me quite cute, often feeding us if we looked hungry and letting us sleep on their floors. Lee was an easy-going character, and together we were like the Three Musketeers, making hundreds of trips to "The Gong" in search of the best surf. We always went to the local stomps on both Friday and Saturday night and often crashed in the twin-spinner or on the beach.

In June of 1961, Lee invited me – along with Gopher, Bernard "Midget" Farrelly and another mate named Les Mulray – to go to Queensland with him. By utilising all the design skills he'd acquired in working in advertising agencies and drawing heavily on the American *Surfer* magazine, he'd completed the first issue of *Australian Surfer* and was quite proud of his achievement. The trouble was that Lee was never very serious about the business side of things – he'd say he had quit the advertising world to follow the surfing lifestyle and wasn't going to compromise that decision – and there was no advertising space sold apart from a few board ads. He'd planned, in a loose sort of way, to go up the coast with us to get enough material for the second edition of the magazine; but when we took off with barely enough money for food and petrol, the business end of things went right out the window.

A wild southerly was blowing as we all headed north from Sydney on a rainy afternoon. But we didn't get far – our first stop was Avoca Point, about 50 kilometres up the coast from the city, and we crammed in a session there until dark. It'd been a big day; we were all exhausted and there were too many of us to sleep in the car so we forced our way into the surf club and slept in the bunks we'd seen through the window. The waves were even better next day, so we surfed hard all day and passed out in the club again that night. Early the following morning, a club member caught us still asleep inside and told us to move on. We were on the road again.

As we drove up the coast most people treated us as a real novelty – to put it kindly. I remember pulling in for petrol at one service station and hearing the owner yelling for his wife to lock up their daughters because the Surfies were in town. Surfies didn't have much of an image back in the early 1960s. When we arrived at Queensland's Gold Coast, Lee's funds were all but gone so the first thing he did was hock the Ford's radio. It was a major blow that left us all a bit downhearted. As we'd cruised up the coast from Sydney we'd spent hours fiddling with the dial in the hope, mostly unfulfilled, that we'd find a station playing rock and roll. Money was tight so we weren't all that mobile, but we didn't care; we had everything we wanted right there on the Queensland–New South Wales border. At night we crashed in our

"Toes on the Nose" - My big foot on Midget's big nose - that was the caption in John Witzig's scrap book. The shot was taken in June '61 at Greenmount, where we were sleeping on the beach. John took this photo on the same surfari as the wonderful photo on the first page of this book.

In the early '60s a good surfer was judged mainly by his bottom turn. Midget had the best, Gopher's (opposite) was "king" and I was really proud when Keyo used this turn of me at Dee Why point in an advertisement for his boards. John took the shot of Gopher.

sleeping bags on the beach around from the old porpoise pool at Rainbow Bay and by day we surfed anywhere from Snapper Rocks to Coolangatta, wherever the break was best.

By the end of that first week, Lee's money had run out completely and if we were all going to keep on eating we had no alternative but to find jobs. Midget borrowed a lawnmower from somewhere and set to work on yards all over Tweed Heads and Coolangatta. Being some five years younger than Midget, Gopher and I decided we'd be better off looking for something a bit more low profile and on the advice of one of the local surfers we walked down to where the prawn trawlers berthed in the Tweed River. We'd never had real jobs before so we felt pretty good when, almost immediately, we were offered work shelling cooked prawns. But there was a catch: we had to work for a week before our first pay. As we worked, we stuffed as many prawns as we could into our mouths. This was survival stuff – would we make it to the end of the week without going crazy with hunger? When on our sixth day we were woken by the pounding of a bigger swell, it didn't look good for our future as prawn shellers but we managed to surf a good long session from dawn through to starting time. On the way to work, Gopher and I talked over our situation and decided to throw ourselves on the boss' mercy; surely he wouldn't be able to resist the pleas of two half-starved little boys. We begged him to pay us for the five days we'd worked so far but he stood fast, so grabbing a bucket of slightly off prawn heads, I tipped the contents over some freshly cleaned prawns and we walked away.

We spent the next day at Snapper Rocks, and the memories will stick with me forever – the waves were fantastic! For some reason I got into a competition with Midget, riding wave after wave, and when we finally walked up the beach, the comments from the spectators seemed to imply that I'd done pretty well. Surf-movie maker Bob "Evo" Evans was there along with a whole bunch of Sydney surfers. That afternoon, Midget left for Sydney with Evo and then, the next thing I knew, Gopher too was abandoning ship, getting a lift home with one of the other surfers who also lived on the Peninsula. This left Lee, Les and I to work out how we would get back to Sydney with only ten bob between us – about enough to buy a gallon of petrol for the big V8. We knew a gallon wouldn't get us far in that fuel-hungry beast, so a bit of creativity was called for. Bearing a length of rubber hose and a drum, we'd front up at the farmhouses we saw on the way and give them a story about having run out of petrol just down the road a bit and needing a gallon to get to the closest town. It worked fairly well, and if we couldn't see a farmhouse we'd wave down a car and give them a similar line. It only took us five days to get back to Sydney that way, sleeping in the car and bumming a gallon of petrol wherever we could. We were keen to get back to Sydney because Gopher's Dad, Meryon Sumpter, had convinced the Avalon Surf Life Saving Club to help him put on the first Malibu surfboard riding championship.

The event was held over the second weekend in May 1961, and more than two hundred competitors, including fourteen girls, lined up at South Avalon for the first event of its kind in Australia. Just about every surfer in Sydney except Midget turned up to have a crack at the 3 to 5-foot lefts and rights in the corner. The late Graham Trelore won a pewter mug in the seniors, with Scott Dillon second and Malcolm Saunders third. The sub-juniors section was really hotly contested but I managed to edge out Gopher and Bobby Brown from Cronulla. Gopher was upset with the result and I remember we had a pretty vocal battle during that next week which soon developed into a Collaroy against Avalon thing. Shortly after, Gopher left Australia for England via the United States. While in the US he convincingly beat the then junior champion Corky Carroll in the 1964 US Championships at Huntington Beach. In England, he continued his interest in surfing, becoming a guiding light for the sport in that country and the first top-class champion to represent Britain in international competitions. Gopher only ever returns to Australia for quick visits to his Mum.

Lee Cross also competed at Avalon, making it to the semi-finals, but in typical Lee fashion his mind was on much bigger things. The second edition of his *Australian Surfer* was as good as the first – in fact the photos were even better – and more ads had been sold, but when the figures were tallied up, his parents were in the hole to the tune of about £3000 and a third edition never got off the drawing board.

While Gopher and I were still in our first year at Narrabeen High, and prior to his leaving Australia, we were given an incredible opportunity for one last adventure together. Around this time I'd started to spend a bit of time with John Witzig, another surfer a bit older than me, and, through him, I'd met his older brother Paul. After four years of studying for a degree in architecture, Paul, who was about seven years older than me, had turned his back on Sydney University to satisfy his lust for surfing. Although architecture was in his blood – his grandfather Henry Budden had been a well-known architect in turn-of-the-century Sydney and had designed landmarks including the Water Board building and David Jones' Elizabeth Street Store – Paul had been bitten so badly by the surfing bug that architecture took a back seat for many years.

In 1959, the American surf-movie maker Bruce Brown had been filming with Phil Edwards in Hawaii and there he'd met Paul Witzig.

Bruce later got in touch with Paul and asked him to shoot an Australian sequence, featuring two young Aussie surfers, for his forthcoming movie *The Endless Summer*. I still don't know why Gopher and I were asked on that trip instead of Midget, who at the time was undoubtedly a much better and more experienced surfer. Whatever the reason, we took off in Paul's Volkswagen Kombi van, with a full load that included a huge projector and a movie camera piled in the back. The projector was to help finance the trip by showing surf movies in Perth, and Paul would use the camera to hopefully get a few hot shots of Gopher and me riding giant West Australian boomers.

It's a long way across Australia, and just out of Adelaide the roads became so bad that Paul decided to put us all on the Trans Australia Railway at Port Augusta, the Kombi included. That train ride was like something from the Orient Express: for the next two days and nights we all sat back in complete comfort while the desert sped by. This was my first time on a train and I found the motion conducive to sleep, while the old-world charm and sophistication of the luxurious smoking and dining rooms was something so new that I was completely fascinated. Paul was going through his white-linen-suit period and he looked a million dollars, especially sitting in the lounge drinking gin and tonic while reading magazines or chatting to other travellers. But Gopher and I felt like fish out of water so we got into the gin and tonic with gay abandon. It was my first taste of alcohol and after a few hours we were both pretty much out of it but having tons of fun pretending we were Paul's spoilt younger brothers. He played his part to a T and we kept the lounge car amused for hours.

In Perth we held a couple of reasonably successful showings of Bruce's movie but the waves were a bit of a disappointment, so Gopher and I were very pleased when the showings were finished and we headed south towards the Yallingup–Margaret River area. We still had plenty of time to explore every sidetrack off the main highway and we found some pretty good waves in the course of a week. Just past Busselton, about 250 kilometres south of Perth, we negotiated the bush tracks for a few hours and finally came on a wide bay where little lefts peeled across a shallow reef. It felt fantastic having the whole bay to ourselves; we could have been the only three people on the planet. We camped there for the next two days, getting covered in smoke and dirt and getting a taste of what south-western Australia is really like.

Leaving the bay, we drove to Yallingup and booked into the Caves House hotel where we soaked up the luxury of a shower and a bed. The next day, we tried to get out through the big, nasty waves at Margaret River, but found ourselves washed back up on the beach

The Great Australian Bight—
a vast plain joining the east
and west sides of this
country - this picture gives
some idea of how big,
flat and old Australia
really is.
I have kept this train
brochure from our
Endless Summer sojourn
to Western Australia for the last 35 years. I
always knew it would come in handy one day.

after only half an hour – we couldn't even get out the back. Standing in front of Paul while he gave us shit, we felt like complete failures and had to admit the waves were too big for mere kids. So it was back to the hotel to work out on the pool table. Our next stop was Ocean Beach, another half-day south and just outside the town of Denmark. It had waves more to our liking and we spent the day enjoying the crisp little rights in the corner and, later, standing in stunned silence at the top of 20-metre cliffs bearing signs warning of the possibility of "killer waves" that can sweep the unwary away.

When we left Western Australia, we again decided to trust ourselves and the Kombi to the railway and we boarded the train at Kalgoorlie, the centre of the State's eastern goldfields. The trip back to the east was a bit of an anticlimax that even an abundance of gin and tonic didn't improve – in fact I was soon to learn what a fickle friend spirits can be! We'd left the train at Port Augusta and after a couple of days' driving reached Geelong, Victoria, where we booked into the Commodore Motel. It was, by my standards at least, a luxurious place, and I still have the letter I wrote to Mum on the motel's stationery.

Next day we went on to surf Bells Beach where Paul filmed a scene featuring the only significant wave that made it to the final cut of *Endless Summer*. It's a typical Bruce Brown send up: "Young Aussie Nat Young has to go one better than the Americans' hang ten and he's seen here hanging body," said Bruce's voice while the camera showed me falling off the front of the board. At first I thought it was a real embarrassment but I loved Bruce's style and laughed when I saw it in the completed movie. Still, it seemed like an awfully long way to go for a couple of waves; but then again, Gopher didn't even get a shot in the movie.

By now, I'd started to develop really severe pains in my chest but I shut up about it in front of Paul and Gopher – but there was no hiding it from Mum when we got home. I'd never really been sick before, and Greta took one look at me and called our local doctor, who ordered me to bed while he did all sorts of tests over the next week. In the end, he told Mum and me that it was a reaction to the alcohol I'd consumed for the first time. While I can't say that the experience warned me off alcohol forever, it did give me a healthy respect for the insidious qualities of spirits.

The next person to take an interest in me was Bob "Evo" Evans, Paul's only opposition in the Australian surf-movie business and the bloke that Midget had gone back to Sydney with after abandoning us on that first trip to Queensland. Evo was a sunset connoisseur. I couldn't count how many nights he'd have me staring at a sunset, watching for the green flash that appears on the horizon immediately after the sun disappears. He first introduced me to this ritual on the north coast of New South Wales and I followed it in Peru, Hawaii and California. Bob was very adept at the social graces and lived for the cocktail hour, his favourite part of the day. His idea of paradise was sitting on some deck in Hawaii, sucking on a Mai-Tai and watching for the green flash, and it shows in the movies he made – they have literally hundreds of sunsets. Bob Evans, or "Surge" as he was also known, was born in 1928 at Manly, near Sydney, and was like a father to me in many ways. Surge – a nickname I never used – had come from his ability to ride across Surge Rock at Fairy Bower on a hollow, 16-foot toothpick board.

At the age of only 21, Bob had been operated on for a serious bowel cancer, the resulting colostomy leaving him with a bag attached to his belly and a need for tailor-made, high-waisted board shorts. According to legend, he'd almost won the Clubbies' 1958 Surfboard Championship and, until 1956, he'd been a dedicated member of the Queenscliff Surf Life Saving Club. In that same year he'd been one of hundreds who watched the American surf team give an exhibition of Malibu boardriding at Dee Why and Avalon, and to say he was impressed with Bob Burnside, Mike Bright, Tom Zahn and Greg Noll is a mild understatement. Bob made a hurried deal to buy Noll's board on his return from a trip to Torquay, Victoria, where he was to compete in the surf-lifesaving carnival held in conjunction with the 1956 Olympic Games.

At that time Bob was working for Hickory, the lingerie manufacturer, and was married to a beautiful Queenscliff beach girl named Valerie. He reckoned that showing surf movies could work in well with his real job selling bras and panties, so he contacted film maker Bud Browne in California. Bud came out to Australia in 1958 and together they showed Bud's movies all over Sydney – with phenomenal success. I can remember one show at Collaroy Surf Club when the audience went wild after the projector broke down for the eleventh time in the first half. They were throwing beer cans, chairs, anything they could get their hands on. The show caused a traffic jam in the main street and the police were called to sort it out.

Bob saw the signs, surfing was going to be the latest craze and with money from the sale of his younger sister-in-law's car he bought an old tripod-mounted Bolex camera and went into the surf-movie business. *Surf Trek to Hawaii* was completed in 1961 and *Midget goes Hawaiian* in 1962, with both films featuring exciting Hawaiian footage with a smattering of local stuff. Then Bob's ambition widened. He reckoned that with himself heading a well-heeled partnership with two other Hickory executives, he could be successful in the surf-magazine business, and so the first issue of *Surfing World* hit the stands in September 1962. Bob's magazine attracted more paid advertising than Lee Cross's *Australian Surfer* – even though it was still fairly plain by today's standards, and sales were higher. However, Hickory was starting to get more than a little peeved at its employee's divided loyalty and so Bob left to go into the surf business full time.

Midget Farrelly – winner of the Makaha contest in Hawaii and unofficial world champion – began to figure more prominently in my life around this time and I sat through Evo's *Midget Goes Hawaiian* five times. One sequence cut to the song *Walk Like a Man* by The Four Seasons and the tune still conjures up a very clear image of the most impressive surfing I'd seen to then – it still gives me goose bumps to think about it. I can remember feeling so proud sitting up like Jackie in the front seat of Midget's brand new 179 Holden station wagon as we accelerated out of Sydney on our way to the second contest at Bells Beach

I knew it was a one-night stand but it was a dream come true. I was going to spend a whole week with my hero and we'd be all on our own. I'd been talking about it for months at school, Henry and all my other mates reckoned I was bullshitting but here I was, gliding down the highway in his brand new chariot. I remember kissing Greta goodbye at the Stuart Street side of Westward Ho, then looking at my younger brother Chris, my Mum, and assorted neighbours' kids through the gap between the roof rack and the car. There they were, watching me actually climb on board, opening the door to that special smell that only new cars have, and I had to pinch myself to realise this was actually happening. The fact that I hadn't been lying to my mates, that Midget Farrelly was going to pick me up that day, would give me enormous credibility.

My family and friends stood in stunned silence, but it puzzled me too! By this time I was aware that I was one of the better surfers in Sydney – certainly in the top bracket of the usual crew that I hung around with every weekend at whatever beach on the north side had the best surf – but why had Midget asked me to go to Bells with him? Why not "Wagga" or John Cormack or one of his mates from his own beach? When I actually thought about it, I didn't even know where his home beach was, all I knew about my hero was that he came from the Dee Why–Freshwater area and that he was the best surfer in the world. How many times had I watched him as he slid through Collaroy in his previous car, a beige single-spinner Ford, usually on his own but sometimes with his girlfriend Tanya Binning by his side. A few years later, we all saw some sexy beach shots of Tanya in a European film called *Mondo Carné*. She was a pretty competent surfer but it was her long blonde hair, height and striking smile that were most memorable. Henry and I once stumbled on them making out in the back seat of Midget's car at Ma Browns, a secluded beach near Long Reef. We couldn't see much but it was enough, Midget had the style of a champion. He was my absolute hero and here I was, sitting in the front seat of his 179 looking up at our two boards strapped side-by-side on the roof rack.

Midget had shaped both boards identically at Keyo Surfboards in Brookvale; I'd abandoned Woodsie's boards to have one shaped by Midget and my turning really improved. Midget's board had his usual three stringers spread evenly across it, and a tee-band of thin balsa on either side of 1/4-inch redwood. Midget was also trying out a design feature he called the "hook tail". Shaped from balsa, the hook made the rail a good two inches longer on the backhand and then cut away into the hook before flowing into the normal lines of the other rail. Midget said the idea was to make the board hold in better on your backhand, and I thought it worked really well. At the time, the object of surfing was to make smooth, flowing turns and these beautifully crafted, 9-foot 6-inch "cadillacs" were perfect for cruising on long clean lines, but we failed to find any on that trip to Victoria. We had a nice time though: shook a lot of hands, drank a few beers, rode a few waves and left for home.

It was a crash course in how to act like a champion and when Midget told me I'd done a good job I felt very proud of myself. In all, I had three more trips with Midget, one being another promotional tour in the 179. We went together, just the two of us, to Newcastle where we put on an exhibition at a place called The Cliff. Midget was gliding so beautifully and with such smooth regularity on every wave, that I felt jerky and lacking in flow. Midget said that we were to go to The Store that afternoon but I didn't have a clue what he meant. When we pulled into the carpark the manager came running out to greet us, shaking our hands and telling us to come in and choose some clothes. I'd already been given a cheque for £25 in payment for the exhibition, and now this! I couldn't believe my luck. I wanted so much to look sharp like Paul Witzig and I really needed a suit. I just knew it was the next step towards becoming a professional surfer, although there was no such thing at the time. Midget's outfit was in a grey fleck and The Store gave me a nice blue suit, which I treasured for years. I wore it when Bob Evans, Midget and I met the Lord Mayor of Sydney just before I left on my first overseas trip the following Christmas.

Midget convinced Greta to let me go on that trip. Mum and Dad had never been overseas at this time and they were very reluctant. He promised to look after me and said that together with Kevin Platt we'd rent a house on the North Shore of Oahu, surf some real big waves and have a ball – it sounded fantastic.

Both these shots were at the 1963 Australian Open
Surfing Championships at Bondi. John took the
presentation picture; Midget on the left, me behind
him and Mick Dooley who placed second to me
that day.
My Dad took the pic of Gopher waxing up, my little
brother Chris is hiding behind his balsa board and
that's Kenno with his arm on the rail of his board.

In early November 1963, a few months before we took off over-seas, I was faced with a bit of a dilemma. The Australian Championships were coming up and the prize for the winner in the open division was a trip to the USA and for the juniors it was just another trophy. I wanted so much to go to Hawaii, so I decided to take the chance and enter the open. Three days before the event, I was running up the beach to Westward Ho to gobble down my breakfast Weet-Bix before catching the bus to school, when I stepped on a broken bottle, ending up with three stitches in my left foot.

I was devastated but even more determined to succeed and I won the 1963 Australian Championships at Bondi. But that didn't make me the best surfer in Australia – Midget was, and everyone knew it, even though he hadn't entered the contest. He was my complete role model right then; I even tried to walk and talk like him – which was pretty difficult as he's such a little bloke and I was already over 180 centimetres tall – and I really believed he was my friend as well as my hero. He'd always be telling me big-wave stories, stories of Hawaii, of girls; then he'd break out in his own rendition of "Bluebottle", a character in the *Goon Show*, before getting all serious again with a heavy story such as the one about the Tenth Annual Makaha Contest he'd won in 1962.

Then the big day finally came and it all seemed a bit unreal. I said goodbye to all my friends at Collaroy and only my girlfriend Marilyn Bennett came with Greta, Harold and me to the airport. My friend John Witzig rushed to the airport between University lectures to present me with a beautiful leather-bound writing case and then the next minute the big new Boeing 707 was in the air. Sydney's *Sunday Telegraph* newspaper had sponsored the contest that got me here, and they'd bought me a first class ticket. I didn't wake up to this until after takeoff when I discovered that Midget and Kevin were in another section behind me. Apparently my first-class status was at the request of the late Sir Frank Packer, the owner of the *Telegraph*, who must have been a sports fan like his son Kerry.

Arriving in Hawaii was so *Hawaiian* in those days. We walked across the tarmac into a big flat concrete building full of friendly customs officials who waved us on and asked if we were "there for the surf meet"; everyone is so surf conscious in the Islands. At the other end of the building there were half a dozen scantily clad Hawaiians, men and women, singing local songs and doing the hula. The atmosphere was incredible: the taste of the fresh Dole pineapple juice they kept pouring down our throats and the fragrance of the *plumeria* (Frangipani) flowers that were everywhere. I had one particularly strong whiff of perfume from behind the ear of the voluptuous dancer who kissed me and whispered "Aloha". Welcome to Hawaii.

All pictures getting ready to go to Hawaii for the first time.

A civic reception at the Sydney Lord Mayor's office before we went.

From the left, Bob Evans, Midget and myself. Snow McAlister took this photo.

Waxing up my new board out the back of "Westward Ho." From the left, Mick Tipping, Belly, Wally, Westie and Chook McClure.

... and getting on the big bird for that first trip.

At last we were able to grab our boards, jump in a cab, and take off in search of Midget's "car man", the guy he'd bought a car from the year before. We threw in $150 each for a really nice '53 Ford wagon and it was off to the North Shore. Midget seemed to change at about this time; he was no longer so happy-go-lucky and didn't smile as much. I put it down to nerves; after all, he was defending his title in what was then recognised as the world championship. After we moved into our rented house off Kenui Road, near Pipeline, we settled into a steady routine of riding big, clean waves all day long and collapsing into bed not long after dusk.

A never-to-be-forgotten experience that winter was the sudden arrival on the North Shore of Peter Troy, the original roving ambassador for Australian surfing, who turned up late one night from some strange and exotic country. We'd all passed out in our little house on Kenui Road after another exhausting day until we were woken by screams and the sound of someone being chased around the house. Through the slatted windows, which in my room reached to floor level, I watched in amazement as Peter, with five men on his hammer, ran round and round the house. On his third lap, he yelled "Open the door", and Midget timed it just right, slamming the door as Peter came flying through. Yelling for Peter's hide, his pursuers milled round restlessly for a while but we held tight, not saying a word or making a move. Eventually, they packed it in and left and Peter Troy got to live and surf another day. I've no idea how Peter knew where we lived. Apparently, he'd arrived in Hawaii by ship late that night and had hitched out to the North Shore. Something happened to lead him into a confrontation with the local boys who'd given him a lift, a row over petrol money or something, and that had led to the late-night race round our house.

Soon after that, the day after I think, Peter surfed pipeline for his first and last time. He went over the falls and hit the bottom and his face needed numerous stitches to fix it up. I was right there and saw the whole thing. Peter was losing a ton of blood and I didn't know where Midget or Kevin were so it was up to me and I had to act fast. I drove Peter to the local hospital in our old Ford. I didn't have a licence and there I was, driving at over 160 kilometres an hour along Kam Highway.

With the day of the Makaha contest rapidly approaching, we were surfing Makaha Beach as much as possible. Late one evening, exhausted and far too tired to cook dinner, we dragged ourselves away from the perfect 6-foot waves and went to a restaurant in Nanakuli. The boiled rice and thinly sliced, marinated teriyaki steak was fantastic on an empty stomach but when we walked back to the car our worst fears were realised – someone had taken all our boards from the back of the wagon. Midget was devastated and rightly so, he was surfing really well and I think, on a board of his own, he could've won the contest for the second time. But with no time to make a new board he had to borrow one and the stress really showed. Every time he went in the water to try a new board, all eyes were on him. The Aussie press had a field day and really played up the fact that our boards had been stolen by the Hawaiians and I do think that the loss of the boards was at least partly responsible for our poor showing in the championships.

In November 1997, 34 years after the robbery, my eldest son Beau and I were sitting around the beach at Makaha, knocking back the odd beer with the locals and enjoying the atmosphere at the World Longboard Championships. In between singing along to the ukuleles I was swapping stories with Jimmy Mendosa, a pig farmer about my age. I'd known him by sight for years but he floored me completely when he confessed that it had been himself and his brothers who'd stolen our boards that night at Nanakuli in 1963. Jimmy just had to get it off his chest. The whole beach erupted with laughter and you could've knocked me over with a feather.

In a way, the loss of my board was a godsend, giving me the chance to ride lots of different equipment. The surfer who really impressed me on that first trip was Phil Edwards, from California. He was a bit older than Midget and taller and smoother to watch, but I could see a lot of similarities between them and perhaps that was why I liked Phil's style so much. Whatever the reason, I started to hang out to watch him surf and one afternoon I found myself sharing the water with him at Pupukea. After many days watching and practising, I was getting pretty good at copying his smoothly flowing, swinging top turn as the lip was about to pitch and I did one right in front of him – not really on purpose, it just worked out that way.

Phil paddled over to compliment me on the ride and we struck up a conversation about boards. He told me about "Baby" the magic balsa board underneath him. Awestruck, I looked along its sleek rails while Phil described how the board was so well trained it returned to him every time he lost it in a wipe-out. He asked if I'd like to ride her. Would I! We traded boards in the line up then and there. Baby was indeed magic, smooth and fast with a balance like a Bowie knife, sort of heavy in the front end but with never a hint of spinning out. I tried to surf just like Phil, a big top turn coming around with the curl and letting the board open up down the line, before cranking a deep, gouging cut back and doing it all again into the shore break. Phil must have been impressed – he offered me the board to keep. I just about shit myself! I declined the offer but I was so flabbergasted I thought my head was about to explode.

Midget Farrelly was the best surfer in Australia and
my first hero. When I was exposed to the Californian
Phil Edwards' surfing I realised that Midget had
modelled his style on Phil's and Phil became my
new idol. I tried to look like him on every
turn as this picture of Kenno's clearly shows.

Living down Kenui Road from us, in a half-cylindrical Quonset hut left over from the Second World War, were three Aussie blokes I'd vaguely known at home. Keith "Natch" Southion, Terry "Bobcat" Adams and Barry "Ugg" Andres had made the surfers' pilgrimage to Hawaii and were loving it. Midget was being a bit of a bastard towards me and Kevin was a real loner, so I fell right in with these fun-loving boys from Maroubra, a beachside suburb in the south of Sydney. They were sharing the Quonset (called a Nissen hut in Australia) with a bunch of "Seppos" from Malibu in California.

We all got on really well together and after a couple of weeks of hanging out, Butch Linden, the best surfer in the hut, invited Natch, Bobcat, Ugg and me to stay at his parents' house in Malibu. A few weeks before we were due to leave for California, Evo asked us all if we'd like to come to the island of Maui with him. Midget and Kevin declined, but Natch, Bobcat, Ugg and I were keen. Evo must have been a bit disappointed by Midget's response because he told me he wanted to shoot some film of us in smaller, high-performance waves. He told us to keep a close eye on the swell size, and when it got too big for Waimea Bay we were to go straight to the airport for an inter-island flight to Maui and the surf at Honolua Bay. As luck would have it, giant waves came up the following week and it was a frantic scramble to gather up boards and essentials and get to Maui before the swell died.

Maui was a real backwater in those days: hardly any traffic, and Wailuku, the largest town, boasting one crossroads with a gas station and a general store. We headed for the old whaling town of Lahaina on the north-west shore and booked into the Pioneer Inn, right on the harbour. There was still tons of swell running, so we headed out towards Honolua. Luckily Evo's mate, the American movie-maker Bud Browne, had joined us and he "sort of knew the way" to the bay. We were convinced we'd caught a glimpse of a wave just around a bend so Bud got us to park where the road seemed to run out, in the middle of a lush profusion of guava trees hung with passionfruit vines that formed a dense canopy over our heads. We gorged ourselves on the fresh, sweet fruit, then grabbed our boards and headed down a path towards the sound of waves crashing on the reef, finally coming out on a boat ramp to front one of the most breathtaking sights I've ever seen anywhere in the world. A majestic Honolua was breaking far out to our right, with billowing white rooster-tails adding to the effect. We couldn't tell exactly how big the waves were until we paddled out, and when we did we found a perfect six feet, with every wave a carbon copy of the one before. You could take off, drop to the bottom, do a big strong bottom turn to propel you along the wave, then crouch low to get inside the cathedral. Honolua didn't create half the fear the North Shore did – I felt really comfortable with it, even when I surfed it much bigger years later. On our third day there, the swell dropped and we returned to Oahu. Another month and we were off to California.

* * * * * * *

On the drive from Los Angeles to Malibu with Butch and ten other members of the Malibu Surfers Association, our car stopped at a supermarket in Santa Monica to buy something for someone. Next thing I knew I was being told to get out of the car by a nasty cop who emerged from a black-and-white police car. He asked for our passports and the American's IDs. Apparently, someone had stolen a tube of toothpaste and the cashier, intimidated by all the surfers, had called the police. Because no-one would own up to the theft, we were all taken in for questioning about our reasons for being in California and where we we'd be staying. At the police station I was questioned by a pleasant detective who asked all the relevant questions then left me on my own for what must have been two hours. Next thing I knew he was handing me a pizza and explaining that there was a problem with my entry into the United States. He said I'd have to spend the night in jail while it was sorted out, but he was going to put me in a cell on my own because "He didn't want the black boys to get at me". It was a memorable night, my first one in mainland USA and one I'll never forget. Alone in my cell I didn't get much sleep, I sat on the bench and bawled my eyes out. I went back over my brief time in California and tried to work out what I'd done wrong.

Next morning, I was handed my breakfast by the same pleasant detective who explained what had happened. Apparently the customs in Hawaii had made a terrible mistake, for under US law, no-one younger than seventeen could enter the country unless they were with a legal guardian, so they were going to have to hold me in jail while things were sorted out between the Australian Embassy in San Francisco, my Mum in Australia, the pleasant detective, and Butch Linden's mother in Malibu. The detective told me he was sorry that I had to remain in solitary but it was for my own good and would only be for a few days. I cried myself to sleep again and waited on the pizza detective with his combined daily food delivery and negotiations update. Things eventually sorted themselves out and after three days I was escorted from my cell to the front desk and the ample bosom of Butch's Mum, Margaret.

In Malibu at last, I was completely overwhelmed: everyone was so nice. The Lindens owned a big house right on the beach but it was much more luxurious than Westward Ho back in Collaroy. Their house was situated in "The Colony" which in 1964, as it does today, contained the exclusive homes of movie stars and the very rich. I probably saw lots of movie stars in my month with the Lindens, but it certainly didn't register. The single biggest difference to my home in Australia was the bar refrigerator full of icy little bottles of coke, which you could grab whenever you wanted. I was amazed by the affluence. I recall pulling a sandwich to bits to find out what the strange taste was and it turned out to be mayonnaise – I'd never tasted it before and it gave a whole new perspective to salad sandwiches.

California in the early 1960s is almost a cliché – The Beach Boys were just coming on the scene, the first skateboard craze had hit, and surfers were pretty cool. Butch had a "Woody", a 1948 Ford Mercury, dark blue with wooden body panels. It was in perfect condition having had all the leather upholstery and paintwork redone in Tijuana, just over the border in Mexico. Butch said he was going to take us down there in a couple of months when the swells started rolling in from the south. I remember thinking long and hard about that. Imagine a place that was so predictable that, like a migrating bird, you'd know when to head south or north. But it was still February and winter, and everyone was thinking about the surf break at Rincon while the swells were from the north. They call Rincon "The Jewel Of The Coast" and it's easy to see why when you see it from above. As with all coastlines, the points are the most dominant features and the round boulders that often line the shore near them make the waves break the way they do.

Depending on their shape and the way the rocks are dispersed, some points are better for surfing than others and Rincon is flawless – you couldn't build it better. There's a little creek about half way along the point which allows you to paddle out even when the surf is big, and the number of houses probably hasn't changed since the place was settled. We had perfect waves there on several occasions and even saw Midget one day, but he virtually ignored us. On any decent sort of northerly swell it seemed like it broke in a perfect line, at right angles to the rocks for some 150 metres, sometimes even longer, peeling in a perfect tube down the form and finishing right on a reclaimed area where the sea eats into the highway. When I was there that first time, Highway 101 was still the main road between San Francisco and Los Angeles and the amount of traffic was incredible. You could still pull up and park on the side of the highway but this was stopped when they had a few accidents and a carpark was built a little way back up the highway.

For most of our time in California, Natch, Bobcat and I hung around Malibu with our new friends. Ugg had returned to his girl-friend in Australia, but I for one wasn't at all homesick. Lying in the upstairs front room of the Lindens big, gabled home as the winter of '63 faded away, I listened to the Santa Ana, the wind off the desert, blowing at 25 knots or more and briefly holding up the waves before they crashed on Malibu Point with a deafening roar. For some strange reason that I've never thought of until now, it seems that in those days every surfer expected one board to work for all condi-tions. It was your trusted friend and you carried it with you every-where you went. My Woodsie "Island Gun" that had been perfect for the islands and served me so faithfully, hadn't arrived on the plane from Hawaii with me and everyone in the Malibu Surfing Association was surfing the new foam boards made by Dave Sweet. I rode a cou-ple of different boards but couldn't get the right feel, then someone or something sent me poking around under the Lindens' house and there I uncovered an old solid-balsa board. Heavy, thick with dust and seemingly neglected for years, something about it seemed right to me. It belonged to Harry Senior, Butch's father, and as he only used it at the height of summer, if at all, he gave me the okay to bor-row it. It wasn't until I'd been surfing it for a couple of weeks and scratched away the old wax, that we discovered the board had been shaped by the famous Bob Simmons.

Simmons is a genuine legend in the sport. He introduced loads of design and structural changes to surfboards. He's still talked about with reverence by older watermen all over the surfing world. Bob died in unusual circumstances while surfing at Windansea in Southern California. He took off on a wave, the board wobbled a bit, Bob fell off and was never seen again. These days a Simmons "Spoon" is an extremely valuable collector's item but in 1963 it was just another board. I surfed that board everywhere from Rincon to a spot just below the Mexican border and I believe it had quite a bit of the Simmons magic. It was the perfect board for Malibu Point which we only got to surf a few times because it's a summer break. Like Phil Edwards' Baby, it was perfectly balanced, with lots of weight in the front end but finer, and the wide front end helped with smooth, fast rail entry on the takeoffs at point breaks and the narrow tail made it sit in the curl. I suppose it was about 9-foot 6-inches, but I never measured it.

The promised adventure south to Tijuana in Butch's Woody came up pretty quickly. It was extremely memorable but not for the surf – as I remember we didn't even take the boards off the roof rack. Tijuana was a wild town in the early 1960s and wide-open is a mild description. The first place we went into was called the Long Bar and apparently it was the most radical place in town though we were told it wouldn't get going for a few more hours. Peering through the darkened doorway, past the numerous bulky doormen, we could see just how the bar had got it's name: it went on forever, disappearing in a smoky haze into a sea of patrons. For some reason we didn't go in, instead wandering aimlessly around the back streets for an hour or more – I can still taste the fish tacos laced with red-hot salsa and more flavours than I ever thought existed – until we decided we were definitely ready for a drink and went into a place called The Blue Fox where we drank beer with the odd Tequila chaser. The entertainment started around midnight with a floor show featuring a charming Mexican girl being buggered by a donkey. The way she managed to dance into exactly the right compromising position beneath the donkey was quite remarkable, but then again, she was an artist! It seemed the donkey was enjoying himself because at one point I stood in front of him and was sure I could detect a faint smile. Certainly we were all getting off on it; the beer flowed, and I even saw a couple of fights.

This was my first live-sex floor show – the first and last time I ever saw anything like it. I'd been to a strip show at Sydney's famous Kings Cross with all my Collaroy mates the year before, and Bob Evans took me to a bar in Waikiki to hear a guitarist called Arthur Lyman play and sing a beautiful song called *Yellow Bird* before we took a plane somewhere. I think of the visit to The Blue Fox in the same way as I think of Arthur Lyman… Evo liked to call it cultural absorption and it involved consuming plenty of whatever alcohol the locals were into – in Tijuana beer and Tequila, in Hawaii a rum-and-pineapple Mai-Tai, it didn't matter, as long as you sat, listened, talked and drank with the locals. For Evo, cultural absorption always took place right at sunset so there'd be the added bonus of the green flash – if you were lucky!

3

The beginning of the end of Collaroy

Being back home after a very eventful six months in Hawaii and California was difficult to say the least. I tried going back to school but it was impossible. I knew that I'd passed my Intermediate Certificate before I'd left for Hawaii – not that I studied for it or cared at the time – but now, after six months overseas, it seemed more important. The Intermediate was a big deal in those days, the first step towards gaining a good education and a decent job. I returned to Australia in May of 1964, around Easter, and I actually went back to school after the break; but after missing the first three months of fourth year, it was no good. I really tried for the first few weeks, I believe I actually realised for the first time in my life that I would quite like an education, but it was too late, I'd blown it. I was hopelessly behind the rest of the class – no doubt I could have caught up if I really tried, applied myself and only surfed on weekends, but I guess I didn't really want to. The door was being shut on that period of my life and now it's one of the things I regret.

At this time I was still living at home with my parents, along with my little brother Chris, who's four years my junior. Chris was a handsome kid, not tall and gangly like me; more the stature of our Dad but with lots of freckles. He was an exceptionally good surfer with tons of natural talent but, according to Chris, his problem was having me as his brother. Apparently, living in my shadow with all the expectations of family, friends and the media to live up to was impossible for him. I could never understand his attitude and found it hard to comprehend why he couldn't make his situation a winner instead of looking on it as an impossible standard to attain. I still love my brother very much; we've talked a lot about our upbringing and differences and I'll continue to keep my door open. Maybe one day he'll quit his vagabond life on the road and settle down – it's something he says he dreams about when he is in one of his more melancholic moods.

Back in 1964, the streetscape and beachfront between Narrabeen and Collaroy were being completely transformed. Almost every day another old house was knocked down to make way for blocks of

This is my favourite surfing photo of my little brother.
It was taken at Little Narrabeen in the late '60s
during the shortboard period when he was
building boards at Shane's.

Looking south from Narrabeen in the mid '60s
showing what no development plan did to our beach.
"Flightdeck" dwarfed everything else on the
beach changing Collaroy forever.

flats and home units and the area where Westward Ho stood was a prime target. Already a thirteen-story concrete monstrosity – the "Flight Deck" – was casting its shadow over the street. Harold couldn't help himself; the offers were too good to refuse and eventually he sold out to the developers. I couldn't understand how he could sell off our beautiful old family home, but Harold had dragged himself up from nowhere and I suppose the desire to "better himself" was just too strong. For me, the sale of Westward Ho was the last straw. Dad and I had never been close; he didn't understand where I was coming from at all.

* * * * * * *

Harold's background had been very difficult. He'd been raised by an Aunt at Bega, on the south coast of New South Wales, where there were many small farms. His father had apparently squandered the small fortune (£6,000) that was left to each of the five sons by my great-grandfather but Harold had made good during the Depression and then worked hard to raise a family. During the Second World War he'd worked at an abrasives factory. I'd no doubt he was a good man at heart – except for his complete obsession with material possessions – though he didn't show much affection towards his wife and children and we didn't have much quality time together. He took Chris and me away with him twice: once to Tasmania and once to Queensland. On the trip to Queensland, Rusty, my golden cocker spaniel, had an attack of distemper in Tweed Heads causing him to run wild in the main street. Poor Rusty was shot then and there; right before my eyes. I was devastated; we were really good mates and several times had run away from home together. Rusty had been given to me instead of sending me to boarding school – I never understood the reasoning behind those alternatives – and I really loved that dog.

I have two older sisters, Pam, and June, thirteen and ten years older respectively. I can't remember them being in my life at all, although June once told me that it was she who rescued me from the maggie that divebombed my pram on the lawn at Westward Ho. Both girls left home at sixteen to marry their boyfriends, claiming they were driven out by Harold's attitude to everything; I can well believe it and sympathised with them. Pamela certainly felt hurt by Dad's strange priorities, and she never reconciled their differences before he died in November 1995. She's a very strong and independent woman, although she has Mum's petite build. Together with her husband John, she worked hard to prove Harold was wrong about their marriage. John was a schoolteacher when they first lived together and Pam worked long hours at a local milk bar to put herself through university, eventually becoming a teacher and head-mistress. When I was about eight or so, and before they had any kids of their own, Pam and John took me away with them for the Christmas holidays. We went to Nirvana, his family's sheep station just out of Narrabri in north-western New South Wales. John showed me how to hold a rifle, and we shot rabbits and crows. The few weeks on Nirvana were an eye-opener for me: the silence; the colours, especially the soft pinks and purples of the dawn; watching the lambs being born and using my new-found skill with the rifle to wreak revenge on the crows who preyed on the new-born lambs, seeking to peck out their eyes. John and Pam gave me my first real taste of the country and I've found over the years that it agrees with me in theory – but I've never found a way to support my family while living the rural life. Finally, after years of schoolteaching at the northern beaches, Pam, John and their two children have returned to the life that John loves best, a big sheep property just west of Orange.

My other sister, June, and her husband Graham, have values similar to Pam and John, but in all other respects, they couldn't be more different. June, a dedicated wife and mother, inherited Harold's large frame and has a quick, warm smile. Graham is a builder; a big, strong, honest man who fathered three sons and always put the welfare of his family first. Their boys, Mark, Adam and Russell were physically very much like Graham, but because they spent their impressionable years living at Dee Why, also on the northern beaches, they ran foul of the drug culture that was burgeoning there at the time. Mark was the eldest, and I built his first board for him – one of many boards in fact – and turned him on to riding waves for all the right reasons. In the early 1970s he was spending school holidays with me and my first wife Marilyn on our farm near Byron Bay.

Mark was the only nephew close to me and as his Uncle I tried to give him advice whenever I saw him, but we never really talked much. I knew he was smoking a bit of pot, we even smoked it together once, but it came as a shock when I found out that he was using heroin. However, after years of using, it seems that with his family's support he finally managed to kick his habit. I hope he is one of the lucky ones who've managed to win the battle and stay winners – about ten years ago, his younger brother Adam died of a combination of overproof rum and heroin overdose in the park at Byron Bay. June and Graham have had a lot of anxiety with their boys, but Mark's been on the straight and narrow for a long time now and Russell, the youngest, is a well-balanced individual who enjoys riding waves, playing music and working hard.

* * * * * * *

After Westward Ho was sold, Harold bought an old fibro house opposite a market garden in Warriewood, about 10 kilometres north of Collaroy and a kilometre or two inland. He wanted to build another kindergarten on the premises, move the business from Collaroy and renovate the fibro house, all at the same time. It was a very picturesque rural setting, half-way up a steep hill overlooking a valley dotted with glass houses full of tomatoes. I can still remember the pungent smell of ripe tomatoes wafting over me as I walked the 2 kilometres home from the bus stop on Pittwater Road.

There was a lot of arguing in the new house. Greta was always being forced to take sides and, naturally, it was really hard on her. My values were, in many ways, diametrically opposed to Dad's but because I'm his son I can sometimes see myself acting in the same way and I'm still fighting against it. I hated his obsession with money but I could understand his love of cars and material possessions. Yet I hated the way this led him to damage relationships with people he'd led to believe he loved – it was all very confusing. I tried awfully hard to show Dad some respect in our home but it was difficult after I'd seen the way some families lived in Hawaii and California. The final showdown came after we'd been living at Warriewood for about six months. After a full-on yelling match over nothing in particular, I committed the ultimate sin by getting in the last word and shaping up! In retrospect, it could've been unfortunate we didn't come to blows. Maybe what I really needed was a good hiding to remind me of my place, but Mum came running in and neither of us got a punch in. In Harold's eyes this meant that Mum had taken my side and it caused lasting problems between them.

To get to Collaroy meant a 20-minute bus ride each way and this became the main problem in my life. The fact that my home was 2 kilometres from the beach when I really wanted to make a career of surfing was really getting to me and it seemed to me that the only way I could get on top of the problems associated with living with Harold, continue surfing and still live at home, was to get a car.

More and more, Bob Evans took me under his wing as the situation on the home front deteriorated and through him I was introduced to Sydney's business world. I can only speculate as to how Bob became the "Mr Surf" of the corporate scene. I was, after all, pretty young at the time, but I'm sure that for many executives, he was their only link with the lucrative market that the youthful surfing culture represented. For his part, Bob was living his life-long dream, supporting his family by doing exactly what he liked doing most – making a new surf movie every year and selling the advertising for his monthly *Surfing World* magazine.

Bob and his wife Valerie had three children: Brett, born in 1958,

side of the situation, explaining that all music was good; it just depended on where you were right at the time. He left that problem and warned me to get my surfing in early the next morning because at 11 a.m. sharp, he'd be picking me up to go to the city, to have a business lunch with Terry Southwell Keally, the advertising manager of Ampol Petroleum.

This was one of many such lunches Bob took me to, and in this way I met a lot of advertising agency account executives and company directors. Basically, Bob wanted me to meet them and talk about surfing – I suppose I added colour when he was making his case to convince an agency executive to advertise in *Surfing World,* or an investor to put money into a movie. Leyland Australia came up with some nice little cars at one time and Rothman's cigarettes were always there until the law changed. One restaurant that I remember frequenting was the French Tavern in the basement of a beautiful historic building in the city. It was there I tasted pepper steak and snails for the first time! I loved it, and though I learnt about food and wine only in a superficial sort of way, it did help me develop a certain *savoir faire* which was to enrich my life greatly.

One of the most important things Bob taught me about dealing with people on this level was the importance of a good first impression. The drill was to always look a man in the eye, greet him with a firm handshake and never be afraid to put your hand in your pocket to buy a new shirt or tie on the way to the lunch or meeting. Occasionally, Evo would invite a female companion along and it was in this way that I got to know Ingrid, his girlfriend of many years. I don't believe my presence ever clinched a deal, I was merely the "local colour".

Bob was a charming man, a smooth operator with great charisma, and it was his style that gave him his finest hour: the securing of Ampol as the major sponsor for the first world championships at Manly in 1964. All the long lunches and sweet talking had finally paid off – no other country could do it, for nowhere else did surfing have such a visible profile. The advance publicity was incredible: surfing was all over the television, in the newspapers and on the radio; and when the invited surf stars arrived in Sydney they didn't know what to think, the media crush was overwhelming and took them completely by surprise. Even the Catholic Church-owned radio station 2SM was a strong supporter of Bob's, having him do morning and afternoon surf reports, another Evo scheme dreamt up over a long lunch.

As soon as word of the contest's location got out, most of the Collaroy Surfers Association members surfed the stretch of beach between Manly and Queenscliff at every opportunity. Speculation over which sandbank would be used was rife, but when the area was finally roped off and the judging dais was being built, we knew for sure – it was the best bank on the beach and we'd been surfing it for weeks. The right was longer and allowed higher performance but the left had a short tight curl on occasions. We thought the Collaroy Surfers Association had a really good chance of providing a winner in the contest. Henry, Tony Raper and I entered the juniors and Kenno, Bob Bell and several of our older mates entered the open. After talking it through with Evo I'd decided to stay in my age group – why, I'm not sure, but I remember feeling comfortable with the decision. My three-stringer Woodsie Island Gun was going okay but it was a little stiff on the smaller beach breaks. When we checked the final entries, we were amazed to find that Bobby Brown was surfing in the open and this meant that "Bonza" Conneeley and I were the front-runners in the junior division.

Robert Conneeley was only six months older than me, but he was the only one of my peers who naturally surfed in feet-down-the-board style and it's significant that he ended up beating me in the prestigious junior division of the 1964 world titles. His style was a unique blend of old and new but because he was using a longboard, the old style dominated. Bonza had grown up at Bondi on the south side of the Harbour and we were fierce rivals, many times battling it out for numerous State and Australian junior titles, but we were always friends. I think we first met through Gordon Woods – I know we were both sponsored riders of his boards at the same time. I remember Bonza's parents inviting me down to their holiday home at Sussex Inlet on the New South Wales South Coast where Bonza and I rode waves at a little right-hand reef the locals named after him and which is called Conneeley's to this day. We ate fish that his Dad caught while he watched us surf and I felt envious of his relationship with his Dad. Bonza and I became pretty close mates although we were from very different backgrounds. He's a talented and dedicated surfer to this day and one of the few that have stuck with it, remaining true to his chosen direction.

Robert Conneeley never felt comfortable on the eastern seaboard and his life was a constant search for the right place to settle down. After a reconnaissance trip across the continent in the mid-1970s, he sold his land at Avalon and bought ten acres at Margaret River, in the south-west of Western Australia. Then in 1976 Bonza sent his wife, Diane, and their two young daughters ahead by plane and, using hand-drawn maps made on previous trips, he and his good friend Craig Leggat set out on the classic surf adventure. The two spent over a month surfing along southern Australia's wild and isolated desert coast. On the rare occasions that I visit Bonza and his family in Margaret River, Western Australia, where the waves can be big and testing, we surf together with complete confidence and security in each other's ability.

But back in 1964 Robert wasn't sure if he wanted to totally commit to the surfing lifestyle, so he took a job with the Commonwealth Bank in Sydney. And then in the space of just a few months he featured in a TV commercial with a surfing theme plugging Lipton's Tea. I was green with envy because I didn't even get to try out for the job. I knew that Bob Evans had been consulted and he must have suggested Bonza. My pride was hurt and I felt let down, so I spoke to Evo about it. He told me, though I didn't understand till much later, that with his excellent manners and winning smile, Bonza was perfect for the job – right down to the way he cocked his little finger. Evo was right; Bonza was a natural for the job, and what's more, he always appreciated a good cup of tea.

After Hawaii, the Phil Edwards influence had become very evident in my style but I began to realise that I wasn't Midget or Phil Edwards. I hadn't yet entirely developed my own style, but I was starting to see that everybody has their own way of standing on a surfboard which is completely natural to them. The main difference between the way I stand on a surfboard as opposed to either Phil or Midget, for example, is that I learnt to stand with my feet across the board, not pointing along it parallel to the stringer. Of course, there are similarities between us but there are differences too, and all the early movies and stills of us surfing show these up. It was not only the position of our feet when we first stood up but also the angle of the feet for the backhand and forehand turns, as well as the important cutback. The differences in stance are fundamental; all the pictures show my feet to be across the board and my body twisting. In 1963 and 1964 it was all body talk but by 1965 I was learning to push and bend at the knees. Early shots of Phil and Midget show very clearly what I'm on about: they are both far more delicate surfers than I am, almost lifting the board out of the water to change direction, then walking to find trim position. My style revolved around walking out of a turn – the difference was just about that simple. This was a period of transition for me and changes in my style almost follow my birthdays.

But there was another surfer emerging as a new role model that winter of 1964, a tall, handsome Californian named Mike Doyle. When he entered my life during the pre-contest practice sessions at Manly, I was totally and utterly infatuated – I wanted to surf just like Mike. An outsider might say my interest was due to the similarity in stature and appearance – even down to the curly hair – but in reality it was because Doyle stood on a board just like me. He was riding a big and bulky 10-foot 6-inch mauve board with white "competition stripes" across its widest point, about 24-inches to the rear of centre. It was a good half-inch wider than the Woodsie Island gun I was surfing in the contest and a good foot longer. With my mates from Collaroy, I sat glued to Mike's every move whenever he hit the water. We were sure Doyle would win the contest but on the final day we thought Joey Cabell had pipped him at the post. However, when the results were announced, Midget was declared winner and 64,000 Aussies on the beach at Manly went berserk.

We did everything we could to console Mike. Henry and I even took the Grunter to his room at the hotel – and smuggling her in wasn't easy, she'd become infamous by this time. Mike thanked us, saying he was stoked by the present and, as he'd be leaving in the next couple of days, he'd come surfing down at Collaroy the next day. We couldn't believe it when he actually showed up! And that wasn't all: he brought with him one of his own handmade, embroidered Mexican shirts as a present for me. It was a perfect fit and became my all-time favourite shirt – for years I'd hand-wash that shirt, only wearing it on special occasions. We surfed right behind Westward Ho, and though the waves were small and a bit sloppy, he made us all feel good by telling us how great our surfbreak was. I was just so impressed with his whole style, taking careful note of his head inclination and everything else he did from the way he paddled to his superb reverse cutback.

The next day I took him to Gordon Woods's factory to meet not only Gordon but also Wally Edmonds, the man who shaped all my boards there. Wally was an excellent craftsman, a cabinetmaker by trade and very efficient with the tools; but he wasn't a surfer so he had to rely on my feedback to assess how a board worked. Wally trimmed a blank and then Doyle pencilled out a template for my new board. Then we talked about the design for a few minutes before turning it over to Wally to continue shaping. The new board turned out exactly like Mike's – as did every board I had made for the next twelve months, except for an Island gun I kept in case the surf was big. I called all those Mike Doyle-inspired boards "Big Red" because their maroon colour was the only thing that made them different from the mauve board that had so impressed me. During this time I did make one board far too long – a big mistake. I thought that its 11-foot 6-inches would smooth my surfing out but it was a complete dog and nosedived on every critical takeoff – 10-foot 6-inches was the perfect length.

One of the long nose rides that let me place
second to Robert Conneeley in the juniors of
the '64 World Titles at Manly.

4
Send 'em up Huey!

Besides its shape, the other thing that set Mike Doyle's board apart at the 1964 World Titles was its "competition stripes". This was the first time the Collaroy mob had seen them, and they were really impressed – they looked so cool! Competition stripes were the latest fashion in California, and in the American summer of 1964 all the hip surfers were sporting them on their boardshorts as well as their boards. While I'd been staying with the Linden family in Malibu, the Malibu Surfers Association had made me an honorary member and I'd been so impressed by the club's energy that when I got back to Australia I took the first steps towards forming the Collaroy Surfers Association, recruiting some of my mates as founding members and holding the first meeting at Westward Ho, just before they knocked it down. We copied everything from the MSA: the shape of our sticker; all the rules; everything except our club colours of red and white – the Malibu club's were blue and white. The club had 35 paid-up members of both sexes and they all painted competition stripes in the club colours across their boards.

I was made president, and the first constructive thing I did was put together a sponsorship deal for the club. I contacted Casben, a Sydney-based sportswear manufacturer, and talked them into giving us forty nylon parkas and boardshorts decorated with the red-and-white competition stripes. They were made for us in a few weeks and a small group of us drove into the city to pick them up. All the people from Casben were so nice that I was amazed when they didn't return my phone call or respond to my thank-you letter, in fact they didn't contact us ever again. I was losing faith in the Bob Evans theory of sales promotion: it seemed very strange that someone high up in Casben could see the commercial opportunity, give us all the clothes and then not take advantage of the marketing potential. In hindsight however, boardshorts were only just starting to be worn by surfers and it was to be another ten years before the general public discovered them.

The Collaroy Surfers Association frequently competed against

KENNO

My third hero Mike Doyle at the '64 World Titles,
with the surfboard that I modelled my future
boards on - for a while.
Tony Raper and Mick Ducatt (standing) watching
Randy Butler paint the Collaroy Surfers Association
"competition stripes" on members' boards.

69

All the original members of the Collaroy Surfers
Association excluding Rick Wright and the girls.
From the left standing with their boards, Ross Bray,
Starky, Henry, Trapper, Twiggy, Bumper, me, Randy,
Willy Dawson, Wally, Paul Drake, Kenno, Elmo,
Blackie.
From the left sitting in the front row, Sexy eyes, Mark
De Jong, Coon, Bunkle, J.F., The Moon, Parko, Coley,
don't know, Jim Atteridge, Radish, Cushy, Mark
Dawson, Marty Vaggs, Pee-rik, Belly, Drooley,
Paul Bavier, don't know, Mick Tipping and Yubo.

other surfing clubs and sometimes we won, sometimes we lost – it didn't matter much as the social interaction was just as important. Our main rival, and the number-one heaviest club in Australia, was Wind'n'Sea. Affiliated with the American club of the same name and with branches in Sydney and the Gold Coast, Wind'n'Sea's membership boasted all the best Australian surfers including Bob McTavish, Russel Hughes, Robert Conneeley, Peter Drouyn, Kevin "The Head" Brennan, Brian Morris and Max Bowman. These guys made up the bulk of the talent that allowed Wind'n'Sea to defeat every other surfing club in Australia – including the Collaroy Surfers Association. In the summer of 1965 we made one last collective effort to beat Wind'n'Sea by forming a club called North Shore Board Riders, which combined all the surfing talent on Sydney's northern beaches – and we almost did it.

I turned seventeen on the 14th of November 1964 and passed the test for my driver's licence on the same day. On a couple of occasions during the few months prior to the test, Harold let me take the wheel of his big Ford Fairlane in order, he said, to pass on a few of his expert driving skills – which was fine, as long as I kept my hands on the wheel in his favoured three o'clock position at all times. I believed I could drive pretty well when I went for the test: after all I'd had months of illegal experience with the Dodge and years of watching Harold from the back seat. Getting my driver's licence was the best birthday present ever and to pass on the first try was pretty rare among all my mates at Collaroy. That same week I bought a car of my own, a used 1962 Ford Falcon station wagon that I christened Fred and I knew I had a good deal when Harold looked it over and gave it the thumbs up. It had been a pretty amazing few months: my licence and a car and, to top it all off, I signed a sponsorship contract – my first – with the American surf-clothing company Hang Ten. I've no idea how they found out about me. Out of the blue a letter arrived from Doris Moore, the owner of the company, asking me if I'd like to be a part of their international surf team. The letter was co-signed by a surfer-come-businessman named Duke Boyd, who later went on to run Lightning Bolt – who made boards, clothes, etc. – with Gerry Lopez, the legendary Hawaiian surfer. I took the letter straight to Evo and together we prepared my acceptance letter and within a few days Hang Ten had fired back a contract and a cheque.

I'd scraped together the deposit on Fred from the bit of money I made repairing boards and working as an apprentice for Gordon Woods Surfboards and my parents paid the balance – on the understanding that I'd repay the money by ferrying the kids to and from Mum's kindergarten. This was a pretty good deal as it gave me plenty of time to surf and meant I had to stick to a routine for five days a week. Every morning at 8, I'd set off to pick the kids up and at 4 p.m. I'd take them home again. I really enjoyed the contact with the kindy kids: we sang songs and played lots of silly games – in many ways I suppose I was still a kid myself. I drove very responsibly and conservatively while I had those kids in the car – which was surprising, given the way I normally drove back then. Fred gave me my independence all right, but looking back I think it's a minor miracle that I survived the experience in one piece. All of us who were lucky enough to have our own cars used to take our favourite chicks along as passengers while we did doughnuts on golf-course fairways at night and it wasn't unusual to come within a hair's breadth of a collision.

Chris – a tall blonde I'd managed to lure away from one of my mates – was my girlfriend at this time. An apprentice hairdresser, she understood my embarrassment with my curly hair and, a week before the 1964 World Championships, used some sort of chemical to straighten it. I was completely stoked – it worked like a dream but unfortunately it only stayed straight for a few months. It was soon after this that I stopped the taxi work. I was working full time – after a fashion – for Gordon Woods Surfboards as an apprentice shaper-come-professional surfer, the sort of deal that was almost completely unheard of at the time. Gordon Woods sat down with Evo and me and worked out a weekly schedule that took into account local surf conditions and Evo's filming trips along the coast – a very practical program that worked well for years. I was paid a weekly retainer of £35, whether I went away surfing or not. In a "normal" week, the schedule had me at the factory every Monday morning at 8 o'clock, where I'd watch Wally Edmonds shape for a while, after which he'd spend a few hours teaching me the finer points of the craft and handling the tools. Wally took a lot of trouble over his work. He'd completed an apprenticeship as a builder when he was younger, and took his task of training me very seriously. Before he let me even touch a foam blank, he spent a lot of time teaching me how to hold an electric planer and cut straight and true. It was a great grounding in the craft and stood me in good stead in later years.

It wasn't long before my work was good enough for me to be put to work shaping "pop out" boards for Nock and Kirby, a big Sydney department store. I learnt years later that Gordon had only made a deal with Nock and Kirby in order for me to gain shaping experience. My work as a shaper was always being interrupted by someone shouting that it was either morning tea or lunchtime. As I was the youngest and not at all critical to the manufacturing process at Woodsie's, I was expected to take the lunch and morning-tea orders, phone them through to the sandwich shop and then pick them up

Getting ready to head out on another surfari, I think.

That's my three stringer Woodsie Island Classic hanging over Kenno's fence (I remember the resin bead fin) from the left, Kenno, Bunkle, Westie (holding himself), Tenfoot, Belly, Wally and Henry.

This was a 1964 advertising shot for my first sponsor Hang Ten in California.

From the left, Yubo, Elmo, Maz, yours truly, Dot and Trapper.

73

at the appropriate times. The other job I didn't like was cleaning up; I always acquired a coating of dust and foam, particularly in my hair and around my eyes. But cleaning up did have its bright side. Every Friday afternoon I would shovel out the shaping bays, break up all the offcuts of foam and load them into Gordon's ute and trailer for the trip to the dump, a bit over a kilometre down the road, which gave me a great chance to thrash the ute.

As I started to feel more confident with the saws, planes and sanding blocks, the boards I shaped were getting better all the time and Gordon thought it was time to remind me of the talk we'd had not long after Mike Doyle had left the factory. Below the big "Jacobs" label on Doyle's board was a little diamond-shaped sticker that read "Mike Doyle Model" and Gordon wanted to put a "Nat Young Model" sticker on some of his boards. I didn't think it was the right time to do it but Gordon knew the surfing industry very well: he was Australia's number-one player in the surfboard business and, what was more important, my boss. So the decision was made and we put out the Nat Young Model in time for the summer of 1964. For each board sold I got a royalty of £2.10.0 as well as a shaping fee of £10, which really boosted my £35 pound weekly retainer and I was on top of the world.

The first shop to buy the Nat Young Model in volume was Richards' Surf Shop at Newcastle. Ray Richards was a friend of Gordon's. and they did a lot of business together over the years. None of my mates at Collaroy rode my boards – it wouldn't have been cool – but just about all of them rode the same design, shaped either by me or Kenno.

There was only one car dealership in Collaroy, a Volkswagen franchise held by a firm called Young's of Collaroy – they weren't in any way related to my family – and I decided to try out my Evans-taught skills on Bob Young, the owner's son and manager of the business. Bob wasn't much older than me and we'd met when the Collaroy Surfers Association had put together a "mile of pennies" – a popular fundraiser in those days – in aid of a children's home. Carrying buckets, the Association members walked among the traffic on Pittwater Road and collected motorists' loose change. We started lining the pennies up along the median strip, from down near Westward Ho, up through the shopping centre and right past Young's of Collaroy. Our community spirit impressed Bob, who talked his dad into having the firm donate around £50 to our charity, so I thought I'd have no trouble bending his ear when I talked to him about a sponsorship. Young agreed to present me with a new Volkswagen 1500 station wagon in return for having my photo taken with the car for an advertisement. That was it, nice and simple.

Styling in the hand-made Mexican shirt Mike Doyle
gave me after the '64 World Titles. Taken at
Collaroy Point, circa '65, with Gordon Woods for
an advertisement.

Counting the results of our club's "Mile of pennies"
in aid of the Children's home in Collaroy. Kenno
took this shot, that's Mick Tipping on the left,
Yubo, Julia Jacobs, Belly, Marty Vaggs and
Elmo's back, in one of our club jackets.

I'd been so pleased with myself that I hadn't mentioned anything to Evo until the deal was all signed up. Evo was pleased for me but reckoned he could have done better with his friends at Leyland fixing me up with a new Mini, which were all the rage. But I knew he was proud of my achievement in negotiating a big sponsorship deal all on my own, no doubt feeling that all the coaching he'd given me hadn't been in vain. The 1500 Volkswagen was new in Australia and while Young's were waiting for mine to be delivered, Bob asked me if I'd hand Fred over in return for the loan of a VW Beetle. It couldn't have worked out better: Rodney "Blackie" Black and I had planned to take our current girlfriends on a surf trip to Gerroa, on the south coast about 45 minutes drive south of Wollongong, and there was nothing like a new car to boost the image! My girlfriend at the time was Belinda Wright, the younger sister of another good mate named Rick, and we had a good relationship. Belinda was tall, thin and very sophisticated, her only drawback, in my eyes at least, being that she smoked like a chimney.

For some reason I can't now recall – probably because I had to pick Belinda up in the city after she finished Technical College for the day – we took two cars. We'd rented a house at Gerroa for the weekend and had a great time together on the first night. The next morning, the little left-hander at the northern side of Black Head was peeling off, made even better because Blackie and I were the only surfers in the area. We surfed for hours until we were called from the water by an hysterical Belinda, running to the water's edge and screaming like a banshee. When we'd calmed her down a bit, Belinda told us she'd taken the VW for a spin and rolled it on a dirt track behind the Seven Mile Beach. Luckily, no one had been hurt but one look at the Beetle told us it was a write-off.

The incident signalled the end of our weekend at Gerroa and the four of us piled into Blackie's little Austin for a cold and very sub-dued trip back to Sydney. Bob Young was a bit upset but under-standing and all our parents were glad to see we were all okay. All, that is, except the parents of Blackie's girlfriend – they sued me for her whiplash injuries and I wasn't even in the car! I was furious with Belinda, she hadn't asked to borrow the car and had put my rela-tionship with Young's of Collaroy in jeopardy. After the accident we went out together for a few more months but we both knew it wasn't happening any more; perhaps if I'd been older I might have been a bit more understanding. As it turned out, "Blackie" and Belinda ended up marrying and having three kids together.

* * * * * * *

This photo with my girlfriend Belinda Wright was taken at a party we had in a house I shared with John Witzig, Nyarie Abbey and Peter Hamill.

I was ready for a change – the waves, the girls, my friends; it seemed I'd been doing the same things with the same people for years – and it was California that again provided inspiration. The idea of the Collaroy Surfers Association wasn't all I brought back from Malibu with me, I'd also brought a new toy – a skateboard – and everyone who saw me ride it were amazed at its speed and the tricks that were possible on it. All my mates wanted one of course but they weren't being imported at the time and no-one was making them in Australia. We improvised by cutting a roller skate in half across the centre with a hacksaw then screwing the two pieces at either end of a piece of timber roughly shaped to look like my skateboard, but of course they didn't work anywhere near as well as the factory-made-and-designed American Hobie. Some shocking cases of gravel rash were incurred while trying to do turns down Alexander Street, the steepest hill in Collaroy, and I reckon many of my Collaroy friends are lucky to be alive after the horrendous wipe-outs they experienced on those home-made skateboards.

I was sure there was a market for real skateboards in Australia and I talked to my good friend John Witzig about it. John suggested we take my board apart, make templates of the pieces and get the components made at various factories around Sydney. It sounded like a great idea at the time and so the Surf Skate Manufacturing Company was born. John had another friend named Michael Roberts and we each put in £500. I was a company director, the only problem being I had no idea of what was expected of me or how to do it; all I really wanted to do was surf! All I seemed to do was collect the rubber wheels and metal castings from the suppliers and bring them back to our little factory in Brookvale. I managed to get free skateboards for my mates but in reality my input to the business was non-existent – and so were the returns so after a year I sold my share of the business for what it had cost me. Not long after, Michael Roberts did the same, leaving John to manufacture the "Midget Farrelly" skateboard. John Witzig's brother Paul, made a hot promotional movie of the Midget Farrelly skateboard team dressed in matching boardshorts and jackets with competition stripes going up and down ramps and around corners. I've never been able to work out why we didn't use my name on the skateboard. I know Midget was paid a royalty and probably made more money out of the Surf Skate Manufacturing Company than the rest of us put together. He and John were sharing a house at Whale Beach at this time and were the best of friends – Midget had been elected president of the Australian Surfriders Association and he nominated John Witzig for secretary – but then the two had a monumental falling out. Exactly what caused that rift is known to no-one other than Midget, but certainly a year or so later the further acrimony between Witzig and Farrelly could be sheeted home to a story called "The end of the era", which was written by John for *Surfing World.*

Since the late 1950s, Midget Farrelly had been the undisputed king of Australian surfing, but after I finished ahead of him at the 1965 World Titles in Peru and a few months later ran him a close second in the Australian Championships at Manly, the crown began to slip. He didn't go to Newcastle in 1965 for the first annual Matara event – which I won convincingly – but the next year I walloped him in the New South Wales, Australian and Matara titles and at the World Championship at Ocean Beach, San Diego. A younger, better surfer had come along and unseated the champion; a natural progression in all walks of life, but that wasn't the way Midget saw it. He was convinced my ascendancy was the direct result of an organised campaign by Evans, Witzig and other people influential in surfing to remove him from the number-one position, a belief he still holds today. Here's what he told the *Sunday Telegraph* in February 1990:

> *Bob Evans needed a surfman for his magazine and his movies. There was me, then Kevin Platt, then Wayne Burton and finally it got around to Nat. It was unbearable. It was the most polarised period in surfing. When you get a collection of people trying to pull you down, what does it suggest? It's the ultimate compliment. I was severely ostracised because my self-preservation mechanism was working okay. Nat was 100 per cent casual but mentally pulled himself down. On the strength of what he did you would have to say he was one of the greatest but in terms of creativity he was very low down on the scale. He pinched good things from other surfers and claimed originality.*

John Witzig claims he covered the events as they unfolded. He was editor of *Surfing World* at that time and, as such, entitled to interpret the events as he saw them. Midget was getting older and it was inevitable that kids who copied him would one day take his place, but he just couldn't cop it; and his enduring hostility to Witzig and myself is testimony to his inability to face the facts. The same thing happened to me a few years later in the early 1970s, when a young Queensland surfer, Michael Peterson, established himself as unequivocally the best surfer in Australia. He'd copied my style to a T but he was better: he could ride deeper in the tube while exercising more control and power than I ever had. Rather than resenting Michael for his ability, I felt comfortable with the inevitability of the changing

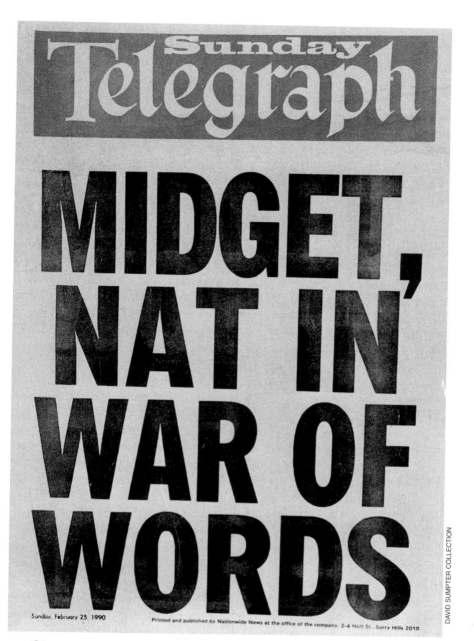

Only in Australia would an editor of a major city newspaper choose to use this as a billboard.

order and wasn't in the least bit hurt. Nor did I feel I was being put out to pasture prematurely. Almost twenty years after Midget distanced himself from me, there's still hostility. Many years after the event, when our then-teenage daughters became friends, I approached Midget and suggested that we sit down over dinner and talk about our differences. He responded by telling me he enjoyed being my enemy and wouldn't even shake my outstretched hand! So I guess that's the way things will stay between us. To this day, Midget Farrelly won't stay in the water if he finds himself surfing the same break as me.

* * * * * * *

My friend John Witzig is an unusual man, who was born in Sydney on July 19th, 1944. John's family was originally from Roseville on the North Shore and they owned a beach house between Whale Beach and Palm Beach and this is where John and Paul were introduced to surfing. Paul's first experience with a surfboard was on a plywood 16-footer in "Kiddies' Corner" at Palm Beach, while John, who had his first ride on a plywood Malibu, could stand up and control his board by the 1958–59 Christmas holidays – though his bandy legs always made him look a little strange standing on a board.

Along with Bob Evans, I give John much of the credit for my education in real life during my formative years. My first Witzig lesson – one I've never forgotten – was delivered with considerable force during my second trip to Byron Bay on what was probably my first visit to a public bar. We were drinking in the old Pier Astor Hotel, when Bob McTavish discovered he didn't have the money to pay for his next shout, so he let the whole bar know that he'd eat a big, black, ugly spider that he was just about to snatch off the wall if anyone would finance him. Someone paid up and McTavish ate the alive-and-kicking spider. Shortly after, a dwarf walked into the bar and, under the unfamiliar influence of beer, I laughed and yelled "Check the baby" – Witzig immediately decked me. Sobbing, I picked myself up from the floor and went straight to the railway station, intending to catch the next train to Sydney. John caught up with me, and after a fairly heavy talk about the feelings of others, talked me into staying. We went back to where we were sleeping in the carpark at the main beach and there was McTavish, out cold on one of the concrete picnic tables and with absolutely nothing covering him against the stiff breeze from the sea. I couldn't believe anyone could sleep like that and thought he was either unconscious from the amount of beer he'd consumed, or poisoned by the spider.

What I learnt from John that night was to think before I spoke or acted, a principle to which I've tried to adhere – with varying degrees of success – ever since.

Both John and Paul Witzig completed degrees in architecture, with Paul eventually becoming a successful architect on the New South Wales north coast while John chose a career in graphic design. The boys were raised in a strict, no-compromises way, and though it gave them both great strength of character, John's singlemindedness could sometimes be almost overbearing. John's approach to knuckles – a game in which one player tries to avoid having his knuckles being rapped by his opponent's clenched fist, the penalty for not doing so a free turn for the opponent – was symptomatic of this. John wouldn't let up, claiming turn after free turn, until my knuckles were bleeding. But despite his painful superiority at knuckles, John and I have remained close friends since 1962.

Our first surfing trip up the coast together, was made with Terry Purcell, another friend, in the cream Volkswagen Beetle belonging to John's mother. On trips north, we always made a diversion to check the surf at Crescent Head, the first north-coast point break, and this trip was no exception. It was raining really hard but not enough to deter us from our mission. We drove to the top of the big hill about 3 kilometres out of Crescent Head and then out onto the flat, where we suddenly found ourselves driving through floodwater that reached almost halfway up the doors. Midway across one particularly deep causeway the VW began to float, just like a boat. We were flabbergasted – one of the many urban myths about the Beetle was no myth after all. But more importantly, at least as far as we were concerned, it meant we could get to the surf in spite of the full-on flood. Every time we came to a deep stretch of water, we'd jump out and push the car across and often had to guide it back onto the road after it lost traction and drifted off into a paddock.

I can't remember how good the surf was on that particular trip, but I vividly remember getting back to Mrs Witzig's house at Pymble where John's mother made us what is still the best soufflé omelette I've ever eaten, and the white poinsettias she screenprinted on my favourite bright-red boardshorts. I wore them until they fell off me.

We thrashed that poor little Beetle so much that on another trip up the coast, it finally gave up completely. On the way back, we'd picked up a young Queensland surfer named Russell Hughes but at the service station where the VW conked out, a friendly truckie agreed to take us all down to Sydney. It was raining, so for half the next day we were jogged up and down under the tarpaulin covering the back of the truck. All the bumping around and the junk food we always ate on those trips had their inevitable effect, and Russell and I began to fart. Seizing the golden opportunity this presented, Russell and I staged a farting competition, finding it hilarious, as only boys can. John was livid: he punched each offender in turn until the stench got the better of him and he was forced up into the rain for air. A funny trip that one, and we did get good surf.

One of the more cerebral characters in surfing, John Witzig proved an immensely provocative writer. His most controversial article was "We're tops now", published in the April–May 1967 edition of the Californian *Surfer*. Written soon after my comprehensive victory in the 1966 World Titles, the article stated categorically that Australian surfers had taken over as world leaders of surfing and that Californian surfers were obsessed with nose-riding to the detriment of other aspects of the sport. John wrote it in response to a story, in the previous issue of *Surfer*, called "The high performers", which was more or less a eulogy of Hawaiian surfer David Nuuheiwa, held to be the world's leading nose-rider. Australia was, according to John's story, in the middle of the so-called "New Era" of McTavish, George Greenough and myself, with shorter, lighter and more manoeuvrable equipment and a more aggressive style of surfing. So there was John, flinging words such as "aggression", "power" and "involvement" into the faces of the Americans. It was like a red rag to a bull. In *Surfer's* 35-year history probably only a photo, published in 1965, of a black man on a Durban beach, with a caption explaining that though he was employed to keep the beach clean, he could not join the swimmers because of the apartheid laws, has sparked so much controversy.

There was an enormous hue and cry after "We're tops now" was published, with hundreds of letters to the editor and an interview in the next issue with Nuuheiwa, Corky Carrol and Mike Hynson rebutting Witzig's claims and even making personal attacks on John and myself. Nuuheiwa, who for many years was a close friend of mine, even claimed – untruthfully – I'd had a fist fight with Barry Kanaiaupuni after a competitive surf session in Hawaii. There was also this offering from Hynson responding to Nuuheiwa's ironic accusation that I was too mercenary: "There's more to Nat's sell-out than that. He's got a big ego and I've seen him burned. I've even burned him shooting pool – broke his ego. I've burned Nat Young's ego so bad shooting pool that he was no longer aggressive. He could not be aggressive because his aggressiveness is his ego and that's a good one too." That these people, all friends of mine, could get so personal was more a measure of the sting of John's article than anything else. They knew he was right, and before long the Australia-born short-board revolution swept the world – including the USA.

Albert Falzon in fashionable check shirt, taking photos with my close friend John Witzig.
Jeff Carter's photo.

5

Second prize
over Buff's shoulder

ALTHOUGH THE 1964 COMPETITION in Manly, New South Wales is
seen by the surfing world as the first World Championship, the
competition in Peru the following year was the first official one.
During the 1964 competition, the International Surfriders Federation
was formed and it was decided that the next international contest
would be held in Peru and that it would be given official status as a
world championship. Peru is a country where what surfers there are
belong to a small and elite moneyed class, and at that time they
could quite comfortably finance the massive obligations demanded
by such an event within their own fraternity – the members of Lima's
Club Waikiki had the power and money.

To get to Peru from Australia in 1965 was a major – and costly –
undertaking. Keen to have the strongest possible Australian presence
at the championship, Bob Evans approached the Nestlé company,
makers of the popular chocolate drink Milo, and asked if they'd pay
the return airfare of an Australian competitor in the World Championship. A company advertising executive told Evo that Nestlé would
cough up the fare, but only as the prize in a contest – and an old-
fashioned board race at that, not a surfing contest. The winner would
be the first person over the line after paddling the 16 kilometres from
Clontarf, in Middle Harbour to Manly Wharf. When the race was
announced in the Sydney press I immediately went into training, as
did every serious surfer and Clubbie in Sydney.

My paddle board was shaped by Wally Edmonds down at
Woodsie's, in fact he shaped a whole bunch of them because there
were quite a few of Woodsie's team riders keen to compete.
Although we didn't know much about paddle boards, never having
built them before, we thought we'd make them as light and as long
as possible. Gordon had a section of his factory set up to make the
polyurethane-foam blanks from which the boards were shaped and
this meant we could do a bit of experimenting. One morning, after
a lot of debate, we decided to try and get a thicker blank by opening the concrete mould before the foam had expanded to its full

Spectators were amazed at Young's lack of fatigue after paddling 4½ miles in 42min. Veteran surfers who watched the race said the performance was probably the best they had seen.

March 3, 1965. EVERYBODY'S—Page 11

I was stoked to beat all the clubbies in the
Milo paddle race from Clontarf to Manly in
January 1965. It was a means to an end as
far as I was concerned. This was a story in
"Everybody's" magazine.

capacity. This sent the stuff spewing all over the floor but we tried it a few more times, varying the interval between blowing and opening the mould. The theory sounded good: we thought if we let the blank thicken with the lid open, this would allow the foam cells to expand, making the blank lighter and more buoyant, but it was a total catastrophe and we spent hours cleaning up the factory floor. We ended up being content with the thickest blank we could blow with the lid firmly shut.

My training program consisted of practising my paddling whenever there weren't any waves worth riding: before, after, and sometimes during school hours. Dad had a mate who was a butcher and in order to put on bulk and build up muscle, I hoed into 50-millimetre-thick steaks every morning for a month before the contest. It worked incredibly well, and by the time the contest rolled around I felt really fit. I won by a mile, which shut up a lot of the Clubbies, who'd always derided the fitness of surfers, and the next day I was holding a free ticket to a place called Peru in my hand – and I wasn't even sure where Peru was.

Bob Evans, Midget and I flew to Hawaii, where Midget and I spent a week training at Makaha, then on to Canada to join our flight to Peru. It was a flight memorable for one incident, and an alarming one at that. Over Central America, the plane was bucking and pitching in a violent thunderstorm when a large section of lining detached itself from the bulkhead and landed on my head but fortunately the plane stayed together long enough to get us to our destination. Lima, the Peruvian capital, was a far cry from suburban Sydney. There was lots of backslapping and laughter when we disembarked at the airport where we were introduced to a very smooth-looking young Peruvian named Pancho, who was to drive us to the hotel. Pancho guided us through the carpark to his gleaming red Pontiac GTO and immediately we were in the car he started sprouting facts about Lima and the waves in Peru. He told us Lima was founded in 1535 and was the capital of Spanish South America until the colonies gained their independence. In 1965, Lima had a population of over a million people – there were 10.5 million in Peru – with half the population claiming Inca ancestry. Everyone, he emphasised, had some Inca blood.

Pancho was talking a million words a minute – he obviously loved his city with a passion – and we couldn't get a word in edgewise. As I looked out the window, I could see we were running yet another red light and then it all became very confused. I remember hearing a shot and Pancho screaming at us to get down as a policeman, angry at our host for failing to stop, pulled out his pistol and fired at the car. We all hit the floor and Pancho unleashed the GTO's awesome power, leaving a trail of rubber as we accelerated up the road. On the strength of our first hour, Peru seemed like a crazy country! Someone must have said something, because we hardly saw Pancho again. Looking back years later, I wondered if perhaps Pancho had been high on cocaine. Certainly the way he talked on the drive from the airport would point to that. Cocaine, as coca leaves or in manufactured form, was readily available and a major ingredient in the lives of the poor, who were mainly Indians, and a few of the wealthy Peruvian surfers.

The surfers were part of Peru's upper crust, the haves, as opposed to Peru's teeming majority, the have nots. To me, at 17, it was all new and, on the surface at least, very glamorous, the surfers we met seemingly possessing amazing wealth and a highly enviable lifestyle. Their exclusive clubhouse, Club Waikiki, was at one end of the beach at Miraflores, the largest and most wealthy suburb of Lima. The beach was divided across the middle by a barbwire fence separating Club Waikiki from the public beach. From my observations over the years, the Latin South American male is incredibly arrogant, but he has such style and charm that he can mesmerise you, convincing you that it's right and normal to have no respect for anyone other than family and friends and I've encountered this attitude, to a greater or lesser degree, on every visit there. The countries of South America always manage to seduce me with their facades of beautiful dusky skinned girls and black-tied waiters, but I think South American attitudes and society are changing. It's becoming less sexist and more equal.

The 1965 World Championships was the most sophisticated and lavish surfing event held up until that time, and I don't think we'll see anything like it again. The Peruvians sent invitations to every country where surfing was known to be a sport: the USA, France, England, New Zealand, South Africa and Australia. Of the 54 sponsored competitors, California's Long Beach Surf Club, with a team of sixteen, fielded the largest contingent – this was at the peak of competitive team-surfing in California – and they looked immaculate, parading everywhere in their blue and white competition-stripe jackets. The Hawaiians were well represented, and got on really well with the Peruvians: perhaps because they have similar dark-olive complexions, giving them that classic "bronzed god" appearance when the sun shines on their wet bodies.

The Hawaiian team, managed by the larger-than-life Chubby Mitchell, who absolutely overflowed with aloha, included such legends as George Downing, Paul Strauch, Joey Cabell, Bob Cloutier and last, but definitely not least, Richard "Buffalo" Keaulana.

What can I say about Buffalo? A mountain of a man, he is revered as head lifeguard and tribal elder on the west side of Oahu and his feats in the waves at Makaha are legendary. He once saved an entire family which was being swept away in huge seas. The wealthy father rewarded Buff with a house right on the beach at Makaha. The generous gift was swept away in a storm a few years later but Buff, in true Hawaiian style, accepted it with equanimity – the sea gives, and the sea takes away. Ten or maybe twenty years older than me – who knows? – I'd met him at Makaha on one of my early trips to the islands. I don't know why he took a shine to me, perhaps it was a big brother thing, though looking back, he may just have liked my surfing. Whatever the reason, later events in Peru were evidence of his liking for me.

I first met Buff in the year of the tsunami. Sirens were going off all over the North Shore and the cops were racing around with loud-hailers warning everyone to move to higher ground, as a "tidal wave" was on its way. Evo and I were just finishing our dinner at the Seaview – back then it was home-made food and the only place in Hawaii to eat – when we heard a real racket coming from the bar next to the restaurant. Evo recognised one of the voices as belonging to Greg Noll, the legendary big-wave surfer, and when we went in to say "Hi", we saw his drinking partner was Buff. The cops came in telling everyone that if they didn't get out, they'd be on their own, as they were moving to higher ground themselves, but Buff and Greg were in no mood to have their evening interrupted and, after buying a carton of beer, stumbled out onto the lawn, Evo and I tagging along, to sit and watch twenty or so small boats being sucked down-river as the ocean receded prior to the arrival of the wave. Greg Noll wasn't content with just a view – he decided that the best place to experience the tsunami would be from the buoy in the middle of Haleiwa Harbor. Greg reckoned that the unique experience of going down with buoy as the harbour drained would be similar to riding a 30-foot Waimea Bay. It wasn't hard to find a boat – there were plenty going past – the main difficulty lay in climbing aboard and steering in our inebriated state. We never actually made it to the buoy but were more than content to sit sipping beer while the boat dropped with the water level as the harbour emptied almost entirely, then slowly rose as it re-filled.

* * * * * * *

Robert "Bonza" Conneeley, Australian Junior Champion, was supposed to come to Peru, but because of some mix-up with his sponsorship he got no further than Hawaii. This left Midget, a Queenslander named Ken Adler and me to surf for Australia. I was really looking forward to hanging out with Bonza and was disappointed when I got the message that he was stuck in Hawaii. We'd

There can only be one high chief, and in my
opinion that man is Buffalo Kahalana, the
Kahuna. Sylvain took this shot of Buff at
Makaha in '97 with his 2nd son Rusty
playing the ukulele in the back of the truck.

Peter Troy was one of Australia's first surfing adventurers - several times we ran into him in one of the exotic countries we visited. This shot was taken in Bali by Dick in the early '70s.

heard months before in Australia that there'd be no Junior Division but it still would've been great to have Bonza in our team. My old mate Rodney "Gopher" Sumpter also showed up, direct from winning a contest in California and vague as to whether he was surfing for England or Australia.

Another unexpected arrival came walking into the club one morning as we were having breakfast. Sporting sandals and a large bushy beard, Peter Troy had turned up just in time to nominate for a heat – the same Peter Troy who'd figured in the previous year's excitement at Kenui Road. Pete had a quick shave, told us a story, then paddled out. He hadn't, he told us, been back to Australia since the events at Kenui Road but had been just drifting along from country to country. After a long and punishing voyage on a cargo ship from Hawaii to South America via the Caribbean, Peter was now doing the Americas from Tierra Del Fuego in the south to Alaska in the north, mostly walking and hitchhiking. The classic gipsy surfer, he used any method of transportation that was going. I always envied Peter Troy and his lifestyle and one of my few regrets is that I never travelled as a free-and-easy vagabond surfer in the 1960s, when I had the chance. Although his travelling had made him a bit rusty as far as surfing went, Peter made up for it with his enthusiasm and fitness and he was a welcome addition to the Aussie team.

While he was on the road, Peter wrote a lot of very colourful, descriptive letters about his adventures to Snow McAlister, who'd let me read the latest whenever I called on him at his flat in Manly. Snow was the oldest surfer I knew and a permanent fixture on the Northern Beaches, always to be seen out riding waves on his plywood ski or spinning yarns on the beach. A confirmed bachelor, Snow had been introduced to me in the early sixties by Bob Evans and he remained an admired friend until his death in 1989. I valued Snow's guidance greatly – he was always considerate of other's feelings – and when I think of him I always think of one memorable north-coast trip taken by Snow, Bob Evans and me. We were rounding a bend in the old dirt track that once skirted the Myall Lakes when Snow instructed Evo to pull off the road because, he said, this was the perfect place to "boil the billy, sit for a while, look at the view and watch the world go by".

Bob Evans was in his element in Peru, it was the perfect stage to display his smooth, sophisticated charm. The high point for Evo was a meeting and cocktails at the Palace with the President of Peru, Fernando Belaunde Terry, a social and economic reformer who lost power in 1968 as the result of a military coup against him, but was re-elected president in 1980.

I always detected a note of disappointment in Bob's voice when

he talked about the contest at Manly not being officially acknowl-
edged as a world championship; I think he saw it as a bit of a slap
in the face. It was, after all, Evo who'd almost singlehandedly negotiated for the massive sponsorships needed to pull the event off and
now it wasn't being recognised. The then president of the
International Surfriders Federation was Senior Eduardo Arena – I
nicknamed him "El Viejo", Spanish for old man – a very dapper
Peruvian gentleman with a wonderfully warm smile and a distin-
guished mane of grey hair. Eduardo, I think, understood what Bob
had gone through to organise the contest at Manly and was personally out to do everything he could to repay the hospitality Bob and
his friends had shown him and his entourage in Australia. After the
championships, Bob was taken to Eduardo's country estate in the
foothills of the Peruvian Andes. The grapes from the estate produced
a big, fruity Riesling-style wine for which the area is famous, the
vineyard going hand in hand with the family's principal business of
liquor importing. The day of wonderful wine and food drew on. Bob
left the room briefly and when he returned the woman he'd been
talking to had vanished – along with all the other women. Over the
next ten minutes, the room filled with thirty of the most ravishing
girls Evo had ever seen – mistresses of the male guests. Evo knew it
was a normal part of Peruvian life, but said he still found the smooth-
ness of the whole operation amazing.

We kids weren't invited to Eduardo's hacienda but we were still
looked after night and day: right from the time we booked into our
luxurious hotel it was first class all the way. Both at the club and at
Punta Rocas an hour's drive south of Lima, beach boys were
assigned to look after and prepare each surfer's board. They waxed
them, carried them to the water's edge and would've paddled them
out the back if asked. When we came in, the boys came running
over the rocks to carry our boards back to the club, wash and wipe
them, and put them away until we wanted them again. We'd never
experienced anything like it.

I'd brought two boards with me, both made at Woodsie's, as the
contest was to have both a big-wave and a small-wave "hot dog"
event. The big-wave event was the official World Championship, the
"Campeonato Mundial Tabla Hawaiiana", and was to be held at
Punta Rocas, while the hot dog contest would take place in front of
Club Waikiki, on the sloppy little beach break that peeled off both
left and right. Eduardo was contest director, the man with the final
say, but when he talked about the small-wave event it was as though
it was just something for the kids and didn't really matter. Back in
Australia, when Evo first told me about the big and small-wave
events, I thought it sounded like a great idea, a step in the right

direction for the World Championships and so I'd brought the two boards with me.

My small-wave board was 10-foot 6-inches long by 22-inches wide, a copy of the one Mike Doyle rode in the world contest in Australia. Coloured the same as its predecessors with deep maroon top and bottom and the red-and-white stripes of the Collaroy Surfers Association, it was also named "Big Red", Red for short, and was wide and very stable, especially while standing on the nose, even in white water. Although the small-wave contest wasn't given any significance by the officials, as far as the competitors were concerned it was the place where all the progressive surfing was taking place. When I stood on top of the big bluff overlooking Club Waikiki and Miraflores, I just knew this was the spot. Seabirds, attracted by the abundance of fish in the cold, plankton-rich Humboldt Current, were diving and wheeling all the way to the horizon. As we clattered down the cobblestone road to the club, I got a closer look at the sloppy little peaks and could see the potential, thinking that it could probably get fairly good.

The semi-finals and finals were held in absolutely windless conditions, the smooth, glassy faces looking a lot like those from southern California, where David Nuuheiwa had moved to from Hawaii. David looked like a cat: smooth and surefooted on every wave, he narrowly beat me in the semi-final but lost the final to Paul Strauch from Hawaii. Then it was time for the big-wave contest, the official World Championship.

* * * * * * *

I'd worked the bugs out of my Woodsie Island gun before I left home. My workmates at Woodsie's at the time were fellow surfers Darryl Holmes, who was the glasser, and his brother John, better known as Stork, who finish-coated the boards. One day I'd just arrived at work, all ready for a morning of shaping with Wally, when the Stork walked in and said we should go up the coast immediately because there was a giant southerly swell and the weather map showed that offshore winds were likely. That was enough for us: we loaded up Darryl's little Austin and were gone inside an hour. Gordon was used to my comings and goings but he wasn't prepared for his other workers to abandon ship on him. I pacified him and justified the trip by telling him I was going to work on the design of the Island gun and needed some help in case something went wrong. I took two Island guns up the coast with me and as it turned out it was a good thing I did. The first afternoon we surfed a spot called Foresters on the central coast and the board I took out was terrible:

I couldn't make any clean turns on the big open faces without spinning out and after an extremely rough trot came in cursing the board and hoping the other one would perform better.

When we pulled up at Lennox Head near Byron Bay the next day, I was awestruck. The surf was a clean 10 feet, with not a soul around, and the offshore wind was peeling big drifts of spray off the back of every wave. I hadn't yet surfed the other board, although I'd had it standing in my bedroom for over a month – to be honest, we get very few quality big waves in Australia, particularly on the east coast, so this was my first chance to try it out. I paddled out full of optimism but extremely cautious after my experiences with the other board, but on those big green faces at Lennox, it felt really positive and fast, without even a hint of spinning out, a taste of what it should go like in Peru. Back in Sydney, I surfed the new Island gun only once more before we left and it was terrible, though to be fair, the waves weren't very big and I found myself constantly wrestling with the board's stiffness on the Sydney beach breaks, but as soon as the waves reached 6 feet, it felt fantastic. In Hawaii, on the way over to Peru, I had another opportunity to test the board and its performance was faultless on every wave I rode.

Punta Rocas – in English, Rocky Point – the venue for the World Championship, is well named being, literally, a huge point guarded by sharp boulders. We surfed without legropes in those days and the big test was in seeing if you could keep hold of your board while "Eskimo rolling" a set of waves on your way out the back. Punta Rocas had no defined break, which made it tricky, especially at around 10-foot. If you lost your board it went onto the rocks where it would at best be damaged, if not broken beyond repair, and the beach boys were kept busy as they scurried like crabs over the rocks to retrieve boards, many of them receiving some nasty cuts and grazes in the process.

On finals day, the waves were a good 8 feet with some slightly bigger sets. I had a long swim and the rocks buggered my board, but then again all the competitors did some swimming that day, with the exception of George Downing and the eventual winner, the Peruvian Felipe Pomar. The result was a huge upset considering that the finals field included the current Makaha champion Fred Hemmings and the talented Paul Strauch, also from Hawaii. My hero Mike Doyle was also in the field, as were Midget and Ken Adler from Queensland. There were lots of suggestions that it was a "home-town decision" and it is a fact that Peru provided two judges and the other countries only one each. Felipe's style was certainly crude when judged against the other finalists, though Bob Evans later wrote that Felipe's style was "ungainly but efficient". By the

AUSTRALIAN WOMEN'S WEEKLY, JUNE 1965

I bought this rug for my mum in Peru. That country was a real eye opener for me.

same token, Bob also said that manoeuvres made in the critical
stages of the waves should have scored higher, which, he said,
would have made me world champion.

I really can't say if I was surfing better or not, and it really doesn't
matter: Felipe is in the record books as the 1965 World Champion.
Perhaps I might have given the impression that I disputed the judges'
decision, I don't know. I was barely dry after winning the 1966 World
Championship in San Diego when Lester Brian wrote: "Nat himself
was not optimistic [of winning] as he has become sceptical of world
contests since his defeat in Peru", and Pomar, upset by my tactics in
the 1966 Makaha final, is reported as saying, "I was disappointed that
Nat hasn't matured and kept step with his unquestioned surfing ability. He appears to be the same poor loser I beat in Peru in 1965."
The truth is, I wasn't a poor loser at all. By the judging standards of
the time, based as they were on "the biggest wave for the greatest
distance", Felipe was clearly the winner. For me, the small-wave
event was where it was really happening.

A couple of days after the contest, Evo and I were lazing around
the pool at Club Waikiki, sucking on cocktails and trying to recon-
cile my losses in both championship events with my win in the five-
mile paddle race. I'd got my revenge on Felipe in that race by
beating him by 2 minutes and 30 seconds, with Peter Troy a close
third, so Evo reckoned I'd earned a drink or two. The alcohol was
starting to take effect when I blurted out to Evo that I'd like to see
something more of the country than just Punta Rocas and Club
Waikiki. The next minute, we were being offered the use of a car by
a striking blonde named Pina. She'd overheard our conversation and
said she was very sorry that Lima didn't have a car-rental company
but she would be happy to be of assistance. Pina, we learned, was
the wife of Pancho – fortunately not the man of airport fame – the
right-hand man of Eduardo Arena and a very successful Peruvian
banker, so successful, in fact, that he owned a bank. Pancho had
been a part of the Peruvian entourage to the Australian contest and
had, I think, asked his wife to do everything she could to assist us.
Whatever; Pina offered to lend us her car so we could look at the
country and hopefully find some waves. Bright and early the next
morning, we met her at the club and after piling all the boards on
her little Chevy Nova, took off to explore the coast to the south,
enjoying the sense of freedom after being prisoners to the contest for
the previous two weeks. Talking to Pina years later, I learnt that her
younger brother, "Shigi" Miro Quesada, whom she'd loved very
much, had died while surfing Pipeline in Hawaii.

Our first stop was at a village street market and a stall selling big,
inviting melons. It was hot in the desert and we were thirsty, so we

cracked it open, then and there, in front of a hundred staring eyes. Looking around the dirt-poor little village, I couldn't believe the poverty the people lived in – it was the first time I'd been exposed to the plight of the Third World's peasants, and it horrified me. I don't think I'd ever before given it a thought, and at the time I didn't think we had anything like it in Australia.

The surf we found on that day wasn't anything to write home about but the trip was made interesting because we found a pier at a beach with a long-running left and I actually got a wave big enough to allow me to surf Big Red under the pier, through the piles and out the other side – I was stoked. Far less uplifting, though equally memorable, was another incident. On the jagged rocks beyond the point were a hundred or more shining black shags drying their wings and resting between fishing expeditions. The last thing they needed was a pack of hoons to start throwing rocks, but this is exactly what we did – we belted the shit out of those poor innocent birds just for the hell of it. I suppose when boys get together and start throwing rocks, reason goes out the door and one thing leads to another, but I'll never forget, or forgive myself for that act of stupidity.

For me the best thing about our time in Peru was the ambience at Club Waikiki… and the girls… and the parties – there was even a picture of me out dancing with some Peruvian beauty that ran in the Australian newspapers. It seemed that every night after dinner we would be going somewhere, either to a night club or a private party. As a young bloke just feeling his oats, I was delighted; the constant string of mysterious, dark-eyed Latin girls was a whole new experience and dancing through the night in my white patent-leather shoes, moving from one señorita to another, was so wonderful that I felt like staying in Peru forever but, luckily, Evo managed to talk some sense into me and put my experiences of Peru in their proper perspective.

The presentation night at the Club Waikiki was a really lavish affair. I was escorting a gorgeous Peruvian girl, courtesy of the club, and everything was going along just fine, though the almost non-stop dancing in a penguin suit – not to mention my second placing – were beginning to get to me. Around midnight, after the banquet had been scoffed and gallons of alcohol consumed, the presentations began. Or at least I'm told that was the case. To say I was under the weather would be a gross understatement – legless would be more accurate. I rolled around the dressing room as a valet struggled to keep me still long enough to straighten my bow tie and get me and my coat arranged in a vertical position. It was no use, I just couldn't stand. Then the next thing I knew I was being lifted up, slung like a

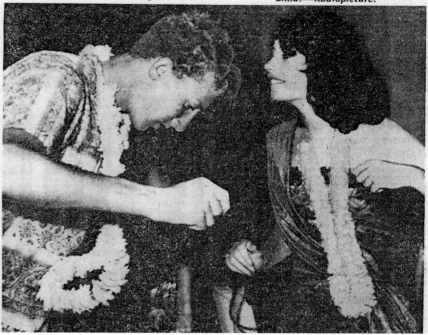

2 DAILY MIRROR, MONDAY, MARCH 1, 1965

SURFING'S SWINGING CHAMP

Robert "Nat" Young, Collaroy surfboard rider, has a swinging time with a dark-haired beauty at a Hawaiian night at the Waikiki Club in Lima, Peru. Nat, 18, won the five-mile surfboard paddling race in the world surf championships in Lima.—Radiopicture.

Dancing with one of the girls from the Club Waikiki in Peru.

rag doll over Buffalo's shoulder and carried onto the stage. The audience was yelling and screaming – apparently they'd been trying to get me up on stage for quite a while – but Buff, in his best pidgin, said: "Nat, he a liddle bit fuckdup jus now. He wud like say 'Aloha'." Everyone clapped and I left the stage the same way I'd come onto it, dangling limply over Buffalo's brawny shoulder.

Immediately after the contest, the official meeting of the International Surfers Federation was held at Club Waikiki, to hold a post mortem on the contest and to decide on the next country to stage the event. I got there a bit late and when I walked into the room, George Downing and some of the Hawaiians were locked in a full-on argument with Eduardo Arena and the Peruvians. It was all getting a bit nasty and turning into a real slanging match with both sides constantly interrupting whoever was speaking. Eduardo could not keep control and it might have erupted into a fight at any moment if it hadn't been for big Buffalo Keaulana, who stood up and said something like, "Let me talk, Georgie". Buff, a former Makaha champion, apparently hadn't said a word all night, but now he showed his true stuff. He'd just started to put the issues as he saw them when all of a sudden the meeting was at it again. Downing was getting verbally stuck into Eduardo, when Buffalo pulled a ukulele out from under his chair and began to sing *Pearly Shells*. When he reached the chorus, he walked over to Downing and signalled with his head for him to start singing. Downing resisted, but Buff insisted and Downing joined in, then someone else started to sing, then another, until everyone was singing along – Buffalo had reminded us that we were all in this together. As I sat there, singing along with the other Aussies, I looked over at Buff and thought that this was what a Hawaiian *Kahuna* must be like: a surfer so in tune with Huey that he could settle the differences and keep alive the spirit of surfing.

6
The end of an era

I ARRIVED BACK IN AUSTRALIA from Peru in March 1965 and was treated like the new World Champion by both the media and the surfing community. Australian national pride has a tendency to exaggerate our sporting successes, especially when the media implies that one of our own has been hard done by, and the 1965 World Surfing Championship was no exception. The media ignored the fact that I'd come second and hailed me as Australia's "runner-up world champ", the Aussie boy who would have been world champion if it wasn't for a flaw in the judging system and a bit of bad luck – and, thanks to that national pride, people swallowed it, many still believing today that I was actually 1965 world champion.

It all boosted my self-confidence tremendously. In essence people were saying I was the heir-apparent to Midget's throne and everyone, including me, believed it. Midget and I were still quite close at this time, surfing together every few days and talking regularly. He was writing a weekly surf column for the *Sun Herald* newspaper and Bob Evans was doing the same for the *Sunday Telegraph*, the only newspaper articles I read voluntarily, everything else I read in the papers was brought to my attention by Mum or John Witzig. When Mum showed me a story about Midget called "the changing of the guard", I could understand why he felt so insulted – the reporter had written him off completely. In reality, Midget's competitive life was far from over – a fact he demonstrated by beating me in the 1965 Australian titles – and the story was nothing more than some newspaper reporter's assessment of the state of Australian surfing as he saw it. Perhaps this was when the rot set in; Midget and I never did get to talk about that article.

There was probably a lot more media speculation flying around, but I wasn't paying much attention to anything outside myself right then. The situation at home had become intolerable and Harold, Greta and I had reached a compromise which we knew was only a stop-gap solution. I was living in a bedroom with separate access at the back of the house that allowed me to come and go as I pleased,

No more heros! I was doing it in my own way. John
took this picture of me perched on the nose at fisho's
in Torquay back in Easter '65. The waves were too
big to hold the contest at Bells that year.
Conneeley won the seniors and I came second.
The juniors were cancelled.

so Harold and I only had to face each other at meal times, if at all; from my point of view, the name of the game was to stay out of his way as much as possible. When Harold and I were forced into close contact, Greta found herself defending me on a regular basis, so seeking an excuse to leave home, I told my parents I was going to get another dog. Harold blew up as expected, and I packed my gear, jumped into my car and drove to Whale Beach to ask John Witzig if I could move in with him. Greta knew it was going to happen sooner or later, and seemed quite relieved when I confirmed the move with her as she'd always respected John, making me promise only that I'd visit her regularly.

John's rented house on Whale Beach Road was a big, comfortable, rambling weekender, typical of the beach houses owned by well-to-do country families at the time. The owners only used them at Christmas or Easter, if at all, and for the rest of the year they were available for rent. Most of the houses on the Peninsula were similar, built in the first half of the twentieth century when the Australian economy rode on the backs of sheep, and John's was no exception. Clad in hardwood weatherboard with wide verandahs, it rested on beautiful sandstone foundations that continued well above ground level, making it almost two floors high. The corrugated-iron roof made a wonderful noise when it rained and the verandah allowed perfectly framed, picture-postcard views of Whale Beach. The high sandstone foundations allowed for quite a lot of space between the floor and the ground, and in the Whale Beach house, as in many other Peninsula houses, the sandstone had been lined with fibro to create a "garden flat". The upper level consisted of the kitchen, bathroom and two bedrooms, one of which was occupied by a guy named Peter Hamill, who was a projectionist for Paul Witzig, and his girlfriend Nyarie Abbey, who worked for John at the skateboard company. I'd known Nyarie, a tall wispy blonde, for years, but we'd never really talked to each other. Dorothy De Rooy, the best female surfer in the Collaroy Surfers Association, my wife-to-be Marilyn Bennett and Nyarie hung around in the same group: with both brains and looks, they were the hot chicks in the top class at the girls high school right next door to ours – Henry and I were always hanging out for a really good perve at the surfie chicks in class 1A.

John Witzig lived in the garden flat – in reality, one large room – and had made it his own private domain. There was a basic kitchen at one end and John used the remaining space for entertaining and sleeping. Sea-grass matting covered the floor and a picture rail and narrow shelf, filled with empty wine bottles, ran round the walls. I knew that John was really into good wine and, along with our friend Terry Purcell, was building a collection. John and I had made quite a few trips up the coast with Terry, who was now working part-time at the skateboard factory and studying for his Doctorate of Philosophy at university. I can remember looking at the bottles lining the walls and when I pointed at one, John delivered a lecture on the quality of the grapes, where they were grown and how the amount of rain and sun had affected the quality of the vintage.

John and Terry were buying wine together in moderate quantities and I decided to start buying a bit also – they'd studied the subject closely and told me what to look for. Buying wine that would be best to drink in five, ten, twenty or even thirty years was a fantastic concept to me at the time. Every few days, or that's how it seemed, one or the other of us would stumble on a dozen bottles of red produced by some well-regarded vineyard or wine maker in the 1950s or 1960s. Often the person behind the bar – most of the finds were in pubs – had no concept of the true value of the wine, and if we inquired about more, we'd occasionally be taken to the cellar. Some of the purchases we shared, at other times we invested individually and in this way I was able to acquire some of Australia's finest reds. A dozen of the 1958 Hamilton's Bridgewater Mill for under £1 each and three dozen 1962 Rouge Homme being my most memorable finds. Now, thirty years on, Terry still has plenty of those irreplaceable wines left but John had to sell his entire cellar to keep afloat through one particularly sticky financial crisis and all my wines were stolen when someone broke into my house at Whale Beach in 1969.

John's flat was a wonderful space to be in. In what became a Sunday-morning ritual, Nyarie, Peter, John and I would sit together, wolfing down hot toast thickly spread with avocado spiced with freshly ground pepper while we browsed through Saturday's *Sydney Morning Herald* – a paper John read religiously every day – to the accompaniment of a Chopin polonaise, while the morning sun streamed through the open French windows. On most other mornings I'd stand on the verandah, squinting through the glare off the water as I tried to assess the waves at The Wedge in the northern corner of Whale Beach, one of only two consistently high-quality lefts on the northern beaches. I remember the day the graffiti "choc wedge 7d" appeared in big white letters on one of the giant boulders above the break, courtesy of my old friend Gopher's elder brother "Mexican". Choc Wedge, price sevenpence, was a popular ice-cream of the day, and we all thought Mexican's effort was quite funny – we'd think differently now, no doubt.

When I moved into the shared house, there were also two Afghan hounds in residence. One was Sian, a very feminine golden bitch belonging to Nyarie, and the other was John's regal black-and-tan young dog, Aram. Aram and I shared quite a few magic moments over the years. Afghans love to roam and so we did, taking long walks on most mornings and afternoons. Whale Beach was a perfect place for dogs at the time: a huge expanse of golden sand to play in and no council dog-catcher to worry about and a fascinating jumble of boulders lining the shore. We spent hours jumping from rock to rock, testing our skills on the 2-kilometre-or-so walk between Whale and Palm Beaches. You couldn't really say that those dogs belonged to either John or Nyarie, incredibly independent and very intelligent, the dogs only shared the house with them.

John had taken Aram's name from a William Saroyen book that had greatly impressed him; though he hadn't given it to me to read, which is strange, because at that time he was influencing not only my reading but Nyarie's also. I did get to read some great books in this period: from Tolkein's *The Hobbit* and *Lord Of The Rings* trilogy to *The Catcher In The Rye* and *Animal Farm*. I also read Ayn Rand's *The Fountainhead* around this time: no other book, before or since, has had such an effect on me and I identified totally with the lead character, a talented architect who broke new ground with the revolutionary buildings he designed, fantasising that I was developing a new, totally different style of surfing.

Another book to impress me – so much so that I named my new red setter puppy after its central character – was *Youngblood Hawk* by Herman Wouk. Driving to the western suburbs to get the pup, I knew exactly what I'd call him, and when the ball of red fluff with the too-long legs bumbled its way to my feet, I swept him up and told the breeder its name was Youngblood. Looking back, I was probably a bit envious of John and Nyarie's relationship with their dogs but it went a bit further than that: my childhood friendship with the cocker spaniel Rusty was so close and had come to such an abrupt and horrible end, that I longed to rekindle all those feelings that only the devoted companionship of a good dog can provide. So now our household contained, in addition to the humans, a red setter, two Afghans and two German shepherds. The shepherds belonged to Peter Hamill and when he began working as a taxi-driver, Nyarie looked after them for him. You'd think that all the dogs would make for a chaotic household, but it was smooth and peaceful most of the time and Nyarie was very dedicated to them. I was very attracted to Nyarie and we often got into some heavy discussions about everything from the hidden meaning in the latest books John had us reading, to the disasters we'd experienced in our personal lives. I was falling in love with her, but it was to be years before anything came of it. All our raves took place over a cup of tea on the front verandah against a background of crashing surf – a very dramatic setting.

THE WIND blows strong from the nor'east but, the water is smooth with only a faint ripple to disturb the surface. Nat Young arrives late one afternoon; the surf is 5'7". It is good long reef and 'Nat' rips. His bottom turns are unbelievable and he snaps his fin on the third wave.

This is my favourite shot of me and Youngblood at Long Reef. Alby took the pictures for Surfing World magazine, Volume 10 #1.

Bob McTavish gave me a crash course in the rhythm and blues and turned me on to boards with thinner rails and lower volume.

One day someone from the ABC phoned – I don't know why they picked us – to ask if they could film a party at our house as part of a television documentary the ABC was making on the surfie lifestyle. We'd been talking about having a party for months and this was the perfect excuse – not to mention that the ABC was paying for everything: food, wine, beer, a band, all we had to do was be there. I can't remember the film crew at all and I never did get to see the finished documentary – titled *This Surfing Life*, it went to air in the summer of 1966–67 – but I recall dancing through the night by the light and warmth of a big bonfire. It was a great party, the only one we ever had at that house, and it was also the last time I saw my girlfriend Belinda. She'd stayed over the weekend, and as I drove her home we talked about our parting company and the possibility that our paths would never cross again.

Bondi's surfing maestro, Kevin "The Head" Brennan also stayed at our place that weekend and together with McTavish we surfed The Wedge on the Sunday morning. Kevin had won both junior and senior State Championships in 1965 and was an incredibly talented surfer on the right day. Bob McTavish was always around at our place when he was in Sydney. I thought he just came by to use the shower but sometimes we got into some deep conversations about surfboards and waves. He was living in a beige twin-spinner Ford parked in the North Avalon carpark on a semi-permanent basis. The front seat had been ripped out and replaced by an armchair, while the back seat doubled as a bed and sofa. Bob still drove that old twin-spinner, despite the modifications: he'd be on the Peninsula for a while, shaping boards at Wallace's in Brookvale, then head up the coast to shape for a board maker in Queensland. One wet afternoon, he turned up and announced that he was going to do what he'd said he would a year previously: give me an education in Rhythm and Blues. Bob had over a hundred records for me to listen to, ranging from black artists like Muddy Waters to Ginger Baker and the other new sounds that were coming out of England back then. It took me a week to play my way through those records and I took it all very seriously, believing it was an important part of my education.

On another of his flying visits, Bob arrived at our place singing the praises of Noosa Heads, a place I'd never before heard of, going on and on about waves that peeled off endlessly around three rock-lined bays. Later that weekend we all went to a barby at Bob Evans' Elanora home and while we were sitting round the fire, sucking on ice-cold beer and munching snags, McTavish kept it up: "Noosa; Noosa; Noosa". Mac didn't have to sell Noosa to us, however. Evo had heard of the surf there and he'd been looking for a fresh location for his surf movies. This, coupled with the fact that neither of us had ever been there, meant we were going as soon as we could get organised.

* * * * * * *

We took off with Bob's wife Val and their three young kids, Brett, Fiona and Glen, heading north along the coast to Queensland. Passing by Crescent Head, Angourie, Byron, and the Gold Coast was a new experience for me, I'd never before driven by these places without stopping to surf. North of Brisbane, we drove into the area known in the tourist brochures as the "Sunshine Coast". The landscape was very different from that of northern New South Wales: no soft, rolling hills, instead, flat coastal plains with the odd mountain jutting up dramatically. We drove through Caloundra, back then an old-fashioned beach resort for Queensland country folk, with lots of guesthouses sporting wide verandas. Arriving in Noosa, we rented an ugly modern house right across the road from Main Beach and once we'd settled in, set off to explore the area. Overhanging the seaward side of the road at First Point was a stand of enormous gum trees and high in the branches of one were two koalas, happily munching on leaves – we were all really impressed.

On the opposite side of the road, up the hill towards National Park, the urban landscape was interesting: it was the first time I'd seen sympathetic development with buildings nestled among trees and overlooking the surf. Hundreds of tall, stately gums had been given the respect they deserved and towered over everything all the way past Johnsons to National Park. Both Johnsons and First Point were very protected and although they were breaking at only 1 to 2 feet, it was easy to see the potential. From Johnsons we could see National Park was about 3 feet and there were only two surfers out on the water – it looked magical and I was all ready to paddle out right then. However, when we watched for a while and got a better idea of the layout, we could see that it was really breaking too close to the rocks. McTavish had told us to follow the coastal walking-track past the "Boiling Pot" for about 450 metres to Tea Tree Bay. From the end of the point at the "Witch's Cauldron" we could see the quality of the waves at Tea Tree and I ended up running the last couple of hundred metres to the water, hardly able to contain my enthusiasm. Paddling out, the waves looked about the same size as at National, but with the difference in swell direction they were breaking away from the rocks and rolling into the bay – and nobody else was out.

Those first few waves are etched in my mind. In surf like this I

Watching McTavish surf National Park at Noosa for my first time was inspirational. Ti Tree bay provided me with a long-running consistent quality curl to further develop my style. John took both these shots.

George Greenough was different to say the least. He still looks and surfs the same as he did in '69 when Alby took this photo of him with his spoons.

could be so much more accurate than in the Sydney beach break. The takeoff exploded in the same spot every time, perfect for a classic Phil Edwards top turn, then into a long-running wall. Sometimes I'd get low and tuck myself into the tube, at others let the curl break on my thighs until the wave started to slow right down. Just before this point in the wave was the perfect time for a nose-ride; either that or a good strong cut back before the final section fizzled out on the rocks. I was so excited by Tea Tree on that first day that I surfed it right into the beautiful winter twilight that only Noosa seems to have. My board was giving me a bit of trouble because it was designed for Sydney's small, gutless beach breaks where you needed volume to get around, both paddling and surfing. Up here, where the waves were finer and more predictable, it was tending to spin out, especially when the waves took on a bit of size and it dawned on me then what McTavish had been saying back in Sydney about thinner boards and finer rails.

McTavish and an American named George Greenough – who rode a kneeboard – later showed up at the Noosa house with tales of bigger and better surf down the coast a few miles. Evo and Greenough got on like a house on fire after Bob got out all his camera gear and spread it out on the kitchen table; Greenough was right into cameras. While they drooled over Evo's toys, McTavish took me out to his car and, taking two golf clubs out of the boot, introduced me to "cane toad golf", which involved using the golf clubs to hit as many cane toads as great a distance as possible. The cane toad was introduced into Queensland in the 1930s, in the misguided belief that it would rid the sugarcane industry of cane beetles, one of its worst pests. It didn't work and the cane toads, poisonous to most Australian snakes and other potential predators, bred in their millions to become a pest over much of Queensland and northern New South Wales, by the 1990s spreading into the Northern Territory. Bob was very accurate at chipping the toads, justifying the "game" by insisting that by getting rid of even a few of the pests, he was doing his bit for the State. I found out the hard way that the game, though novel and exciting at first, resulted mainly in getting bits of cane toad all over myself.

By the next day the swell had dropped so Evo and I went to try a spot that McTavish and Greenough had surfed the day before at the mouth of the Mooloolah River near Point Cartwright. The break seemed pretty sharky and was exciting, though a bit short and too close to the rocks. As these were the days before leg ropes and I was having trouble with my board, I was pretty glad to get out of there. McTavish was working just up the coast from Point Cartwright, shaping for Hayden Kenny Surfboards in a town called Alexandra

Headlands, so we called in to the factory to say hello. When we got there, however, they were all out surfing on the right-hand reef across the road from Booloorong, a swanky little resort about 800 metres down the road from the factory. Greenough was riding a surf mat, lying down and going sideways in a style I'd never seen before, while McTavish and a bloke named Russell Hughes were ripping it up as I would have expected. Sitting ourselves down on the beach to watch the action, we were approached by an older, bearded beatnik type who'd come out of the water when he saw us sit down. I recognised him immediately: it was Bob Cooper, the original Californian gypsy surfer whom I'd met in Sydney the year before. He was from Santa Barbara, California, Greenough's home town and it was he who'd told George about the Queensland waves. Cooper had fallen in love with Wills, an attractive Netherlands-born girl who worked at Booloorong, and when he took us over to meet her, she made me a memorable chocolate milkshake – on the house.

George Greenough and all the Hayden Kenny workers shared a house right on the beach at Alexandra Headland. One evening the boys were feeling the cold a bit – even in Queensland, winter nights can be relatively cool – so George set to work to ease the situation.•
He first cut a hole in the iron roof through which he ran a whopping great piece of pipe to make a chimney. The bottom of the pipe he attached to a tin washbasin which was sat in a second washbasin half filled with sand, forming a fireplace that kept the house warm all winter. When we walked into the living room and saw Greenough's creation we started to get the idea we were dealing with a unique character, a Gyro Gearloose type. The day after surfing Point Cartwright the swell went completely flat so Greenough invited us, along with the rest of the crew, to slide down the front of a place called Wappa Dam. This was a very ballsy experience; you had to jump well out to land 3 metres down the mossy spillway and avoid the bits of metal sticking out from the dam wall. It was 9 metres down once you hit the face, and a full on adrenaline rush. After that we all went back to George's house to eat some of the tuna he'd caught the morning before. It seems that when George knew the fish were coming up the coast near Caloundra he'd paddle out on an old surf ski or air mattress to intercept the school a couple of kilometres offshore. He'd kept the house supplied with fish the entire winter, so naturally the boys all loved having George stay with them.

George taught me his way of fishing and I became totally hooked, so to speak. One variation he showed me involved taking a big chunk of foam and winding about 80 metres of venetian-blind cord around it. On the free end was tied the biggest hook to be bought, baited with the largest slab of meat available. Then you paddled out from

George's surfing was head and shoulders above anyone else I had ever seen - he was showing us how to ride the tube. How did he stop this fin-less rubber mat from slipping sideways?

the shore and let the line unwind until it was just off the bottom, allowing the foam and the rest of the line to float on the surface. After that was done, you paddled back to the beach and waited till something happened. It always seemed ridiculous to be paddling out on an air mattress to the foam doing flip-flops in front of me, having no idea what was on the other end but pulling it up anyway. Greenough said if the pull was slow and steady it would probably be a big shark, while spasmodic bursts of power meant it would more than likely be a stingray. A few times I got towed around to the point where I finally had to cut the line off. It was pretty scary – whatever was on the other end of the line was awfully big. I kept practising this method of fishing when we went back to Sydney until I had to give up because I had a hard time finding friends to do it with.

The surf came back up at Noosa at last and we got to see for ourselves what McTavish was talking about when he said George Greenough was the best surfer in the world. All that previous week he'd surfed lying down on his air mattress, which really made me laugh – the best surfer in the world but he didn't even stand up! It was a Wednesday morning when the swell hit. We'd been at Noosa for a week, only surfed Tea Tree once and could only imagine the potential of National Park. But on that Wednesday we were all out nice and early, jumping off the rocks at the Boiling Pot to eliminate the long paddle back out. It was a solid 6 feet and getting stronger by the hour and George, Bob and I did a few crossovers that Evo recorded for posterity. Greenough was surfing his kneeboard "Velo", a 5-foot long fibreglass spoon with very little flotation and a flexible tail. To say I was impressed is a mild understatement – I couldn't believe my eyes. The thrust and acceleration out of the turns that was sending him hurtling down the line was truly amazing and it looked to me as though George was carving from further back inside the curl than anyone I'd ever seen before. I had to agree with Bob, he was the best free surfer in the world as long as he had some substantial power in the wave. The G-force and foil that George had been gibbering on about all week suddenly made sense: he'd talked about how fish stored energy in their fins, in their whole body in fact, and when they wanted power to propel them forward they released that stored energy. It was so simple, why hadn't someone thought of this before?

The first thing I did when I'd finished surfing that day was change the fin on my board. I sanded off the crude, roughly shaped skegg that did nothing but keep the board straight and replaced it with one of Greenough's foiled fins, copies of a blue-fin tuna's tail, with swept-back curves on a narrow base. George showed me how to lay up the glass and resin for a fin panel. He explained the necessity to get as much resin out as possible to make the fin dry. Fibreglass had the power and ability to store energy, while resin was soft jelly with little or no "memory". The sanding of the fin into a perfect foil was critical. George had experimented with different-shaped foils and determined that those with flat sides delivered the most raw power. He spent a morning showing me how to sand a fin, getting it really accurate by counting the numbers of layers of fibreglass on each side. There was so much to learn!

Then our time in Noosa was suddenly over and it was time to leave. I felt I'd just scratched the surface on understanding surfboard design but my further education would just have to wait until I could get back up the coast again. Back in Sydney, I tried to describe to Woodsie what I'd seen and learned in Noosa. It was difficult to explain but I knew the whole direction of surfing had changed for me. Woodsie's reaction was predictable and straightforward – we changed the fins on all production boards from then on. Woodsie suggested I build a board based on the same principles as the one Greenough was riding and try it out. It was a great gesture on his part, but a really daunting task for me – and, of course, Gordon had no idea of the time involved.

I carefully chose a blank, cutting out the template at 6-foot 6-inches because I was much bigger than George. I then shaped the bottom with tons of curve at the front and flat towards the tail. Then came the tricky part: I had to lay up the fibreglass in a staggered pattern to allow the tail to bend and store energy and I had very little real idea of what I was doing and I could see it was going to be trial and error. After days spent sanding and laying up fibreglass I began to feel pretty good about the board I was creating. The deck was easy, I rolled it over and, as Greenough had shown me, used a sander to remove the excess foam and get the required flotation. When the time came for the maiden voyage, I chose North Narrabeen because it has the best consistent wave in Sydney, paddling out about half an hour before dawn with no one around. The waves looked good but it was hard to see them coming because I was so low in the water. Paddling for a wave was impossible, I got in so late on the first takeoff I got buried trying to get to my feet. It was a disaster, I tried for an hour to get the board up and planing, but to no avail. Dejected, I returned to Gordon's shop to explain to him what had happened and try to rationalise my next move. I worked out that the problem lay in the fact that because George knelt on his board, his centre of gravity was low and stand-up surfers couldn't apply his type of power.

7

Sam

BY THE NORTHERN WINTER of 1965–66, after three trips to "The Rock" – Hawaii – I felt I was getting pretty familiar with the place. However, during a three-week stay on Oahu in November–December the waves were pretty uneventful. It was one of those seasons where I went through the motions: a couple of nice sessions at Sunset but nothing happening out in the water to make the trip memorable. I was surfing a standard Woodsie Island Gun with a Greenough stage-3 fin attached; the board wasn't too different but the fin was and I remember being surprised that no-one asked me about it, probably because I didn't have much credibility in Hawaii at that time. On the inside, I was busting to get home to Youngblood, and back to north-eastern Australia while the cyclone season was still on. After my disastrous attempt at riding the Greenough spoon, and in order to get myself ready for Hawaii, I'd gone back to riding a version of Big Red, 10-foot 6-inches long by 22 1/2 inches wide, and a Woodsie Island gun. I'd made sketches of the board I wanted to shape and hidden away in the loft at Woodsie's was a blank I'd chosen after a lot of searching – I wanted no lift at all and a nice heavy stringer.

But I was in Hawaii, and as the official Australian representative at the 1965 International Makaha Championships, I had obligations. All the guests were billeted in ex-military Quonset huts, close to the contest site at Makaha on the west side of Oahu. The event had been receiving financial support from The Outrigger Canoe Club for a few years, and all the invited participants were extended club privileges including a place to park, use of all its facilities and a chance to meet some of the more affluent Hawaiians. It was great to be able to use the palatial clubhouse – complete with restaurant, volleyball courts, outrigger canoes, pool, etc. – right on the beach in Waikiki, instead of wandering around like a tourist as I'd done in previous years. It was at the club I met the then Hawaiian champion Fred Hemmings, who took me for my first ride in a Hawaiian outrigger canoe, on breaks called Canoes and Number Threes. It's a great experience and

At Honolulu airport with Baron Arnaud DeRosnay after we had finished representing our countries in the International Championships at Makaha.

one that sets the imagination wandering. As you dig your paddle into the water to send the canoe gliding along the waves on the reefs off Waikiki, with the sun dissolving into the ocean behind you, you're constantly reminded that you're in the same type of craft as that used by Polynesians from the south when they discovered and inhabited the Hawaiian Islands. Fred was a superb sportsman, a large-framed, muscular, footballer type from a big, hospitable family and I fondly remember the meal they shared with me one night at their modest home in one of the valleys behind Waikiki.

I had no car, so most of the time I stayed at Makaha, about 40 kilometres north of Waikiki, surfing hard and enjoying the company of the close-knit community. Every afternoon a dozen locals would descend on the beach to watch the sunset, play music and do a little socialising and it was no surprise to find my old protector Buffalo Keaulana among them. One afternoon when the waves were only at about 2 feet, Buffalo paddled past me carrying a spear and wearing a diver's mask. I watched in amazement as, after ignoring the first wave in a set, he shot the spear into the white water of the second, lifting it from the water with a decent-sized *awa* impaled on it. After taking the fish off the spear and throwing it to a kid with instructions to take it to the beach, he went on fishing until he had enough to feed everyone. By the time we left the water the fire had been lit and the fish had been cleaned and were sizzling away on a barby. With the sun melting into the horizon, I sat down under a coconut palm and someone handed me a beer. Buff reached for his ukulele and began to sing *Pearly Shells*, just to remind me of Peru, while everyone cracked up – the story had obviously been told a few times.

After checking the waves at Makaha one morning, I teamed up with my old hero Mike Doyle and his best mate Rusty Miller, who were members of the US team, to go surfing on the North Shore before the heats began that afternoon. We decided to drive over Kole Kole Pass, in the military zone around Schofield Barracks, which would cut a good 20 minutes from the trip between Makaha and Sunset. This was the first time I'd been over Kole Kole and I couldn't understand why security measures were so strict, but I later learned that the Pass was used by the Japanese bombers as they flew in at low level to bomb Pearl Harbor, the incident that brought the United States into World War II. Doyle was great: he treated the armed guards to the same winning smile that I'd first seen in the world contest at Manly in 1964 and explained that we were all "invited international guests" snatching a bit of time to catch a few waves before the heats began. The guards were won over, presenting us with a pass for the return trip and waving us through. I've never since been denied access through this short-cut but thousands of other surfers have been turned around. We surfed Sunset for a few hours then headed back over the Kole Kole Pass. Once through the gate and around the first switchback, Doyle pulled over to the edge of the road, stopping the car to admire the breathtaking view.

We sat on the stone retaining wall, perched on the sheer cliff, with the whole western side of the island laid out thousands of feet below us. I noticed an unfamiliar, aromatic smell almost at the same time as Doyle pushed a hand-rolled cigarette into my fingers. I didn't know what to do or say, it was the first time I'd been offered a hit on a joint and I had no idea of exactly what would happen to me, so I gave a sort of "no", trying not to be rude. It was a strange situation: the marijuana was being offered by one of my heroes and my reaction surprised me. Doyle was like a god to me at that time, so why didn't I take the joint? Thinking about it later, I remembered reading a magazine article claiming marijuana wasn't conducive to competition performance and went on to say that tests on both soldiers and civilians had shown that they lost their drive. The story also claimed that people became passive and lethargic, spending a lot of time just sitting, talking and laughing. It sounded like fun but I'd decided then and there that dope wouldn't help my burning desire to be the world's surfing champion.

* * * * * * *

It felt great to be back in Sydney, covered in foam dust, the electric planer like an extension of my arm as I took the initial clean-up cuts off the blank I'd retrieved from Woodsie's loft. The plan shape wasn't that different from what I'd been riding in Australia all along, with the 22 inch-wide point 6 inches behind halfway, and only 6 inches shorter than what was considered the normal length for someone my height in 1966. But this slight difference was enough for people in the United States to seize on as an explanation of my win in the San Diego world contest in October 1966, their media going on about "the short-board revolution". It may have been the best term they could come up with to describe the difference between the Aussie boards and their own – ours were up to a foot shorter – but length wasn't the most important factor; the most significant difference lay in the thickness of the Australian boards.

One of the most important lessons I'd learnt from McTavish and Greenough was that you had to get a rail down in the water to control a turn, so the first modification I made to the board was to drop the overall thickness by at least half an inch, making a huge difference, both in the flotation for paddling and the amount of rail you could bury in a turn. The new board was $2\frac{1}{2}$ inches thick, at least an inch thinner than a US board made for someone of my height and weight would have been right then. The other McTavish-inspired element was the rail. I'd experimented with a few since Noosa the year before and found that getting rid of the bulk was the key, the soft egg was the best shape for my style of board. This really broke new ground for me, giving me some well-needed control in a turn. The big, fat round rails used on all boards up till then didn't have the responsiveness necessary for drawing a turn out through a section, because under pressure they'd spin out. The final element was the bottom shape, which was really no different to look at than the boards being ridden elsewhere in the world. The nose was flattish, for nose-riding, then rolled slowly into a full-curve displacement hull and was at its deepest right in front of the fin. It complemented the thinner profile and just flowed into the soft-egg rails.

When I'd finished shaping, I handed it over for Darryl to wrap up in the super-strong Volan fibreglass cloth that would give the finished board the light-green tinge I'd always admired, especially with the wide laps that were fashionable at that time. I'd laid up the fin panel before I left for Hawaii, giving it time to cure, and I'd done everything exactly as George had told me, using only enough resin to saturate the 36 layers. In plan view, the fin's shape was that of a normal Greenough Stage Three, with a flat foil to deliver maximum thrust out of a turn – shaping it with the coarse pad on the grinder was like carving butter. I'd learnt a lot about making Greenough's fins since the day at Long Reef when one I'd based on a normal fin panel broke in half from the pressure of a loaded turn.

I'd need a quality wave to test my new board and Sydney surf just wouldn't provide it – unless there was a miracle – and I couldn't go up the coast right then because too many other things were happening. The board had been curing for a week when a miracle in the shape of a strong swell did arrive, and I took "Sam" on his maiden surf. The first problem was in the flotation: just paddling out was much harder on Sam than on any of my previous boards and I was a bit worried; I wanted to surf the board in the State, Bells, and Australian titles. What had I done wrong? I'd probably have dumped the board then and there if not for the fact that it planed really well. Sam had me half under water and catching the waves wasn't easy because I had to paddle so hard, but when I caught a wave with a bit of a wall I could feel the fineness in the rail giving me better control than I'd experienced with any of my earlier boards even though the waves weren't really long enough to give a true picture of the board's performance. Funnily enough, the first place I put "Sam" in the water was at my old stamping ground, Collaroy, at a break called "The Kick" about 100 metres behind the tide-filled swimming pool.

My first time in the water on Sam. I was stoked
when this photo turned up in a magazine but
no one else realised the significance. My board
was magic! Ron Perrott just happened to take
the picture on this pretty big day at The Kick
behind Collaroy pool.

After about an hour of riding the consistent 5-foot, right-hand walls, I fell off, right in front of the pool on an absolute purler of a wave that for a minute actually had me thinking that I could make it around the point and into Collaroy Beach, something I'd never managed to do. Swimming in to the rocks on the point I was really mad with myself. I just knew my new board would be buggered – I couldn't even see where it had gone. But when I climbed over the pool wall, there was Sam, without a scratch and floating in the middle of the pool as if nothing had happened. I couldn't begin to imagine how my board had managed to float across the rocks, over a brick wall and into the pool – it looked impossible, but there he was, surrounded by a crowd of people! Someone who'd seen the whole thing told me that after I'd fallen off, the wave catapulted the board straight into the air, over the wall and into the middle of the pool, where it landed without touching anyone – I began to think there might have been something a bit odd about this board I called Sam.

*   *   *   *   *   *   *

I was still trying to leave Sydney. I knew Sam and I needed time in the thinner waves in Queensland, where the Australian titles were to be held, but every week something else would come up to trap me in the big smoke. Not that I minded too much, autumn is my favourite time of year in Sydney. From March to May is a time of clear, sunny days and plenty of swell. Every week I'd visit Mum to deliver my washing, collect my mail and chat over lunch. As a rule, the mail might contain a cheque from Hang Ten or perhaps a personal letter, but never an official Government letter like the one I held in my hand one day in that autumn of 1966 – I was really worried, never having received anything like it. The letter was from the Taxation Department explaining that they were unfamiliar with the occupation of professional surfer, the term I'd used to describe myself on my taxation assessment forms, and asking me to arrange an interview the next week. At the Taxation Department I was interviewed by a Mr Smyth, who turned out to be a pleasant and helpful man. He'd already spoken to Gordon Woods to confirm my arrangements with the board factory and I showed him the Hang Ten contract and told him how I'd acquired my car from Young's of Collaroy – I also told him that I was thinking about buying some land, which would put me in debt for the first time in my life. (Perched on a sandstone cliff overlooking the ocean towards the Palm Beach end of Whale Beach Road was a block of land that I'd been interested in for some time. I used to go up there and sit looking at the ocean beyond the mini-forest of scribblybark gum trees growing down to

Whale Beach Road. It wasn't a very big piece of land and was wedged between the ugliest house in the world on one side and a rustic little cabin on the other. I did eventually buy the land by naming my parents as guarantors for a £6000 loan from the Commonwealth Bank in Collaroy.) Mr Smyth's response was short and to the point, something along the lines of "sounds like you need a manager". He then went on to tell me that he'd heard that Richie Benaud, the Australian cricketing legend, was working with young sportsmen and that it might be worth my while to give him a call.

* * * * * * *

Richie Benaud was something else, the first truly professional sportsman I'd ever meet. He and his wife ran their business from a flat in Bondi, in Sydney's eastern suburbs, and following a ten-minute phone conversation, Richie invited me over to discuss my situation in more detail. He was a lovely man, totally obsessed with cricket but an absolute professional who spent more than eight hours a day at his typewriter churning out cricketing stories for any newspaper who'd buy them, in Australia and overseas. He also put together numerous short, weekly radio "grabs" for broadcast throughout the British Commonwealth and was part of Australia's team of commentators for test-cricket broadcasts.

Richie wanted to know if I'd talked to any newspapers about writing a column – or if I could string a few words together. I told him I wasn't sure if I could write, and, in any case, I thought I should wait and see what happened at Bells and the State titles before I talked to a paper. Richie's response to that really got me fired up – I was talking rubbish; I should go and talk to the newspapers now; never put anything off; I was going to be State, Australian, World champion that year; everything else was mere details – he radiated such self confidence and positiveness that it was impossible not to become enthusiastic.

Because the *Sunday Telegraph* had given me my first ticket overseas, for winning the 1963 Open Championship, I thought it would have the most sympathetic ear of all the Sydney papers, but Bob Evans was one of the surf writers for the *Telegraph* and naturally I wasn't going to talk to them behind Bob's back. When I told Evo of my meeting with Benaud and what he thought I should do, he endorsed Richie's idea completely. Evo set up a meeting at the *Telegraph* but didn't attend himself, believing the meeting was one I'd do better to handle on my own; he'd give his opinion to the management when and if it was asked for.

I went to the newspaper's head office overlooking Sydney's Hyde

Park, where I met the then Managing Editor, Frank Margan. I had to explain that I had no writing experience and hadn't completed my school Leaving Certificate – but, I hurriedly added, English had been my favourite subject at school. When he didn't immediately kick me out, I thought I was still in with a chance. It didn't take long for me to convince him that the *Telegraph* needed someone like me to give a younger surfers' slant to the two pages of the "Under 21" section, as the other person writing for the surf pages was even older than Evo – the Vice-President of the Australian Surfriders Association, Ray Young. They were really doubling up, I told him, for not only were Ray and Evo older, Ray's position gave his articles a sort of official slant. I concluded by saying that what the *Telegraph* really needed was a weekly column from me to compete with Midget Farrelly's column in the *Sydney Morning Herald*. The meeting came to an end with Mr Margan non-committal, but he did say that I should show him a sample of what I could do by writing about the forthcoming Bells Beach titles, and when I got back he'd get a reporter to work with me in editing what I submitted – getting a newspaper job was going to take a little time. I thought going into the interview without Evo at my side had blown it for me, but there was nothing I could do about it now. I'd given it my best shot and now I had no choice other than to do what I was advised, looking on it as pre-employment training.

As he'd promised, when I came back with my Bells story Mr Margan introduced me to one of the journalists who sat me down, read through the story then took a pair of scissors and cut my painstakingly handwritten piece into its twenty main points and explained why he'd done what he had. My story on Bells that I thought was so brilliant in the way I'd described the size of the surf and the fierce competition seemed insipid when we looked at it back at the *Telegraph* office. They showed me that it was just dry facts anyone could write and I needed to put more of myself into the story. I began to see what they were getting at. I'd won Bells from an unknown surfer from Victoria in big, pounding, 8-foot surf; Midget didn't compete – my story should have been dynamite. It was invaluable training that enabled me to continue writing my column right up till the end of 1972. My next story – detailing my April success in the State titles at Avoca Beach was much better. The surf was really wild and woolly with big peaks in the middle of the beach. Avoca is just like Collaroy in these conditions, being protected from the Southerly Buster, so I knew how to handle the testing conditions and it gave me some great material to work with, especially when I narrowly beat Bobby Brown and Robert Conneeley – not to mention the fact that, once again, Midget failed to show up. Midget had

Each of these people had a huge influence on
my life. From the left, Bob and Val Evans with
Doctor Robert Kinross Spence. Jeff Carter's photo.

This shot of John's is known in the surfing world as "The headless Bob McTavish" for obvious reasons.

missed both Bells and the State Championships: what was going on? Would he show up for the Nationals? This was the first of my stories that the *Sunday Telegraph* published. My rough copy still had to be edited, even to having the last few paragraphs rewritten, but essentially I'd done it all myself. I was now a journalist for the *Sunday Telegraph* with a half page to fill every week for which I'd be paid $100. I was looking pretty good.

It was now mid May. Finally, with nothing more to anchor me in Sydney, I tied Sam to the roof on Evo's Valiant and we left for Queensland. The plan was that Bob would shoot a sequence of me training for the Australian titles which were being held at Greenmount, Coolangatta, and every Tuesday we'd send our columns to the *Telegraph*. Noosa hadn't changed at all in the twelve months I'd been away; a few more houses perhaps, but still the same beautiful linked bays. McTavish, Greenough and most of the crew from the year before were still there but making boards with a company called Cord rather than with Hayden Kenny. McTavish was living in an old ice factory in Mooloolaba and shaping a few boards every week. He seemed stoked to have me around as a sparring partner because as the current Queensland champion he was a definite contender for the Aussie crown.

On a day when the swell was down, Evo, Greenough, McTavish and I made a trip to a relatively unknown area north of Noosa called Double Island Point. Driving along the beach then walking over the headland we camped out for a couple of days in complete seclusion with the most magnificent bay in front of us. The fishing was good, the smooth and glassy waves ranged from only 6 inches to a super-hot 4 feet, and the days seemed to run together in a haze of food, surf, fishing and sleep. Those few days with my mates at Double Island created some lasting memories and were exactly what I needed to recharge my batteries for Coolangatta. Sitting round the campfire talking surfboards and strategy for the Australian Championships, we all agreed on some hard cold facts: in 1966, there were two distinct styles of Australian surfing, or so we said. The older "Functional" style can best be described as take it easy, safe, keep your movements to a minimum and do only what the wave will allow. It was smooth, flowing and beautiful to watch, and Midget had become its greatest exponent. The other style was nicknamed "Power" and was developed by the three of us around the fire. We joked that it was all Greenough's fault, certainly George turned us on to fins and how to build them to store forward thrust. This was the single biggest development in power surfing, because George's fin designs let us, for the first time, get into areas of the wave that we could accelerate out of. The ability to ride in the tube and get out of it by turning and applying pressure was a real revelation; it was like taking a blindfold off.

The weather in Coolangatta was pretty wild that first week in June. As we drove down the coast for the weekend competition we were caught in 110 km/h winds and driving rain squalls; a low off the coast had produced cyclonic conditions with turbulent seas. Luckily, because I was State champion, I didn't have to compete in the preliminaries that Saturday. I felt really sorry for my friends, trying to get a decent ride in the 2-foot onshore mush; it didn't seem fair for them to have their hopes dashed by the fickle forces of nature and I hoped that Huey would send them a few good sets, but, that's competition. On the Sunday morning before the finals I rose bright and early. The swell looked about the same as it had the day before so I asked John Witzig – who was up from Sydney – if I could use his car to check the surf at Kirra. Driving round the point at Kirra my attention was focused more on the waves than the road until the bloodcurdling sound of grinding metal and squealing tyres jerked me back to reality – I'd hit another car.

After the police interview, John made arrangements for his car to be towed away and took me back to our hotel, more worried about me than his car. As I seemed unhurt, he suggested I should do what I planned and go for a warm-up surf at Kirra, – but I'd have to get a move on, there was only an hour or so to go till the final. I took John's advice even though I was still pretty shaken, falling off on the first few waves until I settled down and centred. The warm-up shook out the butterflies and made the final a lot easier than it might otherwise have been.

I felt confident and strong as we paddled out after being photographed. Although the waves were only 3 feet and lacked any guts by normal Greenmount standards, it was contestable surf. I always made sure I caught the first wave in every battle during my career and this time was no exception. However, as I paddled back out I saw Midget on a much better wave and thought he had to have scored well. Then I managed an equally good wave and we were even again, at least in my mind. I paddled out to sit and wait for a set with McTavish and Bobby Brown and as we sat there talking we saw Midget fall off another medium-sized wave. Then the set rolled in and we all got a wave each, as did Russell Hughes, the other Queenslander in the final. McTavish surfed adequately, but the little choppy waves didn't really suit his concentrated powerful style. The dark horse getting all the good waves was Wayne Burton, a guy from Sydney; I knew he was a good surfer, but Australian Champion he wasn't, he just happened to excel on the day. Time after time I saw him flying down the line, finally being put out of the winner's circle when he caught an edge in the north-westerly bump. Robert Conneeley took no risks whatsoever – we both knew he was capable of better – and came in very disappointed with the result.

And then the final of the 1966 Australian Championships was over. I thought I surfed well enough for the conditions but was even more excited by the fact that it was the first time that year I'd surfed against Midget – and I'd won on all six scoring waves. Bob Evans wrote a story for the *Telegraph* the week after my win and other newspapers and magazines took up the "New Era" theme and that was it – Midget was not happy.

Then it was time for the Newcastle and Hunter Valley Championships, held in conjunction with the Matara Festival. I'd won this contest quite easily the year before, but that was without competition from Midget and I had to keep reminding myself that I'd beaten him in Coolangatta and I could do it again. Right from the very first heat there was no doubt that I'd win – Sam loved the place – and the only real battle was with a hot goofy-foot named Richard Harvey. When I fell off in the final, letting Sam wash in towards the rocks on shore, thousands of eyes were watching the board's progress. From the top of one wave I got a glimpse of Sam wallowing in the shore break and I waved and yahooed loud enough for him to hear, then swam as fast as I could towards the rip. As if responding to my call, he floated out in the rip, with us both reaching the same spot in the shortest possible time. I climbed back on and paddled out thinking that Sam really was magic. The word was out all over Newcastle, even the guy at the service station where we stopped for fuel before heading back to Sydney, was talking about Sam, Nat's magic board.

It's hard to put into words exactly what happened to Australian surfing in 1965–66. We said that the new power style had consistently beaten the functional style but really, all that happened was that I'd beaten Midget at every encounter we'd had. Looking from the outside, one would simply say that the younger sportsman had finally beaten the reigning champ, and so the wheel turns; there was really nothing more to it. The team chosen to represent Australia in the senior division at the World Championships was picked directly on national titles results and was comprised of surfers from both the Functional and Power schools.

Those eligible to compete were Robert Conneeley, Wayne Burton, Bobby Brown, Russell Hughes, Bob McTavish, Midget and myself. Everyone was really excited about going to California and the Australian Surfriders Association had team blazers made in green and gold; everything was looking great except, with only six weeks to go before we left Australia, there was no sign of the six promised free

SUNDAY TELEGRAPH, SEPTEMBER 18, 1966.

UNDER 21

California here I come

... SAYS NAT YOUNG

AS usual, the Newcastle Hunter Valley contest was tremendous in every respect.

I was fortunate enough to return to Sydney with the trophy for the second time in succession.

Today finds me in good spirits and good health in Hawaii. Confirmation of my ticket for the world surfing contest came through early in the week from the U.S.A.

However, there was no mention of expenses and on Monday night I found myself with a ticket but no financial support.

Anyway, thanks to the Sunday Telegraph, 2UW, Colan Products Pty. Ltd., Gordon Products Woods and the prize money from the Newcastle contest, "Sam" and I were on Friday's plane for Hawaii.

I guess you are wondering who "Sam" is, and I think a definition would be appropriate at this time because "Sam" really matters to me.

He is a little over the fence in actual age, about one and a half years old this coming summer.

The stress marks of overwork are starting to show, but he still has so much power. "Sam's" vital statistics are from nose to tail about 9' 4" and 21" thick, and 22" in his widest part. I guess "Sam" is a little different even in statistics to most boards.

In fact to float the 12½ stone of me the board should be at least 10' long and nothing under 4" thick.

● Experiments

"Sam" is as much a part of my surfing as I am, together we have experimented and also had a lot of fun, from the early mornings at North Narrabeen to the high pressure of the Australian championships.

To put it bluntly, "Sam" is very me. We can adopt an attitude for high tension contest surfing and still have a ball when we meet each other for a surf every couple of days.

Anyway, after "Sam's" efforts in winning the last six contests this year, I told him about California and promised him a trip.

So here we are.

I think the world contest could be seen best through the eyes of "Sam," because you see nobody knows he is magic. In fact I only found out a few months ago myself, and last weekend proved it.

During the finals of Newcastle contest, in front of about a thousand people, I fell off in the shore break. All eyes were on "Sam" as he floundered in a channel close to shore.

When I pulled myself over a wave and whistled and beckoned for "Sam" to come, taking his time, he made his way through the heavy shore break to me.

"Sam" and I found the flight to Hawaii very pleasant. Next week we will tell you how we found California in our first surf.

SURF STAR Nat Young and his trusty pal Sam at Mascot Airport before boarding a plane for Hawaii this week. Who's Sam? Why, it's Nat's favorite surfboard — the one that has carried him to victory in six successive contests this year.

One of my early columns in the Sunday Telegraph.

tickets. The Association was ropable, we couldn't believe the Americans would renege on their promise, especially after Manly, where six tickets had been provided for the US team. In the end, the American Surfing Association came good with only three tickets, which really let a lot of our team down. The tickets went to Gail Cooper, the winner of the women's division, Ted Wilson the official Australian judge, and myself. It's hard to believe that the Americans could be so mean, and I sometimes wonder if the business with the tickets had any bearing on later events. Wayne Burton gave up surfing altogether, married a Collaroy girl named Roslyn and became a breeder of Afghan hounds. Bobby Brown was simply in the wrong place at the wrong time in 1967 when he was caught off guard at his local pub in a dispute over a pool table. Bobby was only 20 years old, not yet in his prime, when his drunken assailant severed his jugular vein with a broken beer glass and ended his life.

8

The New Era

MY SPONSORED TICKET to the 1966 World Surfing Championships in California, sent by the United States Surfing Association, arrived eight days before the event was due to start. The time needed to adjust to the waves in San Diego was getting cut pretty short and I'd have to rely on the experience gained during my previous trip to California. It sounded good in theory, but in reality I hadn't surfed the San Diego area during that trip. I travelled with John Witzig. It was our first overseas trip together and we were both very excited, though travel expenses were a bit of a problem. John was working as editor of Evo's *Surfing World*, so he had a little help from the magazine along with some money from an inheritance, and I ended up going cap in hand to both the *Telegraph* and Gordon Woods for small advances – I needed a regular income to service my loan on the land at Whale Beach and then, at last, we were on our way. We stopped over in Hawaii and spent the night at the YMCA before flying on to California. Also with us on the trip was Ted Wilson, Australia's official judge. Ted had never before been out of Australia, so wherever we went he went too. From Maroubra on the south side of Sydney Harbour, Ted was handsome, likeable, intelligent and funny, the perfect travelling companion, and we really enjoyed each other's company.

We hadn't been expecting it, so it didn't come as much of a surprise when we found that no-one from the United States Surfing Association was at Los Angeles International Airport to meet us. We rented a red Ford Mustang and drove out to Malibu to visit my American "Mum" Margaret Linden and her family and as Butch wasn't home we hung around playing pool and listening to records until almost midnight then left to spend a rough night in a cheap motel. Next morning I called Doris Moore, the owner of Hang Ten, who invited us to have breakfast with her. We had no idea how to get to her home in Long Beach, a problem made worse by Californian freeway maps – they seemed to be in a language completely different from anything we were used to. After several wrong turns and much

The stately Greenough hacienda in Monticito, 5
minutes south of Santa Barbara in California.
John took this shot and the two on the following
pages.

Sam loved the break called "rights and lefts" at the Ranch, it was the perfect training ground for the World Championships.

George and Ted Wilson doing things that boys do and a bit later seem to regret.

confusion over up and down ramps, we arrived at Doris's at 10.30 a.m., three hours after leaving Santa Monica and a possible world record for a twenty-minute trip.

Back in Noosa some months before, John had arranged for us to spend a few days at George Greenough's home in Montecito near Santa Barbara. Of course we got lost in the maze of freeways again and had to call George to come down and show us the way to his house. George arrived in a vehicle that looked suspiciously like a police car – as it turned out, it was an ex-cop-car complete with the official design in black and white, though the similarity ended there – and when he stepped onto the road, I noticed he was wearing the same jeans and tee-shirt he'd been wearing a few months before in Australia. I climbed into the front passenger's seat of George's car to travel the last few miles with him, while John followed in our rented car. The back seat of George's car was a jumble of clothes, cameras, wetsuits, fins, even an inflated surf mat, and looked exactly like his room back in Alexandra Headlands. The house in Montecito was large and in the Spanish-hacienda style, with lots of black iron and whitewashed walls. George had a private entrance to a bedroom that his mother had long ago given up trying to keep clean or tidy. Mr Hamilton Perkins Greenough was an eccentric millionaire with a passion for collecting old automobiles – he had some true classics in a garage under the house – and every now and then George would be sent to drive the latest acquisition home.

Mrs Greenough was very hospitable, filling us with wonderful, wholesome meals and telling stories about George's childhood. I'd always wondered why George wouldn't eat ice-cream and it was his mother who solved the mystery. She told us George and his brother had a passion for ice-cream when they were youngsters and would constantly pester her for it. To cure them of their cravings, she bought them each a giant barrel of ice-cream, sat them down on the front lawn with spoons and told them they could eat as much as they wanted. It was too much even for them, and they were forced to stop completely when it started coming out of their ears. To this day, neither George nor his brother has been able to stomach ice-cream.

After enjoying the Greenoughs' hospitality for a few days, it was off to a place called "The Ranch", about 50 kilometres north of Santa Barbara. Formerly the Hollister Ranch, after the family who once ran it as a large cattle property, The Ranch was in the process of being subdivided and sold in 100-acre blocks, and though many famous people have since bought land there, in 1966 only a few blocks had been sold. We passed inside after George gave his name to the armed security guard at the gate, and it was like going back in time. With only the original ranch house and a few new homes here and there, it was an oasis of space in overdeveloped California. George and a few of his mates had a private surf area extending for some 30 kilometres up the coast from the entrance to The Ranch, and it was the original surfers' paradise. We wound along a one-lane track, catching glimpses of one perfect point break after another every time we rounded a corner and crossed another ravine. The swell looked quite small, only 3 to 4 feet, so George headed for a break called "Rights and Lefts" – and when I saw it for the first time, I just about wet my pants! It wasn't big but it was a perfect peak going in both directions and no one was out there. The offshore wind was fanning the breaking barrels and it was with a great feeling of relief that I realised I'd found my training ground for the World Championships. Sam loved it, performing beautifully as though the waves were made for him. I'd paddle really low on the board, stand up fast at the last minute and turn very slowly but accurately into position; holding him back, storing the power until the wave was about to break then I'd release him like an arrow from a bow – straight through the tube and down the line.

The days went by in a blur of practice, only occasionally inter-rupted by the appearance of George's friends the Hazzard brothers. They lived in Santa Barbara but had built a surf shack of palm fronds and driftwood facing Rights and Lefts and just above the high-water mark and spent every day possible there. Driving home one after-noon, George commented that he thought I'd get a little more spring out of the turns with a bit more flex in the tip of the fin. I thought the fin felt okay, but it was true that the Californian waves seemed to break a lot slower than those in Queensland so, with nothing to lose and perhaps something to gain, I let George re-sand the fin that night. The next day we waved goodbye to the Greenoughs, telling George we'd see him in "Oz" next January, and headed for San Diego.

The further south we drove, the more obvious it became that we'd been in a time warp for the past week; California was just so crowded and developed. We had breakfast in Huntington Beach with Duke Boyd from Hang Ten, then it was back in our rented Mustang and south on the freeway. San Diego, when we got there, seemed more sane, more Australian, and we were all feeling pretty good when we booked in to our hotel on Chevron Island, in former marshland at one end of San Diego Harbour. Most of the competi-tors were staying in the same hotel which made for some good times: meeting heaps of old friends and making new ones and cruis-ing around in a shiny, soft-top Camero. Chevrolet, one of the main sponsors of the World Surfing Championships, had provided one Camero for each team's use during the week of competition.

There were no waves good enough for the first day of the competition, so it was declared a lay day. The day after, I stood looking at the consistent sets of solid, 6-foot, left-hand grinders at North Jetty and decided I couldn't really expect to win on them – all my training had been done on rights – and I felt frustrated and amateurish, a mood not helped by the knowledge that David Nuuhiwa was in the competition. All along the coast, in Huntington Beach and even up around George's place, we'd heard about David. An Hawaiian who'd lived in California for years, he was about my age, height and weight, and all the magazines I'd read told me he was a goofy-foot who preferred 6-foot, left-hand beach breaks – exactly what I was facing on this, the first day of the World Championships. I wanted to introduce myself to David, but I couldn't find him in the crowd. I was walking round the carpark, asking the other competitors if they'd seen him, when I heard that his heat had started. Hurrying across to the sea wall, I sat down and looked out to sea where I was treated to one of the most amazing sights I'd ever witnessed in surfing.

David moved like a cat and paddled with a style very similar to my own and it struck me that this was due more to the similarity of our physiques than anything else. And did he look impressive – even before he rode a wave. Dropping in to a wave, David carved a smooth forehand turn up into the hook then with precise, delicate steps, perched way up on the tip: hang ten, hang five, hang ten again – I thought he was never going to back off the nose. Five and 6-second nose-rides were common and the longest nose-ride in that first session was officially timed at 10.1 seconds. He was amazing, and by far the best nose-rider I'd ever seen. He repeated the feat on wave after wave, sometimes on the nose for only brief periods but always up there repeating the formula. Could it be that the new spray-on wax called "Slipcheck" that David and the other Americans had all over the front half of their boards really worked? I was impressed by the nose-riding display but it really was repetitive. The American boards also made nose-riding easier because they were so long. Nuuhiwa's board must have been 10-foot 6-inches and some of the others were even longer – Sam looked like a shrimp! I was starting to have doubts about my chances but I put on a good front, telling the newspapers "I'd show 'em when I got on some rights". Nuuhiwa won that first day quite comfortably and I finished second.

The next day I felt my luck had changed when we moved to a right-hand beach break called Ocean Beach: the 4-foot rolling rights would give me a chance to show everyone what I was on about. I still felt a bit stupid, paddling out half submerged when the other surfers in the heat stroked along high and dry. I had to work much harder and John Witzig reckoned I looked like a praying mantis because I had to stretch so much to keep up – but at least he waited till we were

David Nuuhiwa was the best nose rider in the world. He won the first day's competition but failed to make the final.

I think this picture (below) taken by the late Ron Stoner was the best picture taken of me at the '66 World Championships. Little right hand peaks like this one at Ocean Beach were just what I needed to snatch the lead in the contest.

RON STONER

In a lot of ways the waves in San Diego for the world
contest were the same as Noosa where Sam had
been conceived. As you can see, he had almost no
lift in the nose at all. He didn't need it because the
takeoffs were not very steep in either place.

It certainly wasn't a home town decision. I had reached
my goal: I'm the new world champ. Jock Sutherland,
Hawaii, 2nd, Corky Carrol, USA, 3rd, Steve Bigler,
USA, 4th, Rodney Gopher Sumpter, England, 5th.
Granny took this snap.

Driving up to LA and getting my picture taken in
my first prize with a back seat full of Qantas
hosties was not a bad experience.

back at the hotel before he told me. Sam had that bowie-knife feel on every wave: all the weight forward, delicately balanced and ready to propel forward. I felt confident and clean, constantly turning to stay in the waves' power with the fin George had tuned giving added spring. I rode the nose whenever the situation allowed it, but really didn't get anything to compare with David's efforts the day before. David bombed out, as it turned out, not getting the required number of waves to make the final of the round. I felt bad for him, I knew what the pressure to do well felt like, but at least got to meet and talk to him after the heat. We talked about our surfing and the differences in our approach: the main emphasis in his Californian style was on getting those long nose-rides, whereas I looked for the hollow, most powerful sections of the wave and stayed there. David told me he thought his way of surfing was best for Californian waves, but he didn't surf like that in Hawaii. We got on really well and decided we'd go to Las Vegas and do a little partying after the titles.

I won that day at Ocean Beach, which gave me an unbeatable lead of 193 points; even if I finished last in the final, I was effectively the new World Champion. But, of course, that wasn't the end of it. The ISF had a problem: with the finals still to be held it already had a winner; what were they to do? I didn't know what to think. Should I ring home? Should I answer the constantly ringing phone? The media wanted my opinion – it was a heavy 24 hours. After talking it through with John and Evo I told the organisers I'd be prepared to go into the final on an equal footing with everyone else and asked if it was possible for all the qualifying finalists to relinquish their accumulated points. The Federation met and decided against my suggestion, saying the rules were etched in stone. So on that final day I entered the water as the winner but still determined to prove to everyone that it wasn't a fluke, by winning the final heat. As it turned out, winning on that final day wasn't difficult; I'd got riding the little peaks down to a science by then, and I proved my point.

The competition organisers were so strapped for cash that the awards ceremony was held on Ocean Beach itself and the Mayor of San Diego was involved in the presentations. While Joyce Hoffman was being crowned World Woman Champion, a talkative lady sitting next to me on the dais questioned me about my age, my family and my home town. My answers seemed to satisfy her until I told her I was from Sydney when she said, in all seriousness, that she'd never heard of that town and asked what state of the Union it was in. When I whispered to her something about kangaroos, the penny dropped. I was stunned. She was the Mayor of San Diego's wife but like so many Americans she thought the world began in New York and ended in Los Angeles.

This shot of Stoner's taken off the pier at Ocean
Beach is not a drop knee turn. I have my feet
across the board not <u>down</u> the board in the
older traditional style. The shot did get me on
the cover of Surfer magazine and made a
great poster for Paul's movie Hot Generation.

I was crowned World Surfing Champion by Duke Kahanamoku on October 4th 1966. I felt proud of myself and proud to be Australian – even more so because no-one could say it was a home-town decision as had happened in the two previous world contests with Midget winning in Australia and Felipe Pomar in Peru. There were thousands of people milling around on the beach and before getting on the dais I'd left Sam with Rich Harbour, a Californian surfboard maker. We'd had a quick few words about building boards like Sam for the US market, but with so much attention focused on me, I was spread awfully thin. That was the last I ever saw of Sam and in the late 1960s, after many attempts to find him, I finally gave up the search.

The first prize was two big, glitzy trophies in the shape of California and a brand-spanking-new, gold Chevrolet Camero convertible. Possession of the car, I was told, was conditional on my being featured in a print advertisement that the company would run in Canada, with the pictures being taken the following week in Los Angeles. The Camero was a new release aimed at capturing some of the market held by Ford's phenomenally successful Mustang and Chevrolet was keen to get the maximum possible exposure for the car, so their advertising manager told me to drive my Camero as much as I could while I was in the United States. They didn't have to ask twice – I hadn't driven the Aussie team car because I was busy concentrating on the competition, but now it was time to play! My new toy was fantastic, with a big 427, V8 motor under the bonnet. I could get a little squeal out of the tyres just dropping it into third gear and I left rubber at every set of lights on the Pacific Coast Highway between San Diego and LA. I rang Mum on the way up the coast; she told me news of my win in the World Surfing Championships was all over the newspapers – even making the front page of the *Sydney Morning Herald* – and the billboards outside the local newsagent's. Mum was so proud of me.

The advertising pictures were tons of fun to shoot, with four Qantas hostesses piled in the back seat of the Camero with the top down, but to this day I've no idea what market they were aiming for. I couldn't relate to the ad at all, and in fact I've never even seen the finished product. After LA I flew to Portland, Oregon, for a meeting with Hirsh Weis, a division of the American lingerie giant Warner. Another division, White Stag, had in the past made high-quality skiwear, and were now going into manufacturing wetsuits and the company gave me $2000 for one photograph of me wearing a White Stag wetsuit. A Hirsh Weis executive told me they had a reciprocal franchise agreement with Australia's Speedo Knitting Mills; Hirsh Weis made Speedo lines in the United States and Speedo made White Stag in Australia. The executive suggested I contact Speedo when I got back home as that company was thinking of making White Stag wet-suits and it would be a nice tie-in. I phoned my weekly column to the *Telegraph* and looked over the City of Portland from the Hirsh Weis factory complex to magnificent Mount Hood, where I spent the afternoon collecting huge pine cones to take home as presents for family and friends. As I boarded the plane for LA I felt pretty sure that I'd have a lot more to do with White Stag in the future.

*   *   *   *   *   *   *

I jumped behind the wheel of the Camero and thrashed it non-stop to Las Vegas and the weekend party with David Nuuhiwa. About ten of us went out on the town that first night but I just couldn't feel part of the scene, though I thought the floor show was all right. It was at Las Vegas that I discovered I hated poker machines and, in fact, am a terrible gambler. Then, as now, I just couldn't take the necessary risks; my money had been too hard come by. The following day we all got together for a party at some bigwig's house on the outskirts of town; there were lots of pretty girls hanging around but I had no contact with any of them. All the male guests played pool and drank beer all day and far into the night, but I got to meet a guy named Mike Hynson, one of the stars of *Endless Summer* and a really fine surfer in the old functional style. We played pool and he beat me easily – thrashed me in fact – as I'd only ever played once against Gopher in Western Australia years before. I didn't even give the game a second thought until a month later, when *Surfer* ran a story about the incident. I couldn't have cared less about a game of pool; the only reason I'd come to Vegas was to hang out with Nuuhiwa, but that seemed impossible because of all the people around – my talk with David would have to keep for another time.

David Nuuhiwa was the only person I'd seen surf at my level at the World Championships; I wanted to get close to talk about our different paths in surfing – and try to get him off his 10-foot 6-inch log. I'd understood him when he told me that nose-riding was his best option on California's slower waves and in Hawaii later that year he proved his point by showing his incredible ability at the Pipeline. A few years later, David and I were flying to a shoot for the movie *Five Summer Stories* and he got on the plane with a beautiful corsage of flowers for my then wife. He looked stunning: dressed all in white contrasting with his chocolate-coloured skin and shining, black shoulder-length mane of hair. My wife and I were quite impressed. David was a real charmer but he did have a nasty streak. In the mid-1980s I stayed a night at his house in LA, en route to the Oceanside Long Board Contest. After a very pleasant family dinner, David went out drinking and partying with Wayne Mayata, another famous old surfer. Much, much later, around 2 a.m., I was woken by an awful racket and with China, another house guest woken by the row, rushed into the living room where we saw Mayata and David, pissed as newts, screaming abuse at each other as they rolled grappling on the floor. David was a big party animal.

*   *   *   *   *   *   *

Back in Australia I was given a civic reception by the Warringah Shire Council and Mum, Dad and everyone in the Collaroy Surfers Association turned out to witness the Council do a complete about face. Only a month before it had seriously considered a ban on surfboards from Dee Why to Palm Beach.

I'd only been home for a few days when I called Speedo Knitting Mills and asked to speak to the general manager. After a few minutes, Bill McRay came on the line and offered me his congratulations on winning the World Title. He told me he'd already spoken to Hirsh Weis in Portland and said Speedo would like to talk to me about working with White Stag wetsuits in Australia; would I call Ken Stevenson, the company secretary, and arrange a mutually convenient time to meet everyone? I was over the moon! This was a chance to learn something new and gave me a way to finance building a house on the land at Whale Beach. Sure, working 9 to 5 would be a drag but they knew I was a surfer and would give me plenty of time off.

Thousands of pros and cons were going through my head as I sat opposite Bill McRay, his brother, and Ken Stevenson in the luxurious wood-panelled boardroom, discussing my immediate future. They explained that Speedo had just taken over the wetsuit operation in Brookvale and was looking for a manager. They thought I could do the job; what did I think? Speedo would pay me $100 a week and provide me with a company car. I explained that I was already committed to represent Australia at the forthcoming Makaha International in Hawaii, and that although my Hang Ten contract had run out, I'd been approached by Dewey Weber, a US surfboard maker, about making my boards in America. I went on to say that I'd no experience in management, let alone manufacturing, but was prepared to give it a go when I got back from Hawaii. Bill McRay grabbed my hand and shook it vigorously, suggesting I look the Brookvale factory over, meet the staff, and come back for lunch tomorrow, to which I eagerly agreed.

The Brookvale factory was a neat little operation, with piles of rubber at one end of the assembly line and finished garments hanging at the other, and the staff seemed like a capable team. A man called John Truelove was to stay on as pattern cutter; the secretary,

98 SUNDAY TELEGRAPH, OCTOBER 23, 1966

NAT YOUNG tells...
"I did what any other Australian would have done . . . I hit him"

NAT speaks to reporter California — but not a w

SURF TITLE SENSATION

My punch-up at San Diego

AN ugly story is going the rounds about an incident in San Diego that almost cost me the world championship.

I had determined to keep it quiet . . . to say nothing because it reflects badly on the normally good relations between Australian and American surfers.

Now I must speak out. I can stay silent no longer, because only I in Australia know the true fact.

I feel it is important for the facts—and not the garbled version of them I have heard—to be known, if anything is known at all.

Take your minds back to San Diego, nearly a month ago now, just before the world surfboard riding championships are due to begin.

I arrived in San Diego to a full blast of American-styled publicity, with many of the surf writers as good as handing me the championship before the contest started.

I knew I was in with a chance. But I also felt it would take all I'd got to win. I didn't like the atmosphere one bit.

On the morning of the finals I was out training, trying as I always do to get as familiar as possible with the waves.

Out there, off Ocean Beach, I was joined by a top American surfer. I don't want to mention his name because I am sure he is just as sorry now as I was for what happened.

I first noticed him paddling towards me as I took a wave—a hollow, three-footer—and went riding in.

As I approached him he swung on to the wave then crashed his board with all its power straight at me.

I was taken quite by surprise. It was the last thing any surfer would expect to happen.

His board caught my leg, jamming it hard against the rail of my own board. I was blinded by pain, and wiped out.

When I came up I was storming with fury. If I hadn't been in peak condition I might well have been knocked unconscious.

I swam to the beach, collected my board and walked over to the American, who was now on the shore.

I asked him why on earth he had done it, and he muttered something about being very upset at the way the contest had turned out a foregone conclusion even before the finals were held.

I am afraid I lost my temper and did what

Under 21 exclusive

most other Australians would have done. I hit him — and knocked him flat.

For the next couple of hours I hobbled around, watching the bruise on my leg swell up and fearing that my chance in the finals had gone. Luckily it didn't turn out that way.

Later, when I met the American and both of us had calmed down, he admitted he was so pent up about all the publicity I had had that he was determined to do anything he could to stop me.

He very nearly did.

He gave me a profuse apology, and so far as I am concerned the whole thing is over.

To anybody else who wants to make something more out of it, I say: Let it rest. Surfing has enough problems without inventing others that don't exist.

After the ugly side of the world championships, let us talk about the good side.

One great thing, I think, came out of this get-together of world surfers, and I am sure we are going to see the results of it here in our own meetings.

At San Diego, Australians introduced a new idea to the world championships. Most American contests are run on the basis of surfers taking the first five waves and scoring the four best.

We suggested that all entrants should have half an hour in the water, taking as many waves as possible and scoring the best of these.

The idea was adopted, and was a great success. It also will be used at the Makaha championships in December.

I shall not be competing there, and another Australian will get the trip.

I think the world should know that there are plenty more good surfers here than just Midget Farrelly and myself.

One of my Sunday Telegraph columns after winning the title.

Jan, would remain, and the rest of the staff, employed to sew and glue the suits together, would vary depending on the workload. The following day, over lunch in the boardroom of the Artarmon head office, I met the rest of Speedo's executives and learnt a bit more about the company. Speedo was then owned by the McRay family, who also owned the Jockey brand of men's underwear and both brands were household words, the ultimate in marketing – in fact all men's cossies and underpants are still called speedos and jockeys in Australia, no matter who makes them, a feat achieved by very few companies. Also manufacturing some other lesser-known brands of women's clothing, Speedo was a very successful company and I could see a big future ahead for me. I was even more impressed when the table talk turned to the family passion for sailing – not just any sailing but the Americas Cup. Speedo had an intetest in *Gretel*, the Australian challenger for the coveted trophy. Bill McRay said with a laugh that if I was a good boy he'd take me out on her, but in all my time with Speedo I never did get to sail either on her, or on *Dame Patty*, the other 12-metre yacht the company supported.

It was already the end of October and an awful lot was happening in my life. I had a new job to start in January, the offer from Dewey Weber to consider, and my departure for Hawaii was getting closer all the time. I had to keep the whole thing in perspective; I'd achieved my dream, I was World Surfing Champion, but I really had to concentrate and get into the water as much as possible, but it wasn't easy. It was the beginning of the Australian summer and everyone was thinking beach and surf. I was flavour of the month and the media wanted a fair bit of my time: from radio talk shows to the Sportsman of the Year awards, I was in high demand. As soon as I'd arrived back from California, the television station Channel 10 in Sydney asked me to host a five-minute spot every night that summer, an offer too good to refuse. For $25 a segment, all I had to do was sit up straight in a nice clean Hawaiian shirt and announce an artist and song. I recorded for a week in advance, which meant carrying seven shirts into the studio and putting on a different one between each take.

Around this time I decided I needed a place of my own, the house arrangement with Nyarie and John at Whale Beach was coming to an end. When I heard about a garden flat on a quiet street in Newport, with a nice family living above it, I made an agreement to move in as soon as possible – Youngblood loved it; it was just him and me. I wanted to decorate the flat so I could give the odd dinner party, and for that I'd need some decent furniture including a bed, a wardrobe, a table and some chairs. My instructor in interior decorating was a lady by the name of Jackie, the wife of Ross Kelly who was an official of the Australian Surfriders Association. Ross worked in promotions for Rothmans at the time and had worked closely with Evo on the complex job of obtaining the sponsorships for the 1964 World Titles in Manly. Jackie and Ross lived with their four children on Bondi Road, in a beautiful old terrace house with tons of Sydney lace and high, decorated ceilings. We had some wonderful dinner parties in that house with Val and Bob Evans, Ross and Jackie, and, occasionally John Witzig and Nyarie. I took several different girls to these dinners in the course of the next few years but none of them really fitted and all were jealous of Jackie. She was a real flirt. An ex-model at least ten years older than me, she was good looking in a very sophisticated way, and we became very good friends.

Jackie was very worldly-wise, with impeccable taste. I'd been having a heap of trouble finding furniture – I'd looked at everything from modern to old junk, – then one day Jackie phoned and told me to meet her at St Vincent De Paul's op-shop in Paddington, she'd found the perfect wardrobe for me. Built of oak in London at the turn of the century, it was made to be broken down into fifteen components for ease of shipping. When I looked at the ornate carving on the front and marvelled at the skill that had gone into building such a piece, I was overwhelmed. All this for $45? I felt guilty about the price, but the woman working at the op-shop said she was glad to be rid of the "big, cumbersome, eyesore". That eyesore is still among my prized possessions and is a family heirloom. The bed wasn't a problem, the iron-and-porcelain that I liked was one of five we looked at in two different second-hand shops, but the dining-room chairs were another story.

Right where Whale Beach Road turns off Barrenjoey Road in North Avalon was a furniture shop called the Bazaar, and John Witzig introduced me to the owners, Gwendolyn and her boyfriend Edwin, who had designed and built the only castle in Avalon. The castle was built of sandstone Edwin had quarried from the escarpment that runs right along the Peninsula, while the Baltic pine for the ceiling came from huge shipping crates he'd retrieved from the Sydney wharves when some of the first Volkswagens imported from Germany were unloaded. I really admired Edwin, he was an inspiration, and we had long raves about form and design in buildings. He was one of the most talented designer/builders I have ever met and, as well as the castle, he has left some beautiful houses in the Blue Mountains and on the far North Coast. Walking along Palm Beach one day, I came across a weatherbeaten wooden hatch cover, washed overboard from some ship. I put it on the car's roof-rack and took it to the Bazaar where Edwin showed me another just like it he'd found years ago and suggested that by joining the two, I could build a dining table. Under Edwin's guidance I sanded and resurfaced the top and made some legs, the first piece of furniture I'd ever built. Trouble was, it weighed a ton, and took four people to lift it so, somewhere along the line in one of my many moves, it got left behind. But back to the chairs. I decided that American ladderbacks were what I wanted and for months looked in every second-hand shop I could find. At last I came across six of them for $5 each, but they'd been covered with thick enamel paint. I took them back to the Bazaar where Edwin let me use their caustic-soda bath. After a few days in the caustic soda the paint decomposed and I later rubbed the chairs with oil and re-glued their joints.

Also about this time, I traded my Volkswagen 1500 – the vehicle Young's had sponsored me with – for a second-hand Mercedes, a one-previous-owner 220 SE in soft cream with a red-leather interior. It was, I said to myself, a present for being a good boy. I love the style, the solid feel of a Merc and reckon they're in a class of their own, and though I've never owned a new one, I've stuck with them since buying that 220 SE. A 300 TD did 350,000 kilometres in the ten years I had it, and never missed a beat. I only parted with it because when they get old they are one-driver cars with lots of idiosyncrasies. A friend named "Doc" Spence first turned me on to Mercs. He'd always had one and, like many doctors, bought them for their reliability. One day at Narrabeen we'd just come out of the surf and were sitting talking in his 280 SE and I mentioned a Merc I'd been looking at in a car-yard over on Pittwater Road. "Don't compromise," he said. "You only live once, so go for the best." A little later, I drove over to Pittwater Road and did the deal on my first Mercedes.

Robert "Doc" Kinross Spence, one-time president of the Australian Surfriders Association, was one of the great characters of Australian surfing. I thought him a real gentleman, in the classic sense, right from the moment I first met him in the carpark at Narrabeen Beach. With Doc that day was an attractive blonde woman – obviously more than just a friend – named Margaret who, I learnt, was the radiologist at Manly Hospital where Doc worked as a surgeon. Doc was a dignified pillar of society living in a big Tudor-style home at the top end of Collaroy with his wife Jill and four daughters when he met and fell in love with Marg. They were meant for each other, as much playmates as lovers, and even now as Doc approaches 80 with his sight and hearing affected, Marg is devoted to him.

One night is unique in my memory. I was having dinner with Jill and Bob in their house at Collaroy on a night when Bob was on call. With the hospital likely to call at any time, Doc was going a bit lighter than he otherwise might have. When, as expected, the hospital did call, Doc asked me if I'd like to come down and watch him operate on the patient – a woman with a ruptured appendix. When we arrived, he introduced me as "Doctor Young" and told the nurses

Back on the east coast of Australia. This was a weekend trip to Crescent Head with John Witzig and Youngblood in my new Mercedes. Taken by Jeff Carter.

that I'd be "observing the procedure". In green gown and mask, I probably looked quite the part as I watched Doc at work, fascinated to see the organs exposed as flesh was peeled back and the offending appendix removed. By 10 p.m. Doc had finished and we went back to his house to enjoy another bottle of red.

I would have loved Doc to come with me to Hawaii for the 1966 Makaha International: I don't know why he didn't as I'm sure he could have arranged it. The Outrigger Canoe Club paid my fare and that of the Australian judge, John Shackley from Perth, Western Australia. John stuck out his hand to me as I got on the flight at Sydney and though I never did find out what he'd done to be chosen as the official judge, I found him an awfully nice man and we remained friends for years after. It was a heavy time for me and I would have welcomed Doc's company. Everywhere I went other surfers looked at my boards and whenever I was out in the water all eyes were on me – I'd discovered that being the champ is an extremely high-pressure role. Only a year before, no-one in Hawaii cared what I said or what I rode, but now I was top cocky, the guy to beat. My newspaper column that week expressed how much I missed being the underdog, and after the results were announced I felt as though I was, finishing fourth behind Fred Hemmings, George Downing and Mike Doyle. The judging was extremely fair and I did not win because I chose the wrong equipment for the 15-foot waves – it was that simple.

In 1968 Doc did come with us to Hawaii, even though his eyesight had weakened to the extent that he had to wear glasses all the time. Out in the line-up at Sunset he would be always asking me where he was and when to paddle and in what direction – he took some horrendous wipeouts but always came up smiling. When we were on Maui I suffered one particularly bad wipeout, landing feet-first on a carpet of sea urchins at the entrance to Lahina Harbour, one of the most painful accidents I've ever had. Doc spent the entire night slitting each puncture wound with a scalpel and carefully withdrawing the broken-off piece of spine. When I thanked him, he said it was a good excuse to have a long talk and drink a bottle of wine.

My store of Doc Spence stories is huge. I was once surfing Fairy Bower where pipes poured untreated sewage into the water, when Doc paddled up with the remark: "Nice day, particularly turdulent conditions". Another time we were down at Bells and I got something very painful in my eye. Doc bent me over in front of a car's headlights and flushed my eye with water from its radiator, removing the irritation. He's a gem, living happily on Queensland's Fraser Island and still managing to ride a few waves – with Margaret's help, of course.

9

'Evolution' and the big Hooka

FOLLOWING-UP ON HIS PHONE CALLS and letters, Dewey Weber flew into Hawaii in January of 1967 to talk to me about joining his team. I was familiar with Dewey as one of the stars of the old Bud Brown surf movies, popular about ten years before, but when he climbed out of the giant Yank tank at the hotel where John Shackley and I were staying in Waikiki, I almost laughed out loud. Dewey was five-feet-nothing tall with slicked-back blond hair, and was wearing big, bright baggy shorts that made him look like a clown – but a pretty fit clown; a ton of muscle rippled under the tent-like Dewey Weber Surfboards tee-shirt. His gymnast's physique, Dewey told me later, was partly due to six years of competitive wrestling – at High School he'd been Californian Champion – and at 28 years of age, he was still in fantastic shape. When he was younger, Dewey said, he'd played the part of Buster Brown – an American comedian famous in the late 1940s – in an advertising campaign for the Buster Brown Shoe Company, though this meant nothing to me at the time.

Dewey had come surfing in the islands every year since 1956. Every year, that was, except 1966 when he'd been anchored to his surfboard factory in Venice, California. Dewey told me that surfing had really taken off in the States in the summers of 1965 and 1966, the boom years of surfboard making in the United States, with the East and Gulf coasts being responsible for the incredible growth, and 1967 was expected to be the biggest yet. Weber, Hobie, Jacobs, Harbour, Hansen, Noll, Bing, and Surfboards Hawaii were the major players, all building from twenty to one hundred or more boards a day. I was amazed when Dewey told me he produced from 250 to five hundred boards a week in the season which ran from April to the end of August. He had asked me to join his team on a retainer of $300 a month, for which I'd have to appear in ads and do one promotional trip to the USA a year, all expenses paid. I'd have to ride Weber boards while I was in Hawaii and the mainland United States and also had to share my ideas on surfboard design with his head shaper, Harold Iggy. I hadn't mentioned Weber's proposal to

With Dewey Weber at Malibu. The Little Man on
Wheels was his nickname but I always called him
Little Chief. He was looking pretty fit and still
getting in the water regularly in the summer of
'68. Granny's photo.

The 1967 Australian Championships at Bell's; Peter Drouyn 2nd and Midget came 3rd. His expression says it all.

Gordon Woods, thinking he wouldn't mind as long as I continued riding Woodsie's boards at home in Australia, so I resisted the urge to sign up with Weber on the spot, instead telling Dewey to prepare a contract and send it to me. I was trying to be more businesslike and take things a little slower, though it's never been my style, and I signed a three-year contract with Weber in March 1967.

When I got back to Australia it was time to start work at White Stag. There were some exciting things happening at the company. Up until that time, every wetsuit in the world was made of thick black rubber to the customer's measurements, but White Stag was producing suits in bright, colourful prints and florals in a range of four or five sizes – an innovation we believed would make the range easy to sell. I felt inspired. Speedo's advertising agency launched a national campaign and I flew all over Australia, introducing the line to both the public and potential retailers. The response was mixed at first, a lot of people had never heard of a wetsuit, but sales slowly increased and the company began to make money in the second year. Our biggest problem lay in the limited retail outlets available to us – surf shops didn't exist in 1967 and we sold our wetsuits through department stores and stores catering to the recreational-boating market.

In between all the goings on at White Stag, I won the NSW Championships at Maroubra, on the south side of Sydney, with Midget in second place. Then, a few weeks before Easter, I went down to Victoria to follow up previous promotions and write wetsuit orders for the following summer, staying on to compete in the Australian Championships at Bells Beach. I won the first two contests and Peter Drouyn the third and under the system in use at that time this meant that I was still Australian Champion, in front of Drouyn and Midget. Midget Farrelly had finished second in the first two events and third in the last, being placed third overall on points, after Drouyn and to this day I can't understand how the points added up against him.

Bells that year was the first contest in which the surfers were considered first and foremost. Everyone was stoked! There was a huge variation in the size and quality of the surf, the waves ranging in size from 3 feet at the protected break called "Fisho's" in Torquay, to close-out Bells Beach boomers. Most waves were big, however, and so were the nights at the Torquay pub. Most of the competitors were staying either there or across the road in the camping ground – always a bright spot on the Bells Easter-party program.

Peter Drouyn is two years younger than me and hails from Queensland's Gold Coast. A supreme extrovert, both in and out of the water, he's pulled off some classic acts. I remember a cyclone swell we surfed together at Burleigh Heads in the winter of 1965, a session featuring in Paul Witzig's movie *Hot Generation*. As soon as Paul pulled his old Bolex camera out, Drouyn started going for the most insane manoeuvres – and pulling them off. He really was a born performer. When we came out of the water after that session, Peter invited me to stay at his parents' house in Surfers Paradise and I got to know his family and friends as wonderful, hospitable people. It seemed to me at the time that Gold Coast people were very similar to Hawaiians in their way of life. In those few days I came to think of Peter as a noisy little brother with tons of surfing talent, then when I saw him do his first "race call" on stage during the presentations at the 1969 Australian Championships in Western Australia, I realised he was quite an entertainer. Years later when he enrolled at the National Institute for Dramatic Art, I thought he'd found his direction in life.

* * * * * * *

Right outside my office window in Brookvale was the newly completed Warringah Mall Shopping Centre and in one corner of the carpark was an artificial ski slope looking like millions of toothbrush heads on a 45-degree slope – Youngblood actually found it first, on one of his regular jaunts around the neighbourhood. The instructor was a champion skier named Christine Smith, a blonde beauty who had represented Australia in the 1964 Winter Olympics at Innsbruck. For me, it was lust at first sight; surfing was getting a bit boring and though I'd never skied I'd always wanted to and the chance to get close to Christine and at the same time learn to ski was one I wasn't going to pass up.

Before long Christine had me paralleling down the carpet of nylon bristles and we were spending every weekend we could on her uncle's farm, just out of Jindabyne on the Snowy River. The homestead was built of the beautiful grey and white-flecked granite blocks found in the Kosciuszko area, and roofed with red corrugated iron. There was a large library with many leather-bound books, one containing a handwritten notation by the Australian poet "Banjo" Paterson. Once one of the largest sheep stations in the area, Kara was a world totally different from the beach life I was so used to. Some weekends the snow was so deep around the house we couldn't drive up to the ski slopes and it was all hands on deck to help Christine's family bring in the ewes and newborn lambs before they died in the snowdrifts. Youngblood loved it: charging around with his long red coat dragging in the snow, he was in doggy paradise. One weekend John Witzig had come to the farm with us and he dug a tiny lamb from a massive snow drift. From that moment on, Sweet Pea, as we christened the lamb adopted John, not letting him out of his sight. When at last we did get up on the mountain that weekend, the snow was deep and heavy, far beyond my ability and a lot different from the Brookvale toothbrush I'd learnt on. The lift stopped five chairs short of the summit and I thought Christine was going to cry with disappointment. We waited in the cold for 15 minutes, then without saying a word, Christine unbuckled her safety strap and launched herself from the chair, landing in the soft snow 3 metres below. Laughing, she skied away with beautiful linking turns through the powder. Christine was beautiful to watch, smooth and strong. She was a patient teacher and I knew with her help I'd get there one day.

On the way back down the mountain that day, we were held up in a line of traffic. Purely by chance, I glanced at the rear-vision mirror and saw a car hurtling around the bend behind us. I barely had time to yell "brace yourselves" to Christine and John before a very drunk skiing instructor ploughed into us at over 100 kilometres an hour. It was a miracle no-one was hurt – the rear of my car was concertinaed like a crash-test ad and I was awfully glad I owned a Mercedes.

* * * * * * *

Long afternoons were spent sitting around the big open fire that took up one whole end of the kitchen building, telling stories and sipping scalding billy tea. Christine was from a broken home; her Dad had left when she was still a baby, and she'd been raised by her mother Unice and an elderly uncle. She loved her life on Kara and she so loved skiing the nearby mountains that she'd hardly ever experienced the beach or waves, or even the sun on her bare skin, so exploring our differing worlds was exciting and new for both of us; she explained to me what an edelweiss looked like and I told her it sounded like a flannel flower. Chrissy had never jumped from rock to rock around the shoreline on any of our beaches but revelled in it because her balance was so good. She introduced me to snowflakes and showed me how different each one really is and what a crystal looked like when you examined it closely. Chrissy told me what it felt like to ski through snow reaching to her belly button, and about the pain she felt after breaking both her legs with spiral fractures when she skied under a log in Austria; and of the trauma of racing and training every day for months on end, suffering almost continual menstrual bleeding from the constant fatigue. Up in the mountains, she showed me snow gums, whose leaves turn over to the sun, creating a sparkling fairy-light show that never ceases to amaze me and still brings Christine to mind.

Christine Smith was the darling of the mountains in the late 1960s. She'd been adopted by the villages of Thredbo and Perisher as the home-town girl who made good. Visiting the lodges after skiing Thredbo, it could sometimes take hours to have a drink with everyone who knew her and followed her career as the Australian skiing champion. Back in Sydney we were virtually inseparable, and although we both had our own flats, we were with each other a great deal of the time – all very exciting, as she had a previous lover still hanging around. For some reason I wasn't jealous, we were obviously both very good friends of Christine and it seemed perfectly natural.

My Weber promotional trip to California didn't do our relationship much good. Dewey had been trying to get me to come to the States for months and in October of 1968 I at last agreed to go. Christine wasn't happy about it, and although I was only away for a few weeks, when I returned we realised our lives were truly worlds apart. We tried a brief ski trip, spending a few days on New Zealand's Tasman Glacier to get background material for an article for *Chance* magazine, and it was a wonderful experience, flying to the head of the river of ice and snow and skiing through incredible ice formations in every shade of blue, but we didn't make love the whole time we were in New Zealand. The wheels had come off the relationship and we couldn't put them back on again.

I didn't see Christine again after that trip. John Witzig told me that for a time she rented a little house in Whale Beach, where he had dinner with her once. We heard that she married an American named Wayne Gardener and after they broke up had several relationships; one with a polo player who ran with a fast crowd in Double Bay. Frank, a Hungarian much older than her, was another man in her life and was responsible for getting Christine involved in interior decorating in the Eastern Suburbs. Poor Chrissy met a tragic end in a Sydney hotel room – she took a ton of sleeping pills and never woke up, and none of her family or friends understood why.

* * * * * * *

When Sam disappeared, the honest truth is I felt unsure on other surfboards. I really believed he was magic and I just couldn't surf anything else. I tried lots of different boards but it just wasn't the same – I built boards with exactly the same outline and vital statistics but they just didn't work like Sam had. I sort of gave up and severed my relationship with Gordon Woods; what with skiing and Christine, my

The blonde is Australian skiing champion Christine Smith heading off to the '68 Winter Olympics in Grenoble with her team mate Dawn McDuff.

mind was on other things. I'd lost enthusiasm completely after the 1967 contest season ended and didn't go surfing for months.

It wasn't at all difficult to win both contests that year, and it happened almost without me thinking. McTavish was working for Keyo Surfboards just down the road from my office in Brookvale and I'd call in every now and then to say hello and check on his latest shaping job. One day after not having been to Keyo's for a few weeks, I walked through the showroom and there were ten new boards, all in the 8-foot range and all with deep vee bottoms and concave noses. The 4 inch-deep vee held right off the tail, giving them a different look, like nothing I'd seen before. Bob explained that he'd been making them shorter and shorter over the past few weeks and insisting the little "Plastic Machines" were really exciting to ride.

McTavish is a charismatic character when you get him going. As I drank in what he was saying, I felt the fire coming back, I wanted to shape one of these little machines and go surfing. Bob explained how the vee bottom in the tail sat the back of the board in the water, allowing it to roll up onto one side and carve an arc. My first thought was that these boards would have all the action in the rear end; they were really only turners and I wasn't sure that was such a good thing because it struck me that nose-riding had been thrown completely out the window. I thought the concave noses were a feeble attempt to get the boards to nose-ride but they just wouldn't do it like the old boards did. For the first time in my surfing career lightness had become a factor; everyone was building their boards out of stringerless blanks to keep the weight down.

I asked Denny Keyo if I could use Bob's shaping bay and, for the first time in six months, I shaped a new board. It was 8 feet long by 23 inches wide and like McTavish's had a 12-inch pod across the tail with a 4-inch vee. The stringerless blank was really hard to hold while shaping and I had to use a brick to keep it in one place. The thickness of those Plastic Machines also made them appear strange, as they held the thickness of the centre right through to the tail. And I soon found that glassing them was a nightmare. The idea was to get the board as light as possible, so a thin skin had to be put on the bottom to hold the curve, then a couple of layers on the deck to give it some strength and rigidity. I took the new board out in a 3-footer inside Narrabeen "Alley" to test it and thought I'd never get used to the feel, it was so weird. After an hour of practise, and a few long swims to the beach, I began to get the feel of the vee and found how interesting the pocket-riding type of surfing could be.

In October a heavy contingent of Californian surfers from the Wind'n'Sea Surf Club came to Sydney to find out what was happening with the "short board revolution". Twentieth Century Fox film studio was picking up their bill and making a film about their South Seas adventure. With summer coming on, I had a lot of work to do at White Stag, but McTavish spent some time with the Americans and gave them all the relevant information about short boards. I had dinner with the producer Eric Blum, a short, Hollywood type about my age, and agreed to work with his cameraman that Hawaiian season and to talk with Eric in the new year after he'd had a look at exactly what they'd got in the can.

I gave McTavish my free ticket to compete in the Duke Contest at Sunset Beach in Hawaii that year. As the current Australian champion, the ticket had been offered to me and it was a great honour to be one of the 24 invited surfers. I really wanted to compete in the Duke but McTavish was the vanguard of the vee-bottom, short-board thing, and I was really happy for him. I'd had quite a few sponsored tickets over the years but Bob had only been to Hawaii once before and that was as a stowaway. On that trip he'd been assisted by other paying passengers, simply staying on board a Hawaii-bound ship. After he'd been in the Islands a month, he was arrested while working at painting a roof on the North Shore and sent home to Australia. Stowing away – particularly from California to Hawaii – was a sort of exclusive pastime for a lot of surfers in the 1950s and 1960s, before aeroplanes became the main means of transport.

I was still pretty naive in those days, and I thought they'd let me compete in the Duke if I just turned up on the day, but unfortunately all the invited surfers showed up and there were no slots available – so I had to sit on the beach and watch McTavish fly the Australian flag in the 10 to 15-foot shifting Sunset peaks. When I arrived on Oahu I walked into a very vocal media debate over the pros and cons of the short board. There was never any question over what boards we'd take to Hawaii that year, though we'd no idea how the Plastic Machines would go in the big surf. Bob and I had made slightly bigger boards – both 9 feet – and we decided we'd just have to ride them and see what happened. Back in Australia, McTavish had said he wasn't interested in surfing in the old style, cruising along the bottom running away from the power, and could see himself blasting off the bottom and carving all over the face. The Hawaiians weren't that impressed with our boards and they felt justified in their view when McTavish was knocked out in his first heat. Fred Hemmings called him the "spin-out king" but by all accounts Bob proved his point to anyone who took the time to watch.

When we caught up with McTavish a few days after the event he wasn't even surfing his own short board – it was as though he'd given up – and watching him surf Haleiwa on a big conventional board borrowed from David Nuuhiwa, I thought he looked awkward and stiff. Amazed by his about-face, I couldn't understand what he was doing and it was hard to get much sense out of him. But later that afternoon, when I cornered him outside the house where he and Nuuhiwa were living, he sounded fine, promising to follow us to Maui when I told him I'd be going there next day.

I was travelling to Maui with John and Paul Witzig and the hot young Sydney surfer Ted Spencer; George Greenough was going to fly in direct from California and Doc Spence came over for a few days before going back to Oahu to fulfil his obligations as the official judge for the Makaha contest. McTavish and Nuuhiwa arrived on Maui the day after us and while Nuuhiwa went for spiritual enlightenment from the guru shaper Dick Brewer, McTavish hung out with us – things were back on track. Back in Australia the game plan had called for John and Paul to cover the assault on the Hawaiian waves by our Aussie boys on their Fantastic Plastic Machines. John was editor of *Surf International* magazine and was hungry for material for the fifth issue, while Paul's new movie, *Hawaii '68*, was just taking shape. Eric Blum also sent his head cameraman to Maui and he took a few shots of Bob and I that became part of a sequence for his movie *The Fantastic Plastic Machine*.

Going back to the "Garden Isle" was fantastic; it hadn't changed that much since 1963 and it was reassuring to see that mass condominium development still hadn't really hit the island. We had a hot surf at Ho'okipa right near the airport and then on to Lahina, booking into the same old Pioneer Inn on the edge of the harbour. Bob, Ted and I paddled out past the magnificent four-masted schooner *Carthaginian* and surfed the right-hander at the entrance to the harbour. There were just the three of us out and it could have been Whale Beach in Sydney. The little vee bottoms were going incredibly well, carving all over the face and letting you in nice and late.

After a few days cruising around the Lahina area, riding little waves and meeting all sorts of hippy types, I began to understand why it had been difficult to make much sense of McTavish when he was on Oahu – he was stoned! Back on the North Shore, Bob had been smoking lots of high-quality pot with Hynson and Nuuhiwa for weeks. About this time I decided to get stoned myself, the start of an indulgence that lasted over fifteen years. Those next few weeks on Maui, getting loaded before we surfed, were like a religious experience and the reason marijuana became such a part of my surfing life.

One evening, with the swell coming up fast as it does only in the Islands, we went to bed with the ground beginning to shake with the pounding of the surf. Next morning we smoked a big fat one and about half an hour before daylight paddled out at Honolua Bay. It was insane: no wind at all, giant spiralling barrels and out with just a

You can see the discolouration where I broke
the nose off my board.
The vees really worked at Honolau Bay as
this shot of John's shows quite clearly.

handful of friends and I could feel that same excitement I'd sensed months ago when I first got back into surfing on my vee bottom. With no wind to worry about I could carve up and down the face inside the curl and I remember feeling like a fly gripping a vertical surface. The swell kept up for days; I broke the nose off my board and repaired it in a couple of hours, barely missing even one of those Cathedrals. After a week of 4 to 10 feet at Honolua, we'd all had more than enough of waves and exposure to the sun and John and Paul had more pictures than they could ever use, so we left for home.

* * * * * * *

Back in Sydney, my love of surfing renewed itself and I felt excited about it again. The thirteen half-hour episodes I'd made for ABC television in 1966 had just finished airing. Titled *Let's Go Surfing*, it was virtually a "how to surf" series and received very good reviews – surfing was getting a much higher profile and attracting some interesting characters. One such was a young Englishman named Gareth Powell who'd arrived in the "colony" with a dream of creating a magazine-publishing empire, having made several trips to Australia before finally settling here in 1968. Gareth always went into everything with a splash. With experience gained as a successful book publisher back in England, he started a magazine called *POL*, a girlie magazine called *Chance* and a surfing magazine – all within a couple of months. When I first met Gareth he'd tried without success to buy *Surfing World* from Bob Evans and his partners, but not to be daunted he took its editor John Witzig to lunch, offering him complete control of *Surf International*. John was really stoked; he didn't much enjoy being answerable to Evo and he'd finally been offered a decent salary for his efforts.

The editor of *Chance* was a funny little cove named Jack De Lisa whom I'd first met when he worked for Bob Evans on the girlie magazine *Squire* which was put together in Evo's *Surfing World* offices at the sleazy end of Sydney. De Lisa was one of the prime movers in our "Thursday Club", a social-luncheon group which every Thursday met at a different restaurant to taste and determine the contents of the masked bottles of wine that each of the seven members would bring along. I twigged Jack was a bit devious when at one of the meetings I caught him out the back pouring a quality Australian red into a French Bordeaux bottle, the idea being that other members would nominate the wine as Bordeaux after feeling the indent on the bottom of the French bottle or taking a sly peek at the label. Jack convinced me to keep quiet about it and watch the ruse unfold. Evans said the wine was a young Bordeaux and, for the first time,

John Witzig was very non-committal, as was my old editor at the *Telegraph*, Frank Margan, one of Sydney's foremost wine connoisseurs and the editor of Gareth's *Gourmet* magazine. The rest of the company were all thrown off-track by the shape of the bottle. Then it was my turn: I said it tasted like "an old Hunter Valley... the nose was the giveaway... obvious", finally nominating it as a 1961 Tyrrell's. De Lisa removed the brown-paper bag to reveal the French label then produced the original bottle, explaining what he'd done. Everyone was really impressed by me as I'd never been right before. I'd occasionally guessed the area and sometimes the grape, but never spot on the money for the actual name of the wine. I never did have the heart to declare that I'd seen the label on the original bottle when Jack had done his thing out the back with the bottles.

De Lisa and I became friends of a sort. I was looking for a new flat, closer to the city than Newport so I could get more involved in Sydney's night life, still get quickly to my office in Brookvale and keep some distance between old and new girlfriends and Jack had a flat to rent on the side of the hill in Manly. It looked like a brothel but was at least fresh and clean. Jack had papered all the walls a deep aqua blue and the trim was white with a neutral plush carpet. Something seemed not quite right about this flat I was renting for $25 a week but I couldn't put my finger on it, so one day I carried all my furniture and about nine dozen bottles of wine down the stairs and into the front room. I had a couple of dinner parties there with the Evans and the Kellys and it felt all right.

I began to warm to the flat but I never did feel as though I belonged there. De Lisa told me he'd used it as a studio, enticing would-be models there to seduce them into doing all sorts of kinky things and taking hot pictures of them with the aqua walls as a backdrop. He explained that he didn't really need the place any more as Gareth had agreed to his redecorating the *Chance* office as a bordello – complete with a suite for Jack. When the office and suite were finished we held a fantastic party with Champagne flowing freely and twenty ravishing would-be star models and only ten men – I felt like a kid in a lolly shop, dancing with one stunning woman after another. Every now and then Jack would sidle over and whisper some juicy detail to entice me into changing partners, then around midnight he slipped the key to his private suite into my hand and told me not to be too long. I grabbed the exquisite, tall blonde I was dancing with and pushed her ahead of me up the stairs, fumbling at the door with the key. I removed her flimsy top to reveal jutting breasts, firm and pointed, and then she was all over me. This was too good to be true. Who was this girl? Where did she come from? We moved onto the chaise longue – I'd always wondered what they were made for – and breathless with anticipation, I slid my hand down the front of her pants, into her knickers and onto… "her" penis. I freaked, and got up to bolt then, right on cue, the door burst open – Jack and the other partygoers had seen the whole thing through a one-way mirror. I remember hoping they didn't have pictures. Jack was a real prankster, always in there with the carefully planned trick – in retrospect they were fairly harmless and certainly a lot of fun.

One night I came home to the flat in Manly to find the door wide open. Everything was intact but all the wine was gone – I felt really lousy, my privacy had been invaded, so the next day I called De Lisa to tell him what had happened then moved back to Whale Beach with Nyarie and her younger brother Darian. The big sandstone house they lived in belonged to Nyarie's mother, Alma, and was on the most northerly point above Whale Beach, with incredible views of the horizon. I felt so aware of the elements in that house: the noise of the wind, the pounding of the waves on the cliffs below, and the household was constantly full of laughter, thanks mainly to the green powder. I was to learn later that marijuana in this form, with its unique properties, was "kif" from Morocco.

This was the first occasion since I'd met Nyarie that we'd been together at the right time. We'd talked before about how good it might be and finally it happened, it was just us, with almost no other suitors involved. We had dinner and talked, and found we still got on really well. Nyarie's cat, Sharani, was in the habit of coming into our room early in the morning and offering the night's kill to her owner. On more than one occasion this offering took the form of large and bloodied mouse laid on my neck instead of Nyarie's; I freaked at first but got used to it after a while.

One unforgettable morning I heard Nyarie speaking in hushed tones to Darian, so I got up and walked into the kitchen where Darian was rummaging through the fridge looking for every scrap of meat he could find. It was a beautiful sunny morning, with no wind to speak of, and Nyarie was standing on the deck offering steak to a large chocolate-brown shape in front of her. I couldn't believe it; sitting on the balcony rail was a full-grown wedge-tailed eagle. It grabbed the steak with its beak, transferring the meat to its talons, took flight and made giant wheeling dives to check out the situation until Nyarie held another lump of steak aloft and it landed, grabbing the meat and tearing it to pieces. It hung around for a week, coming to the house at regular intervals, and we all took turns at feeding it. It was quite hair-raising, holding a chunk of meat up to be plucked out of your hand by a bird of prey with a 2-metre wing span and the local newspaper came and took pictures. It was like something from

JOHN

Nyarie with seaweed.

REACTIONS MIXED ABOUT THIS BIRD

Some love it, others want it destroyed

Story and photographs by Gary Steer.

Between Whale Beach and Palm Beach lives a wedge-tailed eagle. Some residents fear it and want it shot. Others love and feed it.

The eagle has been there for about four months, and where it came from no one knows.

It obviously was reared by someone, because it shows very little fear of humans.

But humans are afraid of the eagle.

It has been accused of attacking a pup, and taking washing off lines.

'Shoot'

Some residents have requested that the National Parks and Wildlife Service capture the eagle or, if this cannot be done, to shoot it.

This poses a bit of a problem, because in April this year State Parliament, at the recommendation of the National Parks and Wildlife Service removed the eagle from the State's First Schedule (un-

protected list) of the Fauna Protection Act.

Mrs. Abbey, of Norma Road, Palm Beach, one of the residents who feeds the eagle, has fears for its safety.

"If someone shoots the eagle there will be a lot of sad little children round the area over Christmas," she said.

Mrs. Abbey has a photograph of a row of little girls with the wedge-tailed eagle sitting in between them.

"I have a dog, and there are cats in the area, and the eagle has never touched them," she said.

"It's probably true that he takes washing from the line, but what playful puppy doesn't!"

Mrs. Abbey said many residents of the area get joy out of just watching the eagle soar effortlessly round the cliffs, just as they get joy out of watching the yachts sailing gracefully in front of the wind.

'Afraid'

Some residents are afraid that the eagle might be attacking and eating smaller birds in the area.

Mrs. Abbey said it usually was the other way round, that smaller birds— for example, mag-

Top, face to face with the peninsula wedge-tailed eagle.

Above, a fine shot showing the eagle swooping with its prey near Whale Beach.

pies, currawongs and seagulls — harassed the eagle.

In a recent review of the wedge-tailed eagle by officers of the National Parks and Wildlife Service, it was recorded that crows and ravens were included in the diet of eagles in the wild, but they only made up five to eight percent of prey species taken.

"It is interesting, because crows and eagles often share the same table (i.e. carrion) at other times."

Before the Whale Beach wedge-tailed eagle is condemned just because of his arrogant looks and reputation alone, let us look around for the facts first.

The magnificent Wedge Tailed eagle that came to Whale Beach. Nyarie told me it was a simple case of a country mouse visiting the city.

a kid's story book; why would one of these magnificent creatures leave the inland and come to Whale Beach? A shortage of food and water perhaps? I remember discussing this with Nyarie the morning it disappeared and she said it was just like the story of the country mouse who came to the city for a holiday, didn't particularly like it and went back to the country.

On one occasion we went to Falls Creek with Doc Spence and Margaret with the intention of skiing. It was Nyarie's first time in the snow, but we hardly got out of bed; she loved to watch the white stuff tumbling from the sky but wasn't ready to learn to ski.

Then my annual promotional trip to California for Weber Surfboards came round again. Nyarie drove me to the airport in my cream Mercedes and I felt really secure knowing Youngblood, my car and all my worldly possessions were in her capable hands. In California Dewey picked me up at the airport and we went out for breakfast in Santa Monica. Sitting on the pier overlooking the life-less grey ocean, we talked of the advertising campaign we had run-ning in the magazines, the problems with the "backyard" board makers and the sales-promotion tour of the east coast that I'd do the following summer after the 1968–69 World Contest in Puerto Rico.

I stayed with Dewey and his wife Carol in Hermosa Beach and we went surfing at Malibu. The south swell was good and strong and the board I'd made at Keyo's and brought over with me was fit-ting perfectly into the barrel. It was 8 feet long by 22 inches wide and looked a bit like a torpedo, with soft, rolled rails. It was almost the opposite of Sam in that all the area was in the front end with a narrow, square tail. The bottom was rolled, so you had to be a pretty good surfer to ride it, this becoming evident when I let a guy from Malibu surf on it. He was very hesitant, the board was just too advanced for him, and it provided a good lesson – Dewey and I made sure our boards were designed for the average surfer.

At the Venice factory, I worked with the head shaper Harold Iggy, on the final designs of the boards I thought they should be making for America and came up with what was basically a flat-bot-tomed version of what I was riding. Sales were all right, but the backyarders were really starting to affect the big manufactures. The short-board revolution saw a dramatic fall-off in sales by all the major surfboard makers. Whether it was a reaction to the obscenity of the war in Vietnam, the back-to-nature movement, whatever, "country soul" spread like wildfire through the industry. And the problem was real: for the first time a surfer could get a truly custom-made surfboard by talking to the shaper about his surfing style and where he planned to use his new board.

I had a few free days before heading home, so I borrowed one of Dewey's cars and went north to Santa Barbara to hang out with Greenough again. As it turned out, he was in Australia, but I checked around Santa Barbara and found the place where George made his boards. McTavish had hung out with these guys the year before, after going to California from Hawaii, and Michael Cundith greeted me like a brother – we had so much in common – and invited me to stay at his house in an avocado orchard near Rincon. Michael was a serious devotee of Greenough and the whole back-yard board-building thing. He shaped beautiful little custom-made, George-inspired, "pocket rockets" for all the local surfers and his soul mate, Ritchie West, glassed them. Michael lived with one of the most beautiful brunettes I've ever seen, with hair that hung to her waist and pure, lily-white skin. Maureen was absolutely devoted to Cundith, putting his dinner on the table at the right time and making his breakfast just the way he liked it, with the hot muffin on the table at the same time as his oatmeal and coffee. Tall and lean, her body was just like Nyarie's, with similarly shaped breasts and hips, and Maureen even seemed to have Nyarie's well-balanced nature. We did a bit of surfing at Rincon that week and even went up to The Ranch, but it wasn't great surf; it was the end of summer and the north swells were few and small. The avocado orchard was amazing. We'd all get stoned and armed with a knife, spoons, a bottle of tomato sauce and salad dressing, we'd wander off to Michael's favourite spot among the trees. There we'd pluck the avocados straight from the trees, split them in half and apply lashings of sauce where the stone had been removed. After five or so of these, we'd lie on our backs and stare up into the trees; life was perfect.

Back in Australia I was met with open arms at the airport by Nyarie – it felt as though we were married. While I'd been in the United States, the directors of Speedo had decided to move the entire White Stag factory to Artarmon, where the head office was located. The workers were really angry and most of them resigned; they all lived in the Warringah Shire and the move would mean an extra hour's travelling. And Youngblood created a problem. Now that he was almost fully grown, he'd become very civilised and well behaved and was used to curling up in my office, going out to relieve himself when he needed to, but some of the staff complained when the big red dog wandered into their offices to say hello. It wasn't going to work! I went along with the move but I wasn't enjoying the accountability; White Stag was making money and I believed that should have been the bottom line. At one particularly stormy directors' meeting my intention to spend three months in France to shoot Paul Witzig's proposed film *Evolution* was discussed in some detail; what with that and the yearly trip to America for Weber Surfboards, they were starting to

Paul Witziq — The Gnome to his friends. Paul and I
did a lot of travelling around the world with
Wayne Lynch and Ted Spencer, making five surf
movies in as many years.

get a bit tired of my style. I could see their point. It all boiled down to the fact that the managing director, Bill McCray, and his brothers could see that my lifestyle might rival their own and I was given a choice: either lie down and become a good company man, or leave and go and make any movie I wanted. It took all of ten minutes to decide. I walked outside, tried to think of my future, walked back inside and quit. I remember explaining the situation to my secretary, hastily clearing my office, seeing the paymaster, then driving to the nearest bottle shop.

That certainly wasn't the first time I'd drunk real champagne, but from memory it was the first time I'd bought it – even then, vintage Veuve Clicquot was $40 a bottle. I sped through the Parkway, sipping on the champers and feeling better and better about my decision. I was like a homing pigeon, flying straight back to the Peninsula, where I continued the binge with cheaper champagne. Nyarie thought I'd done the right thing and we stood in the kitchen making peanut butter, honey and banana sandwiches with thick Vogel bread and looking at the big southerly swell pounding into The Wedge.

The next day, Paul Witzig fanged his old blue Valiant up the drive with the exciting news that Qantas had come to the party and our airline tickets to Europe were ready whenever we wanted to pick them up. Wayne Lynch had already arrived from his home in Victoria and was staying with Paul at the top end of Palm Beach, while Ted Spencer was hanging around and surfing everything that even looked like a wave, and already I could feel some conflict between us. (I never quite knew why. Perhaps it was our full-on battles in some contests or the fact that we were such different people. Either way, it came to a head a few months later when we ended up having a full-on punch-up in a London hotel.) We had a big raging party at Nyarie's house that weekend and then it was off to Rome. I guess Paul's reasoning was that Italy was the closest Qantas destination to Biarritz in France, but it looked an awfully long way between them when we examined the map in the plane.

Why France? Well Paul had fallen in love with the daughter of Joern Utzon, the architect who designed the Sydney Opera House. While Utzon was in Sydney overseeing the project, he and his family were living at Palm Beach and Paul was absolutely smitten by Lin's blonde Scandinavian beauty. The pursuit of the object of his desires led Paul all over Europe including Biarritz, where he saw, but didn't ride, some beautiful waves. This, then, was the background to the *Evolution* project.

* * * * * * *

The road Napoleon built for Josephine to get to
their palace at the Grand Plage in Biarritz.

Guethary... when a big North Atlantic storm hits
the Basque coast you are bound to spend a few
days indoors hiding from the elements.

We didn't do much sightseeing in Rome – the Colosseum and that was about it – Paul had been there before and Wayne, Ted and I were hot to go surfing. A look at a map of Europe shows that it is indeed a few days drive to the Basque country, so with Ravel's *Bolero* and *Love De Capo* by Ginger Baker and Cream blaring we set off. We managed to blow up the first Fiat Avis gave us and its replacement carked it somewhere around Pau in the heart of provincial France. Fortunately, Paul had the number of someone in the Surf Club De France – I think it was the French Champion, Jean Marie Lartigau, who I'd met at the World Contest in San Diego – and after a day or so a few of the boys came to retrieve us. They were driving a bright-yellow Peugeot De Chevau, an ex-baker's van and it was so exciting to see some of the surf tribe after a week or more on the roads of central Europe that we almost kissed them. In fact, I think we did.

In Biarritz we quickly got ourselves into a flat and a routine of visiting the local markets every morning to get fresh fruit, yoghurt and the magnificent French bread and croissants. I can't really remember where we surfed first, but the most significant wave on that trip was La Barr. That break doesn't exist any more, not as it was then, but it's still pretty good on its day. Back then there was only one breakwater at the mouth of the river Adour and the buildup of sand on its southern side was a consistent triangle with lefts and rights peeling in either direction, the lefts significantly better than the rights. Wayne was having real trouble riding the tube, not fitting in there and not able to manoeuvre without getting wiped out – he was very frustrated – so we decided to build new boards.

I'd met an energetic old Frenchman named Michael Barland in Hawaii in 1964. He was the only boardmaker in France and only too pleased to let us use his factory. Wayne reckoned we could overcome the problem of not fitting in the tube by going a little bit shorter, in the 7-foot range, and a lot finer with thinner rails that ran from high in the front to low and hard in the tail. Things changed overnight and some of the waves that Wayne rode from deep in the throat of La Barr were the most impressive tube rides I had seen up until that time. We spent all our days surfing either La Barr or if the swell was bigger, the Malibu-style rights of La Fatania or the majestic Guethary with its Sunset-style peaks way out in the centre of the bay. In between surfs we hung around Cote Des Basque – it was the thing to do – with all our French friends. The girls were positively awesome, clothed only in tiny gee strings and exposing those wonderful-shaped breasts that I've come to believe are unique to French women.

That was the summer that Jean Pierre first opened the Steak House above Cote Des Basque and by the time we arrived on the scene in August of 1968, the Steak House was really happening. I think it was there I heard The Doors for the first time, their *Soft Parade* had just been released. The food was good, typical French provincial cooked by Jean Pierre's mother, but that didn't matter so much; it was here that anybody who was anybody in the Biarritz surf scene hung out after dark. Usually we'd eat dinner there then go around to some Aussie mate's place to get stoned before coming back to pick up some chicks and go to a party.

It was on one of these routine runs that we ran into The Hooka – a real one – and I was amazed, I'd never seen such a thing. It stood at least a metre high and had five or six long tubes coming from the bowl. It took a good handful of hashish just to fill the bowl and a blowtorch to ignite the thing – not to mention a team of smokers with formidable lungs to keep it going. It was indeed an awesome instrument of destruction and I got the feeling it had a long history of travelling the world turning people on. The first place I saw it was at the Aussie Max Bowman's flat. He swears he didn't bring it to town, reckons he got up one morning and when he walked out of his front door there it was, sitting on his doorstep saying "Feed me! Let's party!" I've a rather fond memory of sitting across The Hooka from Wayne, both of us inhaling deeply on our tube, when suddenly Wayne's eyes rolled back in his head and he fell backwards into a pit of cushions, laughing hysterically. The Hooka hung around Max's flat for a few weeks and became part of our daily routine, there whenever we wanted it. As long as it was fed with liberal amounts of assorted dope from around the world it seemed happy enough. The Hooka took on a real personality and seemed almost alive. It obviously liked to travel because I last remember seeing it at a particularly memorable party at the Darrigrand sisters' family home just outside Bayonne. The police raided that party and perhaps that's why it just disappeared. The dope being smoked in The Hooka was kif from Morocco; not as strong as Afghani or Turkish hash but if you smoked enough of it, it got you laughing hysterically and enjoyment was guaranteed.

While Paul had been studying architecture, one of his lecturers had told him about a model concept in medium-density housing that had been built on the coast at Hossegor, some thirty minutes from Bayonne, and one day when the surf was too small for any of our regular haunts around Biarritz, Paul suggested we go and have a look at the project. The original housing complex was designed like the spokes of a wheel when looked at in plan and each apartment in the spokes had privacy and uninterrupted views of the area's extensive pine forests, yet was right next to its neighbour. We were all very impressed and as we wandered past the whitewashed walls and down by the tennis courts, we thought we might as well

DICK

Morocco in the late '60s. All the locals were
wearing a dress called a jelaba, so we did too.

amble over the sandhills protecting the buildings from the sea and have a look at the surf. There wasn't much wind, just a light off-shore, and as we stumbled through the dunes and stood looking down on Hossegor we were totally awestruck. Was it a mirage, or was that a classic right-hander over there – just beyond that huge concrete bunker left over from the Second World War – peeling along a perfect sand point? It didn't take us long to come to our senses and get into the water before it all disappeared. But it didn't. It was real, and now when I sit back and watch the annual Rip Curl pro contest at Hossegor, with thousands on the beach, I can't help but wonder how long it would have taken the French surfers to discover Hossegor. I think we were the first to surf that break.

After we'd been hanging round Biarritz for six weeks or so, the winter storms began to move in with much more velocity and regularity than we'd expected, so we decided to drive to Morocco. It did not take long to get packed up and soon we were back on the road heading south. Gopher Sumpter came over from England with his girlfriend Simonne, and joined our caravan heading south. Travelling through Spain could be pretty hairy in 1968 – Generalissimo Franco was still in power and the militia were everywhere on the roads, always travelling in twos on old motorbikes. I recall throwing our small hash pipe out of the car window in fright a couple of times, but it didn't matter as we'd just buy another. Mostly we slept on the side of the road under the stars, unless the weather looked threatening, then we'd sleep in the cars. In this way we made our way through Spain and across the Straits of Gibraltar to Africa.

In Morocco we immediately dressed in local attire, the one-piece jellaba, and went hunting for surf. The local people were very friendly and seemed glad to see travelling surfers, inviting us into their houses for mint tea. Communication was somewhat restricted by the language barrier, but every conversation ended with Agadir – Agadir, was the place for waves. And it did turn out to be a good place to stay for a while. As soon as we pulled into town, the local mover and groover, Abdul, pulled us aside and offered us some dates. They were fantastic, the best I'd ever eaten. They had a strange taste I couldn't quite identify until I discovered it came from kif. Apparently the locals cut their dope with the dates to disguise the taste and it was, I think, the most pleasant way to get stoned I've ever come across. In this way we passed a month in Kenitra and Agadir before leaving for London and the Puerto Rico World Contest.

10

'The Fantastic Plastic Machine'

IT WAS VERY HOT AND STICKY when we arrived in the Caribbean island of Puerto Rico during the first week of October 1968. Wayne, Paul, Ted and I landed in the capital, San Juan, after flying straight from London via New York. In typical "surf macho" style, we rented a car, loaded the boards on the roof and tore off to the opposite side of the island in search of waves. We knew the world contest was going to be held in the Rincon area, so that was our destination. Driving out of San Juan past the old Spanish fort, complete with battlements and cannon, I made a mental note to come back and take a closer look at the reminders of the way 16th-century pirates had fought over this tiny island, but I never did get the chance. It was the same as in Italy and England, the surf was the only thing that mattered and sightseeing was not on the agenda.

All around the coastal village of Rincon, development had been taking place for over a year. Roads and houses were built to be used by competitors and officials then handed over to the local people when the contest – sponsored by the tourism department of Puerto Rico – was over. Surely, I thought, only one man in surfing's hierarchy could pull something like this off – it had to have been the work of Eduardo Arena. I was right as it turned out. We booked in to one of the small and spartan, self-contained cabins, dumped our stuff and immediately left to find a wave. Catching a glimpse of the swell from the top of a hill, off we tore down a dirt road on the outskirts of Rincon, ending up at a spot with beautiful 3 to 4-foot right-handers which we surfed hard until dark, helping to clear our heads after the long flight from Europe. When the time came to head back to Rincon, Paul was having trouble backing the car down the long narrow lane when an ancient woman appeared in the tail lights, showing him the best place to turn. She didn't speak any English, but we didn't have much trouble communicating. She got us to understand that her name was Maria, so that's what we called the break at the end of the road, though officially the break was called Rincon Point. The finals of the World Contest were actually held at Maria's and she

President of the International Surfrider's Federation
in '69, Senor Edwardo Arena.

made a few dollars charging cars to park up and down the street, not to mention all over her front lawn.

Puerto Rico was a new and interesting venue for the then fledgling sport of surfing – and in scale and presentation, those 4th World Surfing Championships seemed more like the Olympics than anything we'd experienced previously. The contest was again being run by the International Surfrider's Federation – and its president was still that debonair Peruvian gentleman, Eduardo Arena. At the official opening, held at the Mayaguez Hilton, "El Viejo" greeted me as if the last world contest had been held only yesterday, kissing me on the cheeks and embracing me warmly. The party was crawling with government officials and I didn't have the nerve to ask Eduardo what incredible influence he'd brought to bear in convincing the Puerto Rican government to put up the money for such a large event. El Viejo's contacts were obviously both international and extensive; certainly they must have spread further than just Peru.

There was another surprise at that party – Pina, the woman who'd lent Bob Evans and I her car when we were in Peru, was there, looking just as beautiful as she had in 1965. It was wonderful to see her. We didn't stay long at the party but ended up going out on the bay in a glass-bottomed boat to smoke a joint and watch the fish make phosphorescent trails through the water. It was as though every move they made was suspended in time, the phosphorescence lingering for several seconds before dissipating. It's one of the most amazing sights I've ever seen, especially on the occasions when dolphins were attacking the fish. The bay at Mayaguez is famous for it's phosphorus, attracting thousands of tourists every year, and I could see why; I was completely mesmerised by the display.

All through our final week of training, the size of the waves diminished further, forcing us to drive from one end of the island to the other in search of waves worth riding, and once all the international competitors arrived, it became impossible to find a wave of your own. The most consistent small waves we found were close to Rincon in a bay called Domes. It was a little, rolling, right-hand reef break in the shadow of a huge, white, dome-shaped nuclear power plant set smack in the middle of dense tropical rainforest. It looked like a set left over from a James Bond movie and was certainly one of the most bizarre backdrops I've ever surfed against. This little break was the only one we surfed consistently enough to determine if the boards we'd built in France were going to be suitable for Puerto Rico. I was really happy with the way my board felt: it had good flow, allowing me to link several turns without losing power. If I pushed too hard, the back would break away, putting me into a controlled drift, but the front held on. The soft egg rails with an edge were high in the front end and low in the tail, and the fin was basically the same design as George Greenough had shown me how to shape years before, but with a bit less volume and more flex in the tip. I really got into this drifting feel – it was so me – skating on the edge of spinning out. For months this was the gauge I'd used to assess whether a session was good or bad; I could feel the drift, especially in a hard cutback with all the momentum gained from a good strong bottom turn. It felt like driving a front-wheel-drive sports car through tight bends at high speed, constantly correcting with your foot flat to the floor. Wayne and Ted's boards were very similar, though not as straight in the tail as mine. We'd all shaped our own boards using our individual ideas, but some overlap was inevitable; we'd been living in each other's pockets for months. Ted's boards were more curvy and rounder in plan shape, a bit like the shape of a cuttlefish bone. He liked the softer flow he'd discovered on his favourite board "Little Red" at Maui the year before, and was trying to get that same feeling back again. Wayne decided not to make rails as hard in the tail as mine, but in most other respects the designs were similar, except that Wayne's board wouldn't drift as easily as mine. Wayne, without an ounce of fat on his body, was quite light, and his board was much finer all over, getting him further down in the water, which became quite noticeable when the board was loaded up in a turn.

All our time in the water at Domes had been well spent as almost every morning Eduardo would stand up and announce "the contest today will be at Domes". Translated, this meant the swell was small and everyone came to hate those words. We even got sick of Puerto Rico!

Back home, the World Contest was getting heavy coverage in the newspapers and, in the mind of one pretty young surf groupie from Manly, became a sort of personal quest. Robyn, "the girl with faraway eyes" (well that's what Mick Jagger sang) flew from Sydney just to look after the boys, and look after us she did – ah, the power of the press. Ted knew her, or had seen her at his home beach of Manly once or twice, and Robyn showed us a good time between surf sessions. For a week she rolled neat joints, shared herself with us at night and kept our little cabin clean and tidy; then one day we came back from surfing and she was gone without a trace – no note, just vanished into thin air.

Dewey Weber turned up not long after this: over the top, bounding out of his car, just as he'd been when I first met him in Hawaii, and as nice as ever. He was staying in a hotel at Mayaguez and drove out every day to surf and talk, and with so much development of my surfboards having taken place over the past couple of months, I had heaps of information to share with him: we talked and surfed for

Wayne Lynch in '69 shouting some obscenity out the car window to his friend John Witzig who is trying to take his photo. I believe surfing like this back-hand turn of Wayne's (circa '66) liberated the goofy-foots and inspired surfers like Tom Carrol and Barton Lynch to realise their potential.

hours that turned into days. Dewey was very excited about my board because it was so different from any in America and he could see a big summer for sales. Over dinner one night we sat down and mapped out the advertising campaign: I wanted to call the board "The Young Weber" the name I'd painted on the board in France, but we went instead for "The Ski". We decided to introduce it with a double-page spread in *Surfer*, continuing the campaign with ads in every magazine in the United States, and I'd make a promotional trip to the Gulf and east coasts of America.

While surfing Domes with Dewey one day, I felt something grab my leg. When I looked down through the crystal-clear water I was astonished to see that I was being attacked by a baby squid! It was the weirdest thing, like something out of a cartoon: I was Foghorn Leghorn and the little squid was Henry "Chicken" Hawk. Here was this little animal sucking on my leg and actually trying to drag me under! I didn't know what to think. It was funny but it was also starting to hurt so I reached down, grabbed the animal and pulled it out of the water and it curled itself round my hand. Then the devil got the better of me and I flung the tiny squid in Dewey's direction, watching as it hit him right on the nose and proceeded to try and wrap itself round his face. Weber freaked! He grabbed the squid and threw it at someone else, providing a little light relief in the line-up at Domes that day.

The contest itself was a disaster, plagued by small insipid waves and constant wrangling between the representatives of the participating countries and just before the final day the officials threatened to call the main event off due to a lack of big waves. Everyone competing in Puerto Rico knew the Hawaiians and the Peruvians would insist that in future separate big and small-wave events be held, as had been done in Peru in 1965. The big-wave contest would be the official World Championship and the small-wave contest would count for nothing. As well as the crazy dispute over big-wave, small-wave contests, there was the ridiculous quota system by which a country's surfing population decided the number of entrants it could send. Finally, to top it all off, we had the great debate between the two schools of thought in surfing – the traditional, older-style approach, pulling for the event to be held over until bigger waves came through, opposed by the more radical younger approach, willing and ready to surf anything to get a result. All this hardly seemed to matter at the time, however, as the surf wasn't cooperating in any case.

During that week the wave size stayed very uniform, between 2 and 3 feet, restricting us to surf Domes; it couldn't have been called big surf by any stretch of the imagination. At last the waves did do the right thing and we were able to surf the final on the outside reef at Maria's, in good 6 to 8-foot rights. Naturally, in line with every-thing else at that contest, every judge had his own subjective view about which style was best. Basically, the ISF judging guidelines called for "the longest ride in the most critical part of the wave... on the biggest possible wave... would be deemed the winner". I think on that score at least, the judges' decision was accurate; Fred Hemmings and Midget got the biggest waves and surfed them for the longest distance placing first and second respectively on a count-back. Russell Hughes came third, although he was considered the dark horse. From my perspective out in the water I thought he had won, with his smooth, flowing style suiting the crumbling walls so well. He was riding a bigger board made by Bob McTavish; it was 7-foot 6-inches long, and a traditional gun shape, being high in the front and low in the tail rails, just like our boards. I came in fourth; my board was spinning-out, I failed to control the drift and was not used to the bigger waves we encountered in the final, having only ridden my board in much smaller surf. The board's drift component was too unreliable; although I loved it I couldn't control it and I knew it was directly connected to the rail and plan shape. Naturally Ted, Wayne and I had been looking very carefully at all the other competitors' boards. David Nuuhiwa, Joey Cabell and Reno Abellira had really different rails on their boards, one I'd never seen before: hard, low in profile, and running the entire length of the board from nose to tail. After all these years and after questioning many surfers, I've still no real understanding of who first discovered that important ingredient – the origins of the low rail are still a mystery.

* * * * * * *

On the plane heading for Hawaii, Paul, Wayne, Ted and I talked non-stop about the contest. We couldn't believe that Hemmings was the new champ! Sure he could surf big waves, all he had to do was sur-vive, but his basic manoeuvres and stiff style were a long way from what we considered real world-champion material – we all agreed that the world champion should represent the cutting edge of devel-opment in our sport. Completely disillusioned with the result, we all vowed we'd never again compete in another World Contest. The only positive thing to come out of Puerto Rico was our exposure to the low-rail theory and the fact that we'd proved a point to a lot of our contemporaries by showing them what our shorter boards were capable of.

When we got to the North Shore at Oahu it was raining and the waves were turbulent and mushy, thanks to a big storm that had been blowing for a week. On the way out to the country I borrowed a

Weber Gun from Dewey's Hawaiian shop. It was 8-foot 6-inches long with soft, low rails; Randy Rarick, the shop manager, was about the same size as me so his boards suited me perfectly. But the next day the sun came out, the trade winds started blowing offshore and Oahu was starting to look like the Hawaii of the travel brochures. Sunset was good, around 10 to 12 feet, and though the northerly swell was kind of broken up, I really didn't care – it was Sunset Beach and such a rush to take off deep, press a big bottom turn and have a real wave chasing me down the line. Out in the line-up fifty surfers jockeyed for position, a normal day in 1968, and you paddled for every wave you were in position for; some you caught, some you didn't.

I'll never forget one incident in Oahu that year. A beautiful big set approaches, I'm about half way in the pack and right in the spot. I spin round and drop to the bottom, rolling the board over for my first bottom turn. Just as I'm all banked up and ready to fire the gun, another surfer appears on my left-hand side, inches away from me. "Hey man, don't bum my high" this hippy whispers almost in my ear. I turn to see who it is but I don't recognise him as a surfer I know. He's in a full death crouch, but going hard. Taken completely by surprise, I fell off and I never saw that hippy again – but I'll never forget that one-liner.

The remaining few days on the North Shore were pretty uneventful. There was surf all right, but it was hard for Paul Witzig to shoot film as we were so far from the beach. There were an awful lot of people everywhere, too; out in the water as well as on land. The hippy era really changed the North Shore; not necessarily for the worse, it just made it different. The "country" feel I'd known and loved so much just a year earlier was gone forever, and many streets were taking on the appearance of slums, filled with ugly prefabricated houses with lean-to's off to one side and backyard board builders in every garage.

After Puerto Rico and Hawaii, it seemed to me that surfing and surfboards were heading in two different directions in 1968–69. You were either a big-wave or small-wave rider and totally different boards were used for each. I couldn't wait to get home and build a low-railer, and even though I wasn't sure if the rails would work on our little waves I was keen to find out. Maybe we were just getting homesick or perhaps we'd had enough of each other's company, but either way, when Paul said "Let's go to the land of Oz", we all cheered.

* * * * * * *

Back in Australia, Wayne went to his home in Lorne, Victoria, and Ted, Paul and I went back to the northern beaches of Sydney. Almost

The late Ron Stoner was the best surfing
photographer in his day.
This was the winter of '69 at Haleiwa.

JOHN

Going over the results of a contest in '68. Bob Lynch in between Ted and me. Ted had either won or something was pretty funny.

immediately I got back, I went down to Keyo Surfboards in Brookvale and built a low-rail, short board for small waves, but with an extremely hard edge very close to the bottom. That board caught a lot in the front end when turning but was very sensitive.

I'd been back on the Peninsula about a week when Ted Spencer came round to tell Nyarie and I that he'd received a hand-delivered letter informing him that he was eligible for national service. In Australia at that time, all boys turning nineteen automatically qualified to enter a "lottery", with the prize being conscription into one of the armed forces – and possible service in Vietnam. Eligible birth dates were represented by numbered balls drawn from a barrel by the Minister for Defence and determined who was going to be "called up" for National Service in the Army, Navy or Airforce. Ted was the first of our friends to be called up and we talked over all the different ways we thought he might get out of it, but none of them sounded foolproof or even practical. On the day of the interview Ted had taken some powerful drugs and when one of the interviewers asked him to hold his arm above his head, he did so – but failed to bring it back down. This is a symptom associated with classic schizophrenia and Ted was discharged. When Ted told this story to Nyarie and I, he said he wasn't consciously trying to give a false impression to the Army officers, he just genuinely didn't think to bring his arm down, and they didn't ask him to – he was absolutely sincere, it really hadn't occurred to him to take his arm down. The person who appreciated this story most, and roared with laughter when I told it to him, was Doc Spence.

Ted Spencer was so much a part of the *Evolution* story and the development of Australian surfing in the late 1960s and early 1970s. An incredibly beautiful surfer and an extremely sensitive human being, Ted has always had my respect and friendship, despite our differences over the years. His parents, Doctor and Mrs Spencer, were very supportive when he decided to follow the surfing lifestyle, doing everything they could to make it possible. I've no idea what they thought when Ted became a devotee of the Hare Krishna movement, and in any case, it didn't happen overnight but was more a slow transformation. By the time his conversion was complete, Ted stated that when he surfed, he danced for Krishna. I thought he looked great with his shaven head and saffron robes and for a time his love and devotion to Krishna gave me real strength. I can recall an occasion chanting with him on the Gold Coast and feeling his incredible love and support .

* * * * * * *

Mum and Dad sold the Warriewood kindergarten in 1967 and bought a spacious home unit on the beachfront at Narrabeen. As it had four bedrooms they asked me if I'd like to move back in with them. It seemed like a good idea, though the only thing I liked about the unit was the view from the front balcony of the "Alley" at Narrabeen. As I'd been on the road most of 1968, home-cooked meals and a comfy bed to myself sounded pretty inviting.

While I'd been away on the *Evolution* project, Mum had been constantly hassled by phone calls from Eric Blum, the producer of the movie about the Wind 'n' Sea Surf Club's Australian trip, and he'd left countless messages, asking me to ring him in the States, "urgently". Eric's cameraman had shot some surfing footage on Maui and I'd agreed to work on the movie. Speaking on the phone, he told me he had all the elements in hand and was coming to Australia the next week to shoot one or two more sequences. It was all going a bit too fast; I should have pulled back right then but I agreed instead to meet him at Sydney airport the following week.

We filmed a moody sequence around dawn, shots of me walking along the beach towards Barrenjoey with Youngblood barking and seagulls mewing. The following week we went to Lennox Head and shot a whole lot of surfing footage with Greenough, McTavish and me. I should have been suspicious when Blum's cameraman, John Stephens, up and split before the Lennox Head shoot, leaving Eric to operate the camera himself, but by that time we were all in too deep. Blum flew me to California to do the voice-overs – and when Blum and his brother Lowell put me up at their Hollywood apartment, I really should have twigged that something wasn't quite right with the movie deal. I spent a week crashing in the Blum's apartment, screwing around writing and rewriting the closing segment of *The Fantastic Plastic Machine* and getting more and more frustrated. It was bloody hard work.

Adding to my confusion, the brothers Blum had agreed to give me $15,000 as soon as I finished, after I'd been led to believe the deal was with Twentieth Century Fox. It wasn't looking good, but being young and stupid, I waited until I'd finished my work on the movie before confronting them, at which time they told me it was standard procedure for large studios such as Twentieth Century Fox to contract independent producers, like them, to make a movie for a fixed sum. They went on to say that they were on budget, so I should stay cool and relax. So I left for Australia, feeling confident that the money would be forthcoming; money that would immediately go into the house I was building at Whale Beach.

A year later, when I badly needed money for my new house, I had a lawyer contact Twentieth Century Fox. The people at the studio said

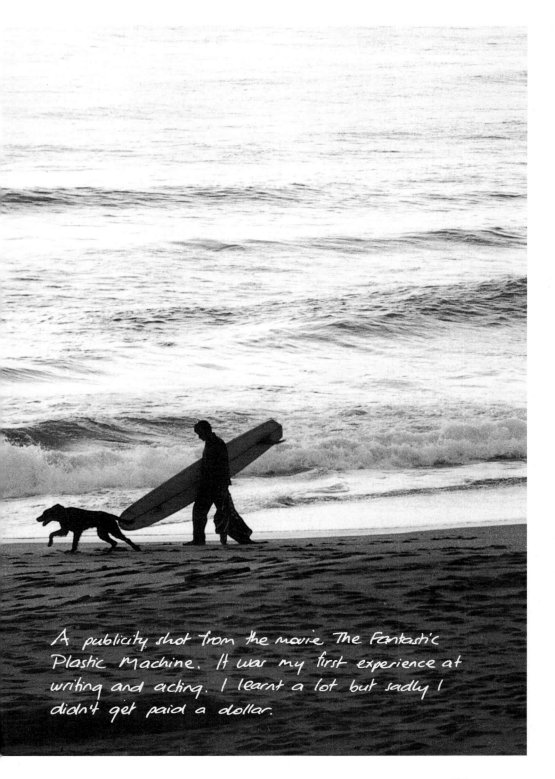

A publicity shot from the movie The Fantastic Plastic Machine. It was my first experience at writing and acting. I learnt a lot but sadly I didn't get paid a dollar.

they'd never heard of Eric Blum and when my lawyer pursued the matter, he found Eric Blum selling used cars in Florida. McTavish had a similar story to tell about going over to the States in December 1968, sleeping on the Blum's couch, working hard and leaving empty handed. Needless to say none of us ever got a brass razoo. But regardless of the fact that it was a financial disaster for George, McTavish and me, it was finished and did have limited success in the United States and Australia. The movie makes a strong statement about the high state of Australian surfing right then and gives an accurate portrayal of the Californian surfers' experiences in Australia.

My house at Whale Beach was nearing completion, a tremendous experience for me; after a gestation period of three years the baby was about to arrive. Since buying the land I'd wrestled with different ideas about exactly what sort of house I wanted. Then through John Witzig I met Ross Thorne, one of his lecturers at university, an architect and an interesting and cultured man. Ross had never been on a surfboard, so in 1967 he came to Noosa Heads, along with John and Terry Purcell, to experience what surfing was like. I took him out at Johnstons, when it was only 6 inches to a foot, telling him to lie down, look up at the 10 o'clock position and to keep his eyes open no matter what happened. I pushed him into a perfect little tube and all I could hear were his sighs and gasps as he flew down the barrel. After just one wave he was content, saying he didn't want another right then – it was, he said, like orgasm and he needed a rest. We went back to the rented apartment and sat on the deck overlooking Main Beach, watching the sun set over the Noosa River and over a couple bottles of wine talked long into the night about the house he was designing for me. After his surfing experience Ross now understood that a wave was a lot like a cave and it was this I wanted him to capture and put into bricks and mortar. I drove Ross back to Sydney in the old Merc and on the way we talked about the house some more, deciding what each room would be used for. I had a Beethoven piano concerto playing very loudly and the tall gums seemed to sway with the music as we sped down the coast. Back at his home in Palm Beach, over a delicious meal he prepared, Ross told me he understood what I wanted and was going to build a balsawood scale model on a plaster-of-paris replica of the building site.

We had dinner again the weekend after, and right from the moment I saw the model of the house I loved it: it was exactly what I'd envisaged when I'd sat daydreaming on the site; a series of cave-like rooms stepping down the cliff, and covered by a single roof parallel with the fall of the land. To get the roof I wanted, I haunted demolishers' auctions, and at last was able to buy a quantity of old roofing slates. Called "Bengal Purples", they were as scarce as hen's teeth, even in

WES STACEY

The buildings we create are some of the few things that remain after we are gone. I am very proud of my house at Whale Beach.

The Whale Beach house was designed by Ross Thorne. It gained a distinction in the Wilkinson Award for architecture.

the late sixties, and were the perfect roofing material, lasting forever and were a perfect blend for the house's surroundings. Ross was really pleased with my find and we could both picture how it would all look: the greys and greens of the eucalypt bark and leaves merging with the colour of the slate. I felt like Moses carrying the moss-covered rectangles of stone up the steep slope from Whale Beach Road, a small stack at a time – it was a very emotional time for me. The only other thing I could help with was selecting the bricks for the walls. A year before we started building I went to the brick manufacturer and put my order in, showing the boss an exact sample of what I wanted – the bricks closest to the fire when the kiln is stacked, resulting in them being contorted, bent and blistered on at least one side. This was to be the face that was visible when the bricks were laid.

So now my castle was finished; I moved my wine into a proper cellar and shifted my few pieces of furniture into their permanent home. The enormous English oak wardrobe I'd bought at St Vincent De Paul at last had somewhere to belong – I'd had a room designed especially for it – and I asked Ross what other furniture he thought I should buy. He came round the next day with some sketches of six benches and Graham, my sister June's husband, made them for me out of chunky Canadian redwood. They were perfect for that house and I still have them. Both Ross and I were very proud of the house on Whale Beach Road. He entered it in the Wilkinson Awards for Architecture and it received an honourable mention. I think the house failed to win because it had only one bedroom, being built for a bachelor, but Ross had allowed for another two bedrooms to be built under an extension of the same roof line. I always thought I should have told that to the judges.

I'd only been in the house a week when Dewey Weber called Mum with the message that he wanted me to do the United States East-Coast promotional tour he'd been talking about ever since I joined him. I didn't feel like going anywhere. I really just wanted to enjoy my home but with Speedo gone, Weber Surfboards was a major contributor towards paying my bills; so I flew to LA, picked up the latest model board, "The Ski", and travelled on to Florida. Dewey's shaper, Harold Iggy, had carved a pretty accurate copy of my original board, with the old high-in-the-front, low-in-the-tail rails – trouble was, I now didn't believe that high rails worked as well as low rails. We were stuck, I had given Dewey the board I'd made in France and surfed in Puerto Rico and he'd made The Ski accurate to the prototype, complete with high–low rails. Back in Australia after Puerto Rico, I'd experimented with different rails and called Dewey to talk about the problem, but he'd said the rails couldn't be changed so early in the season and the shops would get really mad if we tried, as Weber had already delivered hundreds of the model with the old rail shape so I'd have to live with the rails the way they were and slowly change them at the end of the season. Naturally, I wasn't that keen to surf this new board on the tour as I was now using hard, lowish rails on all my boards in Australia.

There was one detail of The Ski that was nowhere near the design of my original board and that was the fin. On the way to Florida I sat on the plane bending the thing in my hands, thinking back to Greenough and all his lessons on fins and how they worked. This fin bent like rubber! Yes, they fitted perfectly into the fin box but because of the way they flexed, I knew they wouldn't work. Weber's representative on the east coast was Mike Tabeling, slightly younger than me but similar in build; tall and lanky. He was a great athlete and a really good surfer, and for several years was East Coast champion. He picked me up in his nice new top-of-the-line Shelby Mustang and we drove down to his home at Melbourne Beach, to check out his Dad's surf shop and have a surf before charging off to visit what seemed to me every other surf shop on the East Coast of the USA, all in under two weeks. We surfed that afternoon at Satellite Beach, right next to the rocket launch site at Cape Canaveral. The waves were terrible by my standards – onshore, 3-foot, close-out beach-break – but not bad for Florida. Mike was running all over them but I felt like an idiot, and the problem was exactly what I'd thought it'd be when I looked at the rails in California and played with the fin on the plane. In every turn it felt as though the tail was sliding everywhere. The rail was too hard in the tail and I had no direction, no drive – the prettily coloured plastic fins were about as useful as tits on a boar! I was not happy with The Ski. I told myself we would fix the rail problem at the end of the season, but the rubber fins were a joke. Weber had been putting them on every board for over a year and they were so bad, we had to do something about the problem immediately. I talked to Mike but he didn't know any better, the fins felt fine to him because at that time he'd never surfed much outside Florida, so I didn't mention the rail problem just then as I thought it would have been a bit much to lay on him all at once. We smoked a big fat joint and Mike convinced me I was taking it much too seriously. It didn't matter, he explained, the East Coast had gutless waves and in any case, most of the people buying the boards couldn't surf. I called Dewey to explain the situation and told him he was indirectly encouraging backyarders to build their own boards by putting plastic fins on ours – we were shooting ourselves in the foot by ignoring the rail developments of the past year and using plastic fins. Dewey claimed it was the shipping and production departments that forced him into building boards with fin boxes and plastic fins

This ad for Weber surfboards announced the launch of The Ski inspired by my contact with Wayne Lynch and Ted Spencer in France and Puerto Rico in '68.

– apparently it was a cost saving measure – and he appeased me by insisting he had chemists developing stiffer polycarbonate fins. "Don't take it seriously," he said, "go and have a nice lunch, relax, listen to Mike, he knows the East Coast."

Mike and I cruised up the coast, taking every one of Weber's accounts to either lunch or dinner, depending on the time of day. We listened to all the shops' problems and back in the motel that night we made notes of some problems for later reference and called Dewey direct with the more urgent matters. As we travelled, we kept hearing about Keith Paull, an Aussie mate of mine and 1968 Australian Champion who I'd last seen in Puerto Rico the year before. The same age as me, he came from Queensland, and on the right day was a good surfer; powerful and smooth with an original, flowing style that was always very pleasant to watch. After Puerto Rico he'd gone to California and hooked up with Bing surfboards where, after doing a bit of shaping he was sent out to do the "real job". Bing Copeland, the owner of the company, had a flash of inspiration when he sent Keith to the East Coast. The American public really wanted to meet and talk to an Australian champion and he was the real McCoy. Australia was flavour of the month – one Seppo even started a business called "Surfboards Australia" and didn't even have any Aussies working for him.

All the money in factory made surfboards was on the East and Gulf coasts, where sales were still good, as California and Hawaii were full on into backyarders by then and, the competition was fierce. It seemed that everywhere we went, Keith had been there and done or said that, the week before Mike and I arrived. Everywhere we went we "just missed him". While Keith was in town they'd had "this unreal summer party with lots of college chicks on vacation" and naturally the waves were perfect. Where were we last week when Keith was here? I had to laugh, or I'd cry – being beaten to the line in every town on the East Coast was really beginning to get to me, our sales out of the shops were suffering and it was beginning to piss me off! I started to see more Bings than Webers on the beach but I shouldn't have worried; Weber's production figures showed 100 boards a day during that summer but you could bet Bing, our biggest competitor, was doing close to that.

My competitive nature was starting to come out and we decided to cut Keith off at the pass by skipping a town and catching up with him in Jacksonville. Tabeling got on the phone to change the dates with the dealers and I cleared it with Dewey. In Jacksonville we walked right into a big summer beach party, spread all over the beach and the boardwalk just down the street from Dave Hart's Weber shop in Jacksonville Beach. The place was going off! Tons of people dancing and drinking and there in the middle was Keith Paull. Tabeling and I grabbed a beer and sat back to listen, just waiting for him to say the wrong thing. However everything he said was absolutely true and could only be interpreted as very flattering to me and our Weber boards and when we went over to speak to him he was elated. We had a full in-depth rave about our different adventures over the last year and as Mike had some killer weed, we invited Keith out for a smoke. He looked at us in a very strange way and said that he didn't do drugs and had nothing to do with people who did. So that was that. I could understand not having a smoke but not having anything to do with people who did? I mean it wasn't heroin! His attitude was a tad hard-line I thought.

We left town the next morning to complete our tour and I flew home to Australia from New York. I didn't see Keith again until the NSW State title – where he came second – at Narrabeen in March of 1970. I saw him at Bells a couple of years after that, in either 1972 or 1973, and he'd shaved his head and was living in his Kombi. As usual at Bells, it was raining, and I tapped on the Kombi's side door and let myself in. We chatted a bit while Keith cleaned the weed and invited me to bust the chillum. "Om dow," I said as I handed him the pipe. I thought back to Jacksonville but didn't say a word.

* * * * * * *

It was a great feeling to be coming home to my own house but my excitement turned to despair when I opened the door. I looked down to the lower level and there, lying on its side in front of the fireplace, was a bottle of Lindeman's 1960 Rouge Homme and most of its contents were spilt over the carpet. I felt like a burst balloon – I'd been robbed again. I cried, I think, to see that magnificent wine growing mould on my floor. Whoever had done this didn't even appreciate wine. The whole scene brought memories of the first time I'd been robbed flooding back, but this was worse somehow – perhaps because this was my own house. When I took a closer look around the house it was a wreck. Broken wine bottles and spilt wine were in every room, even in my bedroom. Whoever had done the damage had a real party before they carried off twenty-odd dozen bottles of Australia's finest wines. I went home to Mum's and phoned the insurance company; at least this time I was covered, I had learnt from my last experience. The insurance company gave me what I'd paid for the wine but it was irreplaceable and the true value could only have been determined at auction.

* * * * * * *

It was December again and the Hawaiian contests were on; time was going all too fast and the years seemed to be running into each other. I promised myself I was going to slow down in 1969 or at least not travel so much. My childhood sweetheart Marilyn came up and spent a weekend with me in the new house. She loved it and we got on really well, for although we'd experienced similar feelings with other lovers in different situations, neither of us had felt the same intensity – we were falling hopelessly in love again, just as we had when we were still at school. Witty and intelligent, Marilyn was petite and almost doll-like, with everything in perfect proportion; she looked as though she really belonged in my house.

Marilyn would walk naked around the house and I loved to watch her. I'd catch her coming from the bathroom, bending over getting something out of the dryer or getting dressed and ready to leave for a nearby school where she was teaching. Then one morning I saw her at the top of the stairs that led down from the bedroom, the soft morning light touching her breasts and making them glow. She looked like an angel and I had to ask her, right then and there. I ran to her, laid her down and asked her to marry me. Marilyn said she wanted to think about it and told me she'd give me an answer when I got back from Hawaii; but I knew that she wanted marriage as much as I did.

The North Shore wasn't that fantastic. People talk about the epic season of 1968–69 but I can't remember many great days – I guess I had other things on my mind or perhaps I missed it because I was only on the Rock for two weeks, though at the time it couldn't pass quickly enough. My two Weber guns were there waiting for me with Randy Rarick and as I lifted them from the nose and looked down the curves, I could see that Iggy had done a great job. They had the traditional Hawaiian big-wave board outlines and the hard low rail popular at the time – lying there all ready to go, the boards looked like a pair of racehorses. Both were finished identically with a big Weber sun sticker on the deck, but the best thing about them was that they had fins that had been fibreglassed on; fins I'd sanded myself in California last summer.

This was the 4th Duke Kahanamoku Invitational, but the first one I'd attended because of the mix-up with the tickets and McTavish the year before. I really wasn't sure what I felt; I was a bit pissed off that I'd not been one of the 24 invited guests in the previous three years, but as the only Australian I felt sort of honoured. Even so, I had to keep telling myself to shut up, it was their contest and everyone knew that Keith Paull, Peter Drouyn, Wayne, Ted or Midget could also surf well enough to be in this prestigious event. On America's ABC television, a man in a white suit, Mr Kimo Wilder McVey, owner

This picture was a fold-out cover of Surfer magazine, another Stoner shot, at Sunset Beach.

of the Duke Kahanamoku Corporation, was telling viewers that they'd "scoured the world to find the true champions". However, the opening party was tons of fun. Imagine a big room full of half-pissed surfers, hula girls in grass skirts and a floorshow by the wonderful Don Ho. The party was at the Duke's restaurant among the magnificent banyan trees at the International Market Place. We were all given two pairs of boardshorts, two tee-shirts and assorted other vouchers for restaurants and bars in Waikiki and rooms at the Royal Hawaiian for the week – though we had no say in which room we were given or with whom we shared it. It came as a bit of a shock when I walked into my room and there was the legend, Micky Dora, sitting on the end of a bed. I'd never met him but McTavish had shared a house with him on the North Shore the year before and all he could say was "He's a classic". I asked Micky if he was in the room because he didn't like the party. "Not much," he replied and asked me if I'd like a nightcap. I agreed, so we took a taxi to a gay bar in Honolulu and over a couple of drinks Micky told me he liked being away from surfers and that he thought they were ignorant pigs for the most part. He said he preferred being anonymous in a totally different environment where no-one knew him, but he always stood out in a crowd.

The next day we drove out to Sunset to start the contest but it was dead flat and stayed that way for two days, then on the third day it was 20 feet and unrideable. The contest was moved to Haleiwa, but it was considered almost too big for that beach when one of the competitors was washed about a mile out to sea from the Harbour. The organisers sent Fred Hemmings out at Sunset to see if the waves were rideable there but after watching him get washed around for an hour they called the day off. The following day was still left-over storm waves, around 15 feet, and in my semi-final I was about to take off when I realised I was too far behind the peak – but I was committed. I ran down the face, but as the right had already closed-out and the thunderous curl was coming at me, I cranked the board around to the left and flew down the line. The wave was a screamer; up till then I didn't know it was possible to go left at Sunset, and live to talk about it. In the next instant I was up on the reef, off my board and getting thrown around in the coral – luckily not live coral, though it still felt pretty sharp rubbing against my right shoulder – and then I was on the beach with microphones shoved in my face and cameras looking for the gory details to take to middle America via ABC. I didn't do so well in the final, placing fifth; the winner was my friend Mike Doyle, who looked just as smooth and polished as ever.

11

'Sea of Joy' and short boards

M Y MARRIAGE TO MARILYN on the 17th of February 1969 was a good excuse for a party. The reception was held at Barrenjoey House, a beautiful old building overlooking Pittwater and still one of the most upmarket restaurants on the Peninsula. Marilyn and I were really excited about going to Europe for our honeymoon but we couldn't get away until June when the contest season was over and Marilyn could get leave from her teaching job. On the contest scene, Ted Spencer was having a fantastic run; he couldn't put a foot wrong it seemed, winning both Bells and the State Championships. The little round double-ended boards he was using were really working for him in the smaller East Coast waves, but how they'd perform in the big powerful waves at Margaret River, Western Australia, during the Australian Championships remained to be seen. The only time I'd been surfing in that area was with Paul Witzig and Gopher back in 1963 and on that occasion I'd ended up crying on the beach and couldn't paddle out; the ocean was so formidable in that part of the world. On the strength of that remembered encounter, I took a full-on Weber Hawaiian gun with me as well as a pretty typical, 6-foot 10-inches long, curved bottom, hard lowish-railed, displacement hull that I'd made at Denny Keyo's.

For publicity reasons, the contest began on one of Perth's city beaches, the idea being to show the residents of the capital how the local surfers stacked up on their home break against the boys from the east. It worked well; some 5000 people streamed out of the city to line the shore break at Scarborough. Midget Farrelly created a bit of a problem when it was announced that he'd be competing as a member of the Western Australian team. A few weeks earlier at Avalon, he'd pulled out of the qualifying rounds for the New South Wales State Championships saying the surf wasn't good enough, and was dropped from consideration for the New South Wales team as a result. A few of the competitors protested over Midget's inclusion in the West Australian team and the officials asked him to withdraw – Midget complied with the request and left for Sydney. After this

Signing the register with Marilyn. I was still competing full on in '69 and Marilyn joined me at Bells. Americans Jack McCoy on our right and Dale Dobson on the other side. Rusty Miller took this photo.

strange beginning we all headed off for the South-West coast.

Right from the minute we stepped out of the car, Margaret River looked exactly as I remembered it: a screaming offshore wind and a solid 8 to 10 foot swell pushed along by the roaring forties – at long last we were going to have a real surfing contest. I stood on the high, windswept cliff overlooking the contest site, squinting at the lines of swell that continued all the way to the horizon and feeling thankful that I'd brought the right equipment. Looking square-on to the Margaret River line-up, the right-handers looked just as good as the lefts – I tore straight out there on my 8 foot 6 inch, 19 inch-wide, translucent green Weber gun. The board felt beautiful; smooth and positive, it was made for this sort of power. This time it seemed, I had just the right board. I took off on a good size right, punched a clean bottom turn and set up the tube, then the curl came over and the next thing I knew I had a long swim through the rocks to the beach. Swimming in, I could see people on the cliff pointing out to sea but I couldn't see my board anywhere. Reaching the shore I realised I needed a little elevation to see beyond the shorebreak and locate my board and I scrambled up the first line of sandhills. I could just make out the green shape tossing in the rip about 200 metres offshore and I turned to run back down to the beach and swim out to get my board when suddenly my heart jumped – there was half of my board being held high in the air by someone way down the other end of the beach. That was it. I didn't even get to surf the board in the first round and I felt that, for me, the contest was all over. I still had the small-wave board I'd built at Keyo's factory a few weeks ago but it was limited, especially if the waves got any bigger, but I took the board out anyway, trying to adjust. It felt fine; not really suited to the size and power of these waves but if I surfed carefully I could live with it.

May is a pretty cold month in southern Western Australia and we had fires going on the beach all the time. We didn't really need them to keep warm through the day, and though the early mornings were pretty cool, we lit fires more because it has become a tradition in surfing – it's very tribal and the social interaction is intensified with everyone standing around a fire on the beach. I still light a fire whenever I get the chance. The day before the finals, we were standing round the fire and our boards were placed with their noses leaning against the first line of dunes. I was standing looking out to sea with my back to the boards when I smelt burning fibreglass. Wheeling around, I saw my board had somehow slid around so that its nose was in the fire and the entire front half was engulfed in flames. Grabbing it by the fin I dragged it into the shorebreak with just one thought in my mind: the blackened and charred wreck promised a long night of repairs if I was going to be ready for the final next day. This 1969 Australian Championship was turning out to be more than a bit of a challenge but I did win the final from Peter Drouyn and Richard Harvey, even though I surfed tentatively.

The juniors were interesting to watch. Wayne Lynch performed on the big predominantly lefts as though he was in his natural element. Swooping and gliding in and around the curl he reminded me of an albatross, just made for a life at sea. Wayne was surfing even better than he had in France and I wasn't at all surprised when he won the junior title. He went on to win four Australian junior titles in a row but I had my doubts that he could hold the momentum into the open division.

At last the contest season was over and Marilyn and I could concentrate on our honeymoon in Europe. Before leaving Australia we traded-in Marilyn's old Volkswagen beetle and my cream Mercedes on a new VW Kombi which we'd pick up in Brussells. The right-hand drive Kombi was fitted out as a camper and at the end of our holiday we'd leave it in Germany for shipment to Australia. I've always been a great believer in mixing business with pleasure so I decided that on our way to Europe we'd spend a month in America doing another promotional trip to the East and Gulf Coasts for Weber surfboards. After the tour Marilyn and I would fly to Europe from New York. Mike Tabeling came over from Florida to meet us in California and in one of Weber's vans, with Mike doing most of the driving, we travelled right across the United States.

The Gulf Coast waves are little and few so I wasn't expecting much surf there but this was more than made up for by the friendliness of the Texans – of everyone in the Southern States in fact. They welcomed us into their homes and had us eating corn grits and hash browns the whole time we were in the South. Mike was very familiar with the Gulf and Eastern seaboard, as this was his territory. Weber paid him a retainer plus a percentage on sales so every few weeks he trod this familiar beat and he was on good terms with all the shops. The tour took on much the same pattern as my previous trip to the East Coast: we'd surf in the morning then take a shop owner out for either lunch, dinner or a beer, depending on the time he had available, and we'd discuss their particular problems. The one major problem the various shops had in common was the threat posed by the dreaded backyarders and smaller boutique manufacturers; they were really starting to eat into the big manufacturers' markets. Weber, along with the other major surfboard manufacturers had been forced to drastically cut production.

Tabeling and I were getting stoned fairly often in order to keep alive our interest in the minuscule waves. Mike knew his job well;

Wayne's surfing around this time on something of a high.
This shot was taken at Johanna, Victoria.

he bought a big bag of quality heads which made things particularly pleasant no matter where we were, how small the surf or how many new faces I had to meet. Marilyn found it interesting but oppressively hot and sticky, as it always is in this part of America at the height of summer – and the beaches weren't much compared to the beaches in Sydney. She told me afterwards that to her, it was like being in a set from *Gone With The Wind*: if she tripped-out on the buildings and accents she could imagine how it must have been before the Civil War. Before we knew it the tour was over and we were waving goodbye to Tabeling at New York's John F. Kennedy Airport and boarding a plane to Brussells.

* * * * * * *

In Europe I tried not to follow the auto routes, intending to stick to the secondary roads all the way to Biarritz, but it was impossible. Surf fever kept creeping in and before I knew it I'd be back on the freeway; driving hard and wondering in which direction the wind was blowing and how I'd ever learn to predict the swell and wind direction from the strange weather maps in the French newspapers. Marilyn handled it. I knew she would have loved to go to the big cities like Paris and Rome but she knew whom she'd married and was prepared to compromise. Only once on the whole trip was she upset. I'd left her alone early one morning in a beautiful camping spot in the pine forest behind La Barr when some French friends picked me up to go surfing and when I returned late in the afternoon, I found the Kombi locked and Marilyn hiding inside. Just after lunch, a man with a gun and dog had surprised her while she was getting dressed and she'd leapt into the van and locked the doors. The man stayed for a while, chattering in French – he was probably a hunter and innocent enough but Marilyn didn't want to take a chance. Nothing at all had happened but she was really scared and I had to promise never to leave her on her own in circumstances like that again. The waves hadn't been as good as I remembered them to be on my first visit to the Biarritz area and there were a lot more French surfers along with quite a few Aussies, Poms and Yanks who were doing the travelling–camping thing in Europe.

We left for Spain and Portugal soon after the incident in the pine forest. Spain in 1969 was a whole lot easier to travel through than it had been on my last trip and the motorcycle police had gone or at least were no longer visible. We followed the coastline as much as we could, enjoying the people and the food, and checking every accessible river mouth and headland for waves. I found a few places to surf that had never before been ridden, if the reaction of local farmers was anything to go by. At one such spot the waves rolled for a few hundred metres alongside a river bank – it was a beautiful break and we camped there for a few days until the swell dropped. Portugal was magnificent, and the wine and seafood were truly memorable. Throughout that country, life seemed to revolve around the sea and it wasn't hard to understand why Portugal had become the leading seafaring nation of the 15th century.

After two weeks on our own in the countryside we were keen to make contact with people who spoke English and surfed, so we camped at Estoril, at the entrance to the river Tagus, with it's impressive castle and battlements protecting the main entrance to Lisbon. The lefts were good and strong, 4 to 6 feet the whole time we were there. Taking off in the shadow of the gun turrets and paddling back out as we watched huge ships entering the river was neat. Out in the surf I met a mob of guys from Newport Beach, California; we went out to dinner with them a few times and ended up getting stoned with them every day for a month. Marilyn and I became quite good friends with this crew; they were renting a nice house overlooking the beach and once when Marilyn was feeling a bit poorly one of their girlfriends invited her to spend a few nights there.

I walked into the house one day and saw one of the guys sitting there with his leg encased from hip to foot in plaster. I'd been surfing with him just a few hours earlier so I was pretty puzzled over how he could have had what must have been a serious accident, visited a doctor or hospital and have his leg put in a cast in such a short time. The "patient" confided in me that the cast was made of compressed Moroccan kif wrapped in a thin white bandage; he was off home to the US that afternoon and the revenue from the kif would pay for his European surfing holiday. Another of the Yanks told me how easy it was to take the motor out of a Volkswagen van and put 50 kilos of drugs in the recess behind the engine compartment. He wanted to know if I was interested, pointing out that I had a van, but I told him I had too much to lose.

On the way back to Germany we stopped off in Zurich at the invitation of a friend, Max Andre, who is about two years younger than me, with a French mother and Swiss father. We'd first met in 1967 when I sold him one of my boards before I left Biarritz for Puerto Rico and I ran into him again out in the surf in France. Max was really hospitable; he put us up in his apartment in Zurich and we had dinner with his family while we were there. Before taking the Kombi over the Alps to Munich, Marilyn and I went skiing in Lech, Austria. Marilyn had never skied before so it was difficult to enjoy skiing with her. I wasn't a very patient teacher and gave up after the first day, putting her in classes for the rest of our stay. Not that I could ski very well, but I was competent and knew, though without quite under-standing that there were similarities between surfing and skiing.

* * * * * * *

Marilyn and I arrived in Sydney just before Christmas 1969 – to a full-on press conference. I still have no idea who organised the turnout but I was grilled by newsmen and had TV cameras stuck in my face. The burning questions were: Why had I missed the Hawaiian season when I'd been invited to compete in both the Duke and Makaha contests? Was I going to compete in the Australian contests? Had I really retired at the ripe old age of 22? Was I getting out of competition? And so on. To the last I certainly let them know they were right off the track – especially taking into account the fact that the 1970 World Championships would be held in Victoria after South Africa dropped its bundle over sponsorship problems. I was the 1969 Australian Champion and of course I'd compete in the World Championships. I didn't let on to the media exactly how disenchanted I really was with the contest system; instead I kept my cool and launched into a rave about how surfing was not a very good competitive sport because it didn't have a line to cross or goal posts, going on to say that surfing would be much better represented as an art form. And then I dropped the "Golden Breed Expression" bombshell. I had a letter from Duke Boyd, my old boss at Hang Ten, who now worked in a surfing clothing company called Golden Breed, in which he told me about a dream he shared with an old surfer friend of his named Richard Graham – a dream they hoped see come to fruition in Hawaii the following season. They planned to have an "expression session" with the world's best surfers performing purely for money and with the television audience in mind; no winner, no loser, presenting surfing more as an art form. I'd fired back a positive response: Yes, I was interested, I'd be there for sure.

Things had really changed on the surfboard front in the six months I'd been away. The average length of a board in Australia was now under 6-foot and most of the better surfers were riding 5-foot 10-inch boards – Wayne Lynch apparently was down to 5-foot 6-inches. The day after I arrived home I bumped into Ted Spencer in Avalon. He was about to head south to Victoria to get ready for the World Titles and was taking three boards with him: a 6-footer, one at 6-foot 4-inches, and a 6-foot 8-inch, all of his "White Kite" design, which were really just slightly bigger Greenough kneeboards. There was the same old problem raising its head again – we were trying to surf kneeboards standing up! The little boards were fantastic when surfing in the curl with plenty of power, but as soon

Alby took this shot of Ted Spencer getting his quiver together for the World Contest. From memory he had made a 5'6" for little waves, 6' for in-between, and 7'6" for big ones.

ALBY

The conditions at North Narrabeen for the '70 NSW State Championships suited my 5'10" perfectly. On this memorable wave I won the contest.

as we left that power we were dead in the water, like shot ducks. Ted was a compact ball of muscle and of everyone I knew, he suited the short board best; his normal board for Sydney was around 5-foot long.

I felt I was right out of touch; all this had happened in six months? I didn't feel confident enough to make my own board and I had no allegiance to any Australian surf board manufacturer. What I needed was a good state-of-the-art short board and as the Weber money was still flowing, I got an Avalon kid named Nigel Coats to shape and build one for me. It was 5-foot 10-inches long by 19-inches wide, with hard lowish rails and a normal Greenough fin. Over the next few weeks the waves everywhere on the north side of Sydney were exceptionally powerful with great shape – the uncharacteristic conditions continuing right up and into the State Championships at Narrabeen – and on the grinding beach and point breaks I couldn't put a foot wrong. In the State competition, with sunny skies and offshore winds fanning a solid 6-foot easterly swell, my short board worked perfectly. I had one left-hander in the semi-final that still lives in my memory as one of the finest waves I've ever caught in a contest: I dropped in late, as was often the case on a short board, snuck in a turn halfway down the face and had the curl constantly chasing me for more than a hundred metres – it was the North Narrabeen Alley at its finest. I won that contest with Keith Paull placed second and Ted Spencer third.

As usual I sat back and watched the juniors with interest. Mark Warren won easily, with slick, polished moves way beyond his years. However, the kid that impressed me most was a newcomer with a weirdly unique style; one knee locked in behind the other and arms out at right angles to his body. The other competitors were calling him the "wounded seagull" but he had something going for him and took third place. That kid was Mark Richards, the son of Ray, the Newcastle Surf Shop owner for whom I'd shaped all those "Nat Young" model boards at Gordon Woods so long ago. I remembered Ray asking me to shape a little one for his boy and seeing Mark surfing so well made me feel old. A new experience for me, but I didn't dislike it too much.

In April 1970, Marilyn and I drove north for the Australian Championships which were being held on Queensland's Gold Coast. It felt good to be leaving Sydney, driving our imported Kombi with the steering wheel finally being on the right side for the road. Having the camper meant we could pull over anywhere to sleep and this we did on our first night. On the second night we called in to visit Nyarie, parking in the garden of her beautiful old homestead at Brooklet, behind Byron Bay in northern New South Wales. She shared the house with Russell Hughes and a tall American named

Garth Murphy. Nyarie seemed happy; surrounded by her dogs and installed in another regal house with incredible 360-degree views of the Byron hinterland.

In the living room were two sleek new boards which Russell had just had made in Hawaii. After his success in the Puerto Rico World Contest he was now being sponsored by Hanson Surfboards of California, Don Hanson paying for the state-of-the-art boards. One, shaped by Dick Brewer, was 7-foot 6-inches long, with the same hard, low rails I'd seen in the Islands. The other was under 7-foot and shaped by Gerry Lopez, with a tucked-under, low rolled rail making a hard edge where it joined the bottom about an inch in from the edge of the board, something I hadn't seen before. The next morning Russell, Garth and I went for a surf at Lennox Head. Russell surfed the Lopez board, saying it was really refreshing to feel the kind of sensitivity it offered; it didn't seem to catch at all. He gave me a wave on it and it did feel very different to all the other low-rail boards I'd ever ridden.

Marilyn and I fell in love with the Byron area. There were hardly any other young people around and when we drove down the main street we noticed that just about everyone seemed to be wearing a blue uniform and either worked at the Norco milk factory or Walker's abattoir. Without discussing it in much depth, we decided to look at property in the Byron area on our way back down the coast after the contest.

The surf on the Gold Coast wasn't much good for the contest. I was having trouble getting the short board up and running in the softer Queensland waves and found myself thinking about Russell's Lopez board back in Byron. Midget was the only contestant not using a short board; he was riding a "side slipper" which did exactly as the name implied, being designed to go sideways when the whole rail was buried. It was a method of stalling the board to give the wave time to catch up, thereby giving more open face to turn on. It seemed to work quite well for Midget but I was having trouble working out why a good strong cut-back wasn't a more effective way back into the curl. The judges didn't quite know how to assess his style of surfing at that time, but it worked out pretty well for him when he came fourth overall.

Naturally the contest was being used to pick the team for the World Contest to be held the following month in Victoria, so it was a pretty important event with the pressure really on. I won one round, as did Peter Drouyn and Ted Spencer. Then in the finals at Greenmount I made an unforgivable mistake – I hadn't surfed Greenmount over the past week but I did know there were submerged rocks just below the water. The waves were really small and

The caption on this picture in the Sun newspaper December '68 said "NAT YOUNG THE SURFER THEY CALL THE ANIMAL".

ALBY

Wide shot of the front of our old farm house at Byron soon after we moved in. One of the first projects was to knock out a portion of the front wall to let us look down the barrel at Broken Head.

the tide was pretty high but it didn't feel right riding waves as close to the point as we were. I got off to a good start with a couple of high-scoring rides, then to my utter horror I felt my fin connect with a rock during a driving forehand turn, knocking the fin completely off. It was gone forever and I didn't have another board – I was furious with myself, my chances of winning had just flown out the window and I just couldn't believe it. I screamed "fuck" at the top of my voice at least ten times, and with hundreds of spectators and competitors looking on, I stomped off the beach, throwing my contest singlet down as I went. The officials were angry and rightly so; it was a childish display and as a result I wouldn't be included in the Australian World Contest team unless I wrote a complete apology. Peter Drouyn was the overall winner with Ted Spencer second, Keith Paul third, then Midget followed by yours truly in last place.

Back in Byron, I healed my wounds with some crisp little tubes at the Pass and rode around looking at property with an old gentleman named Tony Kibblewhite who sold bus and train tickets from his shop full of second-hand bits and pieces and masqueraded as a real estate agent. Kibblewhite was an Englishman who had lived in Byron for years and he had a gammy eye that was a little offputting on those occasions when it wept profusely. However he was the only real estate agent in the Byron Bay of 1970 and in his old Hillman Minx he drove Marilyn and me around to look at every bit of property he thought might interest us. When he showed us an old house and 11 acres on a ridge overlooking Tallows and Broken Head, we made a deal on the spot. It was then Kibblewhite sidled up to me to let me know that the old lady who'd owned the house had lain dead in it for a month before she was missed. I never did tell Marilyn that story, it just didn't seem like something she needed to know. I could see the potential in the old house and was planning to make heaps of alterations when the papers were signed. On the way back to Sydney, we tried to plot our immediate future: I had the World Championships in Victoria in a couple of weeks and then another movie trip with Paul Witzig in June; then it would take a month or two to finalise the Byron deal and find a suitable tenant for Whale Beach. We decided not to sell the Whale Beach house because we didn't know if we would like Byron once we were living there – moving out of the city was a pretty big deal for both of us.

The 5th World Championships were going off in style thanks to a last-minute promise of a large sum of money from the Victorian State Government. Two civic receptions were held, one in Melbourne for the media and officials and the other at the hotel on the beach where most of the competitors were staying. That second party at the Lorne Hotel was a big night; we Aussies weren't going to be outdone by other countries. Everything was first class; everything, that is, except the surf. It seemed these World Titles would be plagued with the same jinx as the event in Puerto Rico – no contestable waves. It went from bad to worse when a full-on winter storm with rain and gale-force winds hit the Bells area the day the contest was scheduled to begin, then many of the international competitors came down with a 24-hour virus, especially those from tropical countries, and to cap it all off, some of the competitors had boards and other possessions stolen. The contest was in an acute nose dive.

Things got under way in a mood of sheer desperation; the waves weren't very good, crumbly with short sections, but at least it was a start. Even at that early stage in the event the writing was on the wall; all over the beach and out in the water everyone was talking about 18-year-old Rolf Aurness, the son of James Arness of "Gunsmoke" fame, and how fast he was going. As Rolf screamed down the line on another Bells boomer, coasting over the flat section before driving through the shorebreak, I wanted to scream – I'd recognised another mistake on my part, my boards had no follow-through and I didn't have a chance. I had another opportunity to watch Rolf surf "Winki Pop" the next morning. He was covering a lot of ground and no-one was in his league – it was all over. He had five boards with him, ranging from 6-foot 6-inches to 8-foot 6 – and every one of them a pintail Hawaiian gun with those same tucked-under-to-an-edge rails, just like Russell's Lopez board.

The surf again went flat in the Bells area but this time the officials moved the semi-finals and finals to Johanna, a beautiful windswept beach-break about two hours south of Bells, where the waves were 6 to 8 feet with a tight pocket. Rolf was on his backhand and I thought I could actually pick up my score in waves like this. I did, but only enough to gain sixth place. Peter Drouyn came third, Midget second and Rolf was the new World Champion. This was the first time – and it was to be the last – that a complete outsider had stepped in and won a major surfing event. With no sponsors other than his father, it was a fantastic effort on Rolf's part, but he was so unassuming. He kept to himself, playing a lot of piano and surfing when the mood took him. I ended up spending a bit of time with him and his girlfriend Chenoa at his Dad's place on the Ranch in the early 1980s. He had a great vegie garden and we surfed rights and lefts at all the old spots I'd surfed with Greenough. Rolf was always the same quiet, super-cool guy, riding waves and playing music. The last I heard from him was when a small carved stone figure turned up in the mail from Easter Island, where he'd gone in search of waves with his dad.

I'd just got back to my wife and house in Whale Beach when Weber called saying his dealers on the East Coast needed me to do a

From the left in the shot above, Edwardo, Rolf Aurness and me. Rolf and his dad James from Gunsmoke fame came to Australia a month before the 1970 World Championships. Rolf's boards were a good foot longer than what we were riding and he won the contest easily. These are both John's pics.

lightning promotions trip to boost sales in the coming summer. I tried to back out, using Paul Witzig's new surf movie *Sea of Joy* as a reason, but I really couldn't refuse, as I was on a pretty good deal with Dewey. I flew to the East Coast via California, stopping there for a day to be briefed on the problem. It seemed that sales had crashed and shops were going broke in every small town along the entire length of the Gulf and East Coasts. I called on twenty shops, from New York through Virginia Beach and down to the Carolinas, and everywhere the story was the same: the backyarders were putting them out of business. I couldn't do anything about the situation and there wasn't much point in going on, so I called Dewey from the airport and flew on to London and then to Mauritius where Wayne, Ted and Paul had been waiting for two weeks. The Beatles' *Let It Be* had just been released and I'd grabbed a copy at Heathrow Airport because I knew Paul had a record player. And in a dingy little concrete box in Tamarin Bay we all sang along to the Beatles' newest release.

Apparently I hadn't missed any surf and hardly any came through while I was there; the elusive, perfect lefts of Tamarin Bay once again proving to be extremely fickle. The village of Tamarin was very rural and quiet, the gentle local people a blend of Indian and African. Walking along the beach one day, right where the river flows out into the bay, I dug with my feet in the silt and the biggest, brightest cowrie shells I'd ever seen came up before my very eyes. We hung around for three weeks and only one swell of any consequence arrived – Tamarin is very sheltered – but being the only surfers on the island we did have Mauritius all to ourselves, though there wasn't much to keep us interested. Wayne had two good boards with him, but Ted's and mine were dogs and we wanted to build new ones – but that was impossible of course. We were in the middle of nowhere as far as resin and blanks went.

South Africa was the next stop. As usual, we hired a car in Johannesburg and drove as fast as we could to the surf, ignoring all the sights along the way. We stopped off in Durban for one night; the waves were small but we met a local named Tony "Ant" Van Der Heuvel, who was very anxious to come along as our guide. Jeffrey's Bay was a real surf town and straight off the bat the waves were cranking – we were all stoked after three weeks in Mauritius without surf. The waves didn't go below 4 feet the whole time we were there, getting up to 10 feet on the biggest days.

Ted and I needed new equipment and Ant tapped into a good connection who organised blanks and a glasser to finish the boards off for us. I shaped mine like a long short board, but added a foot to its length – and of course the rails were tucked under to an edge like the Lopez board. The glasser took it upon himself to use bright

Africa was such a fascinating culture; I loved it but felt frustrated not being able to treat the black Africans as equals. Dick shot this pic and the one on the next page.

Jeffrey's Bay, South Africa, one of the most
fantastic waves in the world— it didn't go under
5 feet in the 3 weeks we were there in July 1970.

yellow pigment, a colour I'd never before had on a board; it was very African. My new "Big Banana" board worked exceptionally well, no matter how big the waves, but while Wayne was surfing adequately on the larger of the two boards he'd brought with him from Australia, he decided he wanted more lift in the front end, so he made some saw cuts across the deck and bent more lift in the nose, afterwards re-glassing the top. He reckoned the extra lift improved the board and it certainly looked that way to me.

Ted's new board wasn't helping him much and I maintain the problem lay in the fact that he refused to go significantly longer and extra length was needed to ride those waves properly. For myself, I was pleased to put the past year's experiences on boards under 6-foot behind me. It would have been really frustrating to ride a short board on waves like those. Sure, we'd learnt a lot by going to the extreme, but it felt so good to be screaming down the line again on a 7-footer with plenty of horsepower.

Ant was a South African surfer to his boot heels; fearlessly patriotic, the only things he loved more than the waves of Jeffrey's Bay were making things out of leather and smoking "Durban Poison", seeming to perfectly blend all these elements into his crazy lifestyle. Durban Poison was a unique type of marijuana and undoubtedly the most potent I've ever indulged in. Smoked in a chillum with a piece of cloth covering the narrow end while someone lit the other, I'm sure the ritual was steeped in tribal culture. We spent three weeks in South Africa, totally intoxicated by the Poison and the awesome barrels of Jeffrey's Bay. The only problem was we couldn't get away from the place; it wouldn't let up. We wanted to go to other beaches but every day was the same: 6 to 8 foot perfect tubes – we didn't even visit any of the nearby wildlife parks. Paul decided to stay on, so Wayne, Ted and I said we'd meet him in Hawaii.

Driving back up the coast in the middle of the night to catch the plane to Australia, we rounded a bend and there, in the middle of the road, was a policeman with his hand up, signalling us to stop. As we were coming to a halt, Ant threw the still-burning chillum out the window and the cop spotted it. Picking up the broken pipe stuffed full of smoking weed, he walked back to the car and accused us of throwing it from the window. Ant started wailing: "It's not ours...it's all a terrible mistake"; he sounded like Brother John, the black man back in Jeffrey's who, when he drank too much alcohol, wailed like a banshee. I can't remember what happened next, I was much too stoned, but Ant's performance obviously had the desired effect, as the police didn't take us in and we made the plane for Australia.

* * * * * * *

The few weeks before I left for Kauai were a delight. Marilyn found a tenant for the Whale Beach house and everything was ready for the settlement up in Byron. We made a quick run up the coast to sign all the papers and while we were there Broken Head was breaking as good as I've ever seen it. I had the yellow board I'd made in South Africa and it was fitting so well into the "Broken Buckets" that sometimes I thought I'd disappear and it would go on forever. Sitting out the back I couldn't see the wave coming, then all of a sudden the bottom just dropped away and I was in the tube. It really is a unique type of wave.

The trip to Hawaii and the island of Kauai was a surfing non-event after Africa. Paul was already tucked away in a nice two-bedroom bungalow when we arrived and we soon all relaxed into the Hawaiian style; surfing Cannons and Tunnels and Hanalei when the surf was up. The only memorable thing about the trip was Rupert, a monkey that had come from somewhere on a boat with my old friend Peter Ray, who gave him to Rusty Miller when he left the islands. Rupert was continuously trying to molest the little girl next door; especially when Wayne sat him down and got him so stoned he couldn't scratch himself.

This was a very nice time to be on Kauai. The locals were, for the most part, happy hippy folk and very family minded and they had a large colony at the end of the road on the northern shore of Kauai. It was named Taylor's Camp after their benefactor Howard Taylor, an architect like Paul Witzig, a staunch family man, and the brother of Elizabeth. We all got on well with the Taylor family and shared many memorable meals at their table. Paul stayed on in the area much longer than we did and ended up becoming good friends with the eldest son, Tom, who a year or two later moved to Australia to work on Paul's surf movie *Rolling Home*. He married a girl from Yamba on the New South Wales North Coast and they had a beautiful son called Kieran before the marriage collapsed and Tommy moved back to Hawaii.

We had a strange neighbour who'd turned up a week after we rented our house on Kauai. His name was Bunker Spreckles, the heir to the Spreckles Sugar fortune and the stepson of the movie star Clark Gable. After Gable died, when Bunker was only ten, he was virtually raised by the beach boys at Waikiki, where he was introduced to the ocean and surfing. He was the archetypal spoiled little rich kid in a lot of ways – he certainly had all the toys even down to Clark's custom-made Jeep complete with leopard-skin seats, which he'd inherited. One day Bunker and I pushed that Jeep to its limits, climbing as high as we could into the rough volcanic interior of the island. We both loved adventure.

Bunker rode really strange but extremely advanced boards. At 5-foot 6-inches they were only minimal in length but they were super-thick, 5-inches, with knife-edge, hard-down rails all the way around. When we went surfing together I was amazed both by the speed Bunker was getting and the lightning-fast directional changes deep in the curl. He was good but not that good; it had to be the boards. I pressed him to let me try one but he was reluctant to give me a go. He never actually refused, but I got the impression that permission to ride the board was only granted to a select group consisting only of Bunker and his mate Vinnie Bryant. The boards had been built by Bunker and Vinnie who developed the design in the deep tubes of the North Shore of Oahu with the aid of liberal amounts of peyote.

Bunker was an extremely eccentric character. The first time we met him he walked unannounced into our bungalow with a pillow-case full of peyote buttons, and every day after that he came by to hand out liberal doses of the hallucinogen before we all went surf-ing. We loved it! Under the influence of peyote I believed I could relate to the Native Americans and with the psylocibin flowing through my veins even felt like I became one. You could have incredible contact with nature on psylocibin and surfing on the drug was perhaps the most wonderful experience I've ever had. I felt I was turning the board in the air and making long, flowing curves, banking off clouds. Sometimes after taking peyote tea it seemed the forces would command us to move and move we did, unconscious of any sense of time or space. It didn't seem to matter whether a day or a week went by.

Where the road to the North-West coast of Kauai ends, just past Taylor's Camp, the Na Pali coast runs in a long line of rugged cliffs and beaches. Bunker and I swam as far as we could around the cliffs, then stumbled up the beach, passed out, woke up, ate fruit and drank more peyote tea before going back into the water to swim for another three hours; it was a heavy program. Clark Gable had taught Bunker a lot about hunting and survival and he was very competent. We were both super-fit, no mountain seemed too high. Bunker was dragging a floating sealed container behind him, containing mainly peyote but also a few meagre rations, and wouldn't give it to me under any circumstances. We spent two days in the majestic Ho-Apu Valley, an amazing place to contact the ancient Hawaiian spirits and explore our minds for the meaning of our existence. I remember feeling like a superman with incredible powers unlike anything I'd ever before felt, able to jump amazing distances off cliffs and with-out fear. The pleasure of finding and lying down exhausted in a cave as our ancestors had done, using it like a womb to shield us from the outside world and the midday sun, is indescribable. Ho-Apu is truly an incredible part of the world although I have never been back. When I heard that Bunker had departed this life on January 15th 1977, I thought immediately of our adventure together on the Na Pali.

Another hero of mine who also used to spend time in the wilds of the Na Pali coast testing his survival skills, was Joey Cabell. One day I just happened to be in the right place at the right time when the waves were so big they were closing-out all over the island. We ended up in Hanalei Bay and got to witness Joey Cabell surf Hanalei at 18 to 20 feet. To this day, I've never seen anyone go so fast; it was a real eye opener for me to see "The Gazelle", in the absolute peak of physical condition, achieve those breakneck speeds. I stood on the deck of the Princeton Hotel and watched him, 800 metres off-shore on the board that he'd shaped himself called "White Ghost", 9-foot 6-inches long with down rails tucked under to an edge and a completely flat bottom. It was a memorable experience indeed, and for the next few years Joey was to be my hero and guiding light as far as equipment was concerned.

I left for the North Shore of Oahu the day the Duke contest was due to start, leaving Wayne, Ted and Paul in Kauai. I'd been invited to compete in both the Duke and the first Smirnoff World Pro-Am Championships, sponsored by the vodka distillers. The Duke was held at Sunset Beach in consistent 12-foot surf but I finished seventh when I'd been coming second behind Jeff Hackman since the beginning of the finals. Apparently I scored a technical interference on Paul Strauch but neither Paul nor I saw it like that. The Smirnoff contest kicked off at Makaha Beach in the last week of November and I was surfing a beautiful 8-foot 6-inch down-rail gun inspired by Cabell, with a 9-foot board as backup. With no surfboard company to appease I'd got Cabell's shaper Steve Teau to shape both of the boards before I left Kauai. Using either one or the other of those boards every surf I had in both contests was a breeze, both boards having incredible stability even when it was 15 to 20 feet and bumpy and I advanced through to the finals in both contests. With only thirty competitors in the Smirnoff it was pretty easy to move from beach to beach, with the only problem being that half the competitors wanted to wait and the other half wanted to surf as soon as possible.

Fred Hemmings, the contest director, decided we all should go and have a look at Makaha which turned out to be 10 feet and coming up fast. On the strength of that we held off surfing until the next day. I was hanging out with Mike Doyle again and he had a good friend called Buzzy Trent who lived with his Hawaiian wife Violet at Makaha. We called in for a beer and ended up staying up late being thoroughly entertained by Buzzy's stories about surfing Makaha. His

Another Stoner shot of me warming up for the Duke
Contest at Sunset Beach in 1970. I was invited to
compete in both the Duke and the Smirnoff that
year. I came 7th in the Duke but won the
Smirnoff at Makaha in solid 12 feet surf. I think
Alby took the shot of me walking up the beach.

understanding of how to best surf all the different breaks was very deep and he even told me how many paddles to take in exactly which direction to get to the best take-off when the waves were 12, 15, 18, 20, or 25 feet, either on the Bowl or the Point. Buzzy was a fanatic when he stuck to surf stories but he was also a passionate John Bircher and laid all of that full-on right-wing political philosophy on us. We passed out late on his couch and woke up early. The waves were a clean 15 feet at Makaha and almost flawless and it was there I won my first and only big contest in giant surf in Hawaii. It had taken a while but it sure felt good and put A$3000 in my pocket.

The "Expression Session" was the final event on my calendar for 1970 and I was really looking forward to it. With the surf being so inconsistent all season, providing only marginal waves for the Duke and giant surf for the Smirnoff, the twenty invited surfers were keen to get in the water as soon as possible. Just as the Smirnoff finished the surf went into the doldrums on Oahu but we heard there were still big waves off Maui so we all flew over to the island and had a great session at Honolua Bay and another off the breakwater at Lahaina. The television crew was stoked, the movie would go to air all over America in the next few weeks and the sponsor was delighted, telling us we could expect bigger and better things next year. All the surfers walked away with big smiles and a few hundred dollars each instead of the bad vibes when just one or two guys got all the money. I jumped on the plane for home thinking that maybe we'd found the answer with exhibitions instead of contests, but in reality I had serious doubts. Like the Romans with their games, the commercial world and human nature would demand that we provide winners and losers. What with the horrors in Vietnam, hippies and the peace movement of the early 1970s, I felt that the Expression Sessions were timely, but knew that in reality it was looking at the world through rose-coloured glasses.

12

'Morning of the Earth' and the Californian wind test

IT WAS DECEMBER 1970 before Marilyn and I were organised and ready to move to the New South Wales north coast. Tony Kibblewhite arranged a place for us to stay on the outskirts of Byron while we made the old farmhouse comfortable enough to occupy. My younger brother Chris came up to Byron with Marilyn on one of her many trips to move all of our worldly possessions out of the city, and it was great to see him; he was a tremendous help to us.

Many older Australian farmhouses were built to block out as much sunlight – and therefore heat – as possible, a design characteristic probably originating in India and brought to this country by the English colonisers, and our house was no exception. Its interior was quite dark, with only a little diffused sunlight filtering through the verandah windows. In an effort to open up the rooms and admit more natural light, Chris and I pulled down the interior wall between the kitchen and the living room, a minor alteration that dramatically changed the feel of the house. We painted the whole interior white, further adding to the feeling of spaciousness and Marilyn and I decided to move our bedroom out onto the verandah facing the sea. Next we painted the exterior walls white and fitted mosquito screens to all the windows and doors.

I built our bed at window level, from old railway sleepers, so I could check the sea conditions when I woke each morning, though Marilyn had difficulty getting in and out of bed during the later stages of her pregnancy. When we first moved into the house we had no electricity so wood and sunshine were our sources of energy: a chip-heater for the bath, a wood stove to cook on and a solar-heated shower I made from an old single bed. I was really proud of that shower. First I fitted a shower rose in the centre of the base, then formed the tank by fibreglassing the sides with black resin. I next raised it a couple of metres in the air on four supporting posts, placed a glass-covered frame over it, then hooked it up to the water supply. It worked perfectly, giving us hot showers for years, but being outside it could make you feel a little bit exposed in winter.

It was now possible to move in; the farmhouse was looking and feeling like home. The only other pressing thing left to do was to let some sunlight onto the garden by cutting back the giant mango tree that threatened to engulf the house. About nine acres of the eleven ran up onto the ridge and were covered in dense bush with banksia, several types of gum, and inhabited by a wide variety of native birds and animals – Marilyn and I loved it. I also liked the idea of having protection from cyclones and strong winds. Not that I'd ever experienced a cyclone first hand and had only a vague idea of the forces involved, but looking back, I realise I was really quite afraid of them. In 1971 Mum and Dad had moved to Sunshine Beach near Noosa Heads, setting up house the same year that a big cyclone hit. The noise, wind and driving rain terrified Mum so much that my parents moved to Port Macquarie on the mid-north coast not long after. I've also never forgotten a story John Witzig told me of a cyclone he'd experienced at Noosa: John, Terry Purcell, Doc Spence and McTavish had been standing on a cliff watching the storm-churned sea, when a wave broke 15 metres up the cliff-face, drenching them all. They had to brace themselves to avoid being pulled out to sea by the receding water.

The power of nature is an awesome thing and something deep down inside told me to take my time and be selective when removing the protective barrier of vegetation from around the house. This meant that it was hard to see the beach through all the greenery in the yard, but if we climbed a tree and strained our eyes we could see Broken Head and from the bedroom window we could see the beach-breaks at Tallows. With the surf and cyclone season just coming on. it was hard to get much accomplished. The surf was either too good to get any work done or the weather was too nasty. We moved into the house between surf sessions but living conditions were still pretty basic and we never did get a phone or TV.

*   *   *   *   *   *   *

It was around this time that I discovered a fascination for the gold-top mushroom. *Psylociba cubensis*, or its near relatives, grows every-where in the world and gold-tops spring from almost every "cow pie" on the north coast following the first decent rains of the season. We were always very careful to leave the cap intact, carefully breaking the mushroom off at the stem. Within seconds the deep blue of the psylocibin could be seen seeping from the cut, the intensity of the colour giving a pretty good indication of the potency of the mushroom. The golden rule in our little group was quite simple: if anyone stumbled on a mushroom while opening a gate or walking

ALBY

No creature comforts when we first moved to Byron,
just a chip heater, no phone and not even electricity
for the first few months.

It's that look you only find on a surfer-searching
the horizon for one more wave-water on the brain!

down a track to check the surf, they had to eat it. It was only on rare occasions that I went to "Psychedelic Valley" to look for mushrooms as we would run into more than enough on our daily outings. They smelt and tasted revolting. The only way I could stomach them was to overwhelm the repugnant flavour with something even stronger. To get the mushroom down without gagging at the taste, I put them in a Vegemite sandwich. The effects of one of these Vegemite-and-fungus sandwiches could last from 5–10 hours, so one had to be prepared to lose two days; one for the effects of the mushroom and the next to recover – quite a commitment as far as I was concerned and I didn't take it lightly.

The effects I experienced from mushrooms were very similar to those from the peyote-button tea that Bunker Spreckles had made in Hawaii. Both contained the active ingredient psylocibin, which has been used over the ages by many different cultures for contacting their sacred spirits and finding direction. As I see it, the main difference between my culture and that of the ancients lay in the way the drug was used. In the old cultures, medicine men and shamans would take it to seek visions, whereas in my tribe everyone used the drug whenever they felt like it – in my opinion, an abuse of the drug's potential. Each time I took the drug I experienced similar sensations: I felt like a warrior; I could do anything; I was invincible! It was an exciting – though in hindsight very dangerous – state to be in.

One day I swam around the furthest rocks off Broken Head and back to the beach then surfed for the rest of the day, feeling as though I was carving turns in clouds and disappearing inside barrels for hours on end. Right on dusk, I went into a tube where everything went dark and time was suddenly suspended; when I emerged, night had fallen. I'd no idea how long I'd been inside the tube – hours, days – although I remember that looking out from inside, the tube looked like wagon wheels in a movie, rolling forward but appearing to be going backwards. Back on the beach, I explained to Garth and Rusty that energy travelled in circles and the spinning tube was just another manifestation of this. I found the illusion that time seemed suspended very interesting – and the rush of energy from the psylocibin was incredible, though not for everyone. I vividly recall the effect they had on one of Marilyn's girlfriends who'd come to stay with us for what I'm sure turned out to be the worst holiday she'd had in her life. After eating some "magic mushrooms" the poor girl was so terrified by their effects that she sat cringing in a small dark space for the entire day, until the demons went away. We were all really concerned and considered taking her to hospital, but she finally came down enough for Marilyn to talk to her.

My friend Edwin, the designer and builder of the Avalon castle, who, with Gwendolyn, moved to Byron at the same time as Marilyn and I, also had a less-than-pleasant experience with mushrooms. The story goes that for his breakfast one morning the Lady Gwendolyn fed him mushrooms on toast, not realising they were gold-tops. I don't know whether or not she put Vegemite on the toast to mask the flavour of the mushrooms, but they must have tasted all right, because Edwin ate a hearty breakfast that morning. When he started to spin, Gwendolyn dialled 000 and Edwin was rushed to the local hospital to have his stomach pumped.

I turned the property's old farm-machinery shed into a surfboard factory, building the glassing stands myself and, with Garth Murphy's help, a shaping stand. It was really satisfying building boards at home; I did everything myself and there were always plenty of orders, what with sales to a growing number of local friends and Ray Richards, from Newcastle, who asked me to make boards for his shop whenever I had time between custom orders. I modelled them on the board I was riding at that time, a scaled-down version of those Cabell had been surfing in Kauai; 7-foot long by 20½ inches wide, a double-ended pintail with soft, low rails tucked under to an edge. I coloured them all in soft pastels and used very small pivot fins, as with that design I found that I didn't need to use much fin at all, the drive coming from the bottom shape and low rails. Over the course of twelve months I kept reducing the fin size until I'd got it down to only 7-inches deep and 3-inches wide at the base.

On one memorable swell in the winter of 1971, the board was really loose, producing that same fantastic feeling of skating on the verge of spinning-out, controlling the drift with the forward rail, which I'd had in France and Puerto Rico, but this time I had much more control. I believe that this period in Byron was the best I've surfed in my life. Those boards were perfect for Broken and Lennox Heads in anything up to a big 6-foot swell – which was what we got 50 per cent of the time. The only other spot we surfed consistently was "The Pass", right in the heart of Byron Bay, but only on big cyclone-raised swells. We took off around the back of an exposed seam of jagged black volcanic rock, being sure to get in the first turn before setting up the tube then settling into a good solid barrel for the next 100 metres and sometimes even further.

My surfing buddies at this time were Russell Hughes and Garth Murphy, who every morning would drive down the hill from Brooklet, where they lived with Nyarie. Together we'd cruise the coast from Lennox Head through to Byron Bay, surfing wherever we found the best waves. A few weeks after Marilyn and I moved to Byron, Russell, after getting back with his former girlfriend Trish, bought a small farm just outside Broken Head and he and Trish later

DICK

Broken Buckets as I remember them in the '70s. Six feet, hot and glassy with no-one out. Below is one of Alby's stills of me from Morning of the Earth.

I turned the old machinery shed on the farm into a
place to build boards for my friends and me.
From the left, Ken Adler, me and Skydog, and Bob
McTavish's daughter Renee in her dad's lap on the
verandah of my farm in Byron.

238

had a son they called Kokee. It really wouldn't have mattered where we all lived though, as we got together to check the ocean every morning and surfed whichever break was best.

Russ, alias La Ruse alias the Fox, loved a yarn and when he told me this one, while we were watching the surf at Broken Head one morning, he swore it was true. I suspect that like "mooning" a well-known figure or performing the "dance of the flaming arsehole", everyone has spoken to someone who knew someone that did it. Still, the performance of "Dick the Tick" makes a good story, and as the circumstances that made it possible no longer exist, it's worth the retelling here.

Up until 1984, all roads crossing the Queensland–New South Wales border were barred by "tick gates", through which vehicles could pass only after inspection by officers attached to the Department of Agriculture, as it was then. The objects of these inspections were two major pests of Australian agriculture, Queensland fruit-fly and the cattle tick *Boophilus microplus*. Anyone caught trying to smuggle fruit through these checkpoints faced a stiff fine, and all cattle were treated before being allowed into New South Wales, neither pest being present in that State at the time. Though pleasant enough, the officers were thorough and tough, and I've suffered many a bout of fruit-induced diarrhoea after gorging Bowen mangoes on the northern side of the gates, rather than have to put the luscious fruit in the bin for later destruction.

According to Russ, who was living on the Gold Coast and pretty much a kid at the time, he and a mob of mates were heading to Byron Bay for a long weekend. As was usual back then, they were stuck in a long line of traffic waiting to pass inspection at the tick gates at Coolangatta–Tweed Heads. Russ decided he'd pull the stunt he'd been hearing about since he was a little kid, so when their car was about fourth in line for the gates, he jumped into the boot (trunk), where he proceeded to strip down to his underpants. Finally they reached the gates and when the middle-aged woman on duty asked if they had any fruit to declare they all chorused an innocent "No ma'am". Of course such innocence aroused suspicion, and she went to the rear of the car to check the boot. As she touched the handle, Russ, with a yell of "I'm Dick the Tick", leapt from the boot and, clad only in his underdacks, dashed off down the road between the cars. He said that the poor woman didn't know whether to laugh or cry, though she took it in good spirits after she'd recovered from her initial fright.

Many other interesting people arrived in Byron within a few months of our moving there, among them Garth's old college friend Bill "The Worm" Engler and his voluptuous cheerleader-type girlfriend Marsha. As friends and business partners, Bill and Garth bought the last nine acres available on our ridge and set about building two houses there. Bill Engler was one of those larger-than-life Americans like a character straight out of the Wild West – a real man's man.

Bill and I had some great surf adventures together and one of the best was my first trip to Cactus, right in the heart of the arid coast of South Australia. We were fastidious over our preparations for that trip and made a giant effort to leave before the end of the summer of 1970–71. I built a fibreglass tank large enough to hold all the water we'd need, while Bill fixed the tent and picked a supply of magic mushrooms. We stored the gold-tops in honey, thinking it would preserve them, but when we took off the lid a few weeks later, the stench was so appalling we threw them out. For over a week, we had no contact with anyone, until another travelling surfer and his girlfriend wandered into our camp – we were overjoyed to see them. It was great roughing it at Cactus, surfing hard and getting heavily encrusted with salt – I seemed to derive some primitive satisfaction about going a few days without a shower. The Southern Ocean is so cold that we had to wear wetsuits; which seemed really at odds with the high air temperatures experienced on land, though there's an almost total absence of humidity because the coast is so arid. After ten days of roughing it, we reluctantly returned to Byron. We made a few more trips to Cactus, with Marilyn and our daughter Naomi who was born in Byron in July 1971, Garth and even Youngblood.

The story of Cactus is an interesting one. Back in the mid-1960s, Adelaide surfers made it one of their regular surf-safari destinations and as its popularity increased sanitation and rubbish became a problem. My old friend Paul Witzig had first gone to Cactus in 1968, to shoot a sequence of Wayne Lynch for his movie *Evolution*, and fell in love with the area. After getting a perpetual lease on 1200 acres of desert in 1971, he and his wife Marianne lived there for four years and during that time Paul decided to do something to preserve Cactus's delicate environment. He set up proper campsites, camouflaged among the coastal dunes and sank a deep water bore. He dug pits for rubbish and even put in a crude septic tank, then set about building a house for Marianne and himself behind the bay to the east of Cactus.

Paul tells a bloodcurdling story about watching a giant fin cutting the water as its owner rounded the point and speeding up behind three surfers sitting on their boards enjoying the sunset. He swears the fin was the same height as the seated surfers. Paul took off from his verandah running; waving his arms and shouting and desperately trying to cover the 200 metres to the beach in the shortest possible

Pasha the Afghan in the foreground with Russ, alias
La Ruse or The Fox styling beside The Worm's car.

time. The surfers were sitting out the back, looking towards the beach completely oblivious to the shark and Paul was running like a madman until he stumbled and fell in his hurry to alert the surfers. Then, when Paul thought it must attack, the shark dived and disappeared, leaving Paul in a distraught state and the surfers unscathed.

Cactus, or Point Sinclair to use its official name, is one of the last contacts with civilisation heading west along the coast. Right at the north-eastern extremity of the Great Australian Bight, its sheer, crumbling cliffs and sugar-white dunes stretch wild and open for the next 1,200 kilometres. Until they were placed on the protected list, huge Great White sharks were regularly caught in the area – and many surfers have been chased from the water and a few attacked. The pub in Penong, half an hour's drive north over a dirt track, is a good place to hear hair-raising shark stories.

On another memorable trip. Garth, Bill and I went north to Fraser Island in Queensland for a couple of weeks. It might be the world's largest sand island but you wouldn't know it, what with its beautiful lakes and the abundance of greenery in the interior. We camped, surfed and made a serious attempt to catch a few of the hundreds of brumbies – feral horses – that used to infest the island. We spent a couple of days watching one mob's eating habits and reckoned the best way to catch one was to stretch out along a branch in a big tree and wait for one of the foraging horses to move underneath. Then the plan called for one of us to drop a strong noose over the unsuspecting animal's neck while it was busy eating. But when we'd tied the brumby to the tree, what then? We didn't dare try to ride the horse we'd captured, the challenge was capturing a wild horse just like the Native Americans used to do; the thrill was in the hunt. I felt a bit sad when I was told a few years later that all the brumbies had been destroyed or moved off Fraser Island.

Garth Murphy always seemed to me to be of Native American descent, although he was pure Anglo-Saxon. He was fascinated by their culture and fed me a steady diet of books by or about Native Americans, *Black Elk Speaks,* being the most memorable. Garth was also proficient with a hammer and saw, having built several houses in California and Australia, and quite an accomplished musician, introducing me to the guitar. He taught me a few simple chords and together we wrote songs about our adventures, or "war parties", surfing the breaks in our area. He turned up to go surfing one morning with Rusty Miller, a famous US surfer whom I'd been friends with since we met in Hawaii in 1965. Rusty and Garth went back a long way; they'd been partners in a business making Surf Research surfboard wax in California. Like so many young Americans, Rusty had become disenchanted with his country over its involvement in the war in Vietnam and had left his homeland for good, only returning for holidays. He has a beautiful wife and family and still lives in the Byron area. I met Rusty through my involvement with my boyhood hero Mike Doyle. Mike and Rusty were the best of mates back then and surfed at a similar level, though I always preferred Mike's style. Rusty also could play the guitar really well and was a good horseman, both excellent attributes for life in Byron in the early 1970s. Sometimes Rusty and I would meet to ride horses hard along the beach at Broken Head which was easily accessible by a track from our property. I even once carried my board on my horse and camped out, hobbling Shondalay in the grass nearby; it was an idealistic "alternative" lifestyle.

We always celebrated birthdays, Christmas and other holidays, both American and Australian, together, the festivities in the form of a big party to which everybody brought a plate, a musical instrument if they owned one, and something to drink and smoke. May Day was an important social event, not for its political implications but because the 1st of May is the start of spring in the northern hemisphere. One afternoon in early March I happened to be in the police station seeing the cops about some trivial matter when I noticed, behind the officer I was talking to, a door leading to a courtyard in which were six superb marijuana plants in perfect bloom; grown apparently to show the less-experienced constables exactly what a marijuana plant looked like. An inexperienced officer, not trained in horticulture, might mistake marijuana for the noxious weed called "stinking Roger" which is as prevalent as lantana – and almost as much of a curse – in the Byron area and bears a strong resemblance to marijuana.

After I'd finished my business with the police, I was having a beer at the Great Northern Hotel and happened to mention the wallopers' "Bob Hope" to a group at the public bar. Not long after, apparently, someone crept around the side of the police station, crawling under the floor of one wing which was raised about 60 centimetres above ground, and pinched the dope plants, pots and all. It was the talk of the town and everyone laughed themselves silly – everyone, that is, except the police. They were hopping mad and buzzed round the district like frenzied hornets. When May Day 1971 came round, I can remember getting totally out of it and dancing around the Maypole to the strumming of Garth and Rusty's guitars; later that night the crew from the pub turned up with some beautiful heads they said were the last of the wallopers' home-grown.

Except for the odd foray elsewhere, all our surfing was done in Byron or at Broken and Lennox Heads. There were plenty of good days (and doubters have only to see the old movie *Morning of the*

Riding Marilyn's horse Shondalay on the farm at
Byron '69. We had a track through this paddock
down onto the beach and Broken Head. These
are Alby's shots from when he came to stay
on the farm. The lower pic shows me about to
hit the water on one of my classic pintails at
the breakwater at Brunswick Heads.

Earth as testimony to the fact) with, it seemed, big southerly swells running up the coast almost constantly. When they weren't, it was cyclone season and lows would form off the Queensland coast to the north and pump northerly swells into the bay. One night a cyclone, ranging further south than most, hit Byron with terrifying force. Marilyn and I were in the house with Naomi, who was still a tiny baby, when the wind began to howl, blowing so fiercely I thought all the windows would go, there and then. One window in the bathroom did give way, shattering on the floor and setting us on edge so much that I decided to do what the old-timers recommended. Starting at the back of the house, I began to open every window. With the wind screaming and the rain blowing horizontally in sheets the first one blew right out of my hand but after that the operation went quite smoothly and I managed to get every door and window wide open. Marilyn was hiding under our bed comforting Naomi and after I'd got everything open I scrambled under there with them; it was an horrific night and day. We were lucky not to lose our roof like some others in Byron had, and I still believe the dense vegetation on the property saved us by breaking the force of the wind and diverting it over and around the house.

During the surf season, from January through to midwinter, we'd get up before dawn and cruise around the area checking the conditions. We came to know a lot of interesting things: where and when the local cop visited his mistress (we talked about telling his wife but never did); and at exactly what time each shop opened its doors so we could buy a bottle of the famous Norco chocolate milk. If the swell was from the east or north, we'd more often than not end up at the caravan park at Broken Head, owned at the time by an ex-prizefighter named Rex something or other, an eastern-European name I could never remember. Rex lived behind his kiosk and really didn't like us much, although we probably contributed a fair bit to his income and were always his first customers of the day. The shop was built of corrugated iron and that may have contributed to his dislike of us. Our rattling the shutter at 6.50 a.m. for our first chocolate milk of the day may have made him nasty and full of venom. Russ put some graffiti on the outside of the front shutter that Rex didn't see for a month or two, as he rarely opened the shutter from the outside. "Do not feed the Rexaramus" it read in bold, red paint, and every morning we watched in hysterics as he opened his cage and blurted out: "What do youse bloody-well want". Ah, Rex, we loved you!

"Broken Buckets" was our nickname for the waves at Broken Head and if you were to rest a bucket on its side you would get an idea of the shape of the break. They were unique waves, very difficult to see coming and therefore hard to catch. We had to paddle our hearts out for the slightest movement and we wouldn't know we were actually on the wave until we broke through the face, pulling our boards behind us as we got to our feet. The waves just sucked out, leaving us plummeting downhill with barely enough room to pull into the curl. A lot of the wave sequences featuring me in *Morning of the Earth* were shot on Broken Buckets.

Looking back on those days, one surf session stands out as particularly memorable and has to do with an encounter with a most inquisitive dolphin. I like to think I'd seen this animal before, but unless there is some sort of distinguishing mark, a notched fin for example, it's impossible – for me at least – to tell one dolphin from another. For similar reasons, I'll refer to this particular dolphin as a he. I've always wondered what was going through the dolphin's mind that morning. Did he know it was me or did he just happen to be on the same wave? I felt he was the same dolphin that featured in an old photo the original owner of the land around "Black Stump" beach, two beaches south of Broken Head, showed to me not long after I'd moved to the area – probably because I had a red setter. With his old box camera, Mr Carter had photographed his red setter and his horse swimming in the shorebreak, and draped over the horse's back was a dolphin. A dog, a horse and a dolphin all playing together in the sea – it was quite a photo.

Pulling into a perfect bucket one morning, I went through all the gears on the pintail in order to stay ahead of the curl and I found myself locked inside a perfect tube, with the inside wall of the wave just centimetres from my face and with me, staring me right in the eye, was a dolphin. There in the green room, the two of us were suspended in time and making full eye contact as we raced neck-and-neck. How long we stayed like that I've no idea, but certainly it was long enough for each to size up the other's form and appreciate the uniqueness of the situation. For years I've told this story to friends and I've always hoped I'd again share a tube with a dolphin, but alas, I never have. At the end of that tube the dolphin was gone and I never saw him again; but I'm sure he kept riding deep barrels for as long as he was able, for that is the secret affinity between surfers and dolphins – we're the only animals to see the unique view from inside a wave; and that's a wonderful experience to share.

*　*　*　*　*　*　*

There were two pubs in Byron, one the newer Pier Astor, up on the beachfront and the older Great Northern, down in the middle of town. I never spent much time in the Astor but I was partial to the odd beer at the Northern. One evening after dusk a car came speeding up our

Garth and Nyarie going surfing at Lennox. No highway
then, just a track through the paddocks skirting the
rocks. The bottom-turn pic was taken by Dick the
same day as the shot above.

The Gnome, Nyarie and Russell up a tree at Apollo
Bay on a surfari during the early '70s Bells contest.

drive, its driver racing up to the door puffing and panting to tell me a Micky Dora from the States was on the phone down at the Northern asking for me. I was alarmed by the thought that it may have been an emergency, so I jumped in my car and raced into town. It was a good 3 kilometres into Byron, and it must have been twenty minutes from the time the messenger left town to the moment I ripped the receiver out of someone's hands and blurted out "What's up Micky?" "How's the surf?" came the reply. "What!" I almost yelled. "I was thinking of coming 'Down Under' and…" he rambled on at ninety to the dozen. It was classic Micky Dora; he had me. I explained that I didn't have a phone at the house as yet and he said he'd figured that out after long involved conversations with numerous operators in Australia as well as some telephone linesmen who worked in our area.

After that first one, everybody knew better than to treat Micky's calls as emergencies, but someone would still drive out to the house to get me while all the boys in the bar had a good old chat to Dora. Micky would talk to anyone and everyone – the town drunk, trav-elling surfers, whoever happened to be in the bar when he phoned. After about ten such calls – which I was sure were costing him a fortune – he told me he was using a phone with a direct link to a satellite, which meant he could make free calls to anywhere in the world, talking for as long as he wanted. I barely knew what a satel-lite was in 1971.

I was drawn to Dora right from the time he and I shared a room together at the Duke Contest in Hawaii. We hardly knew one another, but I liked his style. He was more than a touch eccentric but nice if you liked that sort of thing. I did and still do. Micky Dora is proof that surfing is a subculture within the greater society; a sub-culture with its own values, standards and legends. Within the surf-ing tribe and even beyond it, he's a legend in the true sense of the word – a giant in the collective consciousness of surfers worldwide. Incredibly, this reputation, this legend, was created almost entirely on the fringes of the surfing culture, outside the competition arena, where the outlaws live. Dora's reputation was established by what he said and did; it has nothing to do with surfing contests but every-thing do with not compromising. Although he's been an expatriate for most of the past 25 years, his reputation back in the USA has proved durable and around Los Angeles he's still a cult figure of sorts. Around the time of the 1992 presidential elections, a friend of mine on his way to Los Angeles airport swears he saw a bumper sticker proclaiming "Dora for President".

There have been many stories told about Micky Dora, some true, some complete fantasy, but ever since the mid-1960s, when some-one scrawled "Dora Lives!" on the seawall at Malibu, the legend has continued. It'd take a book much bigger than this to record all the stories and offer any real insight into the man called Micky Dora, but I'd like to add to the record a few of the memorable experiences I've had with "The Cat".

Despite all the phone calls to the pub in Byron, Micky didn't make it to Australia until 1974. When he visited me we surfed and played tennis but I was preoccupied with building a house at that stage and didn't have the time to play every day. Later that same year Marilyn and I made a trip to California and we stayed at Micky's house in Brentwood for a while. America was still The Cat's home then and he both hated it and loved it with a passion. Marilyn was a little alarmed by the bear traps placed at the windows, the guns under the pillows, and Micky's assemblage of paraphernalia collected from around the world. As for me, I was fascinated by the phone he'd used to call me in Byron Bay. I used it to ring my friend Max in France and spoke for an hour.

One of the best stories Micky ever told me about his childhood boarding-school days had to do with a particularly nasty nun who, to get him to do inane things quicker than he wanted to, would sadistically twist his ear. Punishing young "Micklos" was a virtual obsession for the woman until Micky, determined he'd take no more of it, plotted his revenge. Even at that age, he'd already discovered the itch-producing qualities of fibreglass dust and he diligently collected a cupful of the horrible stuff. One afternoon he stole into the nuns' deserted dormitory and sprinkled the dust between the sheets of the hated nun's bed. It all went like clockwork; the poor woman went to bed as usual that night but the next morning she was carried off with a nasty red rash covering her body, a rash no doctor could explain. Not for the last time in his life, Dora knew satisfaction at a stunt well carried off.

Possibly the best stories told to me by Micky dealt with his on-set shenanigans in the era of Hollywood's *Beach Blanket Bingo/Ride the Wild Surf* epics of the late 1950s. Micky's tall good looks and surfing prowess, not to mention his verbal skills, had landed him a job as Frankie Avalon's double, being called on when ever Frankie was required to hit the waves. Micky was constantly riding waves or hanging around at Malibu Point wearing red-and-yellow shorts identical to Frankie's. Always eager to perform a task to his employer's expectations and beyond, Micky would beckon the point-of-view camera boat – full of expensive 35 mm movie cameras – closer and closer to the breaking waves. "You'll get a great shot from over here." Of course the inevitable happened, with the boat capsizing and all the gear tossed around in the line-up, and of course the insurance company would have to write everything off. Micky had timed the disaster for last light and came back on the full moon to retrieve the equipment as the swell dropped. With some thorough rinsing and careful attention to drying, by the next morning the cameras were back in working order and being offered to the original owners – at a specially negotiated price, of course.

To put the Hollywood stories in proper perspective, I have to lay them on you as Micky would. Everything was fair – stealing, lying and basically doing anything to get back at those "suckers" from Hollywood who'd plundered Malibu in order to create a script or produce a movie about this new phenomenon called surfing. According to Micky, the original *Gidget* was all right because "it was real", but the quantity and quality of the following surf movies was "bullshit" and that's why he acted so ruthlessly. At least, that was the way he justified it.

Annette Funicello was Frankie Avalon's co-star in several of the beach movies and rumour had it that to keep her feelings of personal insecurity at bay, she kept $1,000 hidden in her on-location van. Well one day, the money just disappeared and Micky was somehow connected to the theft, ending his on-screen career. But Dora was a master scammer and that was only a minor setback in his career.

Here's another classic Micky story, one that I know is true because I was personally involved in it at a time when I was spending time with The Cat in California. One morning, after a heavy night spent socialising in Hollywood, Micky told me to get dressed, we were going to dine with his father who lived in Montecito, about 80 kilometres up the coast near Santa Barbara. I put on one of my best costumes; a beautiful old shirt that John Wayne had owned (bought from a shop on Vine that sold clothes once owned by movie-stars) and a United States admiral's blazer complete with badges and gold braid. The balance of the outfit I can't quite recall, but it was in good taste for this period in the seventies when *Sergeant Pepper's Lonely Hearts Club Band* set the tone. When I saw Micky's outfit I was stunned; his 6-foot-plus frame was covered in leather from head to toe, a gleaming black-leather, ankle-length coat almost, but not quite, concealing a very official-looking uniform. His hat was of Second World War vintage and had once belonged to a German submarine commander and the gleaming leather boots and gloves were in keeping with his newfound position as a high-ranking officer in some foreign army. Striding out of the front door and beckoning me to follow, he walked around the side of the house to the garage whose doors he opened to reveal a meticulously restored Lotus in traditional British racing green – I was more than a little impressed. We climbed aboard and when Micky fired up the engine, he seemed to become part of the car.

By the time we'd gone a few kilometres down Sunset Boulevard the engine warmed up and Micky started to give the Lotus some stick and as he punched it through the curves, I realised he could drive very well indeed. His confidence and pleasure were obvious when we stopped at the first red light. He looked over at me, his dark-stubbled face grinning out through flying goggles and topped by the rakish navy cap. Right then I had a premonition that we were in for a big day. Between the roar of the Lotus's engine responding to the frequent high-rev gear shifts and the beating of the wind in the open cockpit, conversation was almost impossible and we merely nodded at one another knowingly as we passed a flat Malibu point at a little better than 160 kilometres per hour and streaked past Pepperdine University and out of the city.

I wasn't at all surprised when I heard the siren wailing and looked back over my shoulder to see the black-and-white cop car on our tail. Micky kept going for several more kilometres, then, just before we got to the northern end of the Malibu coast, he allowed the black-and-white to pull us over. Instead of waiting for the officer to come to us, Micky vaulted from the Lotus and ran back to the cop car, thrusting a Romanian diplomatic passport through the window then, in what I can only describe as a classic Micky mumble, strode back and forth waving his hands and repeatedly glancing at his watch. Impatiently reaching into his crested attache case for letters, Dora asked for an escort in order to avoid any further confrontations with local authorities. I heard him thank the officer in broken English as he wrote down the cop's name in a notebook then before I knew it we were back up to 160 kph and running red lights until we hit Highway 101. On the freeway the Lotus really showed its British breeding and our V8 Dodge escort was hardly keeping up. At Mariposa Lane we stormed down the off-ramp, through another red light and up the hill towards the grand old homes of Santa Barbara. At the bottom of one particularly prestigious driveway Micky stopped momentarily to address the officer. Without getting out of the Lotus, Dora thanked him for his assistance and assured him it wouldn't go unnoticed. After a crisp officer's salute, we roared up the drive, waited a few minutes until the cop left, then backed out onto the road again. We continued to Micky's father's house to enjoy a very pleasant lunch with some delightful French Bordeaux, Mr Dora being the American importer of Rothschild wines.

Micky was also responsible for introducing me to Armond, a terror of a man who spent 50 per cent of his time surfing, windsurfing and skiing and the other 50 per cent keeping in touch with every social event worth attending in Hollywood, mostly by telephone. Micky and I have had some crazy times together, and going skiing

Santa Monica,
California in the mid
'70s. Dora and me
with his Lotus on the
way to have lunch
with his father in
Santa Barbara. We
stopped off to see
Californian surfer
Denny Aaberg, and
Denny's mum took this
pic.

with Micky and Armond ranks among the craziest. After pulling into the carpark at one of the large ski resorts near Los Angeles, Micky handed out local ski patrol parkas – in exactly the right colours – from the boot of Armond's Mercedes. Proudly displaying our white crosses and name tags (an added Micky touch), we marched up the road to the lifts. Since we were in a bit of a hurry to get up the hill to the scene of a rather ugly accident that had just been reported, we squeezed in at the front of the line. As we stepped onto the chairlift I glanced over at Micky and saw it again – that dark-stubbled, smiling dial – another successful scam. Of course the powder was perfect that day and as we made our way around the mountain I remember marvelling at what an absolute classic Micky was; a living legend in the true sense of the word.

On another occasion when I had to visit LA, I rang Armond from Australia to see if he could put me up for a few days, as Micky had left for New Zealand. Not only would he put me up, he said, he'd pick me up at the airport. He was anxious to repay my hospitality when he'd come to Australia the previous winter. In retrospect, I believe what followed could only have taken place in America. I arranged for a friend to drop me off at Sydney airport and just before we parted he slipped me a present – a 15 centimetre-long "Thai stick" of marijuana. I quickly stuffed it into one of my fashionable calf-length boots and thought no more about it.

In Los Angeles I was met by a beaming Armond who pulled down the top of his 280 SEL and, wedging my board into the back seat, roared out of the carpark and up onto the freeway. Once on the freeway Armond lit up a big fatty and, caught up in the euphoria of the moment, we failed to take notice of our surroundings. The police later told Armond that the cloud of smoke billowing from the Mercedes was almost blinding when they pulled us over. But we were oblivious to this, enjoying a heavy rave, when cop cars came down on us like a ton of bricks, converging on us from all directions. There was a black-and-white behind us, a plain black across our path and three undercover cars cutting off all possible exits. With guns trained on us and commands to put our hands on our heads barked at us through a loud hailer, the squad cars disgorged a flock of cops. I freaked. The cops opened the car doors, told us to get out and, with my hands still on my head, flung me against the freeway barrier, telling me to spread my legs while I was thoroughly searched. The Buddha stick was taken from my boot and my passport was confiscated. Twenty minutes later after the cops had searched the car, my luggage and my surfboard and spent a lot of time on the radio, we were told to turn around and face the music. Armond and I found ourselves looking straight into the eyes of a

SURF STAR IN COURT

March 18th 1971

Former world surfboard champion Nat Young (above left) yesterday pleaded not guilty to five charges in Byron Bay Court of Petty Sessions.

Young, 23, was charged under the name of Robert Harold Young, professional surfer, of Bangalow Road, Byron Bay.

He pleaded not guilty to charges of resisting arrest, assaulting Constable John Woodlands, of Byron Bay police, using unseemly words, behaving in an offensive manner and failing to produce his driving licence.

Young said he pleaded guilty to a further charge of having driven a vehicle with a smooth tyre.

Police allege the offences took place at the Captain Cook Lookout, Byron Bay, on February 24, this year.

Young's solicitor, Mr. L. Brien, of Ballina (pictured with Young), attempted to have the smooth tyre matter dealt with but the police prosecutor, Sgt. D. Milne, objected. He said all the matters were tied into one.

Mr. A. H. Carless, S.M., said he thought it more desirable all matters against Young be adjourned and heard the same day.

Mr. Brien said it was not possible for the matters to go on yesterday as three witnesses for the defence were not available.

Mr. Carless remanded Young to appear at Byron Bay on August 19 and allowed bail of $100.

plainclothes Clint Eastwood look-alike, complete with aviator sunnies and smooth country and western attire. "Well," he said, "we've checked you both out completely. It's refreshing to know that you're not an international drug smuggler, Mr Young. We've been able to confirm that you are a professional surfer and we know that's how you make your money. Mr Armond has no criminal record and appears to have been slightly engrossed in wanting to show his Australian friend here a good time. So," and here he looked at Mr Armond, "here is a $100 ticket for travelling at such dangerous speeds, Sir. As for you, Mr Young, we've only to deal with the drugs found in your possession." My heart sank, all I could see was the inside of a Los Angeles jail again, a repeat of 1963, only worse; the potential headlines in the Australian press; and the fact that I'd never be allowed into the US of A again – it was too much. I was brought back to the present by Clint asking if I knew what the California wind test was, and of course my response was a polite "No Sir". With that, Clint held up my stick and clapping it between his palms, rolled it into fine dust. He then opened his hands, raised them as if making an offering to the elements and blew the powder into the air. "That, Mr. Young, is the California wind test," he said, peering over the rims of the aviators straight into my eyes. "And it's your lucky day, mister." Before leaving he told Armond that he was well aware of certain local customs and said he understood Armond's excitement and enthusiasm for showing a visitor the sights. However, he went on, his advice was to indulge in such activities only in the privacy of one's own home. "Good day to you both, gentlemen."

13

Same as it ever was?

RUSSELL HUGHES TOLD VERY CAPTIVATING SURF STORIES that always left me thinking: I want to do that as soon as possible, how can I get there? As I recall it was the winter of 1970 when Russell painted a picture of a place that sounded to me like Utopia – perfect waves in a tropical paradise with no other surfers. I was in my shaping room at Byron Bay when he came in raving about the waves he'd just ridden in a place called Bali. Russell and his friend Frank had been stuck in London en route back to Australia when just by chance they wandered into an upmarket Earls Court travel agent who showed them brochures about an island they'd never before heard of. The pictures showed an inviting tropical island only a hop step and jump from Australia, and anywhere away from the English winter would've looked really inviting.

Bali was a total unknown to surfers in 1970. There was no tourist development to speak of other than the Bali Beach Hotel on the Sanur side and on the opposite shore, the Kuta Beach Hotel, which had been fashionable with colonial Malayan–Singapore society in the 1930s. I've seen a photo, taken in this era, of a bloke standing on a surfboard in the Kuta shorebreak. It's a lame shot that says nothing about Bali's waves but it does prove that someone rode a surfboard in Bali long before Russell.

Russell spent time on both sides of the island and surfed Kuta and Sanur, providing material for graphic stories of Sanur's right-hander rifling down the line and finishing on a rusty shipwreck. The board he was riding wouldn't have helped him much. Russell had been away from Australia for some time and was travelling with the sort of board we were all riding in 1969 prior to the World Championships. It was a 5-foot 10-inch Ted Spencer "White Kite" an excellent board for travelling because it would fit anywhere from London taxis to luggage racks in the metro, but he found the size somewhat limiting when he trying to draw a line through a 6-foot Sanur barrel. As the days turned into weeks, Russell got quite lonely. He couldn't find anyone to surf with on the Kuta side either. He took a local outrigger

Wayne Lynch and his girlfriend Kay spent some time at our farm in the winter of '72. Wayne shaped some beautiful keel fin surfboards.

to the reef but got spooked with the solitude that far from the shore. There were a few German hippies camped down the beach towards Legian and they told him about a guy they'd seen wandering around Kuta with a surfboard, but Russell couldn't find him during his month on Bali. The name of that adventurer never surfaced.

What follows is open to conjecture; certainly Russell was the first person I knew who went to Bali, and that was 1970. I was living at Byron Bay when he returned with the story I've retold here, and Alby Falzon was shooting film of me in the Byron area in the winter of 1970; Alby's movie *Morning of the Earth* was released in 1972. He says he can't remember me telling him Russell's story, his recollection being that his partner David Elfick was the catalyst that sent Steve Cooney and Rusty Miller on that first Balinese adventure in September 1971. Regardless of exactly how it happened, the surfing world was aware of Bali from the moment *Morning of the Earth* hit the cinemas and every surfer who saw the movie had a very vivid picture of themselves riding their dream wave in Bali.

Wayne Lynch turned up in Byron in the winter of 1971, having left his home in Lorne, on Victoria's south coast, and opting for a life on the road to avoid being conscripted into Australia's national service. When he turned eighteen on 12th January 1970, lady luck wasn't smiling on him – the ball with his birth date on it was pulled out of the barrel and Wayne, along with thousands of other kids, was required to register. He didn't make any contact with the authorities, rationalising that the best way to keep ahead of the call-up was to go into hiding and keep on the move. He spent most of the summer of 1970–71 hiding out further along the Great Ocean Road from Lorne in a beautiful deserted bay called Castles, living in a caravan behind the beach on a piece of property he'd bought with his parents. It was virtually a hermit's existence, close to nature with very few visitors, but the remote existence and tons of big powerful waves gave him the perfect environment to develop his surfing.

The boards Wayne ended up riding were "Keel Fins"; in the 7-foot 6-inch range and quite narrow; they were only 18-inches wide, with low, hard rails. The only thing really different about them was the keel; its length varied between 15 to 18-inches and was 6-inches deep, the theory being that a conventional fin put the drive up away from the bottom, whereas the keel fin put the pressure right at the base, where the fin attached to the board. An older Victorian surfer named Paddy Morgan developed the keel fin design when he first saw Rolf Aurness joining all the sections together in 8 feet at Bell's Beach while training for the 1969–70 World Titles. As Pat remembers it, all the Aussie surfers on their under-6-foot short-boards were only taking off in the bowl section at Bells, and no-one was covering the distances like Rolf. The length and speed of his rides so impressed Pat that he started to build boards similar to Rolf's, later finding that widening the bases of the fins helped a great deal on the predominantly big powerful waves in Victoria. The wide bases grew longer and longer, finally becoming keels.

In July of 1972, Wayne drove his girlfriend Kay's little Volkswagen bug, seemingly covered in keel-fin boards, up the driveway to our house. Wayne had seen some particularly inviting lefts on the beach-break below my house and wanted me to come surfing and try one of his new boards. Aside from the keels themselves, the boards weren't very different from the Cabell-inspired pintails I'd been riding since 1969 but that session at Suffolk Park was my first on a keel. Wayne was there to explain how much you had to bend and push to keep the pressure down, and it felt unlike anything I'd ever ridden before; almost like being locked in a bob-sled track. From Byron through to Ballina we had waves of consequence almost all that winter; it just kept coming – 10 feet at Lennox one day then back to 6 feet on the beachbreaks until it came back up again.

At winter's end a cheque arrived from *Surfer* magazine for a story I'd written the year before and I invited Wayne to go with me to the snow to try his hand at skiing; a totally new experience for him. What he lacked in finesse he made up for with incredible agility and it seemed that he wouldn't fall over, no matter what. When we got back to Byron the season had changed dramatically, with small and gutless waves every day. It was easy then to see the limitations of the keel fins – they just didn't work in waves without power or size. Keel fin surfboards required something substantial to ride on and the Victorian waves Pat Morgan and Wayne had developed the design for weren't typical of what most surfers ride 90 per cent of the time.

* * * * * * *

When the Labor Party was swept to power in December 1972, thousands of young Australians breathed sighs of relief. As he'd promised, one of the first things its charismatic leader Gough Whitlam did was abolish conscription. After the election results were announced it was a very jubilant Wayne Lynch who phoned me in Byron to confirm our plans for a surf trip to Bali that coming winter. David "Mexican" Sumpter was making a surf movie and would pay for Wayne's ticket, Wayne's girlfriend Kay would pay for hers; we were finally going and it was onto the big Qantas bird and free booze all the way to Bali. Just like everyone else who'd seen the movie *Morning of the Earth*, Wayne and I were totally over the top with the idea of riding the giant barrels of Uluwatu and were determined to get in amongst them as soon as possible. Ever since Russell had told us of his adventure the dream was constantly on our minds and constantly figured in our conversations. Now, with conscription abolished, the dream could become reality.

I was travelling with Marilyn and our daughter Naomi and in my luggage was a beautiful keel fin surfboard made by Pat Morgan – a board of some of the finest craftsmanship I'd seen on a modern surfboard. It was a translucent bottle green with really wide laps, and where the fibreglass came over onto the bottom and buried in the fibreglass on the keel was the image of a winged elephant that Pat had painstakingly copied from the record cover of Osibissa's *Woyaya*. That board performed as beautifully as it looked. When the plane banked low revealing the long running left-hander at what is now known as Uluwatu, we went into shock; everything we'd been told appeared to be true!

Arriving at Denpasar airport that first afternoon was almost overwhelming and an experience I'll never forget. The drenching afternoon humidity after leaving the comfort of the airconditioned jet to stand, dripping perspiration in the queue for customs and immigration was almost too much. There was no airconditioned immigration building in 1973, just a corrugated-iron shed off to one side of the taxiway where the owner of a smiling golden face stamped your passport and waved you through. The formalities were minimal, but it still seemed to take hours to get through customs and immigration. Once outside the shed you were in a typical bustling Asian airport scene with hundreds of people hustling for your attention. The "bemo" ride to Kuta was completely novel; looking through the back window of the driver's cab and seeing burning incense and offerings on the dashboard, we wondered what we were in for. The sweet smell of frangipani mixed with that of clove cigarettes was everywhere and will be forever associated in my mind with Bali.

In 1973 Kuta was still a typical Balinese fishing village with all the traditional charm that these days you have to go miles into the interior to find. There was no tourist trade to speak of, just the travelling hippies and surfers whose needs and desires were very basic by today's standards. I think both the hippies and the surfers were in some respects good travellers because they didn't try to change the local culture; both trod very lightly around the customs and manners of the Balinese. As the number of tourists increased it all changed: showers, hot and cold running water and airconditioning, more restaurants and, eventually, discos – within an unbelievably short time all the trappings of Western society were available in Kuta. I share some of the blame; along with thousands of other tourists I wanted my creature comforts and the adaptable Balinese were only too pleased to accommodate us all. Like so many things it seemed like a good idea at the time, but the infrastructure wasn't ready to cope with sewage, garbage and all the other by-products of our culture. Tourism grew way too fast and I feel fortunate to have experienced Bali before its economy grew dependent on it.

On that first trip we had no problem finding a place to stay in Kuta as private accommodation was available in a few places along Jalan Pantai, the main street that in 1973, was still unpaved. These places were called "losmans" and were pretty basic: one room with a bed and a squat-down toilet down the stairs at the back of the room. There was no running water – every morning one of the children of the family would bring in a bucketful that you could use to wash in or flush the toilet – and no shower, but an extra bucket of water was available on request. After a couple of days I developed a taste for the grainy Balinese coffee but the bread was a little too coarse and I found it virtually inedible. After a few days we managed to get the idea across that we needed fruit in the mornings and from then on everything was perfect. The woman of the family who owned our losman had five beautiful children of varying ages and a husband who, while he didn't say much, smiled a lot and seemed constantly to be patting his fighting cock.

Once you left Jalan Pantai, there were lots of single-file walking paths running down to the beach – all coconut palms and soft brown cows feeding on the abundant grass, either wandering free or tethered by a ring through their noses. We were overwhelmed by the people and their culture and the natural beauty of the Kuta area.

The only surfers we could find were Bill and Mike Boyum, two young Americans who lived in a losman next door to the Kuta Beach Hotel, just down the road from our place. Mike had been living in Bali since 1969, and though at the time he wasn't a surfer, he knew what a good wave looked like and a steady flow of letters and pictures to his brother Bill in Hawaii enticed him to come and have a closer look. Bill arrived in Bali in 1972 and was the first real surfer to take up residence in this paradise; in 1973 he and a friend were the pioneers of Grajagan.

There were quite a few hippy types in Bali at that time, pseudo surfers who paddled out and played around on a surfboard from time to time but never really got into it seriously. My favourite among them was "Big Eddy", 6-feet 6-inches of muscular, bronzed American, with a heart of gold, who was totally dedicated to turning on everyone who visited Bali. Originally from New York, he'd spent years following the "hippy trail" through Afghanistan, Thailand and India's Goa Peninsula, before arriving in Bali. The first time Wayne and I met him he was on his daily stroll along the

DICK

Hard to believe it now— the top pic was the view
out the back of our losman at Kuta. Bali was an
undiscovered tropical paradise when we first went
there in '73.

Dick took this shot of Marilyn with Pookie (Naomi) squeezed between us on the bike.

Trying to hold one of Wayne's keels down at Uluwatu was very exciting for the first few rides.

beach at Kuta with a huge torpedo-shaped bundle of Thai sticks tucked firmly under his arm. We'd watched him coming towards us after he'd greeted a couple 50 metres down the beach, handing them his gift and treating them to his infectious smile. Big Eddy greeted us as he did every tourist he ran into – with a big warm smile and a couple of sticks. Eddy made it a rule never to get into any heavy raves; he just broke off a few sticks, welcomed you to Bali and kept going; a man with a mission to make sure everyone enjoyed their stay in Bali. Every time he needed more sticks he would fly off to Thailand, returning in a few days with fresh supplies. He was like a hippy version of the "Greeter", well known around Laguna Beach, California in the early 1960s. Both were outgoing individuals who simply wanted to spread goodwill among humanity. Big Eddy also did good deeds for locals; I was with him when he brought back a couple of juice extractors from Thailand and set a family up in a shop down towards Legian. He fell in love with a tall, good-looking brunette named Ros "The Body", who came from my home town in Australia. Although she was the same age as me, none of the gang in Collaroy remembered her from the 1960s, so she must have left our area very early in the piece. Ros – who spent most of her time in Asia – met an untimely death in 1978 when she suffered a ruptured appendix in the later stages of a pregnancy. She is survived by her beautiful daughter Roxanne who lives with her father in America.

Another classic "spaceman" we met in Kuta was Abdul. He wasn't a fully qualified hippy in the true sense of the word because he had plenty of money and was determined to prove that he was a real surfer. "Fun in the sun and income too" was Abdul's motto, and he delighted in laying it on you at every chance he got. Micky Dora told me years later that he'd run into Abdul on a prison plane flying across America, with Abdul protesting his innocence over some drugs charge. Certainly when we arrived in Bali in 1973 it seemed that Abdul had everything – a beautiful Balinese house on the beach towards Legian, an exquisite Swiss beauty to cater to his every need and lots of Indonesian servants to look after things. From the time I first met him, I thought he was slightly crazy. He had really wild eyes that promised anything might happen at any time. Abdul financed one of the first motorbike rental operations in Kuta. When we first went to Kuta, there was only a handful of motorbikes; Abdul had one and so did Eddy and Mike Boyam, but that was about the extent of it. Then, Abdul had the totally inspired idea that he'd help one of the local families and at the same time invest a few dollars for his future. He flew to Singapore, bought a bunch of bikes, put them on a ship and within a few days had set an entire village up for life by providing them with motorbikes to rent to the tourists. When Abdul was convicted on drug charges in the States, the village inherited the entire business and Abdul was refused entry into Indonesia.

Abdul had the first 16-foot Hobiecat that I ever saw; a really neat toy that he handled very competently. One night after dinner he sold me on the idea of sailing straight off the beach in front of his house to go and ride some incredible lefts that Bill Boyam had been raving about. Several people had seen the fabled Grajagan from the air in 1973 but no-one really knew exactly where it was. It was a crazy idea, but late that night we set sail totally prepared to the tune of a hat, sunglasses, a pair of boardshorts and a tee-shirt. For provisions we had only a bottle of water and some muesli bars. As we were running out the door, Abdul went back and grabbed his compass while I strapped our surfboards to the transom – really prepared, I don't think. Under the effects of liberal amounts of high-quality marijuana, the night seemed to pass quite quickly and the hiss of the hulls cutting through the swells at speed was very exciting. Daybreak revealed that we were out of sight of Bali, but when we consulted Abdul's compass we thought we were still heading in the right direction. However, with no chart and no way to gauge our speed, it was impossible to tell. Somewhere around mid-morning the wind began to die; by noon it had gone all together and we spent the rest of the day becalmed. When our water and food were all gone, and with no idea how far we'd come or how far we had to go to reach Grajagan, we decided to turn around and head back to Bali. To be truthful, the afternoon sea breeze had sprung up and was blowing us in that direction anyway. Had it been blowing from any other quarter, I'm sure we would have gone wherever it took us. Abdul insisted he could navigate to Kuta, but I reckon that without the following breeze we could've been lost forever somewhere in the strait between Bali and the eastern tip of Java. About halfway through that second night, more by good luck than good management, we dragged ourselves ashore in front of Abdul's house, so sunburnt and exhausted it took me a couple of days to recover. It was an incredible adventure and nice to talk about twenty years later, but one I'd hate to repeat. I haven't seen Abdul since that trip. Wayne and I left our keel fin surfboards at his house when we took off for Australia, but by the time I got back to pick mine up, Abdul's scene had totally disappeared and I never saw my beautifully crafted board again. Abdul was a charismatic madman who did a lot of impulsive things without any forethought.

The waves we rode on that first trip were totally up to our expectations – it was everything we'd seen in *Morning of the Earth* and more. The conditions were really suited to the keel fin surfboards and some of the waves I watched Wayne drive out of at Uluwatu will never fade from my memory.

Other than my youngest son Bryce – who has a very good excuse, being only seven years old at the time of writing – Wayne is the most accident-prone friend I have. Whenever we meet, it seems, he's recovering from some wipe-out or another. The injury that cut short his first trip to Bali was the result of a motorbike accident as we were returning from an Italian restaurant on the Sanur side of the island. Between riding to the restaurant and returning home, roadworkers had left a ditch across the road and in the dark, Wayne, with Kay riding pillion, had hit it, resulting in lots of gravel rash for both of them and even worse for Kay, the loss of several teeth. Wayne was always clowning around on the bikes. Not long before, we'd been riding out on our morning surf check when Wayne, lying flat on the tank of his bike, flew past, yelling "I'm Superman!" at the top of his voice. Next minute he hit a pile of loose gravel, ending up with lots of minor cuts and abrasions. Back in Victoria, Wayne had barely recovered from his injuries when a travel-agent friend offered him a return trip to Bali as an escort for a traveller with his leg in a cast. On this trip he had another more serious motorbike accident, resulting in a serious back injury, and while in hospital he contracted malaria, a disease he's fought for the past twenty years.

I made twelve trips to Bali in the twenty years following my 1973 visit, but the horrible events on a trip I made in August 1993 led me to swear I'd never return. I was involved in shooting a catalogue for Oxbow, a French clothing company I worked with for six years. In a big chartered cruiser called the *Parneer*, we left Bali for Lombok and Sumbawa. After a couple of days surfing on Lombok we sailed for Sumbawa, planning to cruise overnight and arrive at Scar Reef as close as possible to dawn. In the dead of night I was woken from a deep sleep by the sound and shock of a collision. Leaping from my bunk, I raced up onto the afterdeck, where I was confronted by a truly horrific sight – five people were gripping the *Parneer's* stern rail, moaning and obviously in great pain. The first man I pulled on board had lost his foot. My cabin mate and good friend, Francois-Xavier "FX" Maurin, had followed me up to the deck. A dentist by profession and accustomed to giving injections, he shouted to the captain to bring down the morphine while we laid people in varying states of consciousness out on deck. The morphine arrived and I remember the battle I had with my trembling hands as I broke the vials to allow FX to draw the morphine into the syringe. The most serious case was the man who'd lost his foot. We stemmed the flow of blood with a tourniquet and gave him morphine, after which he calmed down somewhat.

One little boy, aged about ten and in great distress, was crying "barpat, barpat", over and over again; our Australian captain, who spoke Indonesian, told us the boy was calling for his father, and over the wails of the other four victims learnt that the boy's father, who'd been in charge of the prau, hadn't been seen since the accident. Our Captain turned on the searchlights and covered the area in an orderly grid pattern but all to no avail; we saw plenty of driftwood but nothing else.

The steel-hulled *Parneer* had mowed down the 5-metre wooden prau, which had been unsighted by the deckhand on watch. It had been making the crossing between two of the 1,300 islands in Indonesia, a routine journey that the island people had been making since the beginning of time. It could have been 1993 or 1693, the prau would have looked exactly the same. It had a small outboard and a tiny sail but no running lights, and we gathered that it had been carrying a ton of rice, a goat and the six people. At the time of the collision, *Parneer* was running on autopilot and cruising at a good rate of knots in order to make the morning surf on the low tide, and when we hit the prau, it was smashed to smithereens – almost an illustration of the impact the twentieth century has had on traditional lifestyles all over the world.

After a fruitless search for the missing man, the skipper set a direct course for the nearest large port, which we reached after several hours of burning up the sea miles, virtually running *Parneer* aground beside the jetty. We handed the seriously injured man up to those on the jetty while one of the deckhands shouted for someone, anyone, to get a doctor and the police, but everyone just seemed to stand and stare. Then we were told we wouldn't be allowed ashore until we checked in with the harbour authorities so we anchored in deeper water and waited. For hours we watched the injured man lying on the dock in the torrid sun; lots of people came and went but no-one helped him. It was disgusting. Finally the police boarded *Parneer* and the men we'd rescued were taken ashore, decked out in Oxbow clothing, the pockets bulging with cigarettes. The police told us we were in serious trouble; having killed the provider of an Indonesian family we were now responsible for the man's family. We gave the officers all the remaining cigarettes and booze and they smiled and talked for a while before telling our captain that *Parneer* was forbidden to leave port. Two armed guards were posted on the boat – for our protection the police said, claiming that the villagers were very angry over our killing of the man – and we stayed on board for another 24 hours. We were getting worried, as the situation seemed to be deteriorating. When the police returned, they laid their cards firmly on the table: for a payment of $6,000 they'd agree to let us

After the disastrous trip on the Parneer it was better
to stay at the Hyatt and take a small boat like this
to finish the catalogue shoot. From the left, Francois
Xavier Maurin, me, Joel Tudor. Up top Tim McKenna
taking photos with Captain Dan. Sylvain took this snap.

leave – but the boat and the captain would be held in Indonesia until everything was sorted out, probably in a couple of months. The sum they demanded was exactly the money we had between us – I was suspicious of this seeming coincidence – and we wondered if the dead man's family would ever see any of it but the Oxbow team was getting really twitchy and wanted out.

It was a lot of energy to have confined in one space: FX, a young Joel Tudor, the two photographers Sylvain Cazenave and Tim McKenna, Jason Polakow from the sailboard team, and myself. Back in Bali we booked into the Hyatt Hotel and I called my boss in France, suggesting we shoot the rest of the spread in the Hyatt's garden as quickly as we could and get the hell out of there – to which he readily agreed. Thinking about it on the plane home, I found it hard to come to grips with the way events had developed. I'd seen the same sort of thing in third-world countries before: in South America, Mexico, and now Indonesia. It seemed to me that serious accidents can bring out not only the best in people, but the worst also – even in Australia. There's often no value placed on a life other than what it might bring in monetary terms.

Rightly or wrongly, the experience turned me off Indonesia and I doubt I'll ever return. The whole episode was only made bearable because my old friend Nyarie was now living in a beautiful house near the Hyatt Hotel and I could go there to talk about my feelings and the ramifications the accident might have for everyone involved.

To me this story is an illustration of what occurred in Bali, as the result of two cultures on a collision course. Indonesia, particularly Bali, changed really quickly in just ten years. When we first visited Bali, most Balinese were absolutely terrified of the ocean and never ventured into it, for it was the domain of evil spirits – only brave fishermen went to sea in boats. Even the route to the beach at Uluwatu has changed. In 1973 it was quite a job to work out which of the paths across the fields to take to eventually reach the canyon with the ladder down to the cave and then the beach. The Uluwatu area is very arid – it gets very little rain at all – and its farmers are very poor. Even by Balinese standards they had nothing, so it's no surprise that they embraced the idea of charging for parking, offering bike rides to the beach and carrying boards up and down the couple of kilometres or so of tracks from the main road to the clifftop above the break. On my last trip to Bali they were talking about building a hotel at Uluwatu; they have one at the Greenball break and probably a hundred more scattered all over the island – all this inside twenty years. I believe a slower rate of growth would have been better for all concerned but still, a lot of people go there for the first time and absolutely love it. You have to look outside the hotel to see the problems.

I'm really not much good at being gloomy for too long; I much prefer to think about the old days and the best Bali surf trip I ever had. It was in August 1989, and by that stage I was keeping a daily diary so I have an accurate record. According to the diary, Sunday August 13th was the best I've ever surfed Outside Corner, the main break when it's big at Uluwatu. If it wasn't the biggest I've ever surfed, it must have been awfully close to it; 10–12 feet top to bottom with 15–20 feet on the faces. I don't think I surfed it any bigger with Wayne Lynch in 1973 and though we paddled out on one big day back then, for some reason it's hard for me to recall a clear picture of the size. Size aside, on all the previous occasions I'd surfed big Uluwatu, the wind had become a problem, increasing in velocity by the hour and around lunch to mid-afternoon blowing hard cross-shore down the bay from Temples, the outside point at Uluwatu. This crosswind creates a chop that makes take-offs on the green mountains very tricky. The critical point of entry moves out wider in the bay and makes it very unpredictable, especially if you're grossly undergunned.

As any surfer who travels overseas a lot will tell you, any number of boards is a hassle to travel with, two is about the limit unless you're a touring professional surfer. Even the most dedicated amateurs can't take their whole quiver with them when they travel. They have to use a process of elimination, taking into account where they're going and the size and type of waves they might get, then making a choice of boards from what they have available. Often it requires a new board to be built, just so the dream can have a solid foundation – but even then you have to be lucky to run into waves that are right for the boards you have. My usual board in 1989 was a 6-foot 5-inch state-of-the-art Thruster, the style of board I'd been surfing for ten years so I felt quite comfortable with it. The other board, at 6-foot 8-inches was a longer version of the first and was supposed to be for bigger waves. I thought that with these two boards I'd have everything covered, but not this time!

I arrived in Bali on Friday 11th of August, on a flight from Paris via Singapore. Looking through the taxi window en route to the Oberoi Hotel, I could see lots of sad European faces in and around Kuta – even if I hadn't been told I'd have known there'd been no significant surf for a while. A fellow guest at the Oberoi told me that the previous Saturday was the first day of real swell for a month. After a frustrating week, the grunts and groans had gone from 6 inches to 6 feet and then back to flat again. Huey had not been smiling on Bali that month. Finally the waves came and it was crowded everywhere, and with a 5-foot low tide at midday there were over 70 surfers out trying their luck in what would have had to have been a

I have no idea where these pictures of me at Uluwatu came from. I think that it goes back to the pintail days of the late '70s, on one of those numerous high quality days that blend into each other. At Outside Corner it's a matter of setting the ball up right and belting it.

6 to 8-foot Outside Corner. The pack was made up of roughly twenty Brazil Nuts (Brazilians), twenty Aussies and thirty or so assorted Eurogliders, Japs and Yanks. Under the crowded conditions it was survival of the fittest; it's a jungle out there and you have to prove your worth to the pack in order to get a wave.

After a couple of big sets the pecking order usually works itself out, a lot of surfers are washed ashore to sit on the cliff and talk about the experience and this day was no exception. After the first substantial set there was only a handful of surfers in the line-up and I knew my time had come. I made a definite move for one of the biggest waves I'd seen that day. I wouldn't see anything like that volume of water until Hawaii the following February. I felt as though I should be doing what I'd seen many novices do in big surf: paddle one stroke forward and two back. It really was an amazing situation, paddling flat-out on my little board for this big nasty mother and then getting sucked up the face backwards as the Sunset Beach-style lip pitched and exploded, squeezing me like a water melon seed straight out into space. The noise of the initial burst was like lightning cracking and all of a sudden I was skipping down the mountain on my belly, my momentum eventually slowing enough to let me enter the face and then I was propelled underwater for a painfully long time; rolling, tumbling, being held under to the point of giving up, then, like a new-born baby, I popped to the surface and sucked in a deep breath – air had never tasted better. That was Saturday 12th of August 1989, a memorable wipe-out in a day filled with deep tubes and vertical back-side turns that were enjoyed by both spectators and participants.

Dinner at the Oberoi that night was really interesting; I've always believed that pleasure in doing something unique is amplified when other people can sit back and enjoy what you are doing, especially people close to you. A lot of surfers don't like to own up to this because the contact between wave and surfer is so personal they consider it an experience that shouldn't be violated, or even talked about for that matter. The spectators' gallery at Uluwatu has changed over twenty years; from half a dozen local fisherman who watched inquisitively as a few madmen ventured out to where the evil spirits were, to a full gallery of tiered seating and about twenty warungs – little huts whose owners sold everything from drinks and massage to a place to leave your board overnight. Over the hotel buffet that night, many who'd seen my wipe-out were commenting on it. The spectators who'd watched from the cliffs thought I must be hurt or, worst of all, really disappointed because I didn't make the take-off. Others, mainly surfers who'd been out in the water, were amazed that I paddled for such an enormous wave on a 6-foot 5-inch board.

All through that night the constant booming of waves breaking on

Kuta's outside reefs reminded me of the cymbals at the climax of Ravel's *Bolero*. I didn't get much sleep, but that's pretty usual when there's a big surf running, and I was up with the first rays of light, doing my stretches in preparation for the testing day of surf to come. The wind was non-existent – Sanur had to be going off – and during the bemo ride across the island I talked with my newfound friends from the hotel about how nice it'd be to ride some big rights. Sanur wasn't big, maybe 8 feet on the sets, but clean and long, running all the way past the wreck if you got the right wave.

One of the nicest things about having a good morning surfing at Sanur lies in knowing that you're in close proximity to one of the world's great breakfasts at the Hilton Hotel and after pigging out on the smorgasbord, we ran the gauntlet of the death-defying Balinese drivers to make it back to Uluwatu in time for the low tide. It's hard to describe the feelings you get with that first glimpse of breaking waves through the canyon. The heat and glare of the noonday sun do funny things to the faces of the shimmering monsters cascading through from Temples, through Outside Corner and peeling off forever down the bay. It seemed to me that the afternoon had the potential to provide the surfer's equivalent of a mystical experience for a religious person; it would give purpose to my existence. I could hear classical music in my ears and I trembled in anticipation. The wind that had been such a problem the day before was dead-still now, a slight hint of an off-shore breeze perhaps, but only enough to riffle the surface of the water; conditions were absolutely perfect. When I finally focused on the take-off zone I was flabbergasted to see that only five guys were out there out; where were all the surfers from the day before? I was amazed; where *was* everyone? There must have been 500 surfers on Bali on that day, the surf was too big at Uluwatu for anywhere else to be any good and there'd been no waves for weeks. I don't know how long ago I formed the theory that it's better to take-off and die than never take-off at all, but obviously all surfers don't feel the same. Anyway that wasn't my problem on that day – I had to find a horse.

After the heavy wipe-out the day before, I was extremely hesitant about paddling out on my little 6-foot 5-incher and I had to find another board. I wandered around the numerous warungs overlooking the break and saw some mighty fine craft, but on inquiring found they belonged to some Brazilian or Aussie who was coming back later. "Yeah," I thought, "I wonder how many of 'em will be back now that it's over 6 feet." The thought crossed my mind to steal one of these boards and take it for a surf, my rationalisation being that the worst thing that could happen was that I'd break it, and after all, that's exactly what boards are made for. I've been told I have a very weird

DICK

Wide shot looking up the Uluwatu Peninsula to the takeoff in the very background.

attitude to this, but I see it as a tribal rite, a bit like burning a board on the beach to make the surf come up. I've always loved it when I break a board, especially if it's a special one, and every year I break one; in 1993 I broke two, a fitting tribute to a vintage year. So I sat on a bamboo bed in one of the warungs, sucking on a Coke and thinking of my Hawaiian Island Creations quiver back in Hawaii, and my boards at home in New South Wales. I couldn't remember the last time I'd been caught with my pants down, I really wanted to ride those waves but perhaps, I thought, I was meant to sit this one out.

I was eyeballing every possibility; so many boards from all over the world with the one common purpose built into all of them, all lovingly created and brought to Bali to fulfil the dream. It finally came down to a choice between two second-hand boards: a 7-foot 6-inch Bradshaw that had been broken once, and a 7-foot 3-inch Dart made by someone I'd never heard of in Australia, and I'm sure that last statement will surprise some surfing community where these boards were testament to their maker's credibility. The bottom shape of the Australian board was simple and straightforward, accurately carved from a roll into a deep vee. The plan was a simple rounded pin with a half-inch maple stringer down the centre; truly this board was the product of a dream of riding 10-foot Balinese barrels. I couldn't help but wonder if the surfer who'd brought this beautiful steed to Bali had ever realised the dream. The die was cast, this board would be the mount on which I'd meet the maker. I loved the feeling of making a choice on the clifftop at Uluwatu, I'd either fly or die by the virtues of the board. I have been told terrible stories of breaking a board and having to borrow a mate's, spinning out on take-off and swimming for hours, but somehow I just knew this board was right.

A deal was made with Jimmy, the local board repairman, who didn't know me from a bar of soap – I know that because after the deal was made he asked me my name. I'd never rented a board before and it was an interesting experience: 10,000 rupiah for the day or one surf, whichever was the longer, and if I broke the board then I had to buy it for $500. Jimmy looked out at the surf and told me he wanted cash up-front which was fine with me as I never felt my money was safe when I left it at one of the warungs while surfing; not that I don't trust the Balinese, I do, it's just that I'd sooner be safe than sorry. Preparing the board, getting ready and climbing down the cliff through the cave, I felt like a gladiator entering the Colosseum, or my other recurring fantasy, a medieval knight off to the Crusades. At almost every big-wave location you hear some amazing raves and excuses from people to explain why they aren't out there – like the young Seppo I met coming up out of the cave; seems he'd been wiped-out and lost his board an hour or two before and still hadn't found it. Scattered about the path and surrounding bushes was the litter of at least six other boards that had broken since the swell had jumped the day before and among them young Balinese worked feverishly, cutting them into pieces suitable for ding repairs and heatedly discussing the best way to stick this or that one back together.

Just getting off that reef at low tide on a 10-foot swell is a trick as relentless boils and rips appear with every surge. You have to fight to get beyond the reef then turn hard right and paddle in between the swells into the bay. How can I explain the feeling of taking-off on that first 15-footer, the water chattering under the board as I accelerated down the ski-jump face, pressing into that first turn and hearing the lion roaring over my shoulder. I was full of confidence as I felt the Dart's deep vee nestling comfortably in the water. Driving down the line into the second and third turns, it was as though the throttle was opening up, achieving speeds the board had never reached before.

Paddling back out I'm thinking what a lucky bastard I am and the music going around in my head is right out of the 1960s – Simon and Garfunkel singing "and you read your Emily Dickinson and I my Robert Frost; Lost in the dangling conversation of the superficial sigh". Talk about a flashback, I've never thought of that tune before, didn't even know I knew the words, it's very strange, the subconscious. Then I'm back in the line-up again thinking about that day with Wayne Lynch in 1973 when I surfed Ulu close to this good. I'm just sitting there spacing-out about how well those keel boards went in 1973 when I'm woken from my daydream by the approach of a huge set. I turn and paddle hard as I can, straight into the pit; next minute it's down, down, down; setting the turn as late as possible, 15 or 20 feet down the face. Just as the board is about to accelerate an invisible karate chop to the back of the neck, the dreaded lip again, and I'm driven under the water for an eternity. The leg rope breaking like a piece of cotton and finally the kiss of life as I struggle to the surface gulping for air. And still the set is coming. I'm in the impact zone and I take five more waves right on the head. Swimming towards the beach I'm thinking about how riding big waves on your backhand is difficult, it's so much easier on your forehand when you can see the lip coming and duck. It took a while to find my board; slowly I paddle back out to the line-up and sit there licking my wounds. I watch Tim from Newcastle get a couple of good ones and then I get a screamer. The afternoon draws on with just the three of us enjoying perfect 15-foot tubes. On occasions Bali is still a magic island.

14

'Neverland' and the Aquarius Festival

"**K**IF IS LIKE FIRE – a little warms a lot burns", is an old Moroccan saying I saw scratched on the side of a mosque while we were in that country in 1969 on the shoot for the movie *Evolution.* Over the years I've found that statement to be extremely accurate but I also think that by surfing under the effects of cannabis I was able to reach a higher level of expertise. Its unique qualities kept that particular channel open long after the initial effects had worn off, and for more than five years, every surfing session started with a toke on a small bamboo pipe. I wore out several over those years and regarded this ritual as a spiritual activity necessary for centring my concentration and keeping my head into the moves I was attempting.

Unlike many others of my generation I never saw marijuana as an innocent fun drug. Sure it was fun to smoke on some occasions but I considered its effects much more profound than just getting stoned for a laugh. Most of the time I gave marijuana the respect I believe it deserved by endeavouring not to abuse it. The number of times I've smoked dope after dark could be counted on the fingers of both hands and it's only happened when I wanted a big night of sex and rock 'n' roll. On those rare occasions when I did indulge in pot for fun, the festivities have been pretty special and I've never let it become a regular part of my life. It's OK to party once in a while but I don't think any professional athlete can be that flippant with either their physical or mental health.

I believe that marijuana is a stimulant that should be taken in as small amount as possible. Some people take too much too often, needing more and more to get them stoned and their bodies adjust to sleeping with the effects still flowing through them. I'm concerned that road leads only one way: to look for a more powerful drug to get you high and another to send you to sleep. I've taken acid a few times, the effects ranging from incredible insight to deep depression. Mushrooms and peyote have similar effects and should be treated with extreme caution. I found the Carlos Castaneda books very helpful regarding these psylocibins, and I enjoyed cocaine for a time but I lost contact

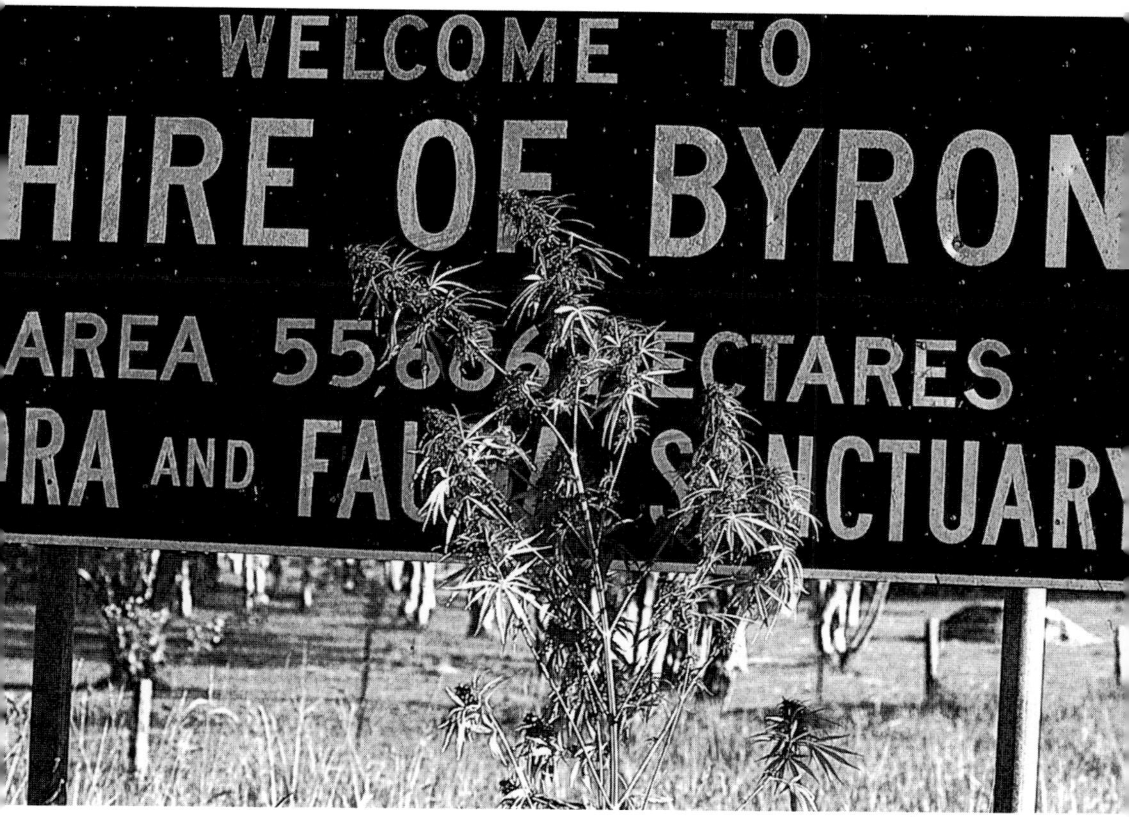
WELCOME TO
HIRE OF BYRON

with reality and that can be fatal – and coke isn't conducive to family life. I found cocaine is a drug that can't be trusted, you're never sure of what you have and the highs and lows are far too extreme.

I was always suspicious of hashish; standards of hygiene in the areas where it's produced are so completely different from ours. I recall being very stoned one day and looking at a big block of Nepalese hash and not being able to think of it as anything more than the deposits of some peasant's fingernails. On the other hand I liked almost everything about marijuana, especially the fact that you could grow it yourself, tending and nurturing the plant and eventually smoking the results of the dedication. It's such a wonderful feeling when, after all that love and attention, the plants bud, to be eventually picked and dried. Hanging them upside down to allow the resin to concentrate in the heads seemed to increase the strength as did drying them away from sunlight. Cleaning the heads of stalks and seeds is a very pleasant ritual but I never really liked the process of smoking anything.

I knew that smoking was bad for me but the alternative, cooking and eating the drug, took too much time and it's really difficult to estimate the amount consumed and so control the effect. I've had some good times on cookies but I found the best way to eat marijuana was to make an omelette, first frying the weed in the butter before adding the other ingredients. However, taking the drug like this meant you could kiss the day goodbye. I've never smoked marijuana cut with tobacco; it made me choke and cough on the occasions when I mistakenly took a hit on someone else's joint. My marijuana had to be pure and of the very best quality, and when I wasn't in a position to grow a plant, I was prepared to pay more for quality – it also meant that less was needed to get high.

It's impossible to write about the end result of my marijuana usage. It's only been twenty years after all, a small amount of time in the scheme of things. However, I'm as convinced now as I was when I first smoked a joint that marijuana has been totally misrepresented to our generation. Prior to 1947 cannabis was completely legal and grown all over the world both for its value as a fibre and for medicinal uses. It's difficult for me to understand why the authorities turned against cannabis; in so many respects I see it as one of humanity's most valuable plants. The worst thing about the legislation against it is that everyone – particularly the "baby-boomers" and their children – believes it's based on a lie and that's why I believe all the anti-drug campaigns are destined to fail.

It was heartening to see the winner of the first snowboard giant slalom event in the 1998 Winter Olympic Games in Nargano, Japan, admit that he'd used marijuana. The IOC took Canadian Ross

Rebagliati's gold medal away when he tested positive for the drug but gave it back when it was decided that marijuana couldn't be classed as a performance-enhancing drug. Snowboarding is surfing in the snow, an extension of our culture, with the opportunity to influence the public's attitude to social issues like marijuana – it may even be at the front line of the debate. As Ross said after the event, he "wasn't going to change his friends".

Over the past few years nearly everyone has become aware of the health problems associated with smoke ingestion and I've completely stopped smoking marijuana as a consequence. I've noticed that it takes only the smallest amount to open the door these days, perhaps it's something to do with my age. However, I feel it's important to get high on occasions so as not to forget the lessons of the 1970s – marijuana cookies or a marijuana breakfast omelette are rare treats that I enjoy tremendously. If this direction continues, by the time I'm sixty I'll be getting stoned only every five years which, come to think of it, is exactly what Mum said would happen when I grew up.

The height of a very intense self indulgent period that I went through was 1973, and to be truthful, it was influenced by my life in Byron Bay. I became a total vegetarian, an extremely fashionable move which lasted a number of years and I also got into the beliefs of an Indian mystic named Meher Baba. His classic one-liner was "Don't worry, be happy". I had a poster of Baba's smiling face on the wall of my Kombi and, later, behind a door in the Byron house; essentially that was as much as I ever wanted to know about his spiritual philosophy. I believe I was doing the best surfing of my life in this period, but ironically, surfing contests weren't happening much at all at this time, and they definitely weren't happening for me. I wasn't really interested in competing and gave up competition altogether after winning the 1970 Smirnoff championships in 15-foot surf at Makaha, Hawaii. I had to push myself to enter and was inspired by the fact that this was the first contest to offer substantial cash prizes.

Looking back at my lack of motivation at the time, perhaps it was brought on by smoking too much after making the move to Byron, and my going a bit over the top with back-to-nature country soul. However there were lots of other underlying reasons for my lack of competitive spirit, and I'd say my feelings at that time were fairly typical of most young people all over the world. Generally speaking, we were disenchanted with our various governments' attitudes to lots of things, including the war in Vietnam and marijuana, and I remember feeling very inspired when the Beatles took out a full-page ad in a London newspaper protesting about the laws on cannabis. The obscenities in Vietnam gave young people a cause, and all over the world we rallied to march against the war; we were

Marilyn and Nyarie opened Neverland in '73
selling hippy clothes and beautiful things. It was
the first alternative shop in the main street of
Byron Bay. That's Garth, The Stork, playing at
the opening party.

united and determined to let everyone know how we felt. In Australia we battled with greedy miners and industrialists who saw the beaches everywhere as mineral-rich sandpits just waiting to be plundered. I fell in with some active surfer-greenies; we protested at every chance we got and I was very vocal in the media about this important issue. The music of the day was all about self-exploration and finding one's self: The Moody Blues, Donovan, The Beatles and Bob Dylan were the guiding lights; their lyrics suggested that marijuana was the key to unlock that inner door.

In mid-May 1973, the first Aquarius Festival was held on the north coast of New South Wales in a little town called Nimbin, about half an hour into the hills behind Byron Bay. All Byron's surfing fraternity went there, camping as a tribe, as did other groups from as far away as Brisbane, Melbourne and Sydney. The Mullumbimby tribe was the model alternative-consciousness group and as they had the best campsite, on the riverbank, all the large gatherings took place at their compound. I think Aquarius was the first festival of its type in Australia and was certainly the first that Marilyn and I ever attended. We were very excited about the collective positive energy being generated, and the fact that it was happening so close to our home in Byron Bay was an added bonus. Through talking, dancing, singing and playing together we got to know that there were thousands of like-minded people all over Australia. Around the campfires at night we talked about the state of the world, past, present and future, and what we were going to do about it. I remember discussions about whales and how all countries would have to help protect them before they were hunted to extinction. Land clearing and rainforest preservation were hot topics that I had not really thought about till then. Some of the people I talked to were optimistic while some were complete pessimists – it was a big cross-section of opinion. Others were there for the free love or a chance to climb into the huge wood-burning plastic-covered sauna with hundreds of other naked bodies. The festival organisers had arranged workshops on all sorts of things. I went to a session on making things from bamboo – which has been useful to me ever since – the teacher showed us how to make everything from a couch to a North-American tepee. Most of the 4,000 people attending were baby boomers but there was also a smattering of older folk who gave the festival credibility. These people seemed to have a grasp of the wider picture. They were able to see beyond a person's looks or the colour of their skin or the length of their hair; they didn't care about the clothes you wore but instead focused on doing the right thing by humanity, in line with the commandments in the Bible. Somehow it all connected much better for me with these older folk involved; I've been back to

Nimbin many times since, but I've never met any of the inspirational souls I met at the Aquarius Festival. They must be very old by now or perhaps passed away as two older members of our group have.

* * * * * * *

Gwendolyn was the oldest member of our Byron tribe and she introduced me to Honey Wilson, a very dynamic friend of hers; it was great to listen to them hit off each other. Totally committed to what would now be called the New Age, Honey was the big, bubbly enthusiastic leader of her family, a straight talker who put you in your place immediately and didn't beat around the bush. She and her husband John, their daughter and son-in-law and their five children were all living in an old schoolhouse at Coopers Shoot; three generations under the one roof. Marilyn and I got to know the whole family pretty well over the next few months; they were all wonderful individuals but the matriarch took the cake. To support their cooperative lifestyle, Honey got the family into importing exotic clothing from Bali and other places and selling it at the many "alternative" markets as well as to shops. They must have been one of the original alternative-lifestyle families in Australia and for me were a real inspiration. John Wilson died in 1985 and in 1994 Honey passed away with liver cancer and the family's collective energy diminished somewhat, but the strength gained from that rock-solid, loving background, gave each member such a good foundation that all of them went on to instigate some very creative projects.

Lady Gwendolyn died in the Byron area in January 1976 after a year of wrestling with a brain tumour. Right until the very end Edwin was devoted, carrying her to the doctor and brewing her potions of Comfrey tea. Gwendolyn is certainly not forgotten by her family and friends, nor by a lot of Australian surfers. In the early days of *Tracks* newspaper she wrote a cooking column and 30 years later I see that some of the recipes are surfacing again in a column named after her.

During our three years in Byron, the population had increased dramatically and to such a degree that Marilyn and Nyarie opened a hip clothing shop (in the main street), which they called Neverland. Originally there had been just a handful of close friends living nearby, but now there were fifty families. The number seemed to be growing every day and people were moving in on all sides of our property; not that they were bad people, far from it, it was just that there were too many people in one place. Byron Bay was becoming a "scene" with no-one doing anything constructive, just hanging out. While it's true that I didn't feel much affinity with these "beautiful people", a couple of events helped me make the decision to leave the Bay. The first involved a younger tourist-type guy who was stopped by a cop in the main street of Byron. Searching his car, the police found 15 kilograms of hash and a gun. I was blown away, it was getting just like New York. The next prod came while we were at a party at Edwin and Gwendolyn's Broken Head beach house one Sunday afternoon. There were lots more people there than the regular crowd I'd become familiar with over the past few months; obviously the word about Byron being the place to be was spreading like wildfire and I didn't know two thirds of the people there. I got into a good gab about cattle and farm life with a nuggetty little bloke, a bit younger than me, named Jim McInnes, a talented ex-Newcastle surfer who had a fruit-and-vegie truck he drove from Ballina to Byron, selling produce door to door. I'd known Jim for years; he'd gained my respect out in the surf at Lennox on days when it was big and solid. I told him about the call I'd had from Doc Spence.

Doc at the time was consultant surgeon for the far-north coast and in Grafton he'd operated on an old guy with a heart condition; the grateful patient wanted to sell his 810 hectare property and offered the Doc an interest-free loan. Doc and his wife Margaret had looked it over but they needed flat land to breed the horses to which they were totally committed and thought its size would also prove too much for them, but they thought I might be interested. When the owner got out of hospital Marilyn and I went down and took a long ride over most of the farm with him; the river ran right past the front 202 hectares and several large creeks flowed out of steep gullies; there was lots of impenetrable rainforest and thousands of gums in varying stages of maturity as the property hadn't been logged for at least thirty years. Lantana was the only problem, the noxious weed infested half the land, but I reckoned on dealing with it later. The truth is that it's still a curse on the property and has never been completely eradicated.

Jim told me he too was fed up with what was happening in Byron so that night at the party we had the beginnings of a deal, fine-tuned over the next few weeks, whereby if I bought a place Jim would run it, and that agreement, with various ups and downs, has been strong and binding since 1974. Jim and I looked at some other acreages closer to Byron but all of them were one-dimensional, strictly cattle properties, and their owners were asking a heap more than the $20 an acre Doc Spence's new-found friend had suggested. I thought we needed some back-up in case the cattle market continued to be a disaster and the ability to sell timber gave me a form of insurance, so when the old farmer agreed to give me the same interest-free terms as he'd offered Doc, we shook hands on the deal.

* * * * * * *

Selling the 4.5 hectares on the ridge overlooking Byron wasn't too traumatic for either Marilyn or me, as we reckoned the move would be better for our family life. Marilyn was pregnant as a commitment to saving our marriage. I was skiing at Perisher Valley when I got the news that my wife had gone into labour seven weeks early, so I picked up Naomi from the Purcell's house in Sydney and drove up the coast. At one stage the radio was playing Dylan's *Mr Bojangles*; Naomi and I were singing along, and we decided that Beau would be the name of the new baby – a very premature boy born in Grafton on 28th August 1974. I had to lift Naomi up to let her peek at Beau struggling for his life in the humidicrib. He was so tiny – less than half the average weight – and as I stared through the plastic crib, all sorts of emotions went through my mind. A baby son – I thought it would never happen. I counted all his fingers and toes, everything was perfect, but it was really difficult to relate to this 3 pound 6 ounce (one and a half kilograms) skinned rabbit. At last, after three weeks in hospital, Marilyn and our son came home to Nymboida. Beau would always be the smallest of my children – hardly surprising after such a shaky start – but he's very strong and a real fighter who enjoys life to the fullest.

The decision on what type of cattle to buy to stock the new farm was made in consultation with a stock and station agent in Grafton. The country was too steep for cows and calves so the original owner had stocked it with store cattle – calves bought at about nine months old and kept for twelve months before selling them as "forward stores" to someone who'd fatten them for market; all-up I invested about $20,000 in cattle. Before I stocked the place, Jim and I checked all the fences; they weren't too bad, but with over 30 kilometres of them to look at, it took a whole day on horseback to do it. There was no house on the farm, but down by the front gate was an old shed which we used for storage and as a kitchen, pitching a tent near it so we could have a bug-free sleeping area. It was much too spartan for our growing family, so we rented an old farmhouse down near the local power station.

The next thing to do was to build a new family home and I wanted the architecture to make a very definite statement, as the house in Whale Beach had done. That house had been bought by a Sydney painting contractor who sanded smooth the rough clinker bricks I'd so diligently collected and painted the interior walls gloss mushroom – Ross Thorn and I wept. I hated living in old houses; I thought of them as someone else's shells and dreams and I needed spaces to inspire me to do constructive things. As I've mentioned earlier, when it came to architecture, Edwin Kingsbury, Gwendolyn's partner, had influenced me greatly. Edwin believed that a family

This is the house we built on the farm.
Completed in '75, it was a huge undertaking
but one of the best projects I have ever done.

home should have one big communal living room–kitchen as its centre or "egg". From this egg, fingers would spread to areas where people big and small could have their private spaces.

After doing up the old farmhouse in Byron I really wanted to try my hand at building a house from scratch but I needed good tradesmen to work with. I had a friend named Jason Smith who had not only completed a degree in architecture, but was also a very accomplished carpenter. After a couple of heavy raves in Byron Bay, he made a working scale-model out of balsa. Without getting a permit from the local council, Jim and I went to one of the highest points on the property and levelled the building site – the view was incredible, you could see for miles up the main valley. We then put twelve poles in the ground to form an 18 x 12 metre semicircle – we were cutting power poles off the farm at that stage and that's what we used. We had an arrangement with a local timber mill that if we sent in a truckload of poles we could get half of them back in whatever form we required, but all the large structural beams were cut with a swing-saw on the concrete slab between the uprights by Jim and a local timber-getter.

On either side of the house was a tower, one of two levels to accommodate the kids' bedrooms and the other of three levels contained the adults' rooms. We boxed-up between the poles and poured concrete for the main living area which was divided in two by a huge fireplace, big enough to sit in, built of old sandstock bricks. Following Edwin's vision, the northern face of the chimney partitioned off the summer-living area including the kitchen and dining room. The entire northern wall consisted of stunning green and purple stained-glass leadlight windows that I'd bought at a church auction in Grafton after a committee of misguided parishioners had voted to replace all that fine craftsmanship with aluminium windows. For next to nothing at the same auction, I also bought enough sandstock bricks for the fireplace and a garden wall around the perimeter of the building site. Jim and I cleaned the bricks at the church and brought them home on the old Ford truck we'd bought for the farm. I really wanted the feeling of space, and according to everyone who's been in it, the main room feels more like a church than most churches. One of the big windows bears the legend "Methodist Church" in heavy scrolled lettering, adding to the religious feel. The three trusses supporting the bulk of the roof are over 8 metres above the floor – just climbing around at that height was a terrifying experience and I'm amazed, and thankful, we didn't have any serious accidents during construction. To get some protection from the prevailing southerly winds, we dropped the roof over the winter living area onto a lower wall and put a section of thick carpet into the quarry-tile floor in front of the fireplace. It took over six months of working every day to get a few rooms habitable. Every morning we'd get up early and start pounding nails, never stopping till the sun went down.

All this while the cattle were doing well under Jim's watchful eye but the market continued to slip and we ended up being forced to sell them for less money than we originally paid. I gave my attention to the lantana as soon as the house was finished. Someone told me that goats love lantana, all you had to do was put them inside a confined space, using an electric fence to hold them, and they'd eat everything within reach. I bought fifty feral goats from the local abattoir for $5 each and put them in an area that Jim and I had secured with mesh fencing and electricity. The next morning I went out at dawn to see how much lantana had been eaten overnight and to my amazement saw the last goat tippy-toeing up the prop against one of the strainer-posts – and that was the last I ever saw of the goats, though people in the area hunted them for years.

Naturally I was still doing a fair bit of surfing while working on the farm. We found some isolated beach-breaks that were a welcome change from the hard work, but the point-break at Angourie was the closest of the quality waves and together with the friends who were helping with the house, hit Angourie point whenever the swell was right. To avoid the crowds we sometimes surfed in the middle of the night, especially if we had the light of a full moon and could keep warm with a big fire on the beach.

Marilyn and I were having our problems; she wanted to go back to Sydney and see if a bit of space would help our marriage and over the course of the next few months looked for a house to buy. A mutual friend from Collaroy days was renting an old fishing shack overlooking Bungan Beach on the north side of Sydney. With a loan from the bank we bought it, then Jim and I set about remodelling it both inside and out. Jim cut all the timber on the farm, bringing it to Sydney on our old truck, while most of the hardware and a big bay window I bought second-hand. We were looking pretty skint; cattle prices were getting worse and Jim's timber-cutting operation required bigger machinery if we were going to make any real money.

The only card left to play was to go back to making surfboards and that meant living in Sydney – I wasn't delighted about it but it made sense and just might save our marriage. I started out shaping my model for Barry Bennett Surfboards and found the classic pintails were in demand, so after a few months with Bennett I struck out on my own and moved to a factory in Mona Vale that I shared with two other surfboard makers. Everything was going OK: I was paying the

We moved back to the city, I started shaping surfboards again and I was not happy about the changes to my lifestyle. This picture was taken outside the old Tracks office in Whale Beach by Frank Pithers.

290

bills and keeping my head above water, but it wasn't exactly what I planned to be doing in 1976.

* * * * * * *

Somewhere along the way, back in about 1970, I got the idea that the public had seen enough of me winning – not that I'd been in any contests since the 1970 Smirnoff, but it just seemed to me that surfing needed a new champion, a new vanguard to follow. It wasn't that I was being a nice guy particularly, it was just that I'd been doing the same thing for over ten years and that was too long as far as I was concerned. In truth I was fed up with the whole competitive scene in the early 1970s. My enthusiasm for Expression Sessions as an alternative to contests had been dented by their failure to develop to expectations and I was turning into exactly what I hated most – a negative bastard with a chip on his shoulder. Even my annual pilgrimage to Bells Beach had become a drag.

I'd been going to Bells each Easter since 1961 and it was one of the high points of my year; I really looked forward to it. Bells had become an institution and I loved everything about it: the cold wind and waves, the pub, the girls, having to wear jumpers, and the solid surfing-community spirit in Victoria. Each year I'd spend the twelve months between Easters recalling fond memories of all the funny situations and people – even trying to get in and out of my wetsuit in the muddy, rain-drenched Bells carpark seemed funny in retrospect. When the road and later the carpark were sealed, another page in the history of Bells turned, but some of us will never forget the way it was.

The natural amphitheatre of Bells gave the Victorians an opportunity to enjoy an annual look at surfing. The spectators at Bells were as responsive as any crowd at a grand final of Australian Rules football in Melbourne. It's the first beach I can remember hearing people cheering and clapping after I rode a good wave – that was back in 1965 after screaming, perched on the nose, across the little Rincon reef and in a perfect finish, being thrown up on dry sand. To my knowledge Bells is the only place in the world where this happens. The Victorian Surfing Association manned the entrance gates, charging spectators a fee to watch the contest and this was another first – they were really well organised. I had great respect for everyone involved – even an old official named Stan Couper with whom I locked horns on a few occasions over the judging system and being made to surf in marginal conditions. But I really admired him and I think he knew my feelings towards him weren't personal.

Two older Victorian mates of mine, Brian Singer and Doug

Warbrick, had started a wetsuit company in the Bells area and called it Rip Curl. They were both keen surfers and always on the lookout for some new angle to promote their product – and the Bells Beach Contest was to be that vehicle. Rip Curl was, and still is, the main sponsor of the contest and with their involvement, Bells in 1973 was the first Australian contest to give money as prizes – professional surfing was about to happen. However, I failed to see my role in this development clearly; something was holding me back from committing to this new direction.

In Easter 1974 I left the farm and went to Bells to have a close look at professional surfing and hang out with Wayne Lynch and a few old mates. Sitting on the cliffs watching the heats and listening to the results over the loudspeaker, I realised that things had changed significantly with the new points-for-manoeuvres judging system. At first the waves were pretty good and I found myself getting quite excited as I compared my estimation of each ride with the announced result. Everyone was surfing so strongly and smoothly, and the new judging system seemed to be working well. I found my estimation of a ride's worth was almost 100 per cent in agreement with the judges, right up until the semi-finals began. Then the waves went consistently downhill.

Michael Peterson was surfing brilliantly before the contest began, ripping every available wave to absolute shreds. Back when I'd been living in Byron and making regular trips to the Gold Coast, I'd watched his development with interest. On a solid easterly swell at Kirra, his performance in and around the curl was flawless and the amount of spray he'd put in my eyes and the size of the wake created by the drive of one of his cutbacks at Burleigh were awesome. Watching him from the top of the cliff at Bells I was thinking that he'd be the one to take my place and not Wayne Lynch as I'd once thought would be the case. Wayne simply didn't have the temperament to win consistently, only on the rare occasions when all the variables came together: a desire to win, good waves and the right board. I had a weird feeling about Peterson filling my shoes on the contest front. He was a real street fighter who'd do anything to win and sometimes watching him ride a wave I felt as though I was looking in a mirror. Michael was making all the same moves as I would, but cleaner and sharper, with more power and direction. It was a very eerie feeling watching him attack a wave, especially on that particular day – looking down I could sense every move before he made it; it was like watching a movie of myself out in the water – I knew exactly what he was thinking.

But watching Michael surf in the heats at Bells also caused me to lose faith in both him and the new scoring system. He took off on a

Alby's picture of Michael Peterson in '69
Just before he took over my position.

ALBY

In the early '70s Michael Peterson was turning harder and riding further back inside the curl than any other surfer competing in Australia.

bad wave – which was his excuse to me later on – made a turn and the wave closed-out, but instead of flicking off and getting another wave he went straight in the foam, moving forward in a crouch position and dangling one foot over the nose all the way to the beach. Under the new system this gave him the necessary points to win but I thought it was a shocking display not worthy of his talent. I was angry at a system that had forced Michael to compromise his surfing to the point of making it look like a game of pinball. I marched down to the officials' tent and gave Stan an earful of how shithouse the new system was and how I felt sick having to watch Michael Peterson performing like a trained seal. In retrospect I took it much too seriously – taking things too seriously is one of my weak points – but I hated the idea of Michael prostituting his talent just to win a contest.

After Bells everyone was off to Sydney for the first Coca Cola contest and I made a point of cornering Michael in the carpark at Narrabeen before the first day of competition began. We smoked a joint together and talked about the new system; by the end of our rave we were both laughing, and it wasn't only the pot – it seemed so funny that the new points-for-manoeuvres system had its weakness just as the old subjective one had. No system works if the waves are bad and I found myself wishing that I'd thought a bit before blowing up old Stan Couper and the Victorian officials a few weeks earlier. Michael pointed out that the problems with the system disappeared as soon as there were waves – tricks were then totally irrelevant.

All the competitors at Narrabeen were buzzing with the news that there was to be a circuit of professional contests developing in the next year. Certainly Bells that year had lots more international surfers, and with Coke's involvement the future looked pretty good. The thought occurred to me that I should be trying harder to make a living out of contest surfing and I did actually make an effort in that direction. Rip Curl was prepared to give me a few dollars to get back into contests and a clothing company called Golden Breed was paying me a small retainer, enough to buy an air ticket to Hawaii if I wanted it.

So I had to make a big decision. I felt a bit of a hypocrite really – I'd made statements against surfing in contests for money and here I was entering the Coke. I didn't mind sponsorship deals, being paid to do ads seemed fair, but I just didn't know what I felt about this latest professional surfer phenomenon. I decided I needed more exposure to professional surfing to make a decision so I'd get as involved as I possibly could in the Coke contest and see if I could get behind professional surfing 100 per cent. The facts were that the giant soft-drink company Coca Cola was sponsoring the biggest professional contest ever and I'd been lucky enough to be invited, so why was I questioning entering? I was doing it just for the money and I sure could use it; making boards was OK but it was dusty, hard work that I didn't want to be doing forever. Things were getting tight financially – I'd lost about $10,000 on my foray into the cattle industry and the payments on Marilyn's new house were a drain. Perhaps this was exactly what I needed to get me out of the soul-surfer role and back in the real world.

The contest started on May 1st 1974. May is usually a very good time of year for waves in Sydney, and it was being held in my old area on the northern beaches. The event was to be portable, moving to the best beach on the day, so the chances of poor waves were minimised. On the strength of all this, my decision to make one last-ditch effort to see what happened seemed pretty reasonable. The first round was held in shitty waves at Warriewood, and as at Bells, Michael did his crouch in the white water and won by miles – he knew how to use the system and leave no stone unturned. The waves were big and lumpy at Fairy Bower next day, but the day after at Winky Pop, the outside ledge at Fairy Bower, saw the best waves of the contest; a good 8–10 feet and everyone who knew how to ride solid powerful waves revelled in the conditions. The headland was covered with thousands of spectators and looked fantastic from the water – I felt like an actor on stage with all those faces staring down at me. I got one very deep, big tube which scored the highest points of the day and my self-confidence was restored; perhaps I really could make a living from professional surfing. I felt as though I was finally surfing up to my potential after the last few years out of competition and riding quality waves on the north coast.

On the typical gutless beach-breaks around Sydney my boards felt stiff and awkward, but they were perfect on the point surf at the Bower. I'd dropped the keel fins before I entered, having realised their limitations in variable wave conditions. I was still riding the classic Joey Cabell-inspired double-ended pintails; all in the 7-foot range with small upright fins. Of course the swell abated the following day and the contest moved to Narrabeen for the duration – and it was there that I decided not to become a professional surfer. It wasn't just one issue that decided me, but there was one I remember most. It involved Peter Drouyn and Ted Spencer, but everyone was doing it and to some Coke executives it must have seemed quite funny. By injecting a relatively small amount of money into a new sport they had all the contestants fighting and squabbling like hungry chooks over a handful of wheat. I found myself doing my best to kill the other guy when it came down to the wire and for me the atmosphere around contests had changed completely. The cash put a whole new slant on surfing from that day on.

Getting ready to go out in my heat at the '74 Coke contest at Manly and the tube at Winki Pop that got me into third place.

I held my own at Narrabeen and the result was Michael Peterson first, Ian Cairns second and me in third. I wasn't disappointed, I felt I'd been judged fairly by the new system but that was essentially it for me. The money had changed surfing contests to dog-eat-dog events and I wouldn't compete again. I'd been lucky to experience professional surfing and I'd made a decision I was comfortable with. By going for public exposure over quality surfing locations, contests were unlikely to be held in good waves and they weren't the conditions I was prepared to compete under – better to bow out now before I get into the survival-of-the-fittest-for-dollars syndrome. It was the end of an era; no more would kids do it as I had, surfing just for the love of it and entering a contest to win a trophy if they were lucky. Now it'd be all about coaching and training and surfing would be just like every other sport. It was another twenty years before professional surfing realised its folly and began holding events at proven locations at the right time of year.

I had one last laugh at the presentations, held at some swanky restaurant in Sydney. When they gave me the cheque for $600 I made my acceptance speech thanking everyone involved and finished off by saying I was donating my winnings to the Labor Party's re-election campaign. The surfers all went wild and all the executives of Coke went the same colour as one of their cans, all, that is, except for their general manager who quickly chimed in with "That speech was written, authorised and spoken by Nat Young on behalf of the Australian Labor Party". Everyone cracked up and the organisers of the contest breathed a sigh of relief. I was absolutely dead serious though. The Liberals had been in power for 23 years prior to Whitlam's election victory in 1972 and I was worried that the Liberals were going to get back in. I felt I had to do my bit, conscription was on the cards again and I already knew some heavy hitters in the Australian Labor Party (ALP) through my position over sand mining on the north coast beaches. I called one of Whitlam's secretaries, explaining my position, and he arranged a meeting with the Prime Minister when he was next available.

When I went to the Prime Minister's Sydney office, the first thing the secretary did was give me back my cheque, explaining that I was doing enough by voicing my feelings about the ALP and its policies. I was then introduced to Gough Whitlam and in the fifteen minutes before his next meeting we talked about a wide range of issues. The man had such a presence – it wasn't so much that he was tall and obviously strong, more that he was powerful but gentle. I'd never met anyone like him and melted like butter as I sat listening to his soft distinctive voice. I was already impressed by his vision for Australia but after that meeting I was sold completely. At the heart

NAA:M155,C7

I believed in Gough Whitlam and donated my $600 prize from the Coke contest to the Labor Party. As a result I was invited to deliver a speech at an election rally at the Sydney Opera House. I was in some extraordinary company: Patrick White, Lloyd Rees and Manning Clark.

NAA:M155,C7

of Gough's beliefs was a fair go for all Australians including the Aboriginals, but he also cared about the arts and saw the need to balance the demands of industry against caring for the environment, and of course he'd already abolished conscription. I loved what I was hearing, it was music to my ears and I just knew he deserved longer than the two years he'd been in office; the effects of his changes were only just beginning to be felt in the community.

Gough Whitlam invited me to speak at an ALP rally at the Opera House along with other prominent Australians: Patrick White, Mike Wenden, Kate Fitzpatrick and many others. When they showed me to my seat I was actually seated next to the great man in the front row centre stage. My friend Terry Purcell and I had written my speech the night before over dinner and a bottle or two of old Hunter red at Terry's house in Whale Beach. All I could really do was give a naive surfer's slant to the same points I'd talked about in Gough's office; halfway through my speech I lost my place but I tried not to stumble too obviously and finished by asking the people of Australia to vote the ALP back into office because they required more than two years to make the dreams of all of us become a reality. I was sure I was voicing the feelings of a lot of young people and Labor was swept back in until the Liberals got Gough Whitlam out of office using the powers of the Governor-General to force an election, which I regarded then – and still do now – as the lowest trick in the book.

*   *   *   *   *   *   *

No-one was allowed to use leg-ropes in the Coke contest. In 1972 the leg-rope, or leash, was invented by someone in America; made of either rubber or latex-covered rope tied to the ankle with cloth and the other end tied through a hole in the fin. Exactly who's responsible for the original leg-rope is a contentious issue but a guy named "Blinky" at William Dennis Surfboards in California is definitely one of the contenders for maker of the first "goon cord", as they were called. Just about all the top surfers frowned upon their use at first, but you didn't have to be a genius to see that they'd catch on, given time. The main reason I didn't like them was because they made thousands of surf-breaks available to surfers who'd previously been scared off these same breaks for fear of damaging both their bodies and their boards. I remember sitting with my friends Russell and Garth in the morning sun at Lennox Head back in the winter of 1972, soaking up the rays on the front of Garth's old car, and the conversation turning to leg-ropes simply because a surfer was putting one on right in front of us. That morning was just like any other; we'd driven as far as we could until the creek blocked us from driving any further on to Lennox Point. As we were all competent surfers, we were unanimous in our opinion that a leash was something Americans used for taking their dogs for a walk, not for going surfing with. Only a kook would use a leg-rope.

Our attitude to goon cords was shared by the majority of the surfing world in 1972 but the simple facts were that we were all attempting to surf deeper in the curl and like it or not every now and then we were all putting a foot wrong, getting knocked off and sometimes even hit by loose boards. I got hit in the neck by a board belonging to guy called John Pick at Lennox in 1972 – he took off on the outside of a wave and let his board go when I yelled at him for dropping in. I had to be carried from the water and driven up to Doc Spence in Casino, who decided to give it some time before operating. I went through years of back pain until acupuncture gave me some lasting relief. On a break like Lennox, having to fix dings after a surf was an everyday occurrence and I always carried resin and glass in my car and if necessary could put a fin back on and be back out in the line-up within half an hour. The point here is that fixing dings was a fact of life, something that happened to all surfers pre-1974. Anyway on this particular June morning, sheltering from the southerly wind in the company of good mates, our attention was distracted from the fast peeling curl to the antics of a newly arrived American named Bob Newlands. Looking extremely primeval, he was clambering on all fours over the rocks with a strap attached to his ankle and the other end tied to the fin. The rope dragging behind him was catching on every rock as he made his slow progress into the surf and when a set wave broke on top of him we almost all died laughing as he attempted to use it to launch from the rocks. Finally he made it and paddled out, taking off on a good-sized wave. As we expected he was wiped out after the first few turns but instead of having to swim after his board he climbed back on and went right back out for another wave, and another; in fact he surfed his brains out with never a thought for the rocks. Finally the penny dropped; who were the mugs here? It was a premonition of what was about to happen – it took a year or more but somewhere within that time frame of 1972–75, everyone started using leg-ropes all the time.

15

Back to the city

I WAS SURVIVING PRETTY MUCH month to month in 1975 – week to week to tell the real truth. It was weird not being under the same roof as Marilyn and the kids. I had my freedom but at what price? I was not a happy man most of the time with feelings of deep remorse causing radical mood swings that depressed me. I wound up spending most of my time with lots of different people from the eastern suburbs of Sydney, an interesting cross-section of city animals. It was a way of life totally foreign to me: staying out all night, getting up late, going for coffee at lunchtime and reading the papers before going to someone's house in the afternoon to get high and do it all over again. I knew I was wearing myself down but I really couldn't have cared less. It didn't matter where in the city I first opened my eyes, I'd lie there wide awake trying to get a feel for the ocean. I've always woken at dawn no matter where I am; it's totally instinctive, something I've been doing since I was nine years old and there's no way I'll ever be any different. Sometimes if I was really tired I hated myself for it, but no matter how big a night I may have had, I'm always awake at first light; "up there with Bobby Limb" as we used to say in the Collaroy days.

My lifestyle had changed so drastically since moving back to Sydney that at times I hardly recognised myself. Whenever I was running low on money I'd come down to earth and head back over the Sydney Harbour Bridge to Mona Vale to make some more boards. Basically I was partying hard and working only as much as was necessary to keep my head above water – anything to take my mind off the failure of my marriage. Luckily all of the surf shops where I sold boards were owned by friends who'd either pay me cash or pay within thirty days, so I always had a few dollars in my pocket. It became a regular pattern: shape and finish the custom orders then build half a dozen stock boards for the shops. After that I could think about getting the hell out of the city or full-on into it. Most times I wouldn't make it up the coast, a party in the city or out on the Peninsula would trap me and I'd drive around daydreaming about

DICK

At times I hardly recognised myself.

special places on the farm or zone out at traffic lights thinking about the beauty of a rain squall over Lennox Head. I could see and feel the raindrops beating all around me, the rainbow after the storm had passed and the sun coming out – my heart was still surfing the north coast and wandering the farm that had been such a huge part of my life for the past five years.

In a good year the cyclone season starts in December and like dedicated surfers everywhere I keep a constant eye on weather maps. When the map showed an intense low-pressure system off Noosa, I made a phone call to a mate up there to confirm that it was creating good waves and left Sydney inside an hour. I didn't even stop at the farm; I needed to ride a real wave. Arriving at the Gold Coast about an hour before last light, I slipped into some shorts and paddled out on my brand-new 6-foot 8-inch pintail to ride a few crisp little curls at Kirra before it got too dark to see. I could feel the potential in the swell even though it was only 2 feet and the new board felt smooth and positive but a bit too stiff for the size of the wave I was riding. However, I reckoned that within the next few days with the swells from the same direction it had to get bigger. It made me tingle just to think about it and I decided to stay on the coast overnight and see what happened the following morning.

Sitting out the back waiting on the sets, I got talking to a local surfer I'd known vaguely for many years and towards the end of our conversation he mentioned a party in Bilambil that night. At the time it sounded like fun and something to do. I booked into a room at the Kirra Hotel, right across the street from the surf, and went downstairs to have a few pre-party beers with the guy and his mates. The party was nothing special though it had its moments. I tried to chat up one of the pretty young girls but all she did was giggle. There was plenty of dope, cold beer and the odd bottle of Jack Daniels floating around and some interesting older surfers to talk to. I was relaxed and having a pretty good time when I heard the police burst through the front door at around midnight. I must have been really stoned or drunk because I freaked and ran, but got nabbed along with a young guy and his girlfriend trying to escape through a back window. After an hour or two in the cells at Tweed Heads, a detective asked me about the night's events and I told him what I knew of them. He put me back in the lockup without comment. During the long, cold hours in the cell, I noticed the weather was getting even more cyclonic, with torrential downpours every half hour or so.

It was around three in the morning when the same detective offered to give me a ride back to the hotel and I jumped at the chance – my car was miles away at Bilambil. When we got to my hotel the copper said he just needed to make a routine check of my room and with nothing to hide I agreed and went upstairs with him. Then to my horror, the walloper opened my toilet bag, producing two bottles he said contained hash oil, and the nightmare began. I was taken to Coolangatta police station, charged, and put in a big open-sided cell not 100 metres from the waves I'd been riding that evening.

All weekend I lay there, listening to the storm moving over the Gold Coast and the howl of the wind as it swung from hard onshore to offshore and the deafening roar of breaking waves. In retrospect I think the sound of the waves zippering along the sandbar was all that kept me sane. I went into a trance, eating no food, and everything was a clean, clear white light and I could take off and get tubed on every peeling barrel. Mind-surfing saved my life that weekend and I reckon I was fortunate that the police station was so close to the beach. I felt as though I'd been surfing for days without rest and was totally thrashed by Monday morning when the detective took me to Southport courthouse for the pre-trial hearing on a charge of supplying a prohibited substance. As the police car passed Kirra Point I snuck a fleeting glance over my shoulder at perfect 6-foot tubes – Kirra was going off. In court, anxiety over my position made me bite a hole in my bottom lip. I told the magistrate I'd be pleading not guilty and was granted bail to appear for trial in Brisbane in six weeks time.

Back in Sydney the work had piled up during my absence and there was a backlog of orders for both custom and shop boards. The activity was another lifesaver – the constant work helped keep my mind off my predicament, and I was definitely over the city party scene after what had happened on my last night out. I pulled my head in and kept a low profile and Marilyn generously let me stay with her until my strength and self-confidence returned.

* * * * * * *

Since the beginning of that summer I'd been running a surf school, teaching ocean safety and surfing to hundreds of kids of all ages, a full-on commitment with morning and evening sessions seven days a week. I also trained and employed three instructors on Warringah Shire Council's behalf, so the surf school was getting my full attention. It was an original idea that I'd worked at long and hard and to my knowledge was the first of its kind in Australia, and probably in the world. Every lesson was written out in detail explaining to instructors exactly what they had to say and do and a water-safety assistant watched over all the classes while they were out in the water in case of an emergency. Building the right boards was relatively easy; each instructor was supplied with a big tandem board on which he took the raw beginners out one at a time and made their first surf experience a memorable one.

I had to work with the Council because as an individual the necessary permits were too hard to obtain and the necessary insurance was ridiculously expensive. The only way I could pull it off and get through all the red tape was to convince Warringah Council that they needed a surf school; that way I could utilise their insurance and they'd handle all the bookings and paperwork. I got to keep all the money after expenses, but because it was being run as a community service the fees were, in my opinion at least, far too cheap. The Council advertised the school in local newspapers and to every school in the district and the response was phenomenal. We were booked out for the whole summer and the Council was getting brownie points for offering such a unique and innovative service to its ratepayers. I was very proud of the whole deal and I know a lot of the councillors felt the same. However, as soon as the Warringah Shire Council heard I'd been busted they immediately suspended me from the project. I felt really hurt; surely I was innocent until proven guilty? Even scores of students' letters and a local newspaper's editorialising couldn't convince the Council that it should think again and the school was put under the control of a young man picked by the Council.

Unbeknown to me, the father of one of the surf-school students was a successful book publisher. The day after my suspension, he called me up totally out of the blue, to say how fantastic the course had been for both his son's and his own surfing, then asked if I'd be interested in putting out a book on how to ride a surfboard. I was flabbergasted. One door opens as another closes, is what my Mum would have said, and I jumped at the offer.

With all the work I'd done in preparing the courses for the school, I'd just about completed a book on the subject. If I bundled all my notes and diagrams together and included the practical experiences that the school had taught me over the past few months, then I'd have something. Reworking the manuscript gave me something constructive to do and allowed me to look at the practicalities of teaching people to cope with an environment alien to many and frightening to some. A.H. & A.W. Reed published the manuscript as *Nat Young's Book Of Surfing* in 1976 and it sold out within twelve months. Instead of doing a reprint I decided to self-publish the manuscript as *Surfing Fundamentals*, now in its fifth printing, which has made me a few dollars and taught thousands of people of all ages how to surf.

* * * * * * *

The court case following the prohibited substance charge was like live theatre and would have been a good drama to watch except that it was me up there on stage. Everything I said would be critical to my future and my freedom and I was terrified. Soon after the pre-trial hearing I'd engaged a solicitor and a barrister from Brisbane recommended by friends as the best outside Sydney. If I'd used Sydney counsel, it would have added thousands to the cost as the trial dragged on for twelve long days. I couldn't stay in Brisbane because seeing and feeling the ocean was really important to me in this time of crisis. Every day after court, I'd drive to the Gold Coast and even if there were no waves I'd paddle out to sit out the back and think about what I'd do if I was sentenced to ten years in jail for a crime I didn't commit. Gloomy thoughts raced through my head: "It happens to lots of people, you've read books about them."; "You have to be prepared for the worst."

Another activity I found very beneficial was spending an hour or two chanting with my old friend Ted Spencer and the Gold Coast Hare Krishnas. The melodic repetition was such a relief after the tension and anxiety of the courtroom and I felt revitalised after each session. Marilyn went with me and her continued support during this period was fantastic. Having a shoulder to cry on and someone with whom I could discuss the day-to-day progress of the case meant the world to me. Despite Marilyn's attempts to keep our marriage afloat on our eventual return to Sydney, I made it difficult by constantly running off to the city while she was either at work teaching or home with our children and we decided to separate.

The court case continued, both sides giving their version of the "events of the night of the 9th of December 1975". I knew that my version was the truth, but would the jury believe it? I certainly wasn't confident, especially when the prosecutor ripped me to bits in his summing up. The biggest flaw in the prosecution case was a very suspect unsigned record of interview in which I admitted to the events described by the police. Then the jury came back with the "not guilty" verdict and it was all over. My first sensation was one of weightlessness and it lasted for weeks. My faith in the system had been restored and my confidence in human nature had been totally resurrected by the jury. I'd been tried by my peers and found not guilty of the police accusations.

That winter back in Sydney, after a constant flow of letters from satisfied students, Warringah Shire Council agreed to take me back the following summer – but not as director of the surf school. I'd have to work instead as an instructor under the same Council man who'd been given my position the season before. I told them very politely where to stick their job and arranged a meeting with the

Mayor of Waverley Council, Ernie Page. I'd met him at a dinner party at Jackie Kelly's house some years before.

Ernie was sympathetic and very positive, giving me the rights to use Bondi for my surf school for as long as I wanted, with no talk of a fee for using the beach. He told me he considered it an honour and a great opportunity for his shire. Waverley's attitude was so different from that of Warringah. The classes went very well, though Bondi wasn't as good a beach for teaching as Collaroy and we were forced to show surf movies in the Surf Club when the sea was too rough, which was about 30 per cent of the time. A lot of parents sent their kids along and even Kerry Packer enrolled both his children. My only problem was with the amount of travelling I had to do every day: driving from the Peninsula to Bondi took over an hour, even at five in the morning; then it was back to Mona Vale to shape surfboards; returning to Bondi for the afternoon classes before heading home again. I sometimes stayed with friends in the city but it was pretty heavy going and I was getting run-down again. I just couldn't go on burning the candle at both ends without something starting to give.

At one trendy media function around this period I met a lot of the staff of Double J – a new, taxpayer-funded youth radio station and the hottest in Sydney. I was already a committed Double J listener, partly because it didn't carry advertising but more so because, unlike the commercial stations, its playlist was varied. I'd become sick to death of hearing the same songs repeated every hour while shaping boards. Double J also had a policy of giving new Australian bands their first airplay and played tons of music not in the mainstream and not pushed by the record companies for that reason. Unbiased news reporting, uncut interviews with a cross-section of people (including one with me on my drug bust) – Double J's quality programming and the attitude of the people who worked there were inspirational and I loved it.

Since its inception in 1975, Double J had been running a surf report by two surfing eccentrics: Phil Jarrett, then editor of *Tracks*, who delivered his report without getting out of his bed in Whale Beach; and Craig "Legrope" Leggat, who later became one of my best friends. At the time of the party Craig had quit Double J to enter an ashram – where he found his destiny was to follow a formal training in law. He is now a barrister and the station was looking for someone to replace him. Over a couple of stiff drinks I convinced the then program manager that I was their man, someone who could talk with authority about surf-related topics and give an entertaining but accurate rundown of conditions at Sydney's metropolitan beaches. They wanted me to start right away and not wait for summer – surfers ride waves all year around they said, so why stop in winter? Double J's attitude to surf reports changed the attitudes of program managers at every commercial radio station in the country.

I got stuck right into this new job and the money was good for the actual hours that I worked. First thing every morning I drove around the beaches on the north side and put in a phone call to a contact who'd done the same on the south side. I'd then sit down and write up the conditions, adding a few witty comments that, hopefully, would light up the switchboard. At the scheduled time, I'd call the station and deliver my report on cue; it sometimes took a few tries to get through, but that was basically it. Surf reporting was also good for my surfing, giving me an inside track on the daily condition of the sandbanks and swell. Often I'd race back and get in a surf before the first report went to air. Sometimes in the water I'd run into other surfers who'd thank me for the tip they'd heard on the radio. At other times locals would tell me to shut up about their home break and not let the cat out of the bag ever again. Like most things, there was a bit of positive and a bit of negative response.

One definite positive was that the reports gave me an opportunity to draw attention to the pollution on the beaches. This was back in the days before the Sydney Water Board had successfully sold its deep-ocean outfall to the public. Everyone was talking about the state of the beaches and sometimes the raw sewage at Bondi and Manly was disgusting, especially when the wind was from the east. This happened was just about every day that summer when I held my surf schools there. I'd go on air choking and gasping and pretending to spew and tell the listeners about the abundance of "brown trouts" in the shore-break at Bondi and that going in the water at these beaches was like surfing in the toilet bowl. Although it was all said laughingly, I was serious as I chatted with the on-air jock. We gave them shit about the shit, which was right in line with Double J policy. It was a fun time, hanging out with the disc jockeys, getting loaded on air at times and going to all the media parties.

I moved into a big modern house, right on the beach at North Avalon, which I shared with an American schoolteacher. He was nice and easy to live with, as I've found most Americans to be, and he didn't mind having my kids around every weekend. Things were running pretty smoothly for a change.

* * * * * * *

The similarities between skiing, skateboarding and surfing fascinated me and I'd started to write about the principle of the "fall line" as it applied to all three. The face of every slope – whether it's snow, water, cement or air (as in hang gliding) – has a path that's the quickest route to the bottom. As you go down that path, your speed increases, and manoeuvres, or turns if you like, are made to either increase or decrease your speed down the slope. If your body doesn't stay "pressed down" during these turns, you'll spin out. I found that it's perfectly natural to breathe out when applying downward pressure during a turn and before making the next, you need to take a deep breath before applying the pressure again – effectively increasing and decreasing your weight. The speed a rider reaches down the fall line can be increased by making the turns less acute, or decreased by turning sharply across the slope or back up the wave face. My experience with the surf schools showed me that you have to reach a reasonable level of competence to appreciate the similarities between these sports. In the old days, skiers were taught to turn leaning out of the slope, with a body position very different from the one used by surfers. Nowadays both sports use exactly the same body position, leaning into the turns, whether you're using two edges or four. Certainly two edges are better on ice or hard-packed snow but in soft snow and water, one edge is sufficient to carve a turn.

I had a dream… I could see a movie with images running on top of one another, turning people on to the real story about all these sports, and I started to gather material I thought would be useful. Alby Falzon gave me a copy of the main sequence of myself from his movie *Morning of the Earth*; Paul Witzig had a work print of the *Hot Generation* sequence of me at Bells and to have a snow element to fade into or flop the surfing and skiing with, my old friend Mike Doyle sent me a copy of a short movie he'd made of himself single-skiing in deep powder snow. When I looked at the footage I was really excited as I knew it'd do the trick, but I really had little idea exactly what the next step should be.

Someone put me in touch with David Lourie, an avant-garde American film maker living on the Peninsula, and when I told him about my ideas he became very enthusiastic; almost within days we were renting some editing time to lay up the dissolves of the surfing and skiing images to see if my ideas worked. When the first prints came back we knew we were on the right track. The Australian Film Commission, set up by Whitlam's Labor Government to help develop Australian cinema, offered assistance in the form of interest-free loans that were non-repayable if the film failed to make a profit. I applied to the Commission for assistance and after a few weeks got a letter back giving me a date for my first interview. I spent as much time as I could putting all my ideas down on paper, complete with a dialogue that I'd lay down over the final image. I had a storyboard showing each shot that we'd need to take and with the help of the assessors at the interview did

I was playing around with film in these days
and I had a dream of making a movie about
the similarity between surfing, skiing, and
skateboarding.

Frames from Fall Line.
This wave has no
name but naturally
it's not where it
appears to be in the
movie. Wayne
Lynch and I almost
drowned leaping off
the cliff near Port
Lincoln, but the shot
really worked.

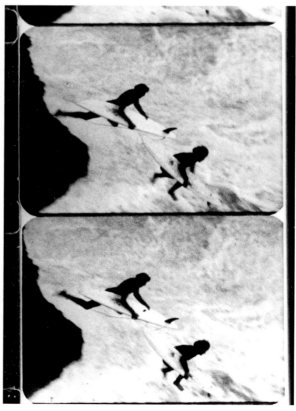

a rough estimate of costs. The next interview was much more casual, the same three assessors, people from the film industry, were there and after we'd completed the formal part of the interview and the five-minute rough-cut was up on the screen, I pulled out a big joint and we smoked it right there in the theatre. I was granted $31,796 over several stages to complete the 45-minute documentary called *Fall Line*, the first payment of $5,000 was to develop the script and at each new stage I had to submit my work for assessment before I received the next payment. It was going to take time and I realised how little I actually had down on paper and how much more I needed before we could even start shooting.

At least the surfing sequence was all planned; what I intended to do was take a top-class water and land cameraman down to Wayne Lynch's part of Victoria. I'd spoken to Wayne and he was prepared to work on it, partly from friendship and partly because it'd be an accurate documentation of a lot of things we'd talked about for many years. He was also well aware that at some stage down the track the sequence would give him a perfect reference to show potential sponsors. The working title of the sequence was "A day in the life" and, as its name implies, it went into every detail of a surfer's day from waking up to getting nailed by a big southern monster. It was extremely difficult to shoot, thanks to the fickle weather around Victoria's Cape Otway area and it took three trips of two weeks to get in the can.

I wrote the scenes very dramatically, overplaying not only the roles of Wayne and myself, but the situations also, to make it look even more terrifying than it would normally be. The beautiful big barrels seen in the final surfing sequence were taken at a spot far away from the jumping-off-the-cliff shots at the beginning of the film. That jumping sequence was filmed where no-one in their right mind would ever surf. It is sheer cliff-face with big waves pounding straight into it and I had to really talk hard to convince Wayne to jump with me. He knew the dangers only too well and respected the Southern Ocean far more than his 26 years might suggest. However, because I knew that on film everything looks so much flatter and less dramatic, I wanted to shoot it at that location and it turned out to be one of the best sequences in the movie – but I reckon we're lucky that we lived to talk about it. From duck-diving under waves and watching the boils coming down to being pummelled underwater after a wipe-out, I wrote every cut. All were situations any good surfer has experienced a thousand times, but no-one had taken movies of that aspect of surfing up till then. The photographer I used for the water shots was an expatriate American named Jack McCoy. He was big and powerful, with a good eye with a water camera, and he'd just finished a surf movie with his partner and was keen for the work. At that stage I wasn't sure of how the expenses would pan out overall, I'd never done any film-production work before, but Jack said he'd shoot the sequence for nothing, provided he could use the footage at some time in a movie of his own. It sounded like a pretty good idea at the time but in retrospect it was one of the silliest things I've ever done – Jack released a short film called *A day in the life of Wayne Lynch*, using all the same shots in the same sequence as *Fall Line*, months before my film was finished. In a curt letter from the director of the Australian Film Commission I was asked for an explanation, which I gave, and after an interview with me, the director's comment was that it had happened because of my ignorance of film production. Most movies go over budget he said and I could have asked for more funds if I found myself short. I had no real contract with McCoy, except for an understanding of what was right and fair and I felt like a fool. He even used David Lourie to edit his film, which was the end of my relationship with David. People would call to tell me how great they thought my surfing was in Jack's new movie and I'd just shake my head. Even Wayne didn't understand why I was so pissed off with Jack McCoy. I was a mug, but I like to think I learnt some valuable lessons from that experience.

Back in Sydney I started to shoot the skateboarding sequences I'd written. David Lourie was still working with me at this stage, both editing and filming. He was a dedicated skateboarder and squash player and through these sports had met a girl named Ti Deaton, from Palm Beach, whose parents had a squash court at their house. David often played squash and skateboarded with Ti and he suggested that I take a look at her as a possible girl for the skateboarding sequence. Our filming had momentarily stalled while we looked for just the right girl – someone tall, blonde and beautiful who could also skate wasn't easy to find, so I thought it wouldn't do any harm to give her a try.

Right from the minute I saw Ti skate I knew she was the girl for the part. We took her to a steep hill in North Avalon and she leapt right out and launched into it. Ti looked older than her nineteen years and her face seemed much too worldly, but she had one of the most genuinely radiant smiles I'd ever seen. She would literally light up every time I spoke to her and with her flowing blonde hair and beautiful lean body, the package was complete. We started to shoot the skateboarding sequences and I got to know her better and every day I found myself counting down the hours till we met – as far as I was concerned, Ti was just too good to be true. I decided I'd ask her out to dinner although I was living with a girl I'd met in the city party scene who now lived at Whale Beach with her daughter. It was

a mutually beneficial agreement with a bit of lust but no love whatsoever; OK for a few weeks but I was keen to get out as soon as the
time was right.

* * * * * * *

At least a year before the events outlined above, I'd still been living
at Marilyn's place in Bungan where I used to sit at the dining-room
table making my notes on the fall line similarities between surfing,
skiing and skateboarding. I remember one day I heard an incredibly
powerful swish, like a giant maggie dive-bombing the house.
Running out onto the newly completed balcony I saw my first hang-
glider less than 50 feet above me; a colourful mass of nylon riding on
the air current created by the wind blowing up the cliff face, pene-
trating that thin line enough to be able to pull around and drive back
the other way. That was it, another fall line sport and I had to learn
to do it. I bought myself a kite and helmet and started gliding down
the front of sandhills. It was still the same fall line principle, carving
turns to either speed up or slow down, but the top of a cliff isn't as
forgiving when hit as snow or water are. I remember the first time I
flew off the cliff at Long Reef. I was so excited that it all actually
worked, pulling the bar in or out to lose or gain height and feeling
the air behave in essentially the same way as water.

Late one afternoon I let my mind wander and was imagining
myself to be an eagle, soaring the cliffs looking for food, and then it
happened: I'd penetrated the area of lift as much as possible and was
just swinging around into a normal turn when I missed a change in
the wind direction and the kite dropped like a stone. I pulled back
on the bar to increase my speed, hoping I'd gain enough velocity to
pull out but there wasn't enough room between me and the top of
the cliff and like a shot duck, I plummeted at full speed into it. As I
stood up all the other pilots came running and, thank goodness,
someone had the presence of mind to grab me before I fell hundreds
of feet to certain death on the lee side of the headland. I was dazed
and my head was spinning, but at least the helmet had saved my
noggin. One of the guys drove me to hospital where I was treated
for a broken toe and a sore spine, but no-one could mend my shattered ego and I never flew hang-gliders again.

Technically, the accident was caused by a tailwind stall, the wind
had shifted without my perceiving the change, but I wasn't to realise
this until years later when I obtained my pilot's licence. The hang-
gliding sequences are the most majestic in the movie. Shot over
many trips at a place called Stanwell Park – the Waimea Bay of
Australian cliff soaring – we had really talented pilots pushing the

kites to the limits in excessively steep manoeuvres to emphasise the similarities with the ground-based fall line sports. Ti, who had now become an integral part of the movie, even went up in a double kite. She looked so good in the skateboarding sequence it seemed a smart idea to have her following the fall line into another sport.

I was falling in love with this girl who liked to do all the same things as I did and it was obvious she enjoyed doing them with me, but I was carrying some pretty heavy baggage around; I was ten years older with two kids and a marriage that still hadn't been formally dissolved. But Ti had a wisdom beyond her years and it just didn't seem to faze her. The most unusual thing about Ti was that she wouldn't smoke dope with me, or even have a drink. All my other girlfriends did and I found it helped loosen things up, made talking easy and heightened sex. However, without the aid of any drug we'd talk at great length about all sorts of topics from religion to having children and if I pulled out a racehorse to get a little stoned, Ti would ask me why I needed it. Was I afraid of something? It wasn't long before the amount of marijuana I smoked declined.

Ti grew to love my kids – it took all of ten minutes – and it was a love that would last. We were really fortunate and when I hear other people's stories of stepmothers and fathers and the hate in some families I shudder to think of the way it could have been. Naomi was five years old, a beautiful little blonde princess bursting with self-confidence either on the beach or out in the water and Beau, at two and a half was very shy and still in nappies. He'd had a bad experience down at Whale Beach the year before when he'd crawled away from Marilyn and down into the shore-break where he'd been cleaned up by a wave and for a few minutes it was thought he'd drowned. Beau was terrified of the water for this reason and the person who cured him of his terror was Ti. Her house fronted onto "kiddies' corner" at Palm Beach and over the 1978 summer she patiently reintroduced him to playing in the ocean and eventually the shore-break. I was really happy for them both; I'd tried but all I got was frantic scratching at my shoulder and high-pitched screams the minute Beau saw I was headed for the ocean.

Also during that summer, Ti and I did the St John's Ambulance first-aid certificate course in preparation for joining the volunteer ski patrol at Thredbo or Perisher. I wanted to put into practice all the things I'd written about the similarity between surfing and skiing and hopefully by spending the season working in the snow I'd get an idea of the right times and locations to finish shooting the final sequences for *Fall Line*. I'd bought a utility with a camper on the back and before the first snows came I drove down to the mountains and left it on a permanent site half way up the road to Perisher. The

My darling Ti when I first met her, how could I not fall in love? Ti's brother Rik took the shot above. An editor friend suggested I talk to her about the skateboarding sequence in Fall Line and the rest is history.

best thing about the ski patrol was that you had to have your boots on by 8 a.m. and you covered the miles checking signs and snow fences. It was good for my skiing and brought me up to the same standard as Ti who'd been fortunate in having parents who skied and who had her skiing almost from the time she could first stand up. Ti had to be in Sydney during the week and I used this time to work on my technique.

I met an Austrian ski instructor named Franz Pickler who took me skiing with him, saying he'd show me how to turn properly. Franz told me to sit in behind him so that he wouldn't have to shout too hard to make himself heard and then we were off, picking up speed as we headed down the fall line at Mt Perisher. Franz told me to let all my breath go as I turned, then in, out, in, out; from the bumps to the open, groomed slopes, fast and slow breathing. Franz had never heard of me and he'd never been surfing, but he proved to me that my theory was valid.

Living in the snow made me more aware of the ties that bound the fall line sports. The crunching sound made when you walked up a snow slope and the squeak of the sand on a beach; the ripples left on the shore by the receding tide and the incredible perfection of a snowflake; the freedom of running all over a surfboard compared to being anchored by tight-fitting boots to your skis. Each was beautiful in its own way.

To fill in the time while Ti was away in Sydney, I took a job picking up glasses at the Valley Inn Hotel and it brought me into contact with a lot of people that I'd never have otherwise met. While working one day I met the head of the Professional Ski Patrol who said he'd noticed my skiing ability improve and was I interested to try out for a vacancy with them. I was dead keen as the only real difference I could see between the pros and the volunteers was that the pros got paid. Ti was the volunteer assigned to me, I was her boss so to speak, which was ridiculous as she skied better and was more competent at first aid than I was – and the few serious accidents we attended proved it.

Towards the end of the season I had the whole thing tightly scripted and it was time to go. I left the ski patrol and flew back to Sydney to organise a cameraman and film stock. I figured a talented boy and girl who were very much in love and shit-hot skiers would give a really nice feel to the snow segment. Somebody told me about a good-looking model called Jane Buckland who could ski and when I rang the number, her sister Kate answered. Jane was out but I told Kate my problem and she said she could do it with her boyfriend Randy Wieman. They were going to be down in the mountains for the professional freestyle ski tour and we could shoot it around that time. I drove over to the eastern suburbs to meet Kate Buckland and see what she looked like, and in five minutes she'd convinced me they could do it without any problem. Kate was extremely confident, we made a deal and she stuck to it right to the end. To finalise the deal I also shook hands with Randy, who was serious, dark and not really tall, but good looking and very much in love with Kate.

I next contacted the management at Perisher to get the use of a Sno-cat to ferry the equipment and cameraman to the different locations I had scouted. It was a perfect contra-deal – good for Perisher good for me, not to mention that I'd just worked for them the month before and knew all the best locations for the shots. Perisher quoted me $5,000 a day for the cat and no rebate on accommodation, so I put in a call to the mountain manager at Thredbo. There the attitude was totally different – no problem with a cat or accommodation, so we were going to Thredbo. I didn't know the valley as well as I knew Perisher and spent a week having a good look around before realising that Thredbo was twice the valley Perisher would ever be. And so we started shooting.

Ti was helping out by running the cameraman around on a ski-doo to get the tight "point of view" shots and we had a couple of hang-gliders on standby to ride the fall line with the skiers. Everything was going smoothly. We took the Sno-cat up to the top of Thredbo before dawn to get shots of Kate doing some ballet routines in that incredible low light and saw a white fox halfway up the mountain. The freestyle competition was very dramatic, with Randy tumbling through the air off the jumps and knocking them dead in bumps – he was a true champion and became a very good friend. Our cameraman was the only casualty: looking with one eye down the barrel of the lens all day, he got acute snowblindness and Ti spent the next twelve hours bathing and dressing his eye.

I'd heard about "surfboards" for the snow. Called Wintersticks, they'd been invented by Dimitrie Milovich in Salt Lake City, Utah. While we were filming, the manufacturers of the popular sweet called Lifesavers phoned me as they wanted a completely different commercial shot in the snow. I convinced their advertising agency that Wintersticks were the way to go then contacted Mr Milovich and got him to send four of the boards out to Australia. We shot the ad with no problems other than Ti landing on her back on the hard pack. Shooting in such short grabs you couldn't see the limitations of the Wintersticks, but when we used them to shoot some footage for *Fall Line*, it soon became obvious that with no edges, the boards were virtually useless in the harder snow conditions, but at least the body movements were the same. Dimitrie was onto something however – he fathered the snowboard.

Back in North Sydney the editing proved long and tedious, with the days turning into weeks and then into three months. All this time the editor and I were locked in a baking little room trying to keep the flow of the movie and stick to the script. Issues kept coming up to stretch the budget, mostly re-shooting interviews or re-recording my voice-overs. The music was one element that had been going smoothly right from the beginning. We had a talented composer working with us who was also a music lecturer at the Sydney Conservatorium and he wrote each section of music when we had the relevant sequence rough-cut, then delivered the track to us for the final edit. Then just by chance I happened to meet the black blues guitarist Taj Mahal after his Sydney concert in August 1978. I told him his version of the traditional *Fishin' Blues* said a lot about going surfing and asked if I could buy the rights to the track for *Fall Line*. Taj sold me the rights to *Fishin' Blues* and one other original piece (that unfortunately wasn't used for the movie) for $2,000, but I should have used more self-control as it was money that hadn't been budgeted for. I asked the Film Commission for more money but they politely turned me down, leaving me with the feeling that they were still feeling a bit toey over the Jack McCoy business. I only needed a few grand to finish the whole thing the way I wanted to, so I played my last card and sold the rest of the cattle off the farm. The cattle were sold at a substantial loss but I finally completed *Fall Line*.

16

Hurry slowly
...and finish what you start

OVER THE COURSE of the next twelve months I learnt that it's one thing to make a movie but quite another to sell it, especially a documentary. There must be hundreds of really good docos made with Film Commission assistance that didn't get a commercial release, sitting around in the vaults gathering dust. *Fall Line* was 48 minutes in total, made to fit into a one-hour time slot on commercial television. The budget allowed for the design and printing of a quality brochure so I was well-armed to market our product. Thanks to my high profile, all the television stations in Sydney were prepared to have a look at *Fall Line* but to my amazement the only one that made a reasonable offer was the ABC or "Aunty" as it's affectionately known. The ABC didn't run commercials and would have preferred my movie to run the full hour, but they still purchased *Fall Line* for one run all over the country.

The feedback was very positive, so the program director asked me to come in and discuss the fee for running it a second and third time. He told me that he'd sent off a memo recommending that the ABC's New Zealand equivalent take a close look at *Fall Line*. Subsequently we made our first international sale six weeks after the movie was finished. I was on a roll and it was really exciting. Someone in the know at the Australian Film Commission gave me contact names at a TV station in Italy and another in Switzerland and after thinking it through, I reckoned they might be interested in *Fall Line*. Skiing was almost a national pastime in both countries and they might appreciate a film giving a different slant to the sport. I had demo tapes made, packaging them up with nice letters and the brochure, and sent them off and within a few weeks both countries came back with reasonable offers. I couldn't believe how easy it seemed; *Fall Line* was getting close to covering its costs and I hadn't even looked at the States.

I changed houses three times during this period without leaving the Peninsula, ending up on the still-water side of Palm Beach sharing a house with an old mate from Queensland. It was great having

Wayne Lynch back in '76. In my opinion he is still one of the finest tube riding technicians in the world. Jack McCoy shot this sequence on Wayne's home turf in Victoria.

a house right on Pittwater because it meant I could have my 16-foot Hobiecat right at the back door. Ti and I had a great summer together, sailing whenever the wind was up and surfing at "Palmy" or "Whaley" when it wasn't. Ti had sailed with her cousin a bit, but I was a complete novice before I bought the cat and made some terrible mistakes learning to sail, the most obvious of them being trying to ride waves way beyond my expertise or the boat's capabilities. I broke two masts that summer, after getting caught while trying to ride waves on the cat as if it were a surfboard.

I had another memorable accident on the still-water side. Ti and I were having a great time, both of us out on the trapeze driving the boat as hard at possible as it flew along up on one hull, when a particularly strong gust pitch-poled us completely in relatively shallow water. We both flew around the front of the mast; I landed right on top of Ti and when we came to our senses we found the mast speared 5 feet into the mud. We spent hours trying to free it from the bottom but couldn't get it to budge. I was standing there, cursing and swearing on one hull with a line over the other. Ti was stretched out with me, giving me extra leverage. We were just about to give up completely and swim to shore for help, when a large wooden-hulled vessel glided to within a few metres of us and someone resembling a dark-bearded pirate threw me a line, telling me to dive under and attach it to the base of the mast. I had no better ideas so I did what I was told. Within minutes the boat had been winched free and was sitting there on the water, bobbing up and down as if nothing had happened. The pirate invited us on board *Duen*, as his boat was called, and while he introduced us to the crew, he made Ti a hot drink, gave me a slug of the captain's whisky and rolled a joint.

Their story was that Mum (Dotty), Dad (Albert) and their numerous kids were sailing around the world. A few years before they'd been farming somewhere in the inland United States when one day they decided they'd had enough. They sold the farm and flew to Scandinavia where they bought an old fishing boat, which they converted into the beautiful three-masted schooner *Duen*. I was really impressed by the family and their big, comfortable ship on which they all had to work constantly to maintain the hull. Albert was good with engines and Dotty kept everyone fed. Ti and I spent a fair bit of time on *Duen* over the next few days as it was such an inspirational space to hang around in. It came up in conversation that captain Albert was the brother of Herbie Fletcher, a surfing friend of mine in California and that brought home to me what a small place the world really is.

This was a period of acute petrol shortages in Sydney and I'd finished half a dozen boards for a friend's shop in Bondi, but had no way to get them to him. One evening over a sunset drink Albert suggested that we sail them down to Sydney. Neither Ti nor I had ever sailed on anything like *Duen* so we were delighted to go for the day. With a stiff westerly wind and almost no swell, we cruised down the coast within one and a half kilometres of the shoreline and delivered the boards into the arms of my friend waiting on the dock, sailing back that afternoon when the sea breeze came up. A highlight of the trip for me was the sight of a 5 or 6 metre tiger shark cruising on the surface as we passed through the Heads, still the biggest shark I've ever seen. With no noisy motor to scare them, it was possible to get really close to sea creatures such as the shark and I remarked to Ti how wonderful it was. With very little to-do *Duen* left Australia and when I next checked with Herbie, she was back in Hawaii after spending a couple of years sailing the South Pacific Islands. Apparently the family was planning to sell *Duen* and buy another farm.

For me it was also time to leave Australia and get on with trying to sell *Fall Line* in the United States. According to everybody I spoke to in the film business, the only place that I'd make any real money with my movie was the States and the Film Commission told me to go and do it, as the trip was a legitimate marketing expense. It felt weird arriving in California with two big cans of 16 millimetre film under my arm instead of a surfboard, but I was on a similar mission – I was going to ride this wave and it would either close-out or be a screamer. I stayed with my Swiss friend Max at Malibu and surfed every day out in front of his house, no matter what the conditions were like. For the rest of the time I hogged Max's phone, calling television stations and agents in Hollywood and Los Angeles, trying to get them interested enough to give me an appointment to show *Fall Line*. I got a couple of nibbles but the doors stayed closed and I was starting to get depressed. After the first few days I ran out of contacts and began sending off sample tapes and brochures to companies picked out of the phone book, then sat round waiting for calls that never came. I needed my girl's shoulder to cry on; I missed Ti.

Ti had arrived in America a month before me in order to go on a pre-planned rafting trip down the Colorado River. Ti, her mother and brother and 25 students from the University of Southern California, had planned to spend three days drifting between the spectacular walls of the Grand Canyon. Unfortunately all of them, apart from Ti's mother and brother, had to be carried out at the other end and spent a day in Mojave General Hospital, flat on their backs with drips in their arms, with the notifiable disease *shigella*, which they'd caught from drinking river water. Ti's older brother Rik was completing a course in business studies at USC and lived across the bay from the port of Long Beach in a unique part of Los

Ti with her Mum and
brother Rik rafted down
the Colorado River in
1979. It was the height
of summer in the
magnificent Grand
Canyon.

Angeles called San Pedro. San Pedro's population was 90 per cent Mexican which gave it terrific character, great restaurants and affordable housing for students like Rik. Ti and her mother stayed with Rik until Ti was feeling better and she had to carry an emergency number for the US Health Department, who had to be contacted if any of the symptoms recurred.

Not until Ti was well and truly back on the road to recovery did she actually stay a night with me in Malibu, but from that moment on, it seemed my luck changed for the better. The first sign of interest came from a company called Churchill Films, a small distributor to the education market. After six weeks without seeing any light, this little glimmer represented a major step forward. Robert Churchill, the elderly owner of the company, rang me to say he liked the demo tape I'd sent and after a few minutes of small talk, he made an appointment for us to call on him at his office.

Max was away on business a lot and he'd given me the use of his Porsche to get around, so with the aid of a street directory Ti and I made our way to Hollywood and Robert Churchill's office where he offered me a good price for a shorter version. The next day in Churchill's editing suite, Robert and I marked up the cuts to make a snappy seventeen-minute version of *Fall Line*. I felt great; if nothing else, I at least had an American sale and a few dollars to live on in California. The fact that I'd had to cut the length of *Fall Line* so drastically was a bit disheartening, but if that's what it took to break into America, I was prepared to do it. Ti helped me put all these negative feelings behind me and I gained renewed confidence that inspired me to try even harder for the lucrative US television market.

Every morning we'd go for a surf or swim at Malibu, then after a leisurely breakfast, hit the freeway into Hollywood. Over a two-week period we must have gone to fifty film companies and door-knocked every TV station in Los Angeles, with a copy of *Fall Line* in one hand and the slick colour brochure describing the movie in the other. Sometimes doors seemed to open with the phone call and at others we even got as far as the secretary, only to have the door slammed shut at the first meeting with the boss. It was hard to stay keen and not get disheartened, but I picked myself up time and time again because I knew in my heart that *Fall Line* had something valid to say.

At last the breakthrough came. It happened at ONTV, a small cable-TV company which, though it had only a few thousand subscribers in the LA area, was growing every day thanks to aggressive marketing and a progressive attitude. If viewers filled in a card each month indicating their favourite TV shows, for example, they were given a reduction in the subscription fee. For me the best thing about ONTV was that they were independent, without network affiliations or head-office protocol, meaning that we didn't have to wait for months to get an answer if they liked the movie. The guy who handled program procurement had grown up at Malibu and was a keen skier who'd surfed when he was a kid. He understood *Fall Line* right away and actually let out a hoot when he saw it the first time, just as I had. He offered us $7,000 on the spot for one screening that month, and said that after it went to air I should call him. We'd "do lunch" after he had a feel for his audience's reaction to the movie.

After *Fall Line* showed on the box, Ti and I sat at Max's biting our nails for a few anxious weeks until ONTV's subscribers sent back their cards with the startling news that *Fall Line* was their favourite sports program that month – we were stoked. ONTV gave us an introduction to Tandem Tat who packaged *Fall Line* and showed it to Showtime in New York, the country's largest cable network. Over the next few years, Tandem signed $120,000 worth of deals for television rights in just about every country in the world – from $100 in Iceland to $80,000 for US cable TV rights. At last I could go back to Australia and get on with my life. Tandem was exactly what I needed. It had two energetic, top-flight agents with lots of clout and the right connections who'd work hard for their share of the profits. They were fantastic and did exactly what they said they would, keeping me informed of every sale as it took place. The only bummer was that before the money even got to Australia, the US Government had taken 30 per cent withholding tax and Tandem its 20 per cent agent's commission and by the time I'd covered my credit card debts for the six months in America and repaid the Australian Film Commission, there wasn't much to actually put in the bank.

As one of my obligations to the Film Commission, I had to take *Fall Line* on the road to give the Australian public a chance to see it, so I hired a 16 millimetre projector and Ti and I hit the circuit. I was the projectionist and Ti acted as publicity agent, selling tickets at the door after putting up posters and passing out handbills the day before. It all went pretty smoothly until the projector blew up in Geelong in the middle of the first half of a showing. Fortunately someone in the audience had a projector at home and we frantically retrieved it while the crowd – in best Saturday-matinee tradition – called for the show to continue by stamping its feet and hurling cans. We definitely didn't make any money out of the screenings, but it was part of the deal and Ti and I had a good time on the road together. *Fall Line* didn't look as good on paper as things like sales of US cable TV rights might suggest, but that's the reality of almost all small business.

* * * * * * *

Our American agent's brochure for the Cannes
Film Festival.

On the plane back to Australia, a woman came up and asked if she could buy me a drink, introducing herself as Dorothy Deger from Palm Beach in Sydney. She sat down and we made small talk about the Peninsula and the inevitable changes taking place there. She then told me she worked for Horwitz, a Sydney-based publishing company, and had an idea for a book, but really needed my help to make it happen. Dorothy said there was a niche in the book market for a little paperback guide to surfing the east coast of Australia. I loved Dorothy's outline – it sounded so nice and simple – and over an airline dinner and a couple of bottles of wine we went through all the details. That was it, all arranged, just like that and Dorothy said she'd pop over to Ti's with a cheque for the advance we'd agreed upon.

Most projects are never as easy as they first seem and this one was no exception. When it came time to actually write about all the beaches, I found I needed much more detail and there was only one way to do it. Ti and I hit the road armed with a pile of Army survey maps and spent the next few weeks writing notes and babbling into a tape recorder. We slept in the car and camped at every beach from Noosa in southern Queensland to Apollo Bay on the central coast of Victoria. It was tons of fun and at each beach we took as much time as was needed to get down on tape the relevant details and my impressions of every surf break we saw.

When we got back to Palm Beach I knocked it into a rough manuscript, and because I'd never learnt to type, Dorothy typed the first draft for me. Horwitz wanted the book to be inexpensive, so colour was restricted to the front and back covers and to illustrate the text a talented local artist named Tony Edwards made black-and-white sketches from my notes. *Surfing Australia's East Coast* had a print run of 20,000 which sold really quickly – the price was right and Australia's biggest book and magazine distributor flooded newsagents with copies. However, within a few weeks people began to complain that their copies of the book had fallen apart after being leafed through only a few times. I called Dorothy at work and Horwitz blamed the printer who discovered that the bindery had used a faulty batch of glue. I swore to Ti that I'd never again write a book for any other publishing company but our own.

* * * * * * *

I'd been travelling a lot in the final stages of producing and marketing *Fall Line*, in and out of Sydney every few weeks. Ti and I had discussed my housing situation and it hardly seemed worthwhile paying the rent on a flat I was only using occasionally. Ti's mother had purchased the house next door, and one afternoon she told me in an off-hand way that it'd be fine for me to use one of its bedrooms. This made it easy for Ti and I to continue our close relationship and see a lot of each other. I got on really well with Ti's mum Veda; she was very much like me in many respects and I could tell how she'd react to certain issues.

One of the things I enjoyed about my relationship with Ti was that we could now ski at the same high level of proficiency. This was fantastic in that I didn't have to help her with her gear or wait for her at the bottom of a run like most guys seemed to do; we were equals in every respect. Ti was right with me, even in a blizzard or on any of the steepest deepest powder runs in the world. A perfect playmate, with all her understanding of mountains on conventional skis, when Ti hit the slopes on a single ski she was awesome.

My Californian friend Mike Doyle had first built a single ski back in the late 1960s simply because it got around the problem of "crossing his tips" when he was learning on normal skis. I'd been fortunate enough to run into Mike and Joey Cabell, another hero of mine, at Mammoth Mountain, California during the winter of 1970. It was heavy snow that day and not many people could ski it well, but Joey and Mike weren't having any problems at all, either riding on the mashed-potato-like surface or spraying giant wakes of snow as they made deep driving turns, gouging deep tracks everywhere they went. This was the equipment for me. Doyle arranged for us to buy four skis: one each for Ti and me, one for Ti's brother Rik and another for my friend Max in Malibu.

These original single skis were made by another old surfer named Bill Bahne, who converted part of his surfboard factory to single-ski manufacturing ready for the boom that never happened. In retrospect I think I was lucky that I didn't know about single skis when I was learning because I know I'd have been tempted to get into them before I'd clocked up the large number of kilometres that I have on conventional skis. All the time spent learning on two skis with Christine Smith and my time with the ski patrol, six days a week, was invaluable. I learnt a lot about mountains and maintain that although you need only one edge – that is single skis and snowboards – to carve in both directions under most conditions, when it gets icy and the snow is hard, there's no substitute for two skis.

*　*　*　*　*　*　*

Armed with the confidence that the single ski had given us, Ti, Rik and I were keen to try our hand at helicopter skiing in the Cariboo Range in Canada's Rocky Mountains. We had a few bucks from the

It was easier for me to apply the Fall Line principle on the single ski as I didn't have to worry about crossing my tips. Rik's pic.

It wasn't long before Ti and I could enjoy heli-skiing together. This picture is in the Monashee range of mountains in British Colombia, Canada.

sale of *Fall Line* and this is exactly what we said we'd do "one day when we can afford it". Every time I saw my Swiss friend Max Andre he was in my ear about helicopter skiing in the Rockies. He'd been one of the first guests of Hans Gmoser, an Austrian mountaineer who back in the 1960s had pioneered skiing in the area and formed a company called Canadian Mountain Holidays. Ti, Rik and I were really keen to experience steep slopes and deep powder; to my mind it was the skiing equivalent of Waimea Bay and Sunset Beach. We were booked to go in January 1979 but Rik broke his ankle in a hang-glider accident while cliff-soaring near his home in San Pedro, so the trip was put back to April. But the powder kept tumbling out of the sky that year, right through till the end of May, with fine sunny days most of the time

We were all amazed by the depth and quality of the snow, even Ti and Rik, with all their years of experience, had never seen snow like it. There were lots of knee-deep days and a few waist-deep and the snow would create a total white-out when you went down for the turn – some skiers used snorkels and face-masks to prevent them gagging on the powder! Of all our trips this was the best. When the snow did get heavy and difficult for those on two skis, the single impressed everyone because it never caught an edge, which was a great help when you were skiing terrain with a tree line and I felt much more confident on the single.

There were, however a few problems, especially when there were three of us on single skis. Without even trying we'd get too much speed up and outrun the guides leading our group down the hill. They'd get really mad, and rightly so. From a safety point of view, to pass the guide is an absolute no-no and it cost me a few bottles of wine with dinner that week. Another problem was reaching the helicopter pick-up point if it was in an area difficult to reach. On two skis you can push and plod through the snow across the flats, but on a single this is impossible. It's an amazing workout: you have to take the ski off, climb onto it, pull yourself along, get off, throw it on top of the snow and do it all over again until you get to the chopper. I've had to do this in waist-deep, soft snow more than once and unless the guide can arrange a high pick-up that you can ski to, it's a major drawback of both singles and snowboards. I don't know how many heli-ski trips we've been on now, somewhere around eight, and certainly they haven't all been perfect powder for six days, but you learn to take the good and bad when you play with nature and it's still one of the highlights of our year when we can afford it.

*   *   *   *   *   *   *

In December 1979 we were heading off on another ski trip to the States and Ti and I had kissed her mother goodbye and were settling into our seats on the plane when a man came up the aisle and said he needed to see me outside immediately. I didn't know what to think; my first thought was that one of the kids must have been involved in an accident or something, but I was way off the mark. When we were back in the terminal the stranger sat me down and told me he was a plainclothes detective. He then informed me that he was arresting me in connection with a marijuana plantation that had been discovered on my farm. As we walked back through Customs I asked that Ti be told what was going on. Someone must have done it as Ti and her mother came to see me later at Darlinghurst Police Station.

First I was taken to Central Police Station where they interviewed me about the drugs, but there was nothing I could tell them. The police told me that my farm manager Jim McInnes had been arrested along with two other men I'd never heard of, let alone met. I think they believed I was telling the truth and after an hour or so I was taken to the old sandstone lockup at Darlinghurst where it was officially charged that I "while being the owner of a property did knowingly permit that property to be used for the cultivation of Indian hemp", or words to that effect.

I called my solicitor and friend Chris Watson who, when I read the charge to him over the phone, started yelling. He couldn't believe the police were going to take me to court in "such a travesty of British justice". "What if you were a simple landlord who didn't even know the tenants? ... Nowhere else in the world was there such an antiquated law ... Talk about a penal colony" and much more in the same fashion. He ended by saying that he'd come first thing in the morning and get me bail.

Sitting in the ancient stone cell I tried to piece my thoughts together. I couldn't believe it. What had Jim done? I mean one or two plants, even a dozen, just to have some good clean smoke around but thousands? Not Jim. There had to be some mistake. I hadn't been near the farm in over a year due to all the work with *Fall Line* and that would be easy to prove. But that wasn't the point. The charge on the blue sheet said that I'd knowingly permitted my property to be used for the cultivation of Indian hemp; "knowingly", that had to be the key word. All night I kept going over this in my mind. I had no answers, just a few questions that I really needed to ask Jim. Exactly what had happened while I'd been away from the farm? My head started to spin so I lay down on the bench and the next thing I knew it was morning, and the solicitor and I were off to court in downtown Sydney.

Of course representatives of the media were all waiting outside the court but the hearing was just a formality. The magistrate set a bail figure that Ti's mum paid and I was given back my passport and told I'd be allowed to continue with the skiing holiday in the States. The stories in the papers didn't hurt me at all but I felt for Veda. What would her hairdresser say behind her back; her friends at the golf club? She'd spent time on the farm and knew my position on everything including marijuana but the old saying is true: if you throw enough mud some sticks. The papers were suggesting that I'd known about the other men being busted the day before and was arrested while trying to skip the country. I had to admit, on the surface it may have looked like this. I certainly wouldn't have gone overseas after the false arrest, if everything hadn't been set up months before and paid for in advance. I think we could have opted out of the heli-skiing in Canada. Max and our friends in the States would have understood, but I quite honestly couldn't think of what else to do right then. Wherever in the world I happened to be I'd still have the problem so I just had to ignore it and get on with my life. I knew I wasn't guilty.

Naturally the trip to the States wasn't as relaxed and enjoyable as it could have been. We went through all the motions, skiing hard for a couple of weeks in good quality powder but always at the back of my mind was the charge waiting to be answered back home. When at last my trial date came round, my solicitor and I were asked to come in to the Grafton courthouse early to have a talk with the crown prosecutor before the proceedings began. The prosecutor told us that Jim and the other men involved had been sentenced to varying amounts of time in jail for their crimes. He then went on to say that the police had interviewed all the people involved and they'd all confirmed that I hadn't been involved or "knowingly" permitted my property to be used for growing pot and they were therefore prepared to drop the charges against me. However, they believed that they could still win the case because I did clearly own the property, but whether or not they'd get a conviction was a moot point. So the actual case took five minutes and was a complete non-event after all that anguish and pressure. I looked across at Ti and smiled as the magistrate pounded the bench with his gavel and declared the case dismissed. Jim was sent to a jail near Glen Innes in northern New South Wales, where I visited him. After his release, he returned to the farm, where he remains to this day.

It was comfortable being back in Palm Beach, Ti and I were getting on like a house on fire. I loved her and knew we were made for each other. I was telling a lot of people we were engaged, though it hadn't happened at that stage. We had the Hobiecat but I really wanted to get into windsurfing, so I went to a factory in Brookvale

Lunch on the mountain, Buqaboos, March '84 with our friends at Canadian Mountain Holidays. From the left, Max Andre, Latanna, Ti (with a mouthful of food), Siqi and the Prince.

and bought a new sailboard. It was a European Alfa, with a giant board that was more like a small yacht, and began trying it out on the still-water side of Palm Beach whenever the wind was up. Ti and I could get it moving, but turning it around was a bastard; even with its deep centreboard it was difficult to jibe. It was fun clipping into the harness and straining the sail against the wind for a few hours, but at the end of a taxing session we were glad we had Mr Charles Richards to take afternoon tea with. He had a flat with big bay windows overlooking Pittwater where Ti and I sailed.

Ti had taken over the care of this lovely old man from her mother who first became acquainted with Mr Richards when one particularly hot summer day she saw him walking along the road at "Palmy". Veda felt sorry for the old man and offered him a lift. It seemed to me that Charles Richards had the whole ritual of afternoon tea planned, right down to the position of the teaspoons. It was as though he lived for Ti's visits, buying fresh scones, jam, cream, and the finest Darjeeling tea. Charles was 96 years old and quite frail, but very dignified and always impeccably dressed and groomed. He'd played second violin in the London Symphony Orchestra and looking over his bow at the oboist one day, he fell in love. They were married and ran away to Australia where they lived happily for the next 45 years. They spent most of their time on the Peninsula, walking everywhere, until Mrs Richards died. Mr Richards still walked every day and kept his life in order just as he had done when his wife was alive. When we had afternoon tea there was always classical music playing in the background and Mr Richards would raise a finger to draw attention to a note or instrument. Charles also had a collection of books about the English Navy and liked to talk of what it must have been like to go to sea in square-rigged sailing ships.

Ti had another older friend in her Uncle Sid and had a Friday-afternoon obligation that they obviously both enjoyed. Whether we were on our way to the city or the surf, every Friday afternoon, as close to four o'clock as possible, Ti would buy a half-kilo of prawns and a large bottle of beer and diligently deliver this offering to her Uncle Sid in Mona Vale. More often than not we'd be in a rush to get somewhere and he'd always see us off with the same remark. "Hurry slowly," he'd say as we walked out the door. That saying has never left me and I think it says so much. These visits to Uncle Sid indirectly led to a very successful business venture.

Ti and I talked about our future. We both loved the idea of owning a surf shop with a factory nearby so I could continue building my boards; she could run the shop and we'd have lunch and morning tea together. I already had a half share in a surf shop at Belfield, in the inner-western suburbs of Sydney; the shop dawdled along paying the rent and selling a few boards but not doing any real turnover. In order to get a feel for the business Ti started working the odd day there, but the ninety-minute drive from Palm Beach was a bit offputting. The shop was in a pretty rough area and break-ins were commonplace; even after we put iron bars on the windows the robbers came through the roof. We considered getting a guard dog and locking it in the shop overnight but our insurance agent told us of a case where the owners of a German shepherd had been sued by a burglar who'd been attacked by the dog. Ti and I eventually bought the partners out, put in reliable staff and stocked the shop properly, but it was the insurance that got us in the end. We had eleven break-ins in thirteen months, every insurance company in the world knew about the shop at Belfield and no-one would cover us. It was time to take it on the chin and put it down to experience.

Just down the road from Uncle Sid's house in Mona Vale was an isolated building at the intersection of two main roads. It was very prominent and highly visible and everybody driving along the Peninsula had to pass the building whether they liked it or not. One side of the building was occupied by the Bazaar, with links to the original shop in Avalon. Edwin had passed on the basics of furniture restoration to Gwendolyn's two sons by her first marriage who, with their father Les, "the Ogre" as Gwendolyn called him, moved the business from Avalon to Mona Vale. Les had a withered arm, so all the heavy work was done by Jonathan, with help from his elder brother Nicky. Jonathan had helped me do up the furniture for Marilyn's house. He was a talented musician and keen surfer and our lives were intertwined on many levels over about ten years.

So in November 1980, with $5,000 each from Ti and me, Fall Line Surf and Ski was born. First we pulled everything out of the shop except the carpet – Ti later hired a steam cleaner and spent long hours getting it back close to new – I built the change rooms, counter and other fittings and at the rear a soundproof shaping room. Finally Ti wallpapered the interior of the shop, and with a few calls to friends who owned clothing companies we were open for business. On a trip to the United States Ti had passed through a town in northern California that had many buildings painted in varying designs, one of which was a breaking wave. Ti's brother had taken a couple of pictures. I called Rik in the States and asked him to send the pictures over and showed them to Peter Stanton, the guy who sprayed my boards. I asked Peter if he could copy this wave onto the side of our shop, to which he replied, "Sure". I don't think I'll ever forget the day we finished spraying the wave on Fall Line. Ti, Peter and I had built the scaffold and Ti and I spent a week cleaning the wall with sugar soap and painting on a base coat. The following day Peter started

SYLVAIN

Fall Line Surf and Ski in 1980. When we opened our shop there were 3 surf shops on the north side of Sydney. When we sold it there were 12!

painting early in the morning and worked on the wall until the wind came up. Cars were banking up at the traffic lights near the building; everyone was curious to know what was going on. Following Rik's photos, Peter did a perfect job that became a landmark in the area and put Fall Line on the map.

When Peter finished the painting around lunchtime on the second day, we didn't even have a good look at his work as we heard the surf was great at Box Head. We just put the lid on the paint tins, grabbed our boards and drove as fast as we could to where I had the Hobiecat on the beach in front of Veda's house. Peter tied the boards on the trampoline, while I rigged the boat and we were off to Box Head. We didn't have to tack once, the stiff north-easter let me set the cat up on one hull and run hard for the next twenty minutes on one swell we caught off Barrenjoey. We anchored at The Box with its magical 200-yard peeling lefts going insane. I was stunned – there wasn't another person in the water. We leapt overboard into a set of waves that were a solid 6 feet. All afternoon we surfed with no-one else in sight, Peter on his kneeboard and me getting constant back-hand barrels until we couldn't paddle any more and it began to get dark. Miraculously, the wind stayed up and we sailed back to Palm Beach with the same ease as we'd sailed down. It was an amazing day, one that Peter and I will never forget.

Fall Line Surf and Ski was a success right from the minute we opened the door. At first we opened five days a week, taking Mondays and Tuesdays off and trying to hold onto our lifestyle without employing anyone. It seems an obvious thing to say but so many surf shops around the world had gone belly up through lack of work by the surfing owners and inattention to overheads, so we were very conservative with our business.

Every day after school the local grommets would be lined up trying on clothes and window-shopping in anticipation of bringing their Mums and Dads back to buy them the boardshorts of their dreams. Quiksilver and Billabong were just getting started with their clothing lines, there were very few surf shops on the northern beaches – nowadays there are eleven – and all the surfing-minded people in our area came to us for their gear. Running out of stock was a regular occurrence. On one Christmas Eve we sold 250 pairs of boardshorts and the speed the business grew at was unbelievable. Towards the end of the 1980s Fall Line was turning over $500,000 a year.

Ti proved to be a genius in the shop, she parried enquiries and would explain to customers that I was busy shaping and couldn't be disturbed. She made appointments for interested customers to see me to talk about their boards and allowed the really committed ones to go into the workshop to watch me shape their boards.

As soon as the word about Fall Line was out, quality surfers I'd been seeing around for years started coming in looking for my boards. I was making the same classic Cabell-inspired pintail I'd been riding since the early 1970s: soft down rails tucked under to an edge, concave in the nose, flat to vee in the tail with a smooth-flowing bottom curve. The boards I made at Fall Line were different in one respect from those I'd made in the past. I was happy and living in one place with someone I loved and they were coming out better, reflecting my general demeanour. I was making truly custom boards and it felt great getting each board in balance for its owner. When I'd shaped as many boards as the car could hold, either Ti or I took the shaped blanks to one of the several glassing and finish contractors we used who'd deliver them, all buffed up and looking pretty, back to us to sell to our customers.

Shaping in the back room was a plan that sounded like a good idea at the time, but was a disaster in reality. The noise of the plane while Ti was trying to sell clothing and the cloud of foam dust that emerged with me every time I opened the door became too much. When the nice old guy in the flat upstairs moved into a nursing home, we took over his garage and moved the shaping room there, from the rear of the shop. The first thing I did with all the new space was shape a windsurfer based on one of my boards. It still didn't feel like a board on a wave, being relatively big and boxy by today's standards but my new sailboard gave me a whole new buzz. Later research revealed that control in the surf depended as much on the shape of the sail as anything, and performance was further improved by developments in fittings.

Whenever there was decent wind I'd get Ti to drop me off at the beach with all my sailing gear then, sailing with the wind and swell, I'd tack a half-mile out to sea and depending on the time of day, sail either to or from the shop. It was such a good space after shaping all day in my garage; stretched out in the harness, flying down the swells, carving on the faces. The speeds I reached were amazing and when I got to my destination, there was Ti at the rendezvous with the comfort of a warm car and a cuddle.

In my new workroom I had enough room to do the experimenting I'd always wanted to. Through the shop I met an American guy who sold epoxy resins and we talked a lot about state-of-the-art boatbuilding technology, which I attempted to apply to surfboards. In line with boatbuilding techniques, I first built a scale model of a board, approximately 6 inches wide by a foot long, then using this as a template I accurately cut and sanded a block of cardboard honeycomb to fit it. I considered myself a pretty good shaper but working in miniature like this was really tedious.

When transferring the model to the full-size board, I saturated the concertinaed piece of honeycomb in thinned epoxy resin and then expanded the shape over the original perfect board inside a big plastic bag. The idea was to make a sandwich with a layer of wood veneer on each side of the expanded honeycomb core. After the sandwich was all laid up, the whole thing was put in a vacuum bag and all the air was sucked out while it cured overnight. When it was a hard form, styrofoam blocks were stuck to the sides and the rails shaped. The ridged, expanded honeycomb was very tough so only a very light layer of epoxy resin was necessary over the board. Attaching the normal fibreglass fins to the timber bottom was a bit tricky, but I managed it. The board was very light and felt really good but the real proof was going to be in the surfing.

Ti, the kids and I took off for a week at the farm and while we were up there we took the new board on its maiden voyage at the point-break at Angourie. It actually felt pretty good and I surfed it hard for the next hour but then it began to float lower and lower in the water – the board was filling up with water and sinking. I caught a little wave back to the beach, rolled the board over and saw that one of the fins had punctured the veneer on the bottom, probably when I was turning. The water had got in and was all through the honeycomb and that, as they say, was the end of that. I was pretty depressed, this was going to be my escape from sucking in foam dust every day. I'd spent a fortune on epoxy resin – not to mention the hundreds of hours spent on the labour-intensive experiment, all the problems getting vacuum bags sealed, learning about epoxy, then everything finally working smoothly, and now the bloody thing had sunk.

I went back to shaping surfboards in the conventional manner for a while, but the health problems associated with breathing foam fumes and dust all day were turning me away from board shaping and towards books, movies and other ways of making a living.

17

Ti and 'The History of Surfing'

T I AND I WERE MARRIED by a marriage celebrant, in the beautiful
tropical garden of her mother's house at Palm Beach at 4 pm on
7th March 1982. On that sunny afternoon, surrounded by family,
friends and tons of flowers the atmosphere was perfect. It reflected
everything we'd felt for each other for a long time, as did the words
for the ceremony, which Ti and I had written ourselves. Ti looked
stunning in an off-white dress, my old friend Terry Purcell was best
man and somehow my 69-year-old Dad was coaxed into leaving his
home in Port Macquarie to sing *Bless This House*. He had a fine bari-
tone voice and I think I can remember him singing in church when
I was a toddler. I'll never forget the joke he used to rattle off whenever someone commented on his voice "Yes," he'd say, "I've sung in
front of the Prince of Wales and King George..." then as the person
stood there obviously waiting for Dad to go on with the story, he'd
deliver the punch line "and several other hotels in Sydney". It never
failed; people in his age group would roar with laughter, while the
younger people just shook their heads. I got off on watching him tell
the story and seeing the audience's reaction.

For a wedding present, Ti's mum paid for a night at a hotel on
Pittwater. We spent that first blissful night together as husband and
wife locked in each other's arms and listening to the wavelets rhyth-
mically lapping the shore outside our room, contrasting sharply with
the constant pounding of the surf we were used to hearing at Palm
Beach.

The very next day we were off to the States on our honeymoon.
For a long time I've tried to live by the principle of never overflying
Hawaii and I always stop over for a few days to pick up on that
unique Hawaiian feel that I've come to love so much. It may have
changed a lot since my first trip in 1963, with a multi-level shopping
centre at the airport replacing the old single-storey cement building,
but the ukuleles and hula dancers in grass skirts are still sometimes
around when you walk into the arrival hall, and sometimes you can
smell the faint perfume of *plumeria* (Frangipani) flowers mixed with

Both Naomi and Beau were made to feel very special at our wedding. My Dad came down from Port Macquarie and Terry Purcell was my best man.

On the way over to
America we spent a
week with Gerry
Lopez in Hawaii.
Sato took these shots
in and out of the
water at Ala Moana.

jet fuel. The aloha spirit is still there, even though it's sometimes hidden underneath the numerous problems caused by the Hawaiians trying to come to terms with the invasion by huge numbers of white Americans who want to make the islands their home. There have been acts of aggression over the issues of race and Hawaiian sovereignty, and, on a surfing level, overcrowding out in the water, but for the most part everyone coexists pretty well. There's no denying that the atmosphere has changed somewhat but if you're humble when you visit Hawaii and go there with the right attitude, you'll have a truly pleasurable holiday.

Hawaii is still the surfer's mecca because at certain times of year those islands have some of the most awesome waves on the planet and the north shore of Oahu has more quality breaks concentrated in a 3-kilometre stretch of coastline than anywhere else in the world. When I hear that the surf is up and I'm within striking distance of the sea, it's really out of my control. I become irritable and impatient and like any other junkie I've simply got to have it. I kept telling myself that I was on my honeymoon and that there's a time and a place for everything – I had to exercise some control over my surfing habit.

We'd booked into a big hotel overlooking the beach at Waikiki, the honeymoon capital of the world, and had only been there a couple of days when I ran into an old surfer friend who was working on the construction site of a new hotel, right next door to ours. He lived on the north shore and said the waves had been cranking all week – that was it, goodbye Waikiki. I've always hated being a tourist or, to be more specific, feeling like one; just looking at things was never good enough, I liked to be doing something at the same time. Ti, on the other hand, had plenty of practice wandering all over the world in a motor home and being a tourist was cool with her.

I rang my friend Gerry Lopez who told me he was sitting looking through his window at an 8-foot perfect Pipeline and we were welcome to come and stay at his place. Gerry was a couple of years younger than me and had become a close friend over the years. He managed to make a living without compromising his surfing or his lifestyle and I admired him for it. He is different from me in so many ways, but a real pleasure to be with. Ti and I spent a week with Gerry, the perfect host, and surfed some wonderful waves in his "backyard" at Pipeline and at Ala Moana. We even flew over to his other house on Maui, where his brother Victor grew the magnificent *Proteas* that they'd been selling to stores as far away as New York and Boston.

Before we left Hawaii, Ti and I had to spend a day in the Bishop Museum. I was curious to see exactly what information they had on the roots of Hawaiian surfing. The exhibition was impressive, with all the old boards lined up in a half-circle behind a typical village scene, and an extensive collection of manuscripts and books with references to surfing. I met the curator of the museum and found out what formalities I had to go through to get assistance with some serious research, because during the next twelve months I intended spending quite a bit of time at the Bishop. I wanted an understanding of the spread of our sport: from Hawaii to New Zealand at the other end of Polynesia; to Australia and throughout the world.

Many of the early photographs of Hawaii were inscribed with the name Ray Jerome Baker, a very prolific photographer who worked at the turn of the century, and we were really impressed with his work. Ti was browsing in the souvenir shop on our way out the door and found a book on Baker by a distant relative named Robert E Van Dyke. It seemed destined to happen; Ti got his number from information and I phoned him and made an appointment to meet him at his studio in Honolulu. Van Dyke's collection of photographs was immense and when I explained that I was particularly interested in surfing-related shots, he said he needed time to look through the thousands of Baker's photographs in his possession. We parted with an understanding that we'd correspond over the next few months and meet on my next visit to Hawaii.

Ever since I'd finished *Fall Line* I'd been looking at the possibility of doing a history of surfing. I wasn't sure if I wanted to do a book or a movie at that stage and to me it didn't really matter much as the project fascinated me. Most people are amazed when I tell them I didn't think the research was daunting, but having been a poor attender at school, and not taking it all that seriously when I was there, I'd never had to sit down and do assignments on topics that didn't interest me. Collecting material on surfing was what I'd always done whether it was surf magazines, letters from surfer friends, or cuttings from newspapers. I still have the 1961/62 registration sticker from one of my first surfboards as well as every one of the hundreds of trophies I've won. The prospect of making sense out of it all was a real challenge and so attractive that I was completely committed.

Some months earlier when I'd looked to see what books and movies on the subject were available in Australia, I found almost nothing. The *Pictorial History of Surfing* was the only book available but really, I thought it was wrongly named. The book extensively covered the development of the Surf Life Saving movement but that's only a small part of the history of surfboard riding. It seemed to me that the subject had never been adequately covered. I began to formulate a plan to obtain photographs and movies of specific eras, following the evolution of the surfboard from its birth in Polynesia to the present day. It was a fascinating subject, so why hadn't someone done it before? Perhaps it wasn't possible. But to me, it seemed the project was meant to be and I was hooked. I decided that first-up I'd attempt a book on the history of surfing and then, if that worked out, a movie of the book. The tried and tested method – it had to be the best way to go.

That was in the future; as keen as I was to get into the history, I had to put the project on the back-burner for the time being. Ti and I were on our honeymoon and the job at hand was to fly to Detroit and pick up a new motor home for Ti's mother then drive it to California. On the way we would take in a couple of weeks of fantastic skiing at Sun Valley, a place my heroes Mike Doyle and Joey Cabell had raved about. A blizzard hit as we left the Black Hills of Dakota but by waiting for snow ploughs to clear the road ahead and stopping when the winds were too furious, we made our way across the Rockies. It was a gruelling two days. Ti and I were both exhausted but we kept up the pace as I knew with the weather the way it was it just had to be dumping in Sun Valley. The landscapes on Idaho's high plains – homeland of the Blackfoot and Cheyenne Indians – were very different to anything I'd ever seen. Peering out through the windscreen I found myself wondering what the winters must have been like for the Native Americans, especially a winter like this, with everything buried under a metre of new snow. The scenery is just breathtaking, billiard-table flat with hills like giant upside-down ice-cream cones scattered all over the countryside.

Mike Doyle had a falling-out with his original single-ski manufacturer and was now getting them made in Sun Valley by a ski technician named Mike Brunetto. This was a major reason for my visit. I was keen to meet Brunetto and hopefully buy some new single skis, both for Ti and myself and for the shop. After *Fall Line* – with its sequences featuring single skis – had been seen on national television, we were getting lots of enquiries about them. The centre of Sun Valley is the town of Ketchum, which at first glance looks like a town from a Hollywood western with a ski hill behind it. In its simplest terms I suppose that's what it is – but that ski hill just happens to be among the most formidable ski slopes in the world. Mount Baldy has a vertical fall of 1,000 metres, making it one of the steepest, longest runs anywhere in the world. Mount Baldy was the reason why in 1935 William Averell Harriman, then President of Union Pacific Railroad, had a branch line built to the then unnamed Sun Valley. Harriman's brief to his Austrian friend Count Felix Schaffgotsch was to choose the best possible site in the Rockies for a ski resort. Sun Valley had a ski lift by 1936 and Mount Baldy was opened up and being skied by 1939. It was adopted by the Hollywood set after the release of the movie *Sun Valley Serenade* and Ernest Hemingway was among the many famous people who had lived in the town. He's commemorated everywhere in the valley with everything from a High School to a ski run named after him.

On the Warm Springs side of the mountain Ti and I found a place to park the motor home within walking distance of the lifts and proceeded to explore the mountain on skis. Some of the pitches on the main runs were so steep I couldn't work out why the snow wasn't slipping down the mountain and the length of the runs in the powder bowls was mind boggling. Because we were the only people skiing the terrain, every run was on untracked snow. As the depth of new snow each day was from 30 centimetres to a metre we were both on our single skis all the time. For Ti and me the greatest thing about the single ski goes back to Mike Doyle's original reason for building them: we could confidently ski the trees without fear of catching an edge or crossing tips – singles really are much safer than conventional skis.

The runs into Warm Springs were so long and demanding that every time we popped out of the trees at the lifts, it felt as though our legs were on fire and until we hardened up we had to have a little rest after each run. At the top of one of the 2 kilometre-long shoots we skied over a 3-metre drop into a big bowl where it was necessary to use short powerful turns to slow down before leaving on the downhill side. Each turn would expose one or two white, seagull-sized birds, blue grouse, that nested under the powder snow. Each time I return to this bowl, I'm greeted by the grouse, sometimes more, sometimes less, but they're there every winter. We mainly skied the avalanche-cleared shoots or coulees – gullies where no trees grew because the slides in the first heavy snows kept them clear of small trees and shrubs. Often the steepest way down the face, they could be very dangerous, especially with a couple of feet of fresh powder on them.

We've never been seriously caught in a major slide; however, we have some rules that we always adhere to. We look carefully before we take off and test that the snow is stable. Accidents are always on my mind when skiing in the back country; you have to ski seperately but still within sight of one another. So long as the person at the rear can lend assistance, most problems can be solved. Invariably I would go first while Ti watched my decent from the safety of the trees. After twenty linking turns I'd ski off to the side while Ti skied down to me and further down the fall line for another twenty turns or so. In remote or avalanche-prone areas Ti and I always carry emergency location beacons just in case we get lost or buried by an avalanche.

R PALMER

Ti and me on our honeymoon in Sun Valley, Idaho USA.

When we first arrived in Ketchum we made contact with the ski patrol and checked our beacons. Some patrollers weren't happy about us going out of bounds all the time but for the most part they were prepared to tolerate us because we'd been on ski patrol in Australia and at least understood their position. The country outside the Sun Valley Company's leased area isn't really the ski patrol's problem but if an emergency did arise they'd be the first to lend assistance.

Skiing at Warm Springs is a real treat with some new discovery on every run. Seeking the cause of a constant knocking sound, we followed it to its source, a woodpecker high in a tree. By listening for the sound we could follow the bird's movements throughout the day. We also discovered that when we were close to the bottom of an afternoon run and momentarily lost in the trees, if we stopped to listen we could hear the sound of the fiddle in the country band that played in the cafe by the lifts and all we had to do was follow the sound back to civilisation. Sometimes if the road had been cleared, we'd drive our camper out to the Board Ranch and instead of traversing back to the lifts, continue down one of the shoots getting another half mile of magnificent untracked coulee at 45 degrees. At the lower levels we ran into elk patiently waiting to be fed by the rangers, and at the bottom of another run was a full-size tepee. Ti and I were falling in love with the Sun Valley area, particularly the Warm Springs side of the mountain.

The carpark at Warm Springs was OK for a night or two, but we really wanted to plug into electricity to run the motor home's appliances. Heating was a must as the temperature dropped below freezing every night and having to drive to the local camping ground for a shower every day was becoming a drag. One afternoon on the way to the showers we stopped to speak to Michael Brunetto, the guy who made Doyle's single skis. Of Cherokee descent, Michael was an immensely talented ski designer who once worked for Head and designed the skis for World Champion, Jean-Claude Killy. After that Michael designed and built "The Ski" with the colourful Bobby Burns and then set up his own small factory in Ketchum using state-of-the-art equipment to make both conventional skis and singles. Doyle had told me to look Mike Brunetto up, but by the time I got around to meeting him they'd had a falling out. However, Brunetto's company, Research Dynamics, was still building single skis.

We found Mike and his assistant Kenny to be really warm and generous people, letting us camp outside the factory and plug the camper in to its electricity supply – they even gave us the key to the bathroom. Mike was an interesting man; with an extensive background in racing and tuning skis, he was also the director of Sun Valley's race program, training the local ski team, and he taught me heaps about tuning skis.

Skiing was Mike Brunetto's life, but hunting was his passion. During the summer he'd fly a little high-wing Piper Super Cub into very short bush strips deep in the back country and with either bow and arrow or rifle, kill his meat for the winter, just as his ancestors had done. Over the years I knew Brunetto, I ate some great meals of tender elk and moose teamed with hearty Australian red wine that we both shared a deep enthusiasm for. The best dinner I ever had with Brunetto was roast wild duck that he'd shot the summer before – he was thinking of me when he plucked them out of the sky, he said – served with a sauce made from flavoursome wild berries braised in the juices from the duck and a generous slurp of wine – magnificent. We spent many happy nights enjoying food and friends in Brunetto's one-room log cabin and listening to Mike play the grand piano that drew your eye the moment you walked in the door. He was a very talented musician and I think he could have made a profession of it.

Then it was time to go. Our honeymoon was over and reluctantly we drove down to LA and leaving the motor home in Max's back-yard in Malibu for Veda to collect later, caught a plane home.

* * * * * * *

Fall Line Surf and Ski was going from strength to strength with the turnover increasing by 100 per cent each year, but it was a vicious circle. We needed more and more stock so we had to keep plough-ing all the profits back into the business. Ti was looking after the shop – we'd employed a couple of young salesmen and a shaper to do the stock boards – while I was buried under a pile of books and photographs, following the obscure trail of the history of surfboard riding. I completed the first draft of the Australian section fairly pain-lessly and in June 1982 made a lightning trip to Hawaii and California to conduct interviews and gather more material. In Hawaii I finished the work with Robert Van Dyke and selected the Baker pictures from those he'd ferreted out in the past few months.

Back in 1965, on my second trip to Hawaii, I'd developed a close association with Wally and Moku Froiseth and their family. Wally was Hawaiian-born of European descent and a wonderful, gentle old surfer who was very easy to get on tape. He also had a good col-lection of photographs to back up what he told me, and under his house he kept his old solid redwood board, a "Hot Curl" with no fin, just a deep vee bottom. This design originated in California, where the boards were also widely used, and Wally surfed it in waves up to 10 feet. My research revealed that the links between California and Hawaii were so intertwined that all I could do was try to talk to as many old surfers as possible. Some accounts of events and times would contradict others and then it would come down to actually asking rather bluntly if they had pictures or other evidence to back up their claims. Some did and some didn't, but it was a pretty good way of separating fact from fiction.

Armed with my trusty tape recorder I spoke to 35 people in two weeks including three days with a researcher at the Bishop Museum. During my week in California, I spoke to as many people on my list as possible, calling ahead to set up meetings. I was given the benefit of the doubt by older American surfers. Even if I was an Aussie, at least I was behaving respectfully and was a good surfer in my own right, so most of them took the plunge and opened up to me. There were so many people to interview, but none more important than Tom Blake, the man who'd first put a fin on a surfboard and the main reason I'd come to the States when I did; his old friends told me that June was the only time of year that he could tolerate the climate elsewhere and leave his home in Wisconsin. When I met him that summer, he was 79 years old. Tom had photocopied *The Voice of the Atom* for me, a work too deep and involved to go into here, but it outlines Tom's principles of blending religion and surfing. I wish one of the surf magazines would run it, as it would be of benefit to everyone. I still read it occasionally and believe it holds many important lessons for surfers as we approach the new millennium.

When my two weeks were up, I felt a bit like Cinderella having to rush away. I hadn't seen everyone I'd wanted to, but keeping to a schedule was the only way I was going to complete the book by 1983. I hit *Surfer* magazine's southern California office like a tornado, filling a big suitcase with all the relevant photographs I could lay my hands on. It was a big deal for Jeff Divine, *Surfer's* photo editor, to trust me with all that valuable material and I felt really relieved when I returned every photo a year later.

Back in Australia the direction of the book became crystal clear and after a few months locked away either at Palm Beach or in complete isolation on the farm, I'd churned out 80,000 words that I was pretty pleased with. Ti and Veda read through it and corrected the spelling and grammar but it was still pretty raw and needed an editor to polish it up. Over the years I'd kept in close contact with my old friend John Witzig who was now concentrating on graphic design after losing a lot of money publishing a surfing magazine called *Sea Notes*. John is very competent. I loved his clean layout and his knowledgeable help with choosing photos was invaluable. John did a fair bit of editing of the manuscript – pointing out many inconsistencies and oversights – and it was really enjoyable to work with him again.

John suggested I talk to Craig McGregor, a well-known Australian journalist with some distant surfing affiliations who lived at Bondi

Junction in Sydney's eastern suburbs. I met Craig at his house and though he had quite a bit on his plate he took the job on. He was interested in the subject and there wasn't much still to do, though he would have to write an opening chapter to give an overview of the whole book. What Craig brought to the project was his professionalism – a huge advantage given the breadth of the subject – and by Christmas 1982 we had a finished manuscript we were all happy with. Photo editing at John's house was an amazing exercise with the floor of one room completely covered in photographs. There were thousands of pictures in hundreds of dated manilla folders and we only had 200 pages to work with – agonising over every photo, we somehow made the cut. John's layout was simple and straightforward with each chapter having a different coloured background tint and we decided to use the highest-quality art paper available.

I called the head of the book division of Gordon and Gotch in Melbourne, Australia's largest distributor of books and magazines. I explained that I was an independent book publisher and requested an appointment at his convenience. John made up a dummy, complete with cover, and armed with this and a pile of sample photographs I sat in the book division explaining how my book was going to fill a gap in the market. I'd done my sums and this made it relatively easy to reach an agreement whereby Gordon and Gotch bought 10,000 copies with no exclusive rights to the book. That one sale covered the printing and binding costs of 25,000 copies of *The History of Surfing* which was printed at the Sydney firm, Deaton and Spencer, owned by Ti's family. We decided not to make it a coffee-table book as we wanted it to be an ongoing definitive history that could be added to every five years or so. As things stood in 1997, that wish has been fulfilled – *The History of Surfing* has been reprinted four times, revised once and to date has sold around 130,000 copies.

* * * * * * *

I stayed with Gerry Lopez at his Pipeline house during another of my short trips to Hawaii the following winter. After three days of riding some incredible big round barrels in his backyard, I was woken one night by the pounding of giant sets closing-out the whole North Shore. Peering into the dawn I could see that surfing Pipeline would be out of the question that day. Gerry hadn't surfaced so I took his pushbike and pedalled down to Waimea just intending to have a look, not having surfed the bay in several years. For ten minutes I stood there totally awestruck at the sight of a light offshore breeze fanning perfectly formed walls of water 15 to 20 feet high. Here was

This wave at Waimea is big by my standards and the subsequent wipe-out was horrific. I ended up with this rip below my lip just from the force of the water.

a golden opportunity, the most coveted big wave in the world was breaking in an orderly fashion and from what I could see no-one was out. I tore back to Gerry's to grab my trunks and the biggest board I could find in his stash. Paddling out through the shore break and over the first big set was awesome and I asked myself what I was doing out there. I hadn't surfed waves like this for five years and even then not very often; there were already enough people looking for fame and glory, and this was the spot to do it.

I thought I was doing pretty well, I could still remember the take-off position from the 1970s and I paddled till I was in the line-up sitting in line with the church tower on the point and as far out as the last palm tree down the beach towards Gerry's. I was right on the button I thought, two more surfers had joined me and a fair-sized set was approaching – the first one was mine. The take-off was no big deal really, I knew what to expect, having done it fifty times in my life and though it's very different at Waimea, a few bad mistakes ensure that you never forget. I paddled really hard, breaking through the top of the wave in a way that is characteristic of the Bay, then plumeted through mid-air. Coming off the bottom I saw a giant left-hander peeling straight towards me and then it exploded all round me. It was like being buried in wet cement and then I was catapulted towards the surface then back down through the water. I felt my leg-rope break like a piece of cotton then the turmoil finally subsided and I was on the surface. Fortunately the rest of the set was not as intense and I could take a good deep breath before diving under each wave.

Retrieving the board, I wandered back up the point to where Gerry and a few other surfers were standing. Gerry got stuck right in. What was I doing taking-off so far over? "I lined up with the church tower and the last palm tree on the point," I defended myself. "Yes", Gerry replied, "but that palm tree got wiped out in the hurricane last year, along with all the houses and everything else down there. You were too far inside. And what about that cut?" I put my hand up to my face and felt a 25 millimetre tear running from my lip towards my chin – more battle scars. It was nothing that a few stitches wouldn't fix but I felt like an old mug.

* * * * * * *

The year 1983 was definitely my biggest so far. Fall Line Surf and Ski was bubbling along and provided a very comfortable living for our family. I didn't have to work in the shop at all as Ti handled everything very competently giving me the freedom necessary to work on the book and still ride a few waves every now and then. I still hadn't dropped the idea of a film but I realised that it was going to take much longer than the book and would need to examine one country at a time so that the story would not get too confusing. During my research in Australia I spent a week at the National Film and Sound Archives in Canberra, screening more than twenty films and returning home with a wealth of information that added greatly to my understanding of Australian beach culture.

I had met a guy named Grant Young, no relation, who'd made a couple of recent surf movies. He had a production company called Dubb's that would be capable of handling the production of my movie *The History of Australian Surfing*. Grant made his big flatbed editing machine and an editor available to me whenever I needed them and I tried to wrestle with the Australian section of the story but it was tedious, time-consuming work and my head was still right into the book. Ti and I threw in several thousand dollars to get sections of the relevant surf movies copied and I spent a few hours each day looking at specific moves and sequences over and over again until the chaos began to make sense. I made notes to give me a record of what was available, but not much more.

*   *   *   *   *   *

Ti and I were determined to continue to have quality time together and indulge our mutual passion for skiing. We rented a house on the North Shore of Hawaii for a week as part of a trip to the United States in February 1983. We had Naomi and Beau, aged eleven and eight, with us and though it was the first time we'd travelled overseas with them, both kids were comfortable with Ti as they'd already spent so much time with her. Neither of the kids surfed, though a year later Naomi asked me to give her a board as a twelfth birthday present and has surfed hard ever since. I got to ride a few waves and squeezed in meetings with a couple of old surfers I'd missed the trip before and we did all the tourist things.

It was a relaxing and enjoyable week, so enjoyable in fact, that Ti became pregnant with our first child, Nava. I'd come across the name during my research at the Bishop Museum. She'd been a high-ranking woman from one of the outer islands who'd been beheaded for surfing at the wrong beach. I thought it was a beautiful name and had only heard it once before, in Mexico, where we'd met the Paskowitz family. Dorian Paskowitz, an energetic doctor, and his beautiful Native American wife had nine kids – eight boys and a girl named Navah. Ti and I liked the name – using the Hawaiian version – and we stored it away in case our firstborn was a girl.

Once in California, we picked up the motor home from Max's

house and drove to Sun Valley. Both kids had skied quite a bit before, but it took a few days for them to feel comfortable. One afternoon early in the stay, Ti and I got talking with a pleasant young man who was just getting rolling as a real estate agent in the Wood River Valley. We told him how impressed we were with the area and the conversation turned to property values and the relatively cheap prices then current. He offered to show us a few apartments and the first one we looked at was the one we bought. It was a "studio loft", meaning that the bedroom was the loft. There was a tiny kitchen, a bathroom, and a living room with three bunks behind the door as you walked in, perfect for Naomi and Beau. The internal layout was brilliant but the best thing about our "House On The Beach", as it became affectionately known, was the view it had of the mountain. About 50 metres away and directly across the road was the lift and then a totally unbroken view of the runs where we skied most of the time – there were sliding glass doors opening on to a deck that looked straight up the barrel. We paid a deposit on the $63,000 full price and the realtor organised the finance through a local bank.

The money from the television sales of *Fall Line* was just starting to flow and that would cover the repayments without having to transfer money from Australia every month. The unit was fully furnished and as we had nowhere to stay other than the motor home the agent spoke to the owners who agreed to let us move in straight away. This made our ski holiday perfect. We could all go off to different areas to ski with classes or friends of similar ability, then meet for lunch and a ski together at the end of the day. It also meant we could have some of our meals at home, which we preferred, as it saved money and we could eat exactly what we liked. Ti had been a total vegetarian all her life which sometimes made eating in restaurants difficult. As Ti did most of the cooking, the kids and I were happy to eat vegetarian most of the time.

* * * * * * *

Back home again it was time to make some decisions about marketing the book. The printing I couldn't really help with at all. I threw in my two cents worth but it was John Witzig with his educated eye who checked the quality of the scans and supervised the printing. Once the pages were collated and the book was being bound I couldn't stay away so I went to the bindery and watched the first copies roll off the machine. I've always really loved a hard-bound book – in an old one it's the musty smell, the shape of the spine, feel of the boards – the type of book that you see a person blowing the dust off in old movies. Some books have been around for hundreds of years and only fire can destroy them, often only with great difficulty. They survive wars and natural disasters, you can throw them against a wall or dump them in water – books will remain long after all the videotapes have gone.

I decided I needed the help of a publicity machine. It wasn't that I didn't know plenty of media people in Sydney; it was just that I needed someone to coordinate the interviews, the bookshop signings and the actual launch. I had more than enough to do making sure we made the ships with the shrink-wrapped pallets of books for South Africa, New Zealand, Hawaii and the mainland United States, not to mention the 10,000 that had to be delivered to Gordon and Gotch in Sydney. The orchestration of all of this was critical because most books are bought as Christmas presents and it was now the second week of October – they have to be in the shops by mid-November at the latest.

I was lucky enough to get Peter Harrison as the publicist and he scored a real triumph by getting the New South Wales Premier, Neville Wran, to launch the book. I'd met Neville Wran once before and I really liked his up-front style and was pleased when he accepted the invitation. The event was organised for the · 3rd November 1983 at the Bondi Pavilion and invitations were sent to all the media organisations and many VIPs. We had excellent television, radio and print-media coverage which is really what a book launch is all about. I picked up Snow McAlister and Ti and Veda brought Isobel Letham – the first person to ride a surfboard with Duke Kahanamoku in Australia.

Isobel and Snow loved being treated like celebrities, though Snow was a little more complacent about it. I'd never heard of Isobel before doing the research on surfing in Australia. Over and over again she'd giggle and tell the same romantic story of her meeting the Duke back in 1918; she was obviously infatuated with him. When I gave her some stills of the Duke and a few of his mates clowning around at the beach – taken from a tiny roll of film that an old friend had found at the dump in Los Angeles – I was her friend for life. Isobel looked like a big yellow buttercup in her matching hat and gown and she and Snow were both absolutely glowing. I'm sure the event was the highlight of their year.

The radio interviews after the launch seemed endless. With "summer madness" sweeping the city, everyone wanted to talk about surfing. The book signings were no different and I could have done one at every bookshop in Sydney if I'd wanted. However, I didn't have a distributor for my books so I eased off a bit while I continued talking to wholesalers in the book trade. The girl who looked after the largest bookshop in the beach-side suburb of Manly advised me to

In 1983 the then Premier of NSW, Neville Wran launched my book The History of Surfing.

I was so stoked to have Isobel Letham (the first person to ride a surfboard in Australia) with my good friend and mentor CJ Snow McAlister to enjoy the launch.

go and see Tower Books, who were located just ten minutes down the road in Brookvale. Tower was a husband and wife affair and although they were just getting started, they were already one of the major independent wholesalers in New South Wales with links to the other States. I really liked Howard Taylor, who was enthusiastic about my book right from the word go. Because Tower was situated close to where we lived, I could hold the bulk of the stock in Veda's garage and drive down with a few boxes when they needed them. I really had no idea how the book would sell so it didn't seem fair to clutter up Tower's little office with thousands of copies of *The History of Surfing*. Howard and I shook hands and our association has lasted all this time, through the numerous reprints of *The History of Surfing* and involvement with various other books.

After sending off a heap of letters to all the big book distributors in the USA and not getting one reply, on 28th of November I flew to Los Angeles and even then, after countless phone calls to all the majors, I failed to get a meeting. It seemed to be a closed door so I decided to try direct marketing, putting an ad in *Surfer* magazine and attempting to sell *The History of Surfing* by mail order. I found a company to handle the orders and it worked pretty well, but was very limited. I had set myself a budget to promote the book and after paying for the ad in *Surfer* we couldn't afford a publicist. A couple of stories in local newspapers and an interview on San Diego television boosted my confidence a bit. It wasn't much really, only a drop in the ocean, but the word on the beach was good and the surfing press was going to review it.

Hawaii was a different matter. A few months previously I'd sold a thousand copies to the buyer for the book section in Honolulu's biggest department store and as a part of that sale I agreed to do an in-store promotion in the lead-up to Christmas. Because the store had some advertising clout the newspapers gave it editorial space and all one thousand books were sold. The store wanted more, but as all the stock was in Los Angeles and Australia, that wasn't immediately possible. The idea of going direct to the retailer worked so well, I decided to try and find a store in California and do exactly the same thing the following summer.

I rushed back to Australia, arriving on 11th of December 1983. I knew Ti's time must be getting close, as the baby was already late. I crossed my fingers and decided to get over my nervousness by immersing myself in the book promotion. The same day I arrived in Sydney I appeared on a television show and two radio interviews and the next week I was booked solid, doing book signings all over Sydney and as far north as Newcastle and Gosford. The book was selling like mad; it was very exciting.

Surfer magazine ad to sell The History of Surfing in the USA.

Ti and I went to a Cold Chisel concert on the Thursday night and the following day the doctors induced the birth. I'd dropped Ti at the hospital on the way to do a radio interview in Gosford before attending a long book signing. All day I was like a cat on a hot tin roof, calling the hospital's delivery room for updates but nothing seemed to change. Ti was in labour and had been given an epidural to help make the pain bearable and she was as high as a kite when I got there that evening. Veda and I helped Ti with each contraction and they began to get closer and closer together until at 10.28 p.m. on 16th December 1983, our baby girl was born. Nava weighed 9 pounds 3 ounces (4.2 kg) – no lightweight, but extremely beautiful.

* * * * * * *

During the early 1980s the longboard or Malibu craze had been slowly spreading up and down the coast. Every Boxing Day a lot of my old Peninsula mates and their families would get together at North Avalon for a barbecue, Vintage Malibu Competition and another competition strictly for the kids. It involved drinking a can of Coke, paddling a Mal around a buoy set way out to sea, coming back to the beach to eat a cold meat pie and a cream bun, then paddling around the buoy again. First one across the finish line without throwing up won a can of Coke. It was a big, fun day. Everyone did a lot of laughing, the camaraderie was fantastic and the waves were generally pretty good. We formed ourselves into a loose social group called The Beachcombers Malibu Club.

Looking back on it, I reckon the whole deal down at North Avalon was the reason I got into riding a Malibu board again. Not that I really needed an excuse, Mals were a lot of fun on the right day and I was living in the perfect place. I spent a fair bit of time going surfing in Kiddies' Corner – the local name for the break in front of Veda's house at Palm Beach – on an old board belonging to Ti's father. His best old board was a classic 1957 Hobie shaped by Joe Quigg. He'd brought it back from California, and because it was by far the best I'd ever ridden, I used it as a template for all the other boards I built.

More and more people were coming in to our Fall Line shop and ordering Mals. At first it was just a trickle of orders, a few old guys too heavy to surf short boards any more, and a few others who wanted to buy a board just like they used to have before home and family had taken priority in their lives. Now, with a dream of getting fit again and their finances in order, it was time to buy a new board and get back to doing what they enjoyed most as kids – going surfing.

Over the next few years the trickle of interest in longboarding became a flood. The rekindling of interest in this style of surfing was happening to a greater or lesser degree on every beach and in every surf shop all over the world – except in California. There, the longboard's popularity never waned, because for 90 percent of the time Californian waves are more suited to them. As well as older surfers ordering new longboards, a whole new generation of people who couldn't get started on short boards, because of the low flotation, were just loving being beginners on longboards. Riding them was such a lot of fun. Girlfriends, mums and kids all started to enjoy riding Malibus in tiny waves and junior, grommets and girls divisions sprang up in all the Malibu club contests.

Around this time, the promoters of the Bells Beach Pro invited me to fly to Victoria to put on a Malibu surfing exhibition. I felt a real sense of déjà vu as, perched on the nose, I ripped across Little Rincon twenty years after I'd first done it – but the crowd and the officials loved it. I could see that this way of surfing could very easily become a lost art if I didn't demonstrate it properly. I tried to stick to the traditional style of longboard surfing, not doing any tricks but adhering to the discipline that I'd come to understand after all my research on the history of our sport. The point I'm making here is that my style of longboard surfing didn't come naturally. I'd never learnt to surf with my feet down the board in the old style, but always had my size 13s planted firmly across the board. So the classic "drop knee" turn that is such a part of my longboard repertoire was developed entirely from looking at old movies and stills and going out in the water and practising the move until I had it down pat.

TONY NOLAN

Changing feet in the tube... my debut back into longboard surfing competitions was in the Beachcomber Malibu Classic in Avalon, Xmas 83.

SYLVAIN

Every year my longboard surfing improved to the point where I could hang ten on my backhand or forehand.

367

18

November Alpha Tango

BACK IN THE EARLY 1980s, every time I flew anywhere with my Swiss friend Max Andre in his plane, we'd invariably end up talking about how much an aeroplane would improve my quality of life. The conversation revolved around the great distances between destinations in Australia and how much more time I could have to spend on the farm, while still going surfing. Organisers of surfing contests all over the country wanted me to give longboard exhibitions and there was now even talk of a contest series like those in the 1960s, except that now the prizes would be money. Then there were the family holidays in remote areas and the dream I'd had of experiencing Aboriginal culture in the heart of Australia. The possibilities seemed endless and I convinced myself, with a bit of help from Max, that I needed a plane to make more efficient use of my time. In the beginning I used to laugh at myself whenever I started daydreaming about it. It seemed so ridiculous to think about owning my own aircraft, but then I'd plan the location for a landing strip on the farm and think about the tax concessions my accountant had said were available and it did seem possible. However, buying anything else would have to wait until I actually had Showtime's money for *Fall Line* sitting in my American bank account.

I can remember March 1980 very clearly. I was sitting chatting away in the co-pilot's seat of Max's Mitsubishi MU2 corporate jet, while he flew us back to California after heli-skiing in Canada, when Max said he'd look into a few types of aircraft to see which would suit me best. As usual he was true to his word and I wasn't at all surprised when he called me at the shop in Mona Vale to tell me he was convinced the Maule was the plane for me. Max sent all the technical literature to read but I had only the vaguest idea of what the brochure was talking about. What I did understand was the fact that I could buy a brand new four-seater Maule M5 Rocket with a 180 Lycoming engine for US$33,000 with another $10,000 for the latest Narco avionics. These included two navigation and two communications systems which would make the plane as safe as possible. I felt confident with Max's decision, but as one last check, he flew down to Maultree in Georgia where the Maule family built every aircraft from the first rivet to the final polish.

Max called me again, saying he was so impressed with the aircraft and the Maule family's operation, that he'd paid a deposit while he was at the factory. It came as a bit of shock – I'd been having second thoughts – but at the same time I was really excited. I asked Max what colour the plane was because I couldn't think of anything intelligent to say. "Anything you want it to be," he replied. "I've ordered blue and white but it can be changed." In the next breath he told me he was going to lend me the money until I could pay him back then went on about choosing the economical 180 horsepower engine that only used nine gallons (41 litres) an hour and that the plane would be ferried out to California next month. I couldn't wait to get over to the States to see what the new toy looked like and learn to fly.

* * * * * * *

With Max at the controls we spent thirty minutes doing take-offs and landings at Van Neys airport. I couldn't believe how quickly the Maule got into the air and how short and slow the landings were. It felt really safe and if something did go wrong the impact would be minimal. Instead of having a nose wheel, the Maule was a tail-dragger and had no nose wheel – apparently George Maule had designed the original tail-wheel for Cessna before he began building aeroplanes with his family. The Maule is designated a STOL – short take-off and landing – aircraft and that was what it did best. Max had seen a promotional movie in which a Maule got airborne in the length of a hangar and landed inside 30 metres, and that, as much as anything else, sold him on the plane.

For a novice like myself a tail-dragger is a bit more difficult to land but once I'd learnt to keep complete control over the rudder at all times and fly it right onto the ground I was fine. Tail-draggers have the advantage of being very tough and are better suited to rough country, particularly beach landings, than any other aircraft. The interior was certainly spartan compared with the deluxe planes that I'd previously flown in. It had two basic bucket seats in the front and, across the back, a single bench seat that could be laid flat in under a minute, creating an open cargo area perfect for boards.

The week after I took delivery of the Maule, Max and I took the plane into Mexico, something we'd talked about for a while. We had a tent, sleeping bags, food and two 7-foot boards all tucked in behind us in the rear of the plane. It all went in quite comfortably,

My Maule M5 Rocket. The top picture was taken on the plane's first trip when Max and I went surfing and camping-out on the island of Natividad off Mexico.

Back in Australia we were given a choice as to what we wanted to call the Maule. There was no doubt about her call sign. The pic above shows Beau loading all our stuff into NAT for another adventure.

once we'd completely removed the back seat, but I could see that no matter what I did, I'd never fit a 9-foot board back there. Something else would have to be worked out to get my longboards to the contests in Australia. Max made a couple of smooth landings on Mexican beaches which was a real buzz; they were just like landing strips, big and wide with a hard surface, but I understand beaches pretty well and could see how it could get tricky. Unfortunately there were no rideable waves where we put down, and in fact, after all my years of flying up and down the east coat of Australia, landing on at least ten different beaches, I've yet to land on a beach, jump out and surf perfect waves then fly off again.

Back in Los Angeles I signed up for a week of lessons before flying back to Australia. The instructor said I had a good feel for landing the Maule, probably because of my surfing skill and certainly it required the same delicate touch as riding a wave. Max flew the Maule in California as regularly as he could for the next year and then it was disassembled and boxed for shipping. We'd rented a 6-metre container into which the fuselage fitted snugly when angled in, the wings were removed and hung in a sling from the roof, then everything was secured for the voyage to Australia. The insurance and freight added another $6,000 to the cost of the plane, but even so, the whole package still cost me less than a fully imported luxury car.

*   *   *   *   *   *   *

In Australia I started taking flying lessons in December 1983 and all through the heat of the Christmas and New Year holiday I drove for over an hour every day in congested traffic from the Peninsula to Bankstown airport in western Sydney. I gave flying all my energy and attention and as a result flew solo on the 9th January of 1984, after just two weeks of lessons. The feeling was fantastic, even better than I'd imagined it would be: to take off from the sweltering city up into the cool, clear air and be flying free of the confines of the earth; to be the actual person in control, the pilot; that first time cruising 1.5 kilometres above the ground is something I'll never forget.

I'll never forget another experience either. One day at Bankstown I missed a turn and got stuck at the end of a taxi-way. Unable to go forward and with no reverse gear, I decided to get out of the aircraft and push it backwards some 6 metres and then have another go at the turn. Frustrated and not really thinking about what I was doing I didn't shut down when I got out of the plane and pushed it backwards, believing that I had no other alternative. When I got back in the cockpit the radio operator at the control tower almost jumped down my throat. He wanted to know where I'd been and who'd been in command while I was pushing the plane? Didn't I know I was never to leave an aircraft while the engine was running? It could have got away and done incredible amounts of damage; and more of the same. I felt like a real idiot, why hadn't I used my head? Back at the flying school all eyes were on me; everyone on that radio frequency had heard me copping it. I felt that my flying days had come to an end before they'd even started, but I escaped with a severe reprimand from the chief instructor. Because I'm not at all bright academically I had to work really hard at my lessons to pass the necessary exams. The practical side was cool, I breezed through that, but the theoretical side, with all the books and maths, reminded me of school and caused a mental block until I got it through my thick skull that it was all absolutely essential if I wanted to fly.

Midway through 1984 I got my restricted pilot's licence which meant I could fly anywhere with a licensed pilot by my side. The Maule arrived in Sydney in early 1985 and was delivered to Bankstown for assembly, once Customs had finished going over it. Registration was the next hurdle. Because my plane was the first of its type in Australia, lots of airworthiness checks had to be made, which meant lots of letters back and forth between the Maule company and the Australian authorities. It couldn't happen fast enough for me and I was getting very frustrated – here I was with the Maule all assembled and ready to go but I couldn't fly it. In the meantime Ti and I decided that my aircraft's call sign would be November Alpha Tango – NAT. It might seem pretty pretentious on my part to use my name for the call sign – even more Yuppified than having a car with personalised number plates – but at least I never forgot it.

It certainly felt amazing to have an aircraft all of my own – not that the Maule was actually mine at that stage. I felt it belonged to Max until mid-1985, when I sent him the last cheque. The little plane handled beautifully in the air but every now and then I could feel what Max and all my instructors had warned me about. If I didn't stay in control of the rudder while landing the whole thing could get away from me in a flash and the plane would "ground loop" without warning.

Not long after I had my endorsement to fly the Maule, I touched down at Bankstown in a pretty strong crosswind. I always felt quite comfortable about coming in with the runway over one shoulder – it was a bit like a side-slip on a wave – but this time as I straightened it up for the final touchdown, it just didn't feel all quite there. As soon as the wheels hit the deck I felt it happen. The plane dived to the right, the left-hand wing smashed violently into the ground, and I went into an uncontrolled slide, the Maule coming to rest on its side after sliding 9 or 10 metres. I was devastated and climbed out to stand looking at nearly a metre of shredded fibreglass, once a perfectly foiled wing-tip, still in contact with the asphalt and smelling of burning resin. I felt sick. The fire trucks raced over with sirens blaring and the first thing the captain did was ask if the fuel was turned off. I told him I thought so but felt like a real mug when he returned to tell me he'd turned it off for me, letting me know that was how fires start.

In a few weeks my baby was repaired and I was back in the air. My ego was damaged, but I'd get over that. The repairs to the aluminium and paintwork were done by experts, but I did the fibreglassing to remind myself that I'd broken it. I promised myself to try very hard not to let it happen again – a promise I kept pretty well, though it was a hard thing to stay on top of. I did manage to ground loop the Maule twice more in 400 hundred hours of flying over the next ten years, with similar results each time. I resigned myself to the fact that, as a veteran bush pilot once told me, there are two types of tail-dragger pilots: those that have ground looped and those that will very soon. He also gave me his theory about landings: "The good ones you walk away from, the bad ones they carry you out".

*   *   *   *   *   *   *

I knew all along that finishing my movie *The History of Australian Surfing* was going to be an enormous task. Until the book was completed in November 1983, I'd been doing research for the movie whenever I could, but with the book finished it was time to pull my finger out and put the movie to bed. During that time Ti and I committed a fair amount of our cash just to keep the project alive: getting old films copied, writing the script and making an accurate inventory of the material available – we had an awful lot of hours invested in the project. In the search for suitable investors we once again turned for support to Ti's family. Their accountant agreed to underwrite the cost of production together with an aunt of Ti's who was in a position to take advantage of the generous tax concessions available. At that time every dollar invested in a film qualified the investor to claim a $1.50 deduction from taxable income – even if the film didn't make a profit the investor did very well on the annual balance sheet. The idea was to take pressure off Australian Film Commission resources and have the film industry supported more by the private sector.

Grant Young produced *The History of Australian Surfing* and did a good job of sticking to the budget and balancing the books, while I endeavoured to make sense out of a very complex story. Every day for nine months I'd sit down with the editor, telling him where to hard-cut or fade, marking up a dissolve and ordering the sections we needed to work with the following day. It was a very complex operation, and with the amount of archival footage at our disposal it was at times hard to tell which was the horse and which the cart. What with having to go out and record interviews and lay down a voice track, I was pretty burnt out towards the end of the project, but by mid-August 1985 we at last had a version I was happy with. Then it was time to organise the music tracks and sound-effects, and with all that completed, hand our finished product over to the neg matcher, who had the laborious task of matching the new and old negatives so we could get the master made.

At this point I approached Coca Cola and invited them to invest in the movie as a part of their summer promotion. They could see the marketing opportunity and a deal was struck whereby Coke would feature both on the posters and a short promotional movie to open the show. Armed with this deal I signed an agreement with Australia's biggest cinema chain to release simultaneously at five suburban theatres and one in central Sydney. The money from Coke covered the cost of enlarging the film from 16 millimetre to 35 and the printing of full-colour posters. Things were going really well; the reviews were good and the audience feedback was enthusiastic but when I talked to the distributor about holding it over for another week they explained that it was impossible, other movies were scheduled for release. The best compromise we could reach was a release in Newcastle, a surfing stronghold, where we did very well by using the local TV station to promote the movie. Figures were very good and we held it over for a second week.

Throughout the movie's production stages my thinking had been not to worry about the theatre release as the television sales would be where we'd make our money. The theatre release was only going to build a good image for the sale to TV. I was under the illusion that the movie was the most sought-after property of all time, that it'd result in an all-out bidding war between the Australian networks with one of them being lucky enough to purchase the rights for $100,000 and that would be the end of that. Twice during the production I'd talked to one of Australia's richest men, a neighbour of ours at Palm Beach. A sports fanatic and owner of a television network, Kerry Packer gave me some good advice when I was confused over the direction a surf-boat sequence should take. "Put in lots of monster waves whenever it's going a bit flat. The man in the street loves 'em," was his advice and I took it whenever necessary. However, I could never get an appointment to see him once the movie was finished, he was always much too busy. I even sent a tape to his office and have never had a reply or a even a word of his opinion. At a meeting with one of his station managers I was offered an embarrassingly low $10,000 for the complete Australian TV rights and none of the other networks were even remotely interested.

I was shattered; the movie had cost over $150,000 to make after paying everyone fairly for their footage and procuring the music rights. I'd counted my time and effort as an investment to keep the budget down, although everyone else was paid award wages, as I believed that the film needed to be made right then or the history of the sport would be lost forever. Since its completion four of those interviewed have died, so if nothing else, their significant contributions have been recorded. I explained the position to the investors, who were naturally a bit disappointed, though they did have the taxation benefits, but I still couldn't quite believe it. After the financial success of *Fall Line* I thought I was on to a sure thing. The product is good and I've no doubt it will become more valuable with time. We decided not to accept any piddling offers and hopefully it will one day be sold for what it's worth. For me it was a crushing defeat, my first clanger. To my way of thinking the real test of how good a product is has always been the amount of money it makes in the end, the bottom line. Forget the art-for-art's-sake bullshit. I know the movie is important and relevant, but I can't watch it any more – it depresses me.

*   *   *   *   *   *   *

The day after the November 1985 theatre release of *The History of Australian Surfing*, I took off for Japan to try to sell the movie and book. It was time; I'd been talking about it for years. Lots of the current crop of professional surfers had told me stories about Japan but I'd never had the opportunity to go there. Over the past few months I'd been contacted by a Japanese company interested in buying my longboards and they wanted to promote them by putting on a Nat Young Surf Contest. In fact they had already held one the summer before without asking my permission. I thought this was a bit cheeky, but also flattering in a way. The route between Japan and Australia goes right over Bali and as I'd never been there in the wet season I thought it'd be a good time to stop there for a while and ride a few waves. While in Bali I stayed with an old friend named Kim who years ago I'd taught to shape surfboards. Married to a Balinese woman named Made, he'd been living on the island since the early 1970s and he and his wife had a beautiful daughter, named Dewi. Kim and I surfed lots of big classic waves together on the Sanur side, mostly just the two of us out in the water, and it was exactly what I needed after the pressures of being in an editing booth for the past nine months. Before I left for Tokyo I thought I'd call a guy I knew vaguely and who'd given me his number while he was in Australia over twelve months before. When I finally got through to his number in Japan, a woman's voice said "Hi". I said "Hi" back and she repeated the greeting. I decided to dispense with the formalities and started shouting the name of the person I wanted to speak to. Kim ran into the phone box, grabbed the receiver and started speaking in rapid Japanese – he'd been going to Japan to shape boards for years and was fluent in the language. Kim stumbled out of the phone box contorted with laughter. "What happened?" I asked. "I was nice, I said 'hi' to the lady." Kim explained that she'd been saying "Hai?" the Japanese word for yes; the poor woman was asking what I wanted and I was saying "yes" back to her.

To say that I felt I was unfairly treated by the Japanese wouldn't be far from the truth. On that first trip, one of the television networks made a copy of *The History of Australian Surfing* while I was being treated to a memorable sushi lunch by their company executives. The deal stalled over the rights I was selling them and when we said our goodbyes the company said it would do some more research into the music rights and get back to me in Australia. However, they failed to contact me after the initial meeting and I heard later that the movie had been shown on Japanese TV and theatre. I contacted a lawyer who gave me a rough estimate of the costs of litigation and I dropped it like a hot potato. A similar thing happened with the Nat Young Longboard Surfing Contest. A Japanese company produced a range of clothing with my name on it and the only things I ever got out of it were some free tee-shirts. Japan wasn't a signatory to international copyright treaties at the time, though I think the situation has changed since.

Anyway on this first trip Kim had set me up to spend a day or two with the guy he shaped boards for in Japan; a young Australian friend of his who was over there teaching English and he was to act as my interpreter. I phoned him from my hotel in Tokyo and he took me sightseeing. Thanks to his communication skills I had a really interesting time wandering through some unique buildings and gardens. I also spent a couple of days in a typical country town and as it was winter I spent a fair bit of time drinking lots of hot saki and soaking in the traditional Japanese bath. I admired the way the Japanese made the best use of even small amounts of land – the terracing was even more precise than in Bali. The train back to Tokyo was something else again; people with colds wore masks over their faces. In so many ways they seemed to be such considerate people. I couldn't believe the sushi bars where you sat and helped yourself from a conveyor belt while a team of chefs kept it supplied.

My moderately priced hotel in Tokyo brought home to me the

A good strong bottom turn. Sometimes a longboard
is the best equipment for the conditions. Sylvain's shot.

value of every square inch of space – tissue-thin walls of rice paper and no en suite bathroom for over $100 a night. It really made me appreciate growing up and living in Australia – thanks to our wide-open spaces, the Australian lifestyle is one the average Japanese just can't envisage.

After everything that had gone on, I didn't make contact with the organisers of the Nat Young Surfing Contest on that trip, but Japan, like everywhere else in the world at that time, was interested in long-boarding. Perhaps because they have so little surfing background of their own, the Japanese were hungry for any surf history but unwilling to pay a fair price for either the book or the movie. I'd given away fifty books to people I met, because I was told it was the custom to give presents when you first meet someone. In the years following I made several trips to Japan, one when we were exporting my long-boards. It was a profitable venture for both parties but Japanese consumers are very fashion conscious and want something different every season. My longboards don't change much at all.

* * * * * * *

The end of 1985 was worth celebrating; it had been another big year and Ti and I were out for a night on the town. We'd been invited to a New Year's Eve party in the city and though we had a great time we left around 1 a.m. as it was an hour's drive home to Palm Beach. I'd been drinking, not excessively, just sipping good red wine all night, and as usual Ti (a non-drinker) drove us home. I slid into the passenger seat of our old British racing green two-door Volvo coupe and promptly flaked out. I was woken up by the siren of a police car travelling in front of us as we went through the bends just before Palm Beach – Ti remarked at the time that it was like having a police escort home. We started passing by big and small groups of people, mainly on the beach but also all over the road and the further we went the more the scene started to resemble Woodstock, with groups huddled around fires.

When we reached Palm Beach Surf Club we came to a dead halt behind the police car; thousands of kids were swarming all over the road. We were obviously going nowhere so I got out of the car and walked up to a group of the cops standing in front of the police car we'd been following. "What the fuck's going on," I said to no-one in particular, more as a statement than a question. The police didn't respond so I kept walking and asked the car directly in front of the cops if he'd move. As I was leaning down talking to the driver through his window I felt someone grab me from behind and I was put in a headlock and dragged to the paddy wagon. Exactly what happened from this point on was debated in court for almost three years. Ti and I knew very well that the police who were present lied through their teeth when they said I hit one of them with an open hand. They all know I didn't – in my head-down, bum-up position I couldn't have even if I'd wanted to – they all agreed I was in a head lock and were lying to protect their jobs and their mates. To be fair the scene that night resembled a riot and the coppers must have been under a lot of pressure; they insisted they'd thought I was a drunken reveller and had no idea we lived nearby.

Just before the paddy wagon took me to the local lockup, I could hear Ti outside trying to explain that we lived at the end of the street and were just trying to get home. I heard the same nasty cop tell her that if he heard one more word he'd throw her in the back, too. At the station I asked to see the senior officer, thinking I could explain to someone that it was all a terrible mistake, but no-one of rank was on duty, they were more interested in taking my fingerprints and giving me a breathalyser which much to their disappointment showed negative. Ti had followed me to the station, which was just down the road from our shop, but by the time I got to see her I'd been charged with unseemly language, assaulting the police and resisting arrest.

The first thing I did on arriving home was write out a detailed account of exactly what had happened. I sent a copy to the Commissioner of Police which never received a reply, but at least my barrister had something to tender in court. It dragged on for the next three years – although the total time spent in court was only five days – and cost both the government and us a lot of time and money. My friend Craig Leggat had become a very efficient solicitor and he engaged Greg James QC to represent me. I'd given a statement at the station but the one tendered in court was another one altogether, concocted from newspaper stories and the cops' collusive account – and, of course, it was unsigned.

On the 8th of September 1988 all charges were dismissed and the magistrate stated that the police had been a bit "high handed". "Why," he asked, "didn't we just talk about the mix-up at the police station on the night?" We later complained to the Ombudsman about the conduct of the police but this was dismissed after half a dozen letters were exchanged. A Royal Commission has since revealed the corruption and bribery reaching all the way to the top of the New South Wales police service, virtually unchanged since the days of the Rum Corps and answerable to none but themselves. One result of the inquiry does seem to be that the service is now trying to improve its image.

* * * * * * *

In Australia the longboard thing went from strength to strength in those summers of 1985 and 1986. You only had to count the recreational Mal riders out in the water to see that something was happening. Old Mals became like hens' teeth to buy and our surf shop never managed to keep a new Malibu on the floor for more than a few hours before it had to be replaced. Because we were selling to both novices and experienced surfers, we had to make two types of longboard. The basic beginners' board was wide and flat and though over 8 feet long it paddled easily and was light enough to be carried by anyone.

The board we used as the basis for custom orders and for my own brand developed over quite a few years. I was using neither new nor old design elements in these boards but rather incorporating all the best design principles I knew to make the highest-performing Mal that I possibly could. I still had all the drawings for Sam, the board on which I'd won the 1966 world championships, and I used his outline and volume as the basis for the new boards. The rest of the updated Sam's elements came from modern technology – Sam hotted up.

I didn't come to fully understand the function of each design element until 1986, when I was invited to California by the Oceanside Longboard Surfing Club to compete in their second annual contest. Donald Takayama, a colourful and dynamic expatriate Hawaiian, was president of the club, and I was completely enchanted with him. He really was and is the man in California when it comes to modern longboards. He's always built magnificent sleek longboards and is constantly refining his plans and now here he was telling me that he wanted to make my boards in America – boards just like the original Sam but with a few improvements.

The first things we worked on were the rails. Both Donald and I had built a whole bunch of longboards with different-shaped rails but being together in California gave us the chance to compare rail shapes during many a surf session and we agreed that the standard low rail tucked under to an edge all the way around was by far superior in all conditions. I'd really only played with the size and shape of the single fin, ending up with one exactly the same size and shape as the original fin George Greenough had sanded for the first Sam back in 1966. After riding hundreds of waves that week and experimenting with different combinations of single and tri fins I found that Donald's three-fin configuration, a large centre fin and two smaller outboard fins, worked best. Although the combination was too powerful for most surfers, I preferred the 12-inch deep Greenough centre fin with two smaller fins out towards the rails. This arrangement makes the board turn quicker and in a tighter curve to the extent that I'd never consider

Both long and short board events were held at the same professional contests in the 80's. South African pro Shaun Tomson certainly enjoyed this event. Dick took the shot at Bondi.

going back to a single fin. I was really trying to be conscious of the elements in both old and new boards and not destroy the unique way the Malibu surfed. We could use lighter blanks and glass jobs but in my opinion the lighter weight didn't improve the performance of a longboard; I was determined that I maintain at all costs the same smooth flow and momentum of the old longboards.

We got one classic surf together that week at a break called Swami's; a long, peeling, peaky reef break in southern California. Donald and I had been surfing hard for an hour or more in pretty crowded conditions and I was paddling back out when I saw Donald run over one boogie-boarder and, seconds later, another. Sitting out the back a few minutes later I asked him what had happened with the boogie-boarders. "Like speed bumps in the parking lot, you roll right over 'em on a long board; go up with the bump then back down. You really don't have to lose your speed, they're only a minor interruption and they're made of sponge." It was classic Donald Takayama.

* * * * * * *

In 1985 there were two Malibu events with substantial purses, one at Newcastle and the other at Bells during the Easter holiday. I flew the Maule to Bells, sending my board by road, and drove to Newcastle as it's so close to Sydney.

It was really fun to be involved in professional competition again and sitting around in a roped-off area I got a chance to talk to lots of young pros, contact that was important to me and wouldn't have happened if the long and short-board events had been held separately. Graham Cassidy, the then director of the Association of Surfing Professionals, was the man responsible for this. As a committed older surfer he could see an opportunity to introduce another style of surfing into professional competition and he and I both believed that longboard surfing was an absolutely valid discipline because it was so different from shortboard surfing. My old friend Doug Warbrick, of Rip Curl, had already used his influence to include longboards at Bells in previous years, so the writing was on the wall so to speak.

After this first year with money prizes the feeling changed amongst the competitors, so Graham, Doug and I got together after Bells 1985 and discussed how we thought the event should be judged. A few weeks later we had it all down on paper and our format has really never been improved upon or changed since. We decided each ride should be judged with 50 per cent of the points awarded for traditional moves including walking the board, nose-rides, etc. and,

Longboard surfing contests got stronger and stronger all over the world. Malibu Rum was a major sponsor in Australia. In Hossegor, France, I'm with the contest organiser Charlie Puyo, the then French President Francois Mitterrand and Marie Pascal-Curren, wife of World Champion of the day, Tom Curren.

because we wanted to open the competition to younger blood, we wouldn't limit competitors' performance at all, giving them room to try the new modern manoeuvres such as re-entries, helicopters and so on, which would be judged as the other 50 per cent of the score for each wave. This awarding of collective points for both new and old manoeuvres was a positive first step, but I believe it didn't make allowance enough for individual styles to be assessed and compared; it was this style element that set each individual apart in the 1960s when longboarding was in its infancy. What makes "good style" is left for individual judges to assess and is a very subjective thing that makes the person judging very accountable – to this day it's a major problem in diving, figure skating and surfing.

* * * * * * *

Longboard competitions didn't really matter to me that much. I equated that way of thinking with cities and tiny waves. They were fun and I loved riding them but it was not the style of surfing I preferred. Max Andre had always raved about Tahiti and in 1983 had asked me to join him and a group of surfers in chartering a yacht out of Raitaia. I just couldn't get away right then, as Ti was pregnant with Nava and the orders for longboards were really piled up at the shop, but I did go on another boat trip with Max the year after and found some great waves at Grajagan, Java. That adventure was a bearable three days long, but I've had five or more longer boat trips in my fifty years and know that I'm not a boat person. I hate the smell of boats, the constant dampness, living in close proximity to other people and what's more I get seasick unless I stay on a constant diet of motion sickness pills. From what I heard later about that particular boat trip in Tahiti, I'm glad I didn't make it, so 1985 was the year I visited Tahiti for the first time.

Max had already made two trips by then, making contact with an old friend of his, Francois Xavier Maurin, "FX" for short. FX's mother hates anyone calling him by his nickname but his complete name is such a mouthful in English, or French for that matter. An absolutely dedicated surfer, he's four or five years younger than me and was French Junior Champion Surfer when I was World Champion. After completing a dentistry degree in Bordeaux, FX and his beautiful wife Dominique decided he should do his national service in French Polynesia. They began their South Pacific adventure in the Marquesas and ended up on one of the islands of Tahiti and their two children were born in French Polynesia. FX worked hard in his surgery but every available minute he spent on the ocean, either paddling a canoe to keep fit or going surfing in real waves.

When he came to pick me up at the airport in Raitaia I was completely on the back foot. Max had said to keep an eye out for a dentist friend around my age and of course my mental picture of what a dentist my age should look like was completely off-track. Striding across the lounge towards me was a tanned ball of muscle at least 180 centimetres tall. He looked 35-ish but the way he was laughing and cracking jokes with everyone in the lounge it was hard to tell his age. This was only a small island with a tiny population and as he was the only dentist he knew everyone. FX was in his element, a cold Hinano beer in one hand and with the other waving to friends. Tearing himself away at last, FX drove along the unpaved and sleepy main street to one of his favourite restaurants, a spotlessly clean cafe – despite its dirt floor – boasting deep-red plastic tablecloths and matching paper napkins. When a girl placed a basket of baguette on our table, we could have been at a sidewalk cafe in Paris.

After we'd eaten, FX took me back to his newly built timber house and once I'd unpacked we went to have a better look at the surf. At the end of an overgrown driveway next door to his house, FX showed me an abandoned mansion, that looked out over the lagoon. The house itself was covered in growth but FX had hacked a path to the front verandah from where he checked the surf. FX told me the house had been built by some Nazis who'd fled Europe after the war; they'd lived in it for years until suddenly and mysteriously disappearing. From the verandah we could see what seemed very rideable waves breaking beyond the lagoon and in a few minutes we had FX's outboard-powered boat loaded up and skimming across the shimmering lagoon. On the way out FX explained that over time, fresh water flowing off the mountains into the lagoons eventually formed openings in the coral reef. There are breaks like this in the reefs surrounding almost every tropical island in the Pacific and every one has waves breaking along its edge. FX's break had a sectioning 6-foot right-hander peeling along the reef. It was about 400 metres offshore and as we approached I eyeballed the coral reef which seemed to be in awfully shallow water on the shoreward side.

However that was the least of my worries. Immediately I arrived out the back and sat waiting on the first set, I saw a shark, and then another, and yet another, hundreds of them – the line-up was in the middle of a feeding frenzy with hundreds of metre-long white- and black-tip reef sharks chomping into a school of surface fish. I tried to keep my cool and hoped they didn't mistake my leg for a fish as FX told me to keep my legs up and relax – but that's pretty hard on a 6-foot 4-inch thruster, my usual small-surf board in 1985.

For the next hour things went pretty well, we were both getting some good clean rides, flicking out before the reef went bare, then

Deep tubes like this sequence taken by Sylvain on a reef off Tahiti are what memories are made of.

Sylvain took this shot of Rico from Brazil, FX and me clowning it up in Hossegor.

towards the end of the session I got a slightly bigger wave that had a barrel. I pulled in but the tight curl eventually got too far ahead of me and I was wiped out and driven into the reef, with the result that my right shoulder looked as though it had been worked on with a giant cheese grater. I hadn't known till then that a wound from live coral will leave the polyps embedded in the cut and if they aren't removed they will cause the scar to break open. The Tahitians have found that the best way to clean a coral cut and kill the polyps is by rubbing fresh lime juice into the open wound – a treatment I accused FX of enjoying. At his surgery, FX covered the wound with plastic skin and with the aid of that and bandages I managed to continue surfing, but I still have a scar from that war wound.

One of the nice things about Tahiti is the abundance of fresh fish. Poisson cru – fish marinated in lime juice, coconut milk and herbs – is a real treat; and in my humble opinion French Polynesia produces the finest sashimi on the planet. Every night Dominique cooked delicious dinners of rice and fish and by day FX and I surfed some wonderful lefts running into the many deep-water breaks in the reef. When the swell got big we flew to the island of Huahine and surfed some big round rights at a break called Fitii and lefts at the Bali Hai break, named after the magnificent hotel nearby.

One day after a long session we thought we'd book into the Bali Hai for a few nights, but when we walked up to the front desk could see no-one. We rang the bell and yelled but still no-one came. Walking around the tropical gardens and peering through the windows we found the place to be deserted. We went into the village and checked into the Hotel Huahine where we were told the story of the Bali Hai. The hotel had been built on an ancient burial ground and when the employees discovered this fact they left on the spot. It took the owners years to find staff willing to work in their hotel.

19

Ralph Lauren, politics and Tahiti

IN JUNE 1986 the sitting member for Pittwater, the New South Wales electorate that includes the northern beaches, retired from State politics and under Australia's parliamentary system this called for a by-election. Around this time I was seeing a bit of Peter Garrett, the shaven-headed charismatic singer with the rock band *Midnight Oil*. I liked his style and had taken more of an interest in politics when he ran for the Senate. After being only narrowly defeated by the allocation of the major parties' preferences, he left politics to concentrate on his young family and his music but I'm hopeful that this won't be the last we see of Peter Garrett in the political arena.

Peter wasn't a board surfer like me but he was a keen body surfer whom I'd first met when he was swimming in the line-up at Narrabeen alley – his manager was also a keen surfer and he introduced us. We later got talking on the beach and cemented the beginnings of a friendship. Though we rarely got together, we regularly talked on the phone, and in 1987 he invited me to the launch of his first book at which he gave a very inspired, patriotic speech. His legal training has helped make him a superb orator, very articulate and concise. Like many other people my age I admired his highly moral stand on such important issues as Aboriginal land rights and the environment.

I think it may have been Peter's birthday when Ti and I were invited to a party at his house in Seaforth. Towards the end of the evening I ended up in a lively discussion about the current state of the ocean at Manly, right down the road from where the Garretts lived. I hadn't surfed the stretch of beach between Manly and Queenscliff for years, but with the Coke longboard contest being held there, I had no choice. It was some of the worst-polluted water I'd ever surfed in; it stank like sewage and looked foul. That was just bearable for fifteen minutes or so, but the water really stung your eyes as well, so if you were unlucky enough to get hit by a wave or fall off, it was excruciating. The water had lost its sparkling blue and most of the time was the same dull grey as the water near Los

FAIRFAX PHOTO LIBRARY

The campaign for the by-election in '86 for the seat
of Pittwater in NSW. We were campaigning for zero
development in our area and an end to ocean
outfalls.

DO YOU WANT *THIS* TO HAPEN TO US?
VOTE YOUNG 1

ILLUSTRATIONS TONY EDWARDS

A handbill for our campaign.

Angeles in California. But the most visible effect of the pollution was the foam – so concentrated were the detergents in the shore-break that when an oily wave broke, it agitated the water like a washing machine, stirring up an unbelievable amount of stinking foam and suds. Peter is a heavy beachgoer and this was his local beach; he wasn't happy about it but I wasn't telling him anything he didn't already know, but other people at the party were astounded.

Australia is known the world over for its ancient Aboriginal culture, its unique animals, the Great Barrier Reef and its thousands of kilometres of magnificent beaches. Now two of these beaches, Bondi and Manly, household words in many countries, were being totally destroyed by pollution and the authorities said they could solve the problem by simply pumping the sewage further out to sea – the watery equivalent of sweeping it all under the carpet. Then someone who'd been listening suggested I take a stand and run in the forthcoming by-election. Ti glared at me but said nothing and in the heat of the moment, perhaps carried away by the good company, I said I'd have a go as long as Peter helped. The next day I nominated and was in politics as an independent candidate.

Our surf shop became campaign headquarters and everyone – Peter Garrett, my secretary Nicky, who luckily had just finished typing my new book *Surfing and Sailboard Guide to Australia,* Ti and myself – dropped everything to hold our first campaign meeting. Peter had been through all this before with the Nuclear Disarmament Party so he knew what to do and had a lot of like-minded friends we could call anytime for advice. We were all willing and capable but we needed a plan of action – Peter gave us that – because we only had two weeks to pull off what the other party political machines had been grinding away at for years.

Firstly the media, something I could take care of on my ear. I wrote a press release, Peter proofread it and Nicky typed it and faxed it out. I took all the calls when the reporters rang back, either setting up interview times or just answering their questions. It was pretty easy because I did it every day with the longboard thing or the latest book or movie; I was just offering them another story opportunity. Ti and Nicky got the fliers stating our policy organised, a pretty easy task for two such competent people, but delivering them to every household was a huge job. Once again our families got involved, dropping them in letterboxes all over the electorate. We held a rally in a local Surf Club one evening and it was standing room only. Peter and I both spoke from the heart and we got an expert to address the rally on the facts about ocean outfalls and how short sighted and environmentally unsound they really were.

The campaign was going very well; I felt I was giving it my best shot, the media were very supportive and the electorate should now understand where I was coming from – what I thought was wrong with the system and what should be done about it, particularly the problem of pollution on our beaches. There was really nothing the Water Board could say in its own defence. It claimed to have inherited an antiquated system that hadn't changed much since the early days of Sydney and needed more funds to address the problems. The Board's public relations department took me on a guided tour of all their sites, assuring me that in the near future industrial and household waste would be separated. My guide showed me dried and treated sewage that could be used as fertiliser, a good first step that I have since learnt was shelved because of the cost of trucking it to farming areas. He also showed me the plans for the deep-ocean outfall they were building, the final stage of which delivered the sludge a couple of kilometres out to sea, cleaning up Bondi and Manly beaches but really just spreading the pollutants further afield – out of sight, out of mind. It didn't sound like a permanent solution to me but the official explained that this was the way every other big city in the world dealt with the problem and that it was a matter of economics. I tried to tell him that some things were more important than money but he was deaf to that argument.

And then it was polling day and Ti and I drove around to all the booths to shake hands with voters and campaign helpers. Just on dusk that evening, as the first results were coming in and in a state of terror, I called Garrett from the election offices. Peter had told me it was impossible to win in this blue-ribbon Liberal seat and not to worry, we were just going to give the major political parties a shake-up to make them aware of what some people thought were important issues. That sounded fine at the time but the first indications from the tally room were that I was winning. I could see my life changing dramatically: picked up in the white Ford Fairlane and taken to Macquarie Street on days when Parliament was sitting; waiting a year to make my maiden speech; the frustration of being inadequate to deal with the relentless debate; but it was academic – when the preferences were distributed the Liberal Party pipped us at the post – just. I was very relieved, I didn't really want to be a politician on any level, but I like to think the 47 per cent we polled helped achieve some of the things that needed to be addressed in Pittwater. Certainly the Government had been given a good jolt about being too complacent with safe seats. And maybe when the deep-ocean outfall chickens come home to roost, the defenders of the band-aid solutions will find themselves out of a job once and for all.

A week after the elections I returned to Tahiti to get my life back in perspective. I actually went back on several occasions during the next few years as FX and I had become close friends. There is an interesting bond between world-class surfers, and I suspect all top-line athletes. They tend to push the envelope that little bit further by doing it together. The standard of surfing seems to get higher when you're doing it with someone you can trust. Conquering your fear in sizeable surf is a huge part of doing it well, but knowing that if you get into trouble your friend has the ability, understanding, and stamina to get you out in one piece is very reassuring. I've been in some hairy situations with FX, reminding me of old times with Wayne Lynch back in the 1970s, when we rode some awfully big waves together on coral reefs miles out to sea. Sometimes it was just the two of us out there and it made for a very intense bond that will hopefully endure for as long as we both live.

Some of these big Tahitian left-hand walls were the most exciting waves I've ever ridden. Taking off with my heart in my mouth; carving hard off the bottom as the curl throws over my head; the awesome power and beauty of a 12-foot high wall of water sucking onto the bottom of my board; feeling like a fly on a wall; driving down the line with the accelerator flat to the floor; not consciously thinking, turning either high or low as my instinct dictates and all the while my eyes are focused 50 metres ahead looking for the first signs that the hidden bowl section might be revealing itself. Sometimes it's a boil in the face of the wave, at others there's no sign at all, the wave just sucks out revealing dry reef, but one thing is for sure; on every wave I know the bowl is lying there waiting to rip my head off if my timing isn't absolutely perfect.

It's a fine line: a heavy wipe-out or a perfect back-door tube; sometimes I went in too high, at others too low without enough power in reserve to drive through the curl – with disastrous consequences. Certainly beating the bowl section was the difference between a good and a fantastic ride. From 3 to 15 feet these sections of slightly shallower coral reef at the openings in the reef create bowl sections on every wave as it breaks, and for me they are the single most exciting element in surfing. I don't know how many times I stayed with FX but whenever I was flying from the United States I'd book the ticket to allow for a few days' stopover in Tahiti. In 1986 Dominique and their kids stayed with us in Sydney on their way back to France – FX would follow six months later. They'd decided it was time to leave the tropics, buy into a dental practice close to where FX grew up in Guethary, get a traditional French education for the kids and see if it was possible to go from living on a tropical island to an old stone house in the south of France.

With FX back in France I needed another exotic location with good waves to allow me a break during the increasing number of flights I was making across the Pacific. Famous fashion photographer Bruce Weber's secretary had been communicating regularly with my secretary Nicky, while I'd been on the road. Ti's mum and Bruce wanted to use some old pictures of me for a story he was doing in an Italian fashion magazine. Nicky told me about it during a phone call and I agreed; I was really flattered but a bit puzzled as to why Bruce Weber would choose me. I recognised his name from somewhere, but not being in the fashion business myself didn't really understand who he was. Nicky sent the photos and thought nothing more about it until they called again, this time asking if I'd come to New York to shoot some pictures for a company called Ralph Lauren. I was amazed. I knew the Ralph Lauren Polo label, having bought a pair of fawn slacks in California a few years previously while attempting – using the Bob Evans method – to impress a television executive to whom I was trying to sell my movie. For years they were my best pants, until a dry cleaner lost them. Not only was Ralph Lauren's agency flying me first class and paying me $2,000 a day, they didn't mind me stopping in Fiji on the way.

* * * * * * *

Someone had told me about a surf camp that two American surfers had opened up on the island of Tavarua, in Fiji. I'd heard that the Fijian islands had good waves but no-one had ever told me exactly where to go. There were literally hundreds of islands, and certainly Fiji wasn't known for its surf – but then again Tahiti wasn't either, until we started to have a closer look. I was travelling with Ti, our baby daughter Nava, Aunty Ina, my friend Legrope and a relatively new friend named John "JB" Bell, a clean-cut, 193-centimetre stunner and a complete surf fanatic. John was really bowled over by the Ralph Lauren deal and he knew very well who Bruce Weber was because he was in the same business. JB was the managing director in Australia of a company called Esprit and through our love for surfing we had become extremely close friends over the past few years.

After a punishing trip by bus and boat from Suva, we stepped ashore on Tavarua and just along the reef from where the boat deposited us was a 3-foot high tubing left that took us completely by surprise. Absolutely flawless, it was peeling for a hundred yards and we jumped right on it, neither unpacking nor realising that we were surfing right in front of the restaurant and meeting area.

We spent the rest of the week surfing Restaurants, as it's called, or when the swell dropped a bit, another quality left called Cloudbreak a short boatride away. John got smacked on the coral reef and needed a few stitches and luckily there was a doctor among

POLO RALPH LAUREN

Cover of a catalogue for Ralph.

MEN

VOGUE

AUSTRALIA

Supplement to *Vogue* Australia April 1989. Not to be sold separately

Nat Young,
champion/surfer,
ecologist, author
and A-1 Aussie hero

Winter's best looks,
from bush to boardroom.
Hot news in power suits:
grey quits,
brown takes over

the guests. The accommodation was in thatched one-room cabins based on the traditional Fijiian *bure* (pronounced booray), or hut, and we were all given a black plastic bag with a shower rose at one end, the idea being to fill your bottle with water in the morning and leave it in the hot sun all day in order to have the luxury of a hot shower after surfing. The only offputting thing for Ti was the absence of things to do while we were out surfing and the abundance of yellow and black-striped snakes on the island; on every walk you were sure to see at least one, although they didn't appear to be aggressive. After a very enjoyable week with a few magnificent waves, I took off for the United States while JB, Legrope, Ina and my family flew back to Australia.

* * * * * * *

New York still had tons of charisma and style and looked the same as it had the last time I'd been there in the late 1970s, though Studio 54, the famous Manhattan night club, had gone. Lauren booked me into only first-class hotels and restaurants and when I did finally meet and have dinner with Bruce Weber it was like getting to see royalty. He was such a nice man, very natural and unassuming. We were shooting on Long Island in a magnificent home they had rented for the occasion. There was a cast of hundreds, from the caterers to the extras who formed the background to individual scenes – it was just like the set for a Hollywood movie. I was overwhelmed by just how wonderful everyone was; I'd expected stuck-up snobs from the modelling world but they weren't like that at all, just a bunch of real people trying hard to get a job done as quickly and efficiently as possible. The first morning was taken up with fittings, trying the new season's range of clothes on the models, using Polaroid snaps taken by Ralph's agency to match clothes with a model and be approved by Bruce. It was a certain look for everyone; someone had obviously really thought about this. I enjoyed modelling, but I definitely had no illusions that I would, or could, make a career out of it. To me it was just like a good wave that came along with me in the right spot and ready to take off.

On the second day I was picked up and taken to wardrobe and hair styling before being shown into the most majestic drawing room I've ever seen. The set designer was just changing the flowers to match the tones of my suit and someone else was wheeling in another antique that was to be used as a backdrop for a certain shot. While I was brought coffee and the morning papers, Bruce's three assistants set up a barrage of cameras on tripods and then, all of a sudden, everyone was being ushered out; the maestro was coming.

Bruce bid me good morning, put his eye to the viewfinder of each camera in turn, stood back and clicked the shutter cords of a dozen aimed and loaded camera bodies and that was it. He told me I looked beautiful and that he'd like to have cocktails with me before the chauffeur took me to the plane that night.

That evening I met both Bruce and the creative director from Ralph Lauren. They explained that the Polo theme for 1987 was to be the "American family" and they needed models for the husband, wife, kids, uncle, aunt and grandparents. They said they were very happy with the pictures of me, asking me to consider modelling the middle-aged husband and saying they wanted to engage me exclusively for Ralph Lauren for a year on both a retainer and per-day basis. I'd made up my mind as they spoke but they told me to think about it, talk to Ti and get back to them before the end of the month.

Ti saw it in the same way as I did; a golden opportunity too good to pass up. The only drawback was that I wouldn't be able to seriously compete in the first official year of the Longboard World Championships because the Polo shooting dates clashed with two meetings. In 1986 I'd finished the year as unofficial World Champion with the highest number of accumulated points but in 1987 Stuart Entwistle, "Twissel" as I'd known him all my life, took the crown, with me a close second. Twissel won because I'd missed a contest; it was cool, I'd made my choice. In 1987 the creative director had a trophy made up and he presented it to me at one of the Polo dinners – I was Polo World Champion. I made several trips for Ralph Lauren that year and another in 1989, but for me modelling was very much a flavour-of-the-month thing. I may have been hot for a while but then I felt like stale bread – they needed someone fresh; c'est la vie.

* * * * * * *

Professional longboard surfing really flourished in the late 1980s, with Brazil, France and the USA all adding Malibu contests to their schedules. I went to every contest possible from 1988 to 1990 because I had good strong sponsors picking up the tab and a desire to be World Champion again. My first trip to Brazil was radical; being exposed to thousands of hysterical fans was bizarre and I now understood why everyone called them Brazil Nuts. It seems that it's normal for international surfers to be mobbed and treated like formula-one motor-racing drivers and they definitely needed security at the beach – it's the only place in the world I've seen fans go to such extremes. Certainly the professional-contest scene in Brazil was like nothing any of us hundred or so touring longboarders had previously been exposed to. I was standing pretty close to my fellow

In '87 the ASP's Longboard tour had contests in Europe, South America and the USA. Consistent high quality surfing like this driving turn at the Bundy Pro on the Gold Coast let me become World Champ again.

401

countryman and friend Twissel, from Manly, when someone shot him with a blowgun dart while we were down checking the surf. Naturally he freaked, thinking it was poison, but thankfully it wasn't, and after a bit of a rest and a cold beer he was back on deck telling the story to anyone who'd listen.

One day, driving on the outskirts of Rio De Janeiro, we rounded a bend after coming out of the last tunnel heading south, when we were forced to slow to a crawl. Creeping along in one lane with the incessant rain beating down on our car we were stunned when we finally reached the cause of the traffic jam. A mass of twisting bodies, one on top of the other, was writhing in a sea of mud covering half the road. Just as we neared this disaster, another wave of people slipped from the *favela*, or shanty town, high on the cliff. These people were living in such poor circumstances that anything more than a cardboard box to live in was a big deal. A mere few days of rain had played havoc with their lives, the subsequent mudslides totally destroying what little they had. All over Rio there were thousands of families living in these conditions, but the majority of city dwellers ignored them. The mud slides happened a few times every year we were told, but after a few days the sun would come out and the *favelas* would be back again. Twissel and I felt pretty uncomfortable seeing people existing like that – Brazil had all this money for professional sport but they couldn't even feed or house the population to a decent standard.

One of the contests was held in southern Brazil in a place called Ubatuba, which has just got to be the best name for a surf-break I've ever heard. The event was the same as in Rio, with hordes of spectators and confusion all weekend and thieving was rampant. The media made a big fuss about three stolen longboards but with poverty everywhere it hardly seemed surprising to me. Holding on to your possessions is a major priority in Brazil and one doctor at Ubatuba had solved the problem by keeping a full-grown lion in his garden; no-one ever broke into the doctor's house.

The Australian leg of the tour was still the richest with the largest number of events and as I was still enjoying flying my plane to every contest, Ti and I left Nava, now five, with Veda and took off for Bells in the week before Easter 1989. Instead of flying the inland, more-direct route that we'd used several times before, I filed a flight plan to fly along the coast. I'd calculated it would take five hours to reach Melbourne in the Maule. John Bell would pick us up, we'd enjoy an evening on the town in Melbourne without the kids and then have a short drive to Bells. Cruising along at 190 km/h, 1,500 metres above the traffic, the police and the twists and turns of the Princes Highway along which I'd suffered tortures for over 10 years, Ti and

I felt very comfortable. Everything was going fine: the ocean off our left wing tip, the purple haze of the Great Dividing Range in the distance to our right; it was truly a magnificent day. I'd been reporting in with my regular radio calls as we passed over the nominated locations and we were right on time.

Not far over the Victoria border I decided to take a short cut by flying cross-country over what I thought was an isthmus to join the coast another 25 kilometres further on. I could still see the coast in the distance so I didn't think too much about the slight diversion. The isthmus was actually a river valley that looked as though it turned and ran parallel to the coast, so I decided to fly along it and then turn left back to the coast when I saw a break. There was a thin layer of cloud above us that, without me noticing, turned into a solid mass and all of a sudden we were in a heavily timbered blind gorge with no room to turn – we were being squeezed between the rising floor of the gorge and the blanketing cloud – the next minute we were flying blind. Through her window Ti saw a tree so close that she could have touched it and when I heard her gasp I instinctively pulled back on the controls and gave the engine full power. I was still cool and hoping that we'd come out of the cloud before we needed oxygen, but it went on forever; 1,800 metres, 2,000 metres and up and up to 3,000 metres, the Maule's little engine was labouring under the load and I was really concentrating on keeping the wings level and not stalling. I was really getting worried when at 3,600 metes we at last broke through the cloud cover and levelled off – I had a sweat up and Ti was really shaken.

I had absolutely no idea where we were and let Melbourne control know our plight. Melbourne handed me over to the National Safety Council in East Sale. This was to be their last emergency because a scandal involving the director had broken; he had skipped the country and all hell had broken loose – and they were going to send a plane up to find us and hopefully bring us down. Waiting for the big twin-engined Dornier to find us was a nightmare; my fuel supply was getting seriously low and there were only about ten minutes of light remaining – I couldn't even contemplate a night landing. And even with the Dornier guiding me, if we didn't find a break in the clouds we were in serious trouble. I'd no experience flying in cloud other than the simulated exercises I'd had to prepare for my licence test. I recalled that it was really scary then – I didn't know up from down which might be all right in training, but this was the real thing.

At last the Dornier arrived and I was told to fall in behind. I tried to keep my cool as we flew in a big arc 6 metres behind the Dornier down to the top of the clouds at 2,100 metres. The captain came on the radio and told me to stick right on his tail as we were going to fly in a big spiral through a small break in the cloud. We couldn't just dive through the cloud as we'd gain too much speed and the wings might be torn off, and we'd also run the risk of running into the tail of the other plane. If luck was with us we just might make it down in one piece. I followed the Dornier down and breathed a sigh of relief when I saw the airport – it was quite dark and the landing lights were all turned on. I did my checks and followed the big plane to just beyond the threshold of the runway, where the Dornier climbed again and went back around, landing behind us. It was another first for me, a night landing. Ti and I both stepped out of the Maule covered in sweat and totally drained. "Never again," I said to her in the motel that night. The next day we caught the train to Melbourne and JB's open arms; he'd gone through a similar experience when he was training for his pilot's licence and he understood completely. Naomi and Nava caught a commercial flight to Melbourne the same day and we picked them up and had a great family Easter at Bells Beach.

I can't remember if I won the contest or not that year, because everything pales in comparison to the flight down. There are no notes in my diary on the contest, only questions about what we would do with our plane. Retrieving the Maule and getting back in the air were hard to do for a couple of reasons. Investigators had come in and locked and secured the private jet belonging to the head of the National Safety Council and in the process had trapped the Maule in the hangar behind it. However, the Council employees came to the rescue again and went to great lengths to get NAT out and in a few hours we were on our way back to Sydney. It wasn't as easy as it sounds. Ti and I were both quietly freaking, but we had to keep our cool and go through the motions because we had the kids with us and the slightest hint of apprehension would be picked up by them. It was a bit like getting back in the saddle after falling from a horse. You have to do it if you ever want to ride again and I really did want to continue flying.

Ti and I were both very relieved when we finally landed at Bankstown. Thankfully, it had been an uneventful flight from Melbourne and I was feeling more confident about piloting my plane again. However, it was really nice to be back on solid ground and enjoying the day-to-day activities around the family home at Palm Beach: reading a good book and riding a few waves in preparation for the next leg of the Longboard World Championships in France.

Not long before I was to leave for France, a friend named Bryan Brown invited me to lunch at his house in Whale Beach. I'd met Bryan in the late 1970s, on the set of a movie called *Palm Beach*, in which we were both doing our best to play our respective roles. I thought then that Bryan was a good actor and obviously lots of other people did too, as he went on to become a star with leading parts in a whole swag of Australian and Hollywood movies. A few years after that he married a beautiful Englishwoman, Rachel Ward, and they had a daughter who was going to Palm Beach kindergarten with Nava. We saw a bit of each other through school activities, but this was the first time he'd invited me to his house. I drove over to Whaley around lunchtime and parked outside their house. I could hear kids screaming around the house and garden, so I ambled up to the back door and yelled out his name to see if any one was in. Bryan answered, telling me to grab a beer out of the fridge and come on through, so I walked into the living room via the kitchen fridge, taking a quick glance through the big bay window to see what had happened to the surf in the last hour. I'd been surfing some beautiful little lefts at the Wedge earlier that morning and conditions looked as though they were improving.

As I greeted Bryan I noticed another person seated on the couch opposite but didn't really focus until I sat down and put out my hand, saying, "My name's Nat". The stranger's hand appeared from around a kid he was consoling as he replied, "Mick". "Shit," I said, doing a double-take, "Mick Jagger". "Yep," said Mick as I tried to cover my embarrassment. We sucked on our beers and ate seafood while the kids climbed all over Bryan and Mick. It was quite a gathering and we all chatted about everything and nothing, from the state of the planet to pollution. One observation Jagger made that afternoon was how dead, dirty and tired the ocean at Los Angeles looked compared to Sydney. He had no problem getting his head around the concept of riding waves, it's the same as making music with other musicians and then riding the energy line together. I told him how I'd based a segment on that theme for a movie I'd yet to make, how it would cut to one of his tracks called *All down the line*. I knew Mick could see what I was getting at and I was stoked. He really was one of my idols and the chance to talk to him and take him down the beach to watch Tom Carrol wind down a few little Wedge barrels – giving Mick a graphic display of the music/surf theory – was something else. It obviously happened for a reason, but I still haven't quite figured out why.

* * * * * * *

In April 1989, Ti and I changed our life completely, selling the surf shop and moving back up the coast to the farm. We'd owned the shop for nine years and it was time for something new. City life was really getting to me even though Palm Beach was definitely the best place to live in Sydney, but traffic lights were taking over, and there always seemed to be a crowd, both in and out of the water.

The country life was really good for our relationship. Ti and I could spend more time together and with Nava, who was really enjoying going to a little school with only a handful of other kids. We were a family in our own home for the first time in our married life and it felt really good getting everything comfortable on the farm again and not having to worry about every penny we spent. Ti and I knew the money accumulated from the sale of the shop, modelling, books and Ti's inheritance from an Aunt had to be invested wisely if we were to continue to enjoy our new lifestyle on the farm, but right then it seemed better to enjoy spending it and not make too many rash decisions. I cleared a paddock to put in a short airstrip for the Maule and we made lots of short flights around the area looking for some sort of investment.

The closest quality surf-break to the farm was at Angourie and I'd been surfing it every time I came to the farm, loving the fact that I could always get a wave regardless of wind direction. One day after a particularly memorable session, I was introduced to an elderly woman who owned a lot of property in the village. We got talking and I explained to her that I loved Angourie but couldn't really afford to buy a housing block because I needed an investment. She told me that she'd followed my surfing career with interest and liked my style and because of that she would be prepared to sell me a piece of commercial property across the road from the beach. She said that if I came up with the dollars for one block, she'd finance the other and would even throw in the pick of her litter of cocker spaniels which Nava had fallen head over heels in love with.

Ti and I started to agonise over the prospect of building holiday units on this property; they would change the look and feel of Angourie forever. We thought about what had happened in Byron Bay, but perhaps we could do it well and not rape the place. In some ways it seemed like a horrible idea as there were only four other units in Angourie, but it was only a matter of time until there were more. It was more a matter of how they were done. In the end we decided it was going to happen sooner or later and perhaps by doing it properly we might influence others.

Paul Witzig and I were still in contact with each other. Paul and his wife and family had left the arid country near Penong in South Australia and moved back to the Northern Rivers, buying a cane farm on the Clarence River. Architecture was in Paul's blood and it wasn't long before he'd set up offices in Byron Bay and Maclean, just inland from Angourie. We had a meeting with the local council who told us they could approve a hotel on the site but Ti, Paul and I argued that

MARTIN TULLEMANS

The possibility of riding waves like this and living in a clean environment keep me stoked on the Angourie area.

IAN STEED

407

it was too much for a village of only fifty houses, and anyway, there was already a pub 5 kilometres away at Yamba. The council was adamant; we had to have a separate business on the commercial site. We finally reached a compromise by which Paul would design a beach house for us, a restaurant and five rental units. We were all of one mind that if we were going to do this it had to fit in with the area and be a good design. I'd long held the view that good design was not just personal preference but rather a collection of ingredients that change, depending on the climate, the number of inhabitants and their personal requirements.

We didn't know whether or not the whole thing would work, so we decided to go in cautiously. Each unit would have one bedroom and a loft, which meant a high roof which, with breezeways, would provide the ventilation needed in the stifling heat of high summer. Spacious covered verandahs were essential, as they were an important component of the north coast lifestyle. Sitting outside in the evening has always been an important part of my day, taking me back to Bob Evans and his search for the green flash. That was the extent of the brief; Paul went away to do the drawings and I ran back to the farm with a list of timber that Jim could cut while I was away on the French Pro Longboard tour.

* * * * * * *

I think the French phrase is *savoir faire*, which translates as "the right thing" or something close to that. For me France has always represented an abundance of just about everything I really love about life, fine food and wine, and good friends to share these pleasures with. French beaches in summer are a 24-hour party. With daylight-saving time you can still be surfing at 11 p.m. and it's not uncommon to start dinner at midnight, even later in Spain. On previous visits it was often 3 or 4 a.m. before I climbed into bed – only to be back at the beach ready to compete at 8 a.m. It's a gruelling pace that gets to you after a while and when you're burning the candle at both ends something has got to give after a few weeks. Staying with FX and Dom and their kids in the quiet old farmhouse was much more my style these days and it was much nicer having Ti and Nava with me. Checking into one hotel room after another, the lifestyle associated with following the tour wasn't something I found at all attractive any more. The travelling had become a chore – professional sport is a single young man's game – or perhaps I was just getting old.

On the way to France we had a stopover in Bali, a really sensible idea as you fly right over Indonesia on the way to Europe anyway and Nava was now an active 5-year-old who needed to run around.

I felt really good about the fact that I was sticking to the "fun in the sun and income too" principle and we'd arranged to meet up with some old friends and spend a week recharging the batteries and getting in shape for the Pro contest. Once in France we took the train. Railways are efficient in Europe and to get to Biarritz you can leave from the airport with only a change of train in Paris before going on to Bayonne. It was a really tight squeeze trying to fit a 9-foot 6-inch Malibu up in the overhead luggage rack. It takes up three spaces, and the other travellers all looked at the board, though no-one said a word. I saw one elderly lady breathe a sigh of relief when she saw me pull out a short length of rope and secure the board. I always travel with this little aid, using it to tie the board to the roof of a taxi, to secure a car boot over the board or even on one occasion to secure a crazed dog on a local flight in France. It has to be the only place in the world where you can take your dog in your lap on the flight with you.

FX was waiting at the train station in Bayonne and it was great to see him and catch up on all the news. We sped across the river Adour, stopping off at his house to drop off our belongings and pick up boards, Dominique and their kids, and belt down to Boucau, the local beach right at the mouth of the majestic river. As soon as we paddled out I could see how disgusting the ocean had become. The water was so polluted it looked dead and it stank, with every imaginable type of garbage floating on the surface. The French blame the Spanish in San Sebastian, on the other side of the Bay of Biscay, for pushing their garbage over a cliff into the sea. The prevailing winds blow it onto the Basque coast where it litters over 100 kilometres of coast and seems to get worse every year. It was even worse than Manly once was and nearly as bad as Chigasaki in Japan, which is still the worst pollution I've ever experienced. At Chigasaki the ocean had been so abused that it had become a stinking mass of chemicals and detergents – and people still surfed in it. Apparently at Boucau the water can be either good or bad, depending on tides and the winds. FX and I used the area to get ready for the contest because it was so handy to his work. He could see the odd patient at his dental practice and meet me on either side of the Adour.

Boucau is right across the river from La Barr where the authorities extended the breakwater, wiping out a surf-break that was among the finest left-handers in the world. The remaining break, Cavaliere, is a far cry from La Barr but when the wind is from the north at least it's offshore. France in summer, especially the Biarritz area, has masses of tourists in July and August and it's impossible to get normal service. The beaches, hotels and roads are crowded with holidaymakers from every country in Europe. I knew my way around the back roads like a local and could get just about anywhere in reasonable time but the roads were really frustrating, especially getting to Hossegor, as it effectively has only one access road in and out.

This was the same classic beach-break we'd stumbled on all those years ago with Wayne Lynch, Ted Spencer and Paul Witzig. Of course it had grown a lot in the twenty-odd years since we'd first seen it. It took me a while to find the original award-winning housing development, but the sandhills behind the beach and the waves remained the same and the third old bunker south from the main carpark seemed to always have well formed lefts or rights on the sandbank. We were all really hoping conditions would be similar to last year's longboard event which had been held in solid 8-foot rights. In that contest Wes Laine, a talented short-boarder from Virginia Beach in the USA managed to get three incredible rides and pip me at the post. As much as we all wished for the contest to be held in real surf, the waves simply didn't materialise in the scheduled time and we ended up surfing 2-foot junk. Huey had deserted us, but it wasn't so difficult for me to win under these conditions.

Towards the end of the contest FX asked me if I'd have dinner with Fabrice and Isabelle, the owners of a French sportswear company named Oxbow. The meal was superb, with some excellent Bordeaux reds to wash down the fresh fish and made even more enjoyable by the fact that the couple spoke good English. This was just as well, as my French was limited to queries about the state of the weather, swells and wind direction. Fabrice asked about the possibility of me joining their company and as I was only sponsored by an Australian surf label at that time, and they didn't plan to sell Oxbow in Australia, it sounded feasible. I told Fabrice that I'd call him from home in the next few weeks.

In the course of the evening I understood that Isabelle controlled the design of the garments while Fabrice plotted the course for the promotional side of the business. They'd started off with motocross garments but the year before had fallen totally in love with surfing, both seeming to appreciate surf, especially the artistry of longboard surfing. Isabelle in particular saw surfers as bronzed gods who deserved the most beautiful threads and colours possible whenever they chose to wear any clothes. I was really impressed by them both and the offer seemed much too good to be true. I'd seen some of their clothes on FX and they looked really interesting, unlike any other surf brand I'd seen.

Fabrice and Isabelle invited Ti, Nava and me to come to the head office in Bordeaux and choose some clothes; one of them would pick us up from the station and we'd have lunch on the way back to Paris. My head was spinning, I needed a few days to think before my meeting with Oxbow. As it was September and the tourists were just beginning to thin out, I remembered the perfect spot to hang out for a few days; somewhere protected from the approaching winter storms and with reasonable quality waves. Ti, Nava and I went to La Fatania, a hidden beach near the village of Guethary and nestled between high, rugged cliffs just off the main road from Biarritz to the Spanish border. A tiered caravan park switchbacks its way down the hillside right beside the steep path to the beach but most of the tourists' vans had gone.

Walking down this path each morning brought back a flood of memories: Micky Dora and I had hung out here in the 1970s, playing tennis just up the road in between surfs, taking coffee, paddling out at Guethary when it was glassy or coming back to the tight little right-hand reef at La Fatania when a northerly storm was blowing.

Every morning I'd load up all the boards, drive around the beaches then call FX with a surf report. As soon as he finished work for the day he'd jump on his motorbike and burn down to the surf, managing to get to La Fatania almost every day. We'd have an espresso from the kiosk at the beach, talk about how his day had been and then surf as long as we wanted while Ti sat and watched and Nava played in the shore-break.

20
Church of the open sky

MY THREE-YEAR CONTRACT WITH OXBOW began in January 1990 but it took me a few months to actually sign on the dotted line; Oxbow seemed just too good to be true. On the surface the deal seemed a definite step up, offering a glamorous lifestyle, but there were also many advantages in living on the farm and I tried to consider the consequences such a radical change would have on our family. During this period of uncertainty I gave their garments a really good thrashing. Within the first few weeks of the clothes' arrival, Ti, Nava and I went skiing at Thredbo in the Australian Alps, and the following January I went heli-skiing in Canada with Max – a thorough test for their skiwear. For everyday wear I wore walk shorts and tee-shirts, which were washed and ironed constantly and everyone always commented on how great they looked; they really were of a much better quality than any other surf brand I'd worn before. Ti and Nava have worn two of the ski jackets for more than eight years. They're cut so well they look almost as good as the day they were given to them and they're still waterproof after all that time. My initial impression about Oxbow and its products was not ill-founded.

I saw my role with Oxbow as that of a surf consultant rather than a professional surfer and to my mind it had the makings of a perfect partnership, the old experienced pro and the progressive young company. I tried not to rush and to be methodical and responsible in all my dealings with them, but it wasn't easy with such an inspired team behind me. When I first joined the company, Isabelle's design assistant wore a kilt and flowing gowns to work each day. He was a wonderfully creative Parisian destined for high fashion more than the surfing world, but his unique style was indicative of the company. I was very impressed. But more important than my liking for Oxbow's striking blend of colours and patterns were my developing feelings for the owners. Isabelle and Fabrice were rapidly becoming good friends and it was the first time in my life that I could relate 100 per cent to the philosophy of a company.

I'd always had fairly typical sporting contracts in the past, simply

SYLVAIN

Laughing with Isabelle at the first World Contest in Biarritz in '91.

413

receiving payment for wearing garments and surfing in competitions with the company's logo all over my boards. I was just coming to the end of one such lucrative agreement with Bundaberg Rum, an Australian institution, when I started with Isabelle and Fabrice. My Oxbow contract called for the same involvement and I was also to help represent them at all the big surfing trade shows around the world. This was totally new ground for me and was to become part of an evolving pattern of events. On the surface my involvement with Oxbow appeared to be the perfect marriage, but it produced tremendous conflicts: between family life and the constant travelling; between the quiet of the wilderness and the frenzy of travel, promotion parties, meetings, making decisions, representing the company. This was far different from the life of a professional surfer. I wasn't completely naive, I knew they were buying my credibility because they had almost no background in surfing to speak of and though they had two short-boarders and FX on their team, I was to be the vanguard of Oxbow's developing surf image. I loved that first year; it involved a lot of international travel, catching up with old friends in Europe and the USA and going to some great parties all over the world, but my family time was getting cut down to a few short weeks before I'd have to leave for the next contest or trade show.

Every time I managed to spend a few weeks back home, I really came to appreciate not being surrounded by people all the time. The feeling of open spaces you can get in Australia is a rare pleasure in an increasingly crowded world and so different from Europe or the Americas. The 1,200 hectares that made up the farm provided an almost idyllic lifestyle and in the two years we lived there we were almost totally on our own, except for Jim the farm manager, who called in whenever I needed an extra hand with something. Other than the contact with Jim the only other visitors were either invited friends or family. There was an older hippy couple living on 20 hectares next door but they lived over a kilometre away. With Jim's help cutting timber they'd built a compact little house on our common boundary. He was a qualified electrician and we often gave one another a helping hand as neighbours in the country tend to do.

Around this time my younger brother Chris had reappeared in our lives and one day he talked about tackling the river on a raft. When Ti's elder brother Rik turned up with two Canadian friends and expressed a desire to go on an adventure, we approached the neighbours to take care of Nava while the six of us spent a day on the mighty Nymboida River. Ti and I had been doing a fair bit of rafting, so much so that we'd bought our own raft and equipment rather than paying to be part of an organised group each time we wanted to go out. Not that all this development as "wannabe river rats" had taken place overnight. Over a few years we got everything slowly organised to the point where we could go for a night or a few days with only a few minutes notice. We got to know the river pretty well after a dozen trips or so but my expertise as a helmsman didn't improve much. Rivers are very different to waves, they tend to hold you under a lot longer and with my limited skills we were really at the mercy of the river as soon as we got into any substantial rapids.

Ti and I loved the wilderness – the animals we chanced upon, having an open fire and camping on the banks of the river – but on this particular occasion we were making it a one-day adventure in order to get back to our young daughter and the babysitter before last light. From survey maps it appeared that we could get closer to the headwaters of the river from the inland or western side although we'd never before attempted to enter from that direction. Jim had to finish cutting a big order of timber that day, so the babysitter said she'd be happy to take our four-wheel-drive to the closest point on the western side, drop us off and come back that afternoon to pick us up at The Junction, a spot we knew very well. Although I didn't know exactly where on the river we'd be putting in, I did know how long it had taken me to come downstream from Platypus Flat a few months earlier, so I could calculate the time spent on the river pretty accurately. Daylight saving was in force and the light would still be good till 8.00 p.m. so I thought by telling the babysitter to meet us at 7, it would give us plenty of time to deflate the boat and get all the gear up to the roadside. Everyone was wearing swimsuits, tee-shirts, life vests, hats and tennis shoes except Chris, who was barefoot.

The river was big that day, not huge, but with plenty of class-five rapids with major 2 to 3 metre drop-offs, a half dozen steep races that ran at 45 degrees through huge granite boulders, spilling over in mini waterfalls. It was exciting stuff guaranteed to get the adrenaline pumping. Having been down this part of the river before I sort of knew what to expect and I opted to carry the raft around a particularly heavy section called The Devils Cauldron, a 10 metre-high cascading waterfall impossible to raft. We must have gone through six different classes of river that day; each time we came around a bend and could hear an ominous roar, we'd attempt to pull into the bank and have a closer look at what lay immediately ahead. At every drop we gunned it and hoped for the best, sometimes going over the falls sideways and sometimes even backwards!

When at 7.00 p.m. we arrived at the Junction I felt we'd put in a pretty big day. It had been hot, the temperature was still in the mid 40s, and I was really looking forward to that first cold beer. We broke the gear down and were all sitting around reflecting on what a great day it had been when someone in our party found a note pinned to a tree; the babysitter had left it to say that she'd arrived a bit early and would go home to feed her animals and return as soon as possible. We interpreted that to mean we could be waiting a couple of hours till she returned, but that was cool, at least she'd be back by dark. We re-inflated the raft in order to have something comfortable to sit on and sat round telling jokes and yarning till nightfall, but 9 o'clock came and still she hadn't arrived. The mosquitoes were starting to get a bit ferocious and we were getting a little irritated. I could see that Ti really looked worried, and this was confirmed when she pulled me aside and told me quietly that she feared the very worst had happened, the neighbour had rolled the four-wheel-drive and she had visions of Nava wandering around in a daze crying for her mummy. Ti said that if the babysitter hadn't arrived by 11 she was going to walk the 27 kilometres of dirt logging tracks back to the sealed road, and then to the police station; Rik said he'd go with her.

By the time 11 o'clock came round we were all pretty worried, fear is very infectious, and though the night was dark and moonless, Ti and Rik set off to find help. We tried to settle down for the night by covering ourselves with newspapers and a garbage-bin liner we'd found at the picnic grounds and they did help to keep the worst of the dew and a few of the mossies at bay. Just around dawn the police van, with Ti and Rik aboard, came steaming up the track to pick us up and drive us back to our farm. It was about five hours from the time they'd left us until they'd stumbled onto the local constable's verandah. Wiping the sleep from his eyes, he told them he'd been informed by the babysitter that our party was caught on the river and that she'd pick us up at the agreed meeting place the following afternoon.

Back at the farm it didn't take Ti and I more than a minute to jump in our own car and tear over to the babysitter's place. When we tore up their farm track they must have thought it was a drug bust, but when a very concerned Ti leapt out calling Nava's name they must have had a clue what all the commotion was about. The babysitter explained that she'd been about to drive out to the Junction to get us; a river expert had told her there was no way we could come down that stretch of river in the seven hours I'd estimated and she thought we would have decided to camp out somewhere for the night. I was so blown out I didn't say a word in case I exploded. "What about the note on the tree?" Ti asked. "Yes, well, I put that there before I talked to my friend about the river," the babysitter replied. Ti grabbed Nava and we left; we couldn't understand someone who'd be stupid enough to leave a note and then not stick to what it said. It was a classic screw up, but one that certainly would never happen again.

In October, Ti gave birth to a beautiful baby boy in Grafton Base

Hospital. Bryce was born healthy and strong and weighed 9lb 4oz (4.2 kg) but seemed to get weaker as the weeks turned into months and every time we took his nappy off we were confronted by blood-stains. After visits to numerous specialists and a trip to the Children's Hospital in Sydney we were none the wiser and Ti and Bryce seemed in worse shape than ever. I could see my beautiful wife and baby disappearing before my eyes; I had to do something. My farm manager Jim had helped cure his own cancer by removing meat and alcohol from his diet and eating only raw vegetables and fresh-squeezed juice. The woman who'd put him on this strict diet and overseen his recovery was a naturopath in Grafton so on Jim's advice we turned to her. She seemed to know immediately what the problem was; a reaction to the antibiotics that Ti was taking and Bryce was getting through her breast milk. She threw out the drugs and put Bryce on slippery elm powder and acidophilus mixed in with his mashed banana. Right from the first night I could see a change in both mother and son and within a few days the blood slowly disappeared from Bryce's nappies and he and his mother started to get colour back in their cheeks.

* * * * * * *

The first stage of the Angourie project was up and running in April 1991. We'd left the farm and moved into a caravan at the building site and then into one of the completed small units while waiting for our beach house to be finished. The units were occupied from the day they were built and once we'd hired a chef and waitress the restaurant opened to serve Mexican food. I got out all the old boards that I'd been collecting since the 1960s and decorated the restaurant with these and some surfing mementos. Looking back, I've no idea what possessed us to open a restaurant – neither of us had any training or experience – we must have had rocks in our heads. I recall discussing it with Ti and rationalising the strange move as being the only way we could come up with an idea of a fair rent for future tenants of the fully equipped cafe. There must have been another way, but at the time we just kept going without thinking about it. Ti and I must have had masochistic tendencies; washing the floors, cleaning up after everyone left, dealing with the odd drunk; life became a nightmare. We just couldn't keep it up for more than ten months and I'd been travelling for Oxbow half the time, leaving Ti with an awfully big responsibility and that made me feel guilty and depressed. Finally after several disasters we found a good tenant; she had no money but was prepared to work hard, pay the rent each week and provide a service to guests in the apartments. She took all my surfing memorabilia down while I was overseas, changed the decor to Mediterranean and put in an espresso machine – the coffee was like that in Europe, you could stand your spoon up in it. I love good espresso and still allow myself one every day. Unfortunately late-night noise from the restaurant led to complaints by guests in the apartments, mostly surfing-oriented families who wanted a holiday involving early nights and early mornings.

On one of my numerous trips to Europe in my first year with Oxbow, I talked to Fabrice about quitting the pro tour. I felt it was essential to try to reduce the conflict between my work for Oxbow and my family life, and the stress it caused. Fabrice offered to discuss it at the end of the season; he understood I wanted more time at home with my family and growing business at Angourie, but we agreed it required some careful timing. If one of our major competitor's surfers became world champion it wouldn't be particularly good for business. Fabrice agreed that as long as I did the trade shows, promotional tours and helped with the surf team's direction, it shouldn't affect Oxbow's big picture. My involvement with surf-team management really meant using my expertise to choose the best longboard surfers in each market so they would be surfing for Oxbow and not someone else. Advising Fabrice about who to choose for this team was easy as I felt I could speak straight from my heart as to a true friend. Longboarding was continuing to expand in all of Oxbow's main markets and as none of the other surf brands in Europe were using it at that time, we decided to build that year's promotional campaign around longboarding.

* * * * * * *

I had a really memorable trip to Hawaii in November 1992; memorable because I was travelling with my 18-year-old son Beau. He'd been there once before with the family when he was a kid, but this was his first serious trip to the islands; he'd decided he was ready to ride some real waves. I guess all serious young surfers have to do it, as there comes a time in every committed surfer's life when it's necessary to bite the bullet and this was it for Beau. On the plane over I could feel his fear and we talked about overcoming it and the waves we'd ride together to achieve that end. I recounted my own first experiences and he dozed off to sleep, not waking till we landed in Honolulu.

We rented a beautiful old house right on the beach in front of Laniakea, and started to ease into the size and power of the North Shore. I'd arranged to share the house with Bryce Ellis, an Australian friend from Avoca on the New South Wales central coast. Always clean-cut and neat, Bryce is one lasting friend that I made through my

Summer '91. Dawn on Spooky beach with Nava, and Bryce, 6 months.

TOM AUGUSTINE

involvement with professional surfing. Hanging around the pro contests all over the world, watching him compete under every conceivable type of condition, I came to really appreciate his smooth flowing style, connecting full rail turns that are rarely seen in professional surfing. That was his downfall really, he wouldn't compromise. It was a period of change in professional performance; there were a few like Bryce on the circuit, but not many, and I hated to see what the system was doing to their surfing, making them ride waves as if they were playing pinball, scoring points for every manoeuvre with no consideration for overall style. Bryce needed waves to surf on, not the insipid slop that the majority of contests were held on in those days. I voiced this opinion at the ASP board meeting in Hawaii that year, but the sponsors controlled the timing and venues for the events and professional contests held to produce videos for sale were still in the future.

Bryce Ellis was a pleasure to live with and one of the first truly committed professionals I've ever had the pleasure of hanging out with. That winter in Hawaii I believe he was surfing at his peak and some of the sessions we had together were awesome. One day we went out in giant 12-foot Haleiwa, just the three of us. It was a real breakthrough for Beau; after that session he realised he could comfortably step up to another bracket of sizeable surf and ride it with total confidence. My little boy had grown up.

It wasn't always big that year, far from it, but we surfed every day regardless of the size. One day when we'd been surfing Backdoor till right on dark, we were cruising home along Kam Highway when a little Japanese guy with a board under his arm ran right in front of the car, bringing us to a screeching halt. He began shouting in a mixture of Japanese and English through the open window but the only words we could understand were, "friend", "shark" and "lifeguard". He was hysterical and kept pointing back down the road repeating the word "lifeguard", "lifeguard". We threw him in the car and wheeled it around back to Waimea tower. It seems that he'd seen his boogie-boarder friend being taken by a shark, right in front of his eyes. For the next few days and nights big powerful sport-fishing boats cruised up and down trying to catch the shark, but the only things found were a fin and a few days later a mauled hand. The shark experts all thought the culprit was a tiger shark as there'd been a lot of sightings around that time. Possibly a shark mistook the boogie-boarder for a turtle, as, seen from below, the silhouette is very similar.

* * * * * * *

Since 1986 Donald Takayama in California was continuing to shape beautiful longboards with both his and my name on them, but really

DICK

Tiger sharks increased in numbers in Hawaii when the turtles were protected from humans.

Friend's birthdays have always been important to me.
We were in Hawaii for Donald Takayama's 50th-
naturally Buff was around- and also when Joey
Cabell turned 55 in 1993 - still riding waves
every day except when it's time to snowboard.

they were all Donald's with a few of my subtleties thrown in. Both models surfed like Cadillacs which is still the best description I can think of for the masterful feeling of gliding you get on one of his "Hawaiian Pro" designs. All the Oxbow outlets in Europe wanted longboards and Donald made as many as he could, but they were much too refined for someone just starting out surfing on the coast of Holland or Germany. It was like giving a Ferrari to a learner driver and I stayed right out of the business side of selling Donald's boards to Oxbow outlets.

One early morning before the 1990 Jose Cuervo Pro in Oceanside, California, Donald asked me to meet him at the beach to have a surf with his protégé, a 14-year-old kid named Joel Tudor. The 157-centimetre, 48-kilogram kid had obviously learnt his lessons well; he was a super-smooth goofy-foot like Donald and it made me feel good inside to be paddling over the back of a wave that he was riding and getting almost washed off by the wake of one of his strong carving turns. His surfing that first morning set aside my concerns about the direction of longboarding among the younger generation. With his flowing blond hair halfway down his back and impish smile I could just see him on an Oxbow catalogue cover – and he became the cover model in autumn 1992.

In that Cuervo contest I still had the draw on the kid. I had my rhythm and I knew it. My closest rival was another old surfer from California named Dale Dobson, whom I only narrowly beat into second place, but I could see the future was with young Joel Tudor, who came a very close third. To my mind, the party afterwards was a far more memorable event than the surfing. The liberal amounts of the sponsors' Tequila drunk at the official presentations guaranteed that everyone invited back to the contest director's home to watch the Californian sunrise and have Margaritas for breakfast wouldn't forget the evening in a hurry.

Besides the party, the best thing about that trip to California was introducing Oxbow to Joel Tudor. Fabrice was very happy, as effectively it was an ace in his hand. For my part I could get out of contests knowing that I'd delivered potentially the world's best longboarder to the company. It seemed an alliance made in heaven and one that would take some of the pressure and stress of constant travel off me. The first time I shot pictures with Joel was in Victoria in April 1992, the week after the Bells contest. We had a ball, Joel, FX and I, constantly sparring, in and out of the water, laughing and putting each other on all the time. I really liked Joel and after that particular trip could count him as a close friend. We were shooting on the Mornington Peninsula and staying in a big hotel close to my friend John Bell's lovely little weekend house in Portsea. JB was delighted to entertain us during our short stay, in between flying trips back to the Esprit head office in Melbourne.

One morning we were surfing a tight 2-foot beach-break and Joel was surfing in one of his new pink wetsuits, a colour Isabelle had chosen to match his aura. When we surfed together we always competed wave for wave, however, for some reason I was caught out the back in between sets while Joel milked a little one through to the beach. Just then another surfer paddled up to me and asked if Joel was a boy or a girl, saying that he had 14 grams of hash on the thing in the pink wetsuit with the hair down around its bum being a girl. I told him his hash was safe and as Joel paddled up I yelled at him to take off his wetsuit and show the guy his tits. Joel looked at me, then stood up on his board, reached around and unzipped his suit like a stripper. I explained to the growing number of surfers that "she" was only just reaching puberty and wasn't very well developed, hence the small boobs. "Bullshit," said a surfer who'd bet on Joel being a boy. So I said to Joel, "Could you be a dear and give these gentlemen a peek at your pussy?" Joel cracked up, he ran to the nose, hung ten, stumbled to the tail on one leg, where he seductively rolled down his wetsuit and hung his old fella out over the pink fabric. Everyone was in stitches, I thought FX would drown, even the guy who'd lost the 14 grams was cracking up. Joel definitely left his mark on Victoria. From that moment on Joel Tudor became "Boris the Clitoris" to me and everyone else who's ever heard the story. I still smile when I see a picture of him "hanging ten" in his stunning pink ensemble.

Boris won the first tremendously successful Oxbow Longboard Contest held during the summer of 1991 in Biarritz, a contest held with all the pomp and style that you'd expect on Oxbow's home turf. A few weeks later Oxbow signed a three-year contract with the ASP to sponsor the Longboard World Championships. I had joined the ASP's board of directors as it seemed the best way for me to stay involved in longboard surfing. I had a lot of strong opinions and wasn't competing on the professional circuit any more, so no-one could accuse me of feathering my own nest. The first thing we dropped was the travel circuit on which contests constantly moved around the world. Many saw it as too elitist, allowing those with good sponsorships to travel to every contest and accumulate more points than the talented underdog who because of family and financial restraints could only compete in his home territory.

With the Oxbow publicity department carefully massaging the European media, Boris was a big hit. The French particularly loved the "wonder boy" seemingly perched on the nose forever; he became a star in every country where we sold clothes. Everything was going according to plan until he was beaten fair and square in

Joel Tudor... wonder boy.

Oxbow poster designed by Chris Lundy.

the first official World Championship by another American kid named Joey Hawkins. We were all blown away, but life went on. Boris had so much charm he just needed a little luck to win the World Championship. It's now six years into the prestigious event and Joel has yet to win, even if he still is regarded by some as the best longboarder in the world. What seemed a marriage made in heaven was never really consummated for Oxbow, while for me it just added to the pressure I was feeling over decisions I'd made on Oxbow's behalf.

* * * * * * *

The northern hemisphere winter of 1992–93 had me running around the world at a pretty frantic pace. Fabrice had given me the reins of the next World Championship after he'd enjoyed a holiday in Makaha and discussed with some of the Hawaiian families the idea of having the contest there. I had lunch with Buffalo and some other family heavyweights at the Makaha Sheridan and the representative of its parent company agreed to let us use their hotel for accommodation and help out with competitors' airfares. I was elated; this was more than I'd hoped for. Unfortunately at the eleventh hour the contest had to be moved to Haleiwa on the north shore of Oahu; after strong persuasion from an opposition company, the Hawaiian families withdrew their support and the deal with the Sheridan was off. I was really wild after all the months of negotiations. I could understand how it happened but it was a terrible time for me. I felt I'd not only let Oxbow down but all the longboard surfers who were so excited about having the contest at Makaha. I had failed and our competitor had finally won.

The publicity department had to change all the press releases, though luckily the artwork wasn't locked in because we were waiting on the winner of the $10,000 prize for the best poster and tee-shirt designs to be announced by Fabrice. My brief for the contest poster had been clear and simple, the design should "endeavour to give the true spirit of that year's event, giant waves, Hawaiian heritage, longboards and flowers". The winner was a local Hawaiian surfer/artist named Chris Lundy and I still maintain that his was the best design for any surf contest poster I've ever seen. I asked my friend Randy Rarick to take on the job of contest director. Born in Hawaii, he'd been a friend since the late 1960s when he was the manager of Dewey Weber's surf shop in Honolulu. Randy was, and still is, the Hawaiian representative on the board of the ASP, but as his day-to day-business he runs most of the big surfing events in Hawaii. We had a lot to do with each other in the year prior to the 1993 Haleiwa meet.

One day, after Randy and I had had our heads down in his office working pretty hard for a while, we took a break and walked up to check the surf from his backyard. Sunset was giant, a clean 15 to 20 feet, with no-one out because the sets were closing-out. We both knew Waimea had to be breaking. Randy was still red hot in big waves, he will ride anything and surfs there every time it breaks, but I hadn't surfed Waimea since the accident when the force of the wipe-out tore my cheek, so I was a little gun-shy. Randy convinced me to drive down and have a closer look, so I borrowed a beautiful 9-foot 6-inch board from a mate of his and we took off for Waimea. It was good, perhaps a little too much cross-shore wind creating a little bump, but hey, it was Waimea Bay, breaking clean at 20 feet. However there were a lot of people out, twenty hotties getting ready for the Eddie Aikau contest that was on hold right then and another 20 wannabees. The days of going for a surf at Waimea with just a few mates are gone forever. Then Randy had an idea. What about an outside reef-break called Blowfish? The wind was just right he thought, but I discovered later that he hadn't surfed there for years. We had Porter, one of Randy's best mates, with us as well as the great-grandson of the Duke, David Kahanamoku. I was really pleased to meet and talk to David as I'd never really had a chance to talk to the Duke before senility overtook him.

Randy drove down the coast to the closest point from where we could check the waves at Blowfish. My three friends were peering through their binoculars and after five minutes someone handed me a pair, but I couldn't see a thing. It looked like mountains of foam everywhere; nothing even resembling an organised break that we could surf. The rest of the crew were all talking about what they were seeing but I felt like the odd man out until it was pointed out to me. On Randy's instructions I followed the river channel with the glasses and there, after really concentrating, I got to see one of the most amazing sights of my surfing life: an 18-foot, perfectly bowling right and left with not a ripple on the face from the light offshore breeze. I was dumbstruck, all my life I'd waited for this. We waxed up and paddled close together in the channel for a half an hour, slowly closing in on the magnificent beasts grazing in the one spot, wave after beautiful wave. I watched everyone get one, saw them all tear off down the line, disappear for ten minutes then come paddling back out through the channel. I'll never forget my first wave at Blowfish; it was probably 20 feet, the biggest one I caught in the four hours I stayed out. After the session I paddled back to the beach feeling guilty because I'd been out on my own for the last twenty minutes. I'd simply lost all track of time. The unique thing about that day at Blowfish was that the break seemed just like small waves on a perfect reef; it was like riding 4-foot Angourie magnified five times. I've never surfed big waves with the same freedom I did that day. I got a couple of perfect tubes, probably the only ones I'll ever get at that size unless I'm lucky enough to one day have a go at tow-in surfing where the surfer is towed into the waves by an inflatable boat. I flew home to Ti and the kids on a high. What a trip.

* * * * * * *

The Friday afternoon following my return, I rolled the little Maule out of its hangar at Palmers Island near Angourie, topped up the tanks, washed her and checked everything. She was just perfect, needed a little air in the tyres but as we were taking off and landing on grass strips it wasn't critical. Next day I took off for the farm, Ti next to me and Bryce and Nava in the back. It was an easy twenty-minute flight that we'd made a hundred times and I wasn't too alarmed when I realised I had overshot the landing a little. I hadn't flown for 3 months and as it was a short strip I decided I'd go around and set the landing up again, giving me more room to roll out after touchdown. We were at seven and a half metres and halfway down the runway when I applied full power – the engine jumped to life and we climbed to about 30 metres when suddenly the engine died. I told Ti to tighten the kids' belts, it looked as though we were going in, then I gave my full attention to trying to get us down in one piece. Frantically moving the throttle in and out gave no response and the hill at the back of the runway was coming up fast. Jim and I had cleaned all the trees off the paddock to put in the strip but it was pretty rough country with stumps and holes everywhere. I held the Maule off, just clearing the hill and hovering over the first big stumps before putting it gently in on the downhill slope. I felt one of the wheels collapse; that side dropped, scraping along the ground and sending us careering into a stump and one wing was almost torn off. When we came to a stop, Ti got the kids out and I automatically turned off the fuel and disconnected the battery. We were all in one piece, that was the main thing, but very badly shaken up. Bryce was crying and Ti was comforting him and Nava. Then the neighbours came running across the paddock; I told them we were OK, but I looked down at my hands, which were shaking, and as the neighbours walked away I watched the shaking get worse. I guess it was shock from the fact that we'd walked away from what could have been a fatal accident. It was a traumatic experience and this, when added to the problems of the past year, called for some serious recovery time – but I was too stupid to do it.

I was stressing; I just couldn't understand why the accident had happened, what made the motor quit? Back at the farm I rang the

Department of Aviation who said that I'd done well; no-one was hurt. They told me to ring my insurance company if I wanted an investigation into the accident as the Department wasn't really interested. The neighbours had told the police about the accident, and they came belting across the paddock, leaving after they'd looked at the crash site. They in turn called the media and it was on the local news within an hour. I couldn't get to sleep that night for worrying about the cause of the crash. We went back to Angourie that night and I picked up the investigator at the airport in Grafton on the Monday morning. He spent a day pulling everything down but couldn't come up with any reason for the motor having given up. I stood round like an expectant father, holding tools, going over the accident in every detail and trying to come up with what I'd done wrong. Just on nightfall the investigator asked me to put my ear to the main fuel tank while he blew into the air inlet. When I heard bubbles I was to give him the thumbs up. I strained my ears and though I could see the investigator go red in the face from blowing, I heard nothing. "That's it," he said, telling me to get him 6 metres of light-gauge wire. He started feeding the wire into the air breather and within a few minutes we were both covered in wasp larvae and the mud from the nest. Mud wasps had built a nest, cutting off the flow of fuel which in turn stopped the motor. Well at least I knew how the accident happened, but my prize toy was broken. I kept telling myself it could have been worse and it really didn't matter, the plane was simply a material possession.

In the official accident report published in its magazine, the Department's summing-up was brutal but accurate: "the pilot failed to check the air inlet before flight resulting in starvation of fuel in flight, no injuries sustained". Max sent me a cutting from the States where there'd only been one other reported accident like this; the aircraft had been left idle for a month at the wrong time of year and mud-daubers' nest-building activities had brought down a helicopter with fatal consequences. That put it into perspective. We were all still alive to talk about it and I felt strangely comforted.

Despite having started so well the year was turning into a complete disaster. Perhaps I wasn't really cut out for the jet-set lifestyle. I found myself starting to question my work for Oxbow, though whenever those negative thoughts started to surface I put them out of my head. I liked the people and the job. All my life it seems that everything happens for the best and I had to have faith. Sure the crash was a bummer, but we were going to collect a big lump-sum insurance payout as the Maule was regarded as a total write-off.

I got back into the job at hand, the next stage of the development at Angourie, a new house for us and six larger units. It had been a

TOM AUGUSTINE

Another perfect tube.

SYLVAIN

From the left, me, John Bell, FX and Hans Hedemann
at Portsea, Victoria, Easter 1990.

fight just getting the project to the final planning stages, though buying the land had been a classic case of being in the right place at the right time. My friend JB had wanted to live at Angourie from the first time he visited the place. He'd always stay with us and over time his three-day weekends became a regular occurrence every few weeks. At a crown-land auction in 1992, JB was the successful bidder on a beautiful house block overlooking the ocean and we were just walking away from the sale when I realised that there was no-one left to bid for the larger parcels of development land. We went into a huddle and formed a partnership just before the auctioneer announced the details of the parcel to be sold. I put up my hand and made a bid, there were no other bidders and so Ti and I, representing the hastily formed partnership, had bought another piece of real estate. JB, one of his Melbourne friends and I were of like minds about the way the project should look but the fourth partner had very different ideas. Ti and I convinced JB that a unit in Angourie was much more practical than a house; somewhere he could call his own and we could rent it out for him when he wasn't around. I called an old mate on the Gold Coast and re-sold the house block that week for the same amount JB had paid for it.

* * * * * * *

Paul Witzig was again the architect for the job. Ti and I looked after all the council details and over many meetings with Paul methodically worked through all the same problems that we'd encountered a few years earlier with the first stage of "Nat's at the Point". The council told us we could have eleven units, but that wouldn't have allowed for any green areas, so we decided on seven. Paul had very strong feelings about what constituted good design for the north coast, the place he'd lived with his family for ten years. He had come to understand what was practical in a residence for either short-term or permanent living. The first requirement is a big deck. One of the real delights is being able to sit in the open and over a drink watch the fading light change the colours of the clouds. The next consideration is the heat; it is very hot and sticky in January and February and unless the ceilings are high and natural breezeways are created, staying indoors is totally out of the question, even in the dead of night. Paul's designs were beautiful and extremely practical. It's quite incredible, really, that I didn't at first understand the implications of his designs and their effects on the public. Many guests come here because of the architecture. It inspires them to do better, live better, surf better, be a better person. Sure the fact that we have protection from both northerly and southerly winds makes Angourie special, and it has a few good waves occasionally, but it's the inspirational buildings that keep them coming back year after year.

* * * * * * *

When the quotes had come back in, JB flew up from Melbourne. In a heated meeting with one of the partners, we decided that the only way we could resolve our differences was by allowing him to build his own two units, providing he stuck to Paul's plans. We signed the contract with the successful builder and JB left for a wedding in Sydney. At one dinner during his week in Angourie he was sitting next to Ti and I noticed them having a heavy heart-to-heart. JB confided to her that he'd had death threats during the past month and was really worried. Ti mentioned it to me after he'd left and I tried to call him but could only get his answering machine. JB's body was found jammed under the wooden seat of the spa in his backyard; that was on 26th September 1993, six days after he had been with us in Angourie.

The police said that it was suicide but at least the coroner ruled that out as it would have been impossible for him to get himself in the position in which he was found. Besides, John had many close friends who knew exactly where he was at, and suicide was completely out of the question. Just the week before he'd got me to hold a ladder – Paul had had to calculate exactly where JB's bedroom would be and he climbed the ladder to get an idea of the view he'd have, a bedroom looking down on the surf at Angourie was his dream. He loved life so much. Sitting in the line-up at the Point on the day he died, I heard his infectious, big horsy laugh and had another sleepless night. I had to take sleeping pills every night for the next week. I kept flashing back to all the good times together: JB and me taking Nyarie to dinner in Bali; putting the lime juice on his coral cuts in Fiji; sitting back watching the Australian Open tennis at Melbourne's Flinders Park. I was devastated. I had lost my best friend, not to mention my business partner, and it really hit me hard.

I noticed a tremor in my hands again. Beau and I cried our eyes out at the funeral but I tried to conceal my feelings in front of everyone. In retrospect two major emotional events in close succession added to my stress and made me very irritable. I found myself flying off the handle easily and I couldn't concentrate or even think about Oxbow. It's interesting to look back on that period of my life. It seemed as though all my emotions had snuck up on me and something had to give – in reality none of us are Superman.

Things weren't improving in my life, it felt as though one wheel had come off the wagon and it was careering out of control down the track. On the whole, the media were sympathetic to JB. They dug up a lot of good and bad facts, but given his high profile, his friends and family had expected it. I did one national interview just to put people right about the suicide speculation and then Ti, the kids and I left for a few days at the farm. We all needed to be with John in our own way; constantly on the phone or staying with us every other week, he'd been a big part of our family's life. I wanted to hide, to go away and not face the problems associated with the building project but the builder was off and running and there were decisions to be made. We had to go ahead but first we had to find some way of working out the financial problems resulting from JB's death. These were major moves for us and it was pretty heavy. We sold every asset that could be quickly turned into cash, including the apartment in Sun Valley and another property we'd received in part payment for the surf shop in Sydney, but we were still short. Then the insurance cheque for the wrecked aeroplane turned up, making our mortgage more manageable – at least the banks were happy and the project would be completed. We would soon own a new house and two units and the remaining two were sold to people who shared our dream for better-designed buildings in Angourie.

That was the year of the big bushfires that threatened most of northern and southern Sydney – what a year it was turning out to be for everyone. We were down in Sydney spending Christmas with Veda at Palm Beach and one afternoon Ti and the kids were at a children's birthday party being given by an old friend. The kids were playing in the front yard when the birthday boy's big brother swung a cricket bat, accidentally smashing Bryce in the face. With blood everywhere Ti flew down to the local hospital where it was confirmed that he'd loosened several teeth and punctured his lips, but worse still, he had a hole straight through his tongue. Bryce was admitted to Mona Vale Hospital and put on a drip for the next three days – with follow-up appointments for years to come with plastic surgeons, dentist and speech therapists! Nava and I stayed close all evening until we were asked to leave by hospital staff as firemen were very close to evacuating the building. From the sixth floor of the hospital Ti and I had discussed how we'd get out if the fires should engulf the building. After sussing out the various exits, we reckoned she could grab Bryce and run to the beach. The orange glow in the west looked really threatening through the windows and I was really worried on the way home. We stopped on top of Bushranger Hill, the highest point on the Peninsula, and overlooked one of the most amazing sights I've ever seen. Two houses on the distant hillside just exploded into flames; one minute the fire touched the building and then with a boom the whole thing went up. Five minutes later another was destroyed in the same way.

21

It's up to you – make it a beautiful life

THINGS HAD TO GET BETTER, they couldn't get much worse. By my reckoning this was the most disastrous period of my life. I had to put the wheels back on and get my family back on track. Spending a few weeks skiing in Sun Valley was the normal program for us at this time of year so we left Bryce, our little wounded soldier, with Grandma and in January 1994, Ti, Nava, Naomi and I took off for America. I had to represent Oxbow at the main USA surfing trade show in San Diego at the end of the month. Fabrice had arranged for me to meet Oxbow's new Japanese importers to discuss next summer's longboard promotion, so combining a family holiday with work seemed absolutely rational.

Naturally Oxbow was paying for my ticket and as Naomi had started work as a flight attendant with Qantas she got hers for next to nothing and I had more than enough frequent flyer points for Ti and Nava to travel anywhere in the world. Getting to Sun Valley was a familiar, well-polished routine and as a family we'd followed it, with minor variations, for five years: getting a lift out to Malibu from Los Angeles airport, picking up our old Chevy station wagon from behind Max's house and spending the next two days driving through the magnificent Nevada desert to the high plains of Idaho. We were all enjoying the secure feeling of being on familiar turf with only family members for company. We stopped at the same hot springs in the middle of the desert, bathed in the mineral waters and laughed at our mental images of cowboys stumbling into this old shed, stripping off and enjoying their first bath in months.

The Sun Valley ritual, the drive there and the arrival, was like putting on your favourite old tee-shirt, and after the traumatic events of the past year we were grateful to sink into the routine of life in the mountains. After a breakfast of Ti's "downhill porridge", we spent every minute, from the opening of the lifts till the last chair up, skiing down the multifaceted Baldy – the main mountain in the resort. At 9 a.m. Nava and Naomi would go to ski classes and Ti and I would get back into the same program we'd followed the season before. It was always cold first thing in the morning and we tried to stay in the sun as much as possible, skiing fast and smooth on the groomed open ridges to get our legs in. Then it was time to dive into a few runs at high speed, all the way from the top to the bottom on the perfectly manicured corduroy. We always stopped for coffee at 11, then off to the Bowls if the snow had softened sufficiently to ski bumps, until meeting the kids for lunch. Most afternoons were a family cruise and I loved having Nava ski right on my tail as I talked to her about breathing, just as Franz Pickler had done for me all those years ago in Perisher Valley.

I'd picked up some brand-new skis from Michael Brunetto – they were now called Mackwa, Sioux for "wolf" – which reminded me of the Coyotes I'd skied on the previous year, but they were even more stable when you skied the variable snow typical of Baldy. In the course of the 800-metre run down the mountain you could ski through every conceivable type of snow from powder, to crust, to ice, and these beauties handled it all; they never once gave way or lost track at high speed. I grew very confident on my 203 cm GS Mackwas. Whenever necessary I went in to Michael's ski-tuning shop out the back of the factory and worked on all our equipment. I still really like doing this as it makes such a huge difference to the skis' performance and the physical contact with files and wax makes surfing and skiing even more closely related.

After a couple of weeks Joel (Boris) Tudor came up from San Diego with Terry English, a really hot snowboarder from Santa Barbara. Though Ti and Nava were a bit reluctant, the rest of us were dead keen to try snowboarding and Terry was really keen to give us all lessons. Oxbow had sent samples of the new line of snowboards, a winterstick with edges, a single ski that I could stand on in a surfing style. After a few hours of adjusting, we were all ripping down the beginners' slopes on Dollar Mountain. It was simple, all the breathing and movements were exactly the same as skiing. Why had I resisted for so long? The carving potential seemed incredible and I found I could drive a turn even longer and more solidly than on my single ski. During the next few days we all got stuck into our snowboards, then one day, for some reason Ti and Nava decided to stick with their conventional skis. Naomi and Boris went back to Dollar for a few more lessons with Terry, but I decided I was good enough to board Baldy for my first time.

I loved the feeling of being on a real mountain with my snowboard. All the runs had about an inch of groomed powder and I carved all over the mowed corduroy with some boarding mates I happened to meet in the lift line. I was amazed at the amount of power that could be loaded into the board on one turn and then the turn linking to it and the next. It was a carver's heaven, at 50 km/h my face would sometimes be only a few inches from the snow. Where had this been all my life? I was converted completely, I'd never go back to two skis or even the single. I met Ti and Nava midway through the afternoon and I took them to see what a board could do. On the final run late in the afternoon we came to one of the steeper slopes called Flying Squirrel. The girls went on ahead and I waited for the run to clear of people before taking off. I was doing big driving turns down the edge of the groomed slope, trying to get as much soft snow as possible, when right in the middle of one gigantic carve the board let go. I know now that it was where a faulty jet on the snow maker had been spewing out water during the previous night. The water froze rock solid and was then covered with a dusting of powder from a light snow fall. After hundreds of skiers had shaved off all the soft snow a big area of sheet ice was exposed, just waiting for a hoon like me to come belting along at top speed. I didn't see it at all and spun out, losing it on the ice; one edge is just not enough to hold in at that speed. I really didn't know it had happened; I was so into the carve and had so much power loaded into the turn that I went up in the air, over a small cliff and into the forest, coming in contact with a tree as I landed. The next thing I was aware of was Ti's voice. It took her over 45 minutes to get back up the mountain and another 10 minutes for the ski patrol to arrive. The fastest way to find me was to go up on the lift and ski down to where Ti had last seen me. She and Nava then split up and side-slipped either side of the run, looking for me in the trees and calling my name. I must have been close to consciousness, as I replied when I heard my name being called, enabling them to find me. Ti took the still-attached board off my feet and steadied me, while the patrolman stuffed a bandage in the gaping wound in my head. Then they strapped me into the banana boat for the ride down the mountain to the waiting ambulance.

It was hard to think clearly, but in the hospital when Ti and I talked about the accident, it was possible to make sense out of what had happened. I'd always held to the "shit happens" theory and if you do the things I do then some day the shit will hit the fan, as they say. The shit and the fan seemed to be coming into contact with amazing regularity as far as I was concerned. The snowboarding wipe-out on top of the plane crash, JB's death, Bryce's run in with the cricket bat, not to mention all the dramas with the partner over the second stage of Angourie. It was enough to make me want to give up and I wondered if anything else could possibly be thrown at me.

The cut in the back of my head took 28 stitches and I had severe concussion, hypothermia and my kidneys and hip were badly

MARK REINEMANN

Mount Baldy in Sun Valley is a formidable mountain, one of the most challenging in the world. I put it down to Murphy's Law that one of the snow guns was faulty on the night of January 17, 1994, creating a big area of ice by the next morning. I hit the ice at full speed resulting in my worst ever skiing wipeout.

439

bruised. My head was the worst injury but I was passing blood for the first few days and that got me really worried. The nurse caring for me was an Aussie girl from Angourie, a real coincidence. I don't remember the doctor at all, but Donna's care and attention seemed to bring me around in record time. After several days in hospital I was feeling good enough to get into a heated discussion with Ti over our next move. The brain scans showed no blood clots and though there was a fair bit of bruising there was no permanent damage. As far as I was concerned that was reason enough to parry Ti's insistence that I call Oxbow with the news of the accident and we all go directly to Australia. She wanted me to see a doctor in Sydney then re-charge the batteries for a few months at home in Angourie. I resisted, convinced that I was OK. I could feel something wasn't quite right with my head but being the stubborn fool that I am, I put on a brave front and insisted that we all go ahead with the plans we'd made prior to the accident. I did make one concession however: number-one daughter Naomi could come with me to the trade show in San Diego so she could be there to hold my hand and keep me company.

We drove back to Los Angeles from where Ti and Nava flew back to Oz, and Naomi and I booked into a luxury hotel next to the convention centre in San Diego. I had a good time seeing all my old friends, talking to loads of shopkeepers about buying Oxbow and trying to go easy on the number of parties we attended. During one intense meeting with the Japanese I looked down and saw my hand was shaking again and then my head started to throb. I tried to ignore it but I'd never had a headache like it before. The pain was indescribable. I excused myself from the meeting and went to my room, where I took the strongest pills Naomi could buy at the drug store and went to bed. Naomi knew I was sick, we were both scared and I knew I had to avoid that pain again. We left for Australia a few days later and the minute the plane got to 10,000 metres the headache started again. I took everything I had and asked the steward for more.

Ti had been home for ten days by this time and I collapsed into her arms at Lismore airport. I felt faint, but incredibly relieved to have actually made it back to her in one piece. She was worried about me, saying that I looked pale and drawn and worse than she'd ever seen me. I pacified her explaining that it was all the travel; a few days at home resting would see me right, but I knew something was seriously wrong. I mentioned the headaches to her but played down their severity and intensity. I had come so close to asking the hostess on the flight home to call for a doctor to help me, but the number of pills I took knocked me out cold for the whole flight. I was having trouble concentrating on any level, even telephone numbers were difficult to dial, and it was impossible for me to meditate, something I'd been doing religiously every day since 1984. I couldn't get any clarity but I still tried first thing every morning. However, every time I'd try to breathe deep and relax, even before I started repeating the mantra, a stabbing pain would shoot into my head and intensify. I'd been taking the strongest pills I could buy over the counter in America, but they gave no relief any more. Something was radically wrong with my head and it was time to come clean and tell Ti how bad I really was. Ti insisted that we go and talk to our friend and doctor David Hope about the accident and my problems. He explained that serious head injuries take time to heal and gave me a prescription for stronger pills to relieve the pain. David also said he needed the advice of a specialist and that he'd contact a psychiatrist to get a second opinion – it was a bit out of his league as a country GP.

Back at Angourie the waves were really pumping. I watched for a week, trying to stay out of the water, but it was impossible. There's an old saying: "only a surfer knows the feeling" – it really is a type of addiction. I had no control over it and just had to have my fix. I like to think it was my destiny, but was it just stupidity? I know now that I wasn't facing up to how sick I really was, telling myself that my problems were all physical. Surely a big strong guy like me could overcome a little belt in the head. When Doctor Hope took the stitches out of my head I was feeling fine and that was the signal to go. I went home and grabbed my board, paddled out at the point and took off on a solid 6-footer.

I didn't even get to my feet before the lip pitched me over the falls. I guess my leg-rope snapped, I can't remember. While swimming in I reached down to feel what I thought was a knock on my leg and felt two of my fingers slide inside a 15-centimetre gash in my calf muscle. On the beach I could see that the cut was all the way to the bone. One of the outside fins on my thruster had been driven into the flesh like an axe, breaking the fin off the board. I left my board on the beach and stumbled home, holding the muscle together with one hand and supporting myself with the other. That was it; now I had no choice, I had to rest because I could no longer walk. It seemed so very simple when I thought about it later, if I wasn't going to rest off my own bat, the option would be taken away from me. Unfortunately the accident happened on a Sunday when our doctor was out sailing with his family so Ti drove me to the local hospital where the doctor on duty stitched me up but for some totally unknown reason didn't put in any internal stitches. Ti noticed this and questioned him about it, but was told: "I do know how to sew up a wound!"

After a week of staying in bed the muscle and the wound were still really swollen and painful and pus began oozing from between the stitches. I had a serious infection because the doctor at the hospital didn't take the time to stitch the inside of such a deep cut. Doctor Hope came out to see me, giving me antibiotics for the infection and a strong sedative to ease my recurring headaches and I stayed flat on my back for a month. I had plenty of good books, a loving family and loads of interesting people coming by every day, so it was tolerable. With all the care and rest the headaches started to subside and David Hope changed pills after talking to the psychiatrist. I could see some light at the end of the tunnel; I was getting better. The specialist said the brain would repair itself in time and I just had to go easy and take the sedatives he prescribed until the headaches stopped altogether.

* * * * * * *

The Oxbow licensee in Japan signed up a young Japanese man who'd been given one of the finest educations I'd ever heard of, starting with schools in Japan and Switzerland and ending with Pepperdine University in Malibu. I met Takuji Masuda or "Tak" as I came to know him, through Boris. He had the most determination I've ever seen in a young man and wanted to master surfing in the shortest time possible, as he really needed to prove his worth to his father. At the last trade show I'd attended he'd asked if he and a few Japanese friends could come and visit me in Angourie. I'm not sure what they thought when they arrived to find me lying flat on my back after the fin-through-the-calf job though. Tak explained to me later that in ancient Japanese culture a man was judged partly by the number of battle wounds on his body – providing he was still alive, he gained respect. After a week of talking at my bedside, the Japanese left for home and I'd agreed to go to Japan as soon as I was feeling up to it.

I hadn't had a migraine for over a week and I was stoked, I really began to believe I was getting better. The calf wound had healed and it was time to hit the road again. It was time for the Oxbow summer tour, a prearranged promotional event for the European importers that we'd been working on for the past year. Our longboard surf team from Hawaii, California, Japan and Australia would fly into Pisa, Italy, to be met by Oxbow's ground staff. Together we'd visit France, Holland, England and the Channel Isles, putting on surfing displays and staging a longboard contest in each country we visited. It was scheduled as a six-week tour and the publicity department had planned just about every minute of every day, in a surf shop, on the beach or with the media, all of which I was really looking forward to. Under normal circumstances this would have been a real pleasure, but I was sick and not admitting it.

On the way to Italy I kept my promise to Tak and went to Japan. I took Beau with me as Fabrice and Isabelle had both let me know how impressed they were with him after they'd met in Europe. Japan was a blast; we had very little surf for the longboard contest but that really didn't matter. We weren't expecting any waves, it was all about meeting people and setting the wheels in motion for selling Oxbow to one of the potentially biggest markets in the world. The parties were big; karioke had just hit Japan and a lot of the executives of the importing company were delighted to let their hair down for what seemed like the first time in their corporate lives.

Tak, Beau and I flew to Paris and then on to Oxbow's head office in Bordeaux to pick up some of the new season's clothes and to allow me to get some up-to-date information on the state of the surf market in Europe that summer. I was having a drink with Isabelle in her new rooftop garden when she asked me about the effects of the snowboard accident. I brushed it off with typical masculine bravado, telling her I was fine, never felt better. I've no idea why men always react that way when a woman asks them an honest question. I just blurted it out without even thinking. We got on to other topics and she told me that Boris had cut his hair. I'd never told Boris outright not to cut his hair, but he knew he wasn't supposed to, as long hair was part of the image. But Isabelle thought he still looked cool and he was still my friend Boris to me.

One of the things I intended to do while I was at the office was to have a serious discussion with Fabrice about the effects of the accident. I'd had another migraine on the flight to France and was taking heavy sleeping pills to get to sleep at night. Unfortunately Fabrice was too busy to talk to me right then, so I decided we'd do it on the phone in the next few days. There was plenty of time. Whatever we decided wouldn't change the situation I was in right then and I had to finish the promotion. I always tell my kids it's not what you start that counts but finishing is everything!

The three of us then flew to Italy to meet the rest of the team. The "roady" and his girl had already arrived, driving a van with all the gear and towing the 1956 Ford "Woody" station wagon. On Fabrice's authority Terry English and I had gone out the year before and bought the best Woody we could find and shipped it to France. The idea was to travel with the timeless symbol of surfing and create a lasting image in the kids' minds that could be triggered anytime we wanted by returning with the Woody, even without the full team. It was my idea that Oxbow buy the car and I'd chosen it from among the twenty or so available in California at the time. It had a fully reconditioned chassis, new timber on the exterior and a big powerful V8 under the bonnet – it was in immaculate shape. Under the insurance conditions, the roady was the only one allowed to drive the vehicle. I said I didn't mind, but the restriction defeated the whole concept of the hot longboard surfers driving the Woody from the surf shop to the beach. It pulled the key element out of the promotion and I was a bit pissed off, though I didn't tell Fabrice. Basically the roady's job was to pay the bills, set up the beach with flags, tents and so on, and look after all the day-to-day details of keeping the circus on the road – but when I started to really go under he ended up doing a lot more than that.

I'd met an Italian surfer while playing tennis in Biarritz the previous summer. President of the Italian Surfers Association, he kept in touch throughout the year and came to pick us up in Pisa, along with representatives from Oxbow's Italian importer. Everything went like clockwork for the promotion in Viareggio. We had a really strong team with Tak, Boris, Beau, and a young Hawaiian kid named Duane DeSoto, and of course FX, who flew in for the weekend. Having no waves of any consequence in the Mediterranean led to other diversions and for the youngsters that involved chasing the local girls. I didn't deal with the problem at all. I really didn't even know about it until it was too late. I should have sat them down and talked about how far they could go. But I couldn't make decisions, the headaches had started again in earnest and were becoming a daily event, especially with the intense summer sun and the necessity to be out on the beach or in the surf most of the day. I was feeling so bad it was impossible to operate at all unless I was loaded up on pain killers and sedatives to sleep at night and I suppose I was passing many of my responsibilities and problems on to the roady. Not speaking a language other than English made it a bit difficult for the boys, after a big night out dancing at the disco they inevitably ended up in one room for a smoke before falling asleep. No-one was exactly sure how it happened, but one night young Boris ended up in the arms of the roady's girlfriend. The romance continued for the whole tour with the couple finally setting up a love nest in London until they were coaxed out of it.

By the time we crossed the English Channel to Cornwall, I was feeling really crook. I was sure the sun was making my headaches worse so I was staying out of it and going to bed straight after dinner every night. The tour was becoming a personal nightmare but I had to see it through and I still hadn't talked to Fabrice about what was happening. I don't know why; it just didn't happen, but I learnt later that the roadie had been talking to Fabrice because of the problems.

Naomi with me in France. She stayed on, learning French fluently, and that helped her get a job with Qantas.

Bryce aged 5 years. On safari in Zimbabwe.

Tak and Beau arriving at the Headland Hotel in
Cornwall, England.
(That's the rear of the Woody we used for the
European tour in '94).

Naomi was flying in to London on one of her first overseas jobs as a flight attendant with Qantas and it was also her 23rd birthday. All the time she'd spent in France learning to speak the language fluently had been the key to her getting the job with Qantas. Ti and I had to force her to go and stay in France, as she'd wanted to get married at 17, and it had been a tough fight for both us and Naomi. It was worth an extravagant birthday party to let her know how proud I was. After a month on the road Beau was also keen to see his sister; they've always been tight and Naomi mothers him.

The English importer's girlfriend and I chose the menu and laid out the place cards for fifty people in the main dining room of the Headlands Hotel. With its magnificent big bay windows looking out to sea and the craggy rocky islets, it was a dramatic and fitting setting for Naomi's birthday dinner. A few old friends came down from London including Jackie Kelly and her daughter Lisa whom I hadn't seen for years. It was a wonderful night and cost me a fortune, far more than I'd ever spent on any party before, but I didn't consider the money. I was high on spending and caught up in the euphoria of being in one of the most beautiful banquet rooms in what is still my favourite hotel in the world. Not that the Headlands is five-star, it isn't, but it's clean and big, with style and ambience. Perched on the end of the point, it's actually an old castle and overlooks Fistral Beach in Newquay. I fell in love with Cornwall through that hotel, or more correctly, a house 100 metres across the golf course from the hotel. With absolutely nothing to obstruct the views of Fistral Beach and the coast, it was built for the owner's mother in the same style as the hotel and was for sale. I couldn't resist, I had to have it. I know now that this reaction and the fantastic but grandiose party were symptoms of the sickness I had, but at the time I saw it as a solution to all my problems with travelling between Europe and Australia.

I'd talked to Fabrice about moving to France but I don't think he thought I was serious. Ti and I had discussed a move like that on several occasions when I became depressed with Australian politics or the abundance of uncaring people that seem to live in Australia. Ti didn't really like France after having had one particularly bad experience while skiing in the Alps as a kid. She sincerely believed it was "a nice place to visit but wouldn't want to live there". I was trying very hard to convince her that living in Europe would cut down a great deal of travel for me and would be a good experience for the kids and anyway, we could go home for holidays. It all seemed so logical to me and when she seemed to come around a bit during one call I made an offer on the old mansion near the Headlands Hotel. It had six bedrooms and an observatory, atrium,

Beau asked me what to say... I said to ask the Hawaiian Princess what she's got under her coconuts.

stables and established herb garden. When I woke Ti up that night after making the offer and asked her to organise a deposit, she called her mum for a quick loan. For some unknown reason we were gazumped on the house deal, the agent told me only that he had a better offer and sent the money back. I didn't even have a chance to discuss the matter with him but for some reason I was more relieved than upset. Ti had known how unrealistic it all was and I think I was relieved because at some level I knew it too.

I didn't tell Fabrice about the house, or my idea of living in Cornwall and coming to work in Bordeaux each week. When we finally did get a chance to talk it was on the phone from Jersey in the Channel Isles, our last stop before the team members headed off to their respective homes. The pills were making me behave irrationally and it was impossible to get early nights. The Oxbow importer had organised some beautiful parties but I hated the state I was in.

Beau was very worried about me and kept telling me to rest and not come to the beach but I couldn't stay away. Fabrice was also very worried, having heard stories of my irrational behaviour from the roady. Along with everything that had happened on the way to the Channel Isles, I'd driven the Woody when I knew I shouldn't and at one of the parties in Jersey I'd grabbed Duane DeSoto by the throat when I thought something he'd said to a girl wasn't Oxbow style. Then there was the issue of buying the house in Cornwall – Fabrice was blown out, the pills, the headaches, obviously all bought on by the accident in Sun Valley. He told me to go home to Australia and see a doctor as soon as possible. I understood what he was saying.

On the flight home the migraines were the worst ever, so bad in fact that I broke the journey in Singapore in an attempt to relieve the pain before going on. David Hope sent me to a specialist in Sydney who did a bunch of tests over the next year or so, helping me to understand the effects of the head injury and deal with the situation. The most important thing, the psychiatrist said, was to change my lifestyle; no more travel for the time being. When I thought back to the month I had stayed home after returning from the United States, I remembered the headaches had got much better. I had to stay in one place, give it some time, and slowly my head would mend.

* * * * * * *

Over a period of a few weeks I was able to get back into twenty-minute meditations, and that was the first breakthrough. I also cut out the sleeping pills most of the time and through staying at home and surfing every day just for exercise, I got my body and mind back

SIMON WILLIAMS

MIKE LARDER

Above, with my darling Nava at Noosa Heads in the summer of 1997-98. She is a keen competitor which makes me very proud.

Opposite at the top, this cutback was taken at home a few months ago. Below, the second stage of our Angourie project was completed September '94.

in working order. Now when I think about it, I wonder how it was possible to live for ten years at the pace I had. I was an accident waiting to happen. My priorities were totally wrong and the accident was a blessing in disguise, alerting me to the fact that I had to slow down, that I was behaving in a manic way and that I had to take the time to smell the flowers. I stopped all international travel for two years, resigned from the ASP board, and Fabrice and I adjusted my position with Oxbow so that now I only work as a model for the catalogues. Most of all I admitted that I was sick and put my faith in the professionalism of the local doctor and the psychiatrist. It hasn't all been plain sailing. In situations where I've been under stress I haven't always handled things rationally, but if I'm kind to myself I have the ability to consider other people.

* * * * * * *

Working on the book you are reading has been very therapeutic. The psychiatrist in Sydney and our local GP both agreed it was a good idea to sit and think and write my memoirs at my own pace. It's taken years, pulling the relevant sections from a book of short stories I'd almost completed after *The History of Surfing* was finished and putting them in chronological order. Certainly it would have been impossible without Mum's ten scrap books in which she kept a faithful record of all her little boy's movements up until she died in 1972. I kept my own diaries from the late 1960s on, so tracking my movements and thoughts has been a real trip.

And so I sit comfortably in Angourie with my loving family and good friends to play with. Sometimes I don't drive a car for a week. Going out for me involves a walk to the point to check the surf, sitting down quietly watching the waves and trying to decide which board to ride if it's any good. If it's junk weather, I decide whether to dive in the pool or ride a few waves on a Malibu for exercise. Often, I think back to those parting words of Ti's 90-year-old Uncle Sid: "Hurry slowly".

The 7th of March, 1998, at the Noosa Surf Festival. Bryce is 7, Beau 23, Ti 40, I am 50 and Nava is 14 years of age. Peter Simons took the photo.

Glossary

ABC, the: Australian Broadcasting Commission (now Corporation). Australia's public, taxpayer-funded radio and television network.

Barby: A barbecue, both the event and the cooking appliance.

Bob: A shilling; twelve pence; one twentieth of one pound. See also Pre-decimal currency.

Bob Hope: Australian rhyming slang for dope, i.e. marijuana.

Bobby Limb (up there with): Bobby Limb, a popular TV personality in the 1960s and 1970s, co-hosted a show with his wife Dawn Lake. Exercising their rapier-like wit, young males of that era (including this editor) would describe rising before daylight as being "up there with Bobby Limb", i.e. at the crack of dawn.

Boil the billy: Make a cup of tea. A billy is a round, metal container with a looped handle used to boil water on a campfire. These days, the term extends to plugging in an electric kettle!

Bombora, (Bombie): From a Darug Aboriginal word for a submerged or partly submerged reef that causes waves to rise and sometimes break; the breakers themselves.

Boomer: A superlative for anything large or exceptionally good.

Bottle shop: A liquor store; an off-licence.

Boxing Day: The day after Christmas Day, believed to be so named because in bygone times it was the day on which boxes, or presents, were handed out.

Brass razoo (didn't get a): The smallest conceivable amount of money.

Carked it: Dead, given up the ghost; also to cark it. In Australia at least, probably from the sound made by ravens and crows, the wardens of the dead (Ed. personal comment).

Chip-heater: A device connected to the bathroom water supply and in which woodpile chips, twigs and scrap paper were burnt to heat water – with surprising efficiency – for the bath tub. Collecting fuel for the "woofer" was the bane of many a youngest sibling's life.

Christmas holidays: In Australia, the long school vacation of approximately six weeks begins just before Christmas.

Chunder: To vomit, especially after over-indulging in alcohol.

Close out dumper: A wave that breaks along its entire length at once, virtually collapsing on itself.

Cyclone: A hurricane. The cyclone season, (approximately December to March) coincides with the monsoon or "Wet" season in northern Australia and cyclones can have effects reaching far inland and down the coasts.

Deck, to: Knock someone to the ground.

Dinky: Brand name – used generically – of a range of sturdy metal toys, both miniature and of a small ride-on size. In this case, Nat refers to a child's tricycle.

Fibro: Asbestos-cement sheeting, popular as a cheap building material in the commodity-scarce days after the Second World War.

Gammy: Crook; not functioning properly, e.g, a gammy leg is a lame or injured leg.

Gong, the: Abbreviation for Wollongong.

Grommet: a young surfer.

Gyro Gearloose: Wacky Disney character known for his eccentric behaviour.

Hitch/ing: To hitch-hike.

Hostess: Female flight attendants in less-enlightened times.

Huey: the surf god, bringer of waves, e.g., "send 'em up Huey".

Leash, leg rope, goon cord: a line from the surfboard attached to the ankle by a velcro strap.

Lolly: Candy, sweet.

Maggie: Australian dialect for *Gymnorhina tibicen*, the Australian magpie, a bird superficially resembling its European namesake. Common in urban areas, the maggie is a much-admired, bold, black-and-white bird with a beautiful song. During the breeding season some individuals become extremely aggressive, "divebombing" passers by and sometimes even inflicting head wounds with the powerful beak.

Measurements: In common with many other sports, surfing still clings to the imperial system for many of its measurements. 30 centimetres are roughly one foot, one metre is equal to 1.09 yards, one kilometre is about 0.621 of a mile, an ounce equals 29.3 grams, and a gallon equals 4.55 litres.

Milk money: Money left out each night, in or under the empty bottles, to pay the milkman for the delivery. For most people back then, running an account with the "milko" would have been unthinkable.

Mug: A term of derision, often used to describe football umpires, "Put yer glasses on yer dirty mug", and slow-scoring batsmen at cricket matches, "'ave a go yer mug".

North Shore, the: The suburbs over the Harbour Bridge from central Sydney and often a synonym for wealth and privilege. Also the northern shore of the Hawaiian island of Oahu.

Out the back: Further out to sea, behind the break.

Peninsula, The: As its name implies, a peninsula on the north-eastern outskirts of Sydney, famed for its many fine beaches and bounded on one side by Pittwater and on the other by the Tasman Sea. Its suburbs, including Collaroy where Nat grew up, are known collectively as the Northern Beaches.

Perve: (Noun, verb and adjectival noun.) To ogle in a lecherous way.

Pissed: Drunk. To be extremely drunk is to be as pissed as a newt, among other things.

Pom: (sometimes Pommy); an Australian term, mostly derogatory, for someone born in England. Its origins have been hotly debated for most of this century but remain obscure.

Pram: Perambulator; baby carriage.

Pre-decimal currency: In today's values, ten shillings – the equivalent of the present Australian dollar when decimal currency was introduced in 1966 – would be worth almost $8. One pound, ten shillings and sixpence (366 pence) is written £1.10.6. Abbreviations included: shilling, s or /- and pence, d.

Purler: Something outstanding; incredibly good.

Pushie: A bicycle; also pushbike.

Quid: £1. See also Pre-decimal currency.

Racehorse: A very thin joint.

Railway sleepers: In the USA, cross-ties.

Recess: In Australian schools a short break from studies taken mid-morning and mid-afternoon. In the 1950s, free milk was given to schoolchildren as part of a health program. Most schools of the time lacked refrigeration facilities and the milk was often left standing in the open, even in summer. I doubt there's an Australian who attended school in those days who can't still taste that sun-warmed, not-quite-sour "school milk".

Roaring forties: The region of the southern hemisphere roughly bounded by latitudes in the 40-degree range. It is characterised by almost constant winds, of gale force and beyond, whose effects are felt along Australia's south and south-west coasts.

Rum Corps: The New South Wales Corps, the English regiment charged with upholding the law in New South Wales when it was still a prison settlement. Its officers controlled the illicit rum trade and through it the infant colony.

Saturday matinee: Afternoon or mid-morning screenings of films for kids, usually of the B-grade western variety, and usually featuring a serial.

Sausage board: A surfboard rounded at both ends.

Seppo: A citizen of the USA. In the classic tradition of Australian slang, this is a slang word for the rhyming slang for another slang word: Seppo=Septic Tank=Yank.

Sets: a group of waves.

Sharky break (or water): A break likely to be frequented by sharks, such as near a river mouth or estuary.

Shout: To pay for a round of drinks. Also the round of drinks itself.

Single-spinner: A Ford car; named for the bullet-shape decoration in the radiator grille; a twin-spinner had two.

Sitting up like Jackie: Like a peasant riding in a king's coach. This peculiarly Australian expression once had racist connotations – Jackie was formerly a generic name for an Aboriginal man – but age and usage have mellowed it.

Snag: A sausage; also snarlers, snorkers and mystery bags.

Southerly Buster: A wild southerly wind that springs suddenly to life along the coast of NSW – particularly around Sydney on hot summer afternoons – especially following a day of hot, offshore winds.

Station, sheep/cattle: In Australia, any large property – often leasehold – used mainly for grazing sheep or cattle is called a station.

Stomp: Both the function and the dance.

Strainer-post: Heavy fenceposts, placed at the corners of paddocks and braced with a wooden stay, that keep the fence anchored when the fencewires are "strained" or tensioned.

Sydney lace: Decorative cast-iron railings on balconies, etc. widely used on terrace houses.

Surfari: A surf trip in a car, taken mainly in pursuit of waves.

Surf Club: The commonly used abbreviation of the official, Surf Life Saving Club.

Terrace house(s): In the USA a row house. A feature of Sydney, they were built mainly last century to accommodate workers. Chiefly two-storied and narrow, the end houses in a row have one interior wall in common, those between the end houses, two.

Test: International contest; chiefly used in reference to cricket and both codes of rugby football.

Tick: A blood-sucking mite-like animal of the *ixodidae* or *argasidae* families. Common in the Australian bush.

Toothpick: An early type of surfboard, about 4 metres long, made with a plywood skin over a wooden frame.

Ute: Utility; an Australian institution. A light truck based on a car design. Small pick-up.

Wag it (to): Play truant from school.

Washing: Laundry.

Walloper: A police officer.

Westie: The derogatory nickname for someone from Sydney's western suburbs, a sprawling area containing the majority of the city's population and home to some of those at the lower end of the socio-economic scale. Many of these people were displaced from the inner city when the rows of old, run-down terrace houses where they lived were bought and "gentrified", mainly by moneyed professionals.

Yank tank: The large, ostentatious motor cars that were once synonymous with the USA; also Detroit barge.

Frank Povah, editor

SIMON WILLIAMS

The Point is a very proud wave sometimes. It makes you bow your head in respect.

Acknowledgements

Without the following people this book would hardly have been possible: Howard Taylor, Denny Aaberg, Mark Trevitick, Micky Dora, Peter Garrett, Rik Deaton, John Doorley, Andrew Watson, Mark Reinemann, David Knox, Craig Leggat, Drew Kampion, Isabelle Cachot, Frank Povah, Jeff Divine, Simeon Barlow and the people at the National Archives in Sydney, Unice Bishop, Dawn Hyde, Gerald Jenkins, Kim Bradley, Max Schachenmann, Marilyn Burmingham, Robert Kennerson, Terry Purcell, Dusty Whitney, Doug Anderson, Kim Smith, Nyarie and Alma Abbey, Anne Kern, Susie Agoston-O'Connor, John Witzig and Ti Deaton Young.

Nat Young
Angourie, July 1998

Photo credits

John = John Witzig
Alby = Albert Falzon
Kenno = Robert Kennerson
Dick = Dick Hoole
Granny = LeRoy Grannis
Slyvain = Sylvain Cazenave
Rik = Rik Deaton

First published in 1998 by Nymboida Press, 8 Bay Street, Angourie, NSW 2464, Australia. Reprinted 1998, 1999 (twice), 2003.

Every effort has been made by the publisher to trace the copyright holder for each photograph reproduced in this book. In some cases it has not been possible to do so and the publisher sincerely regrets any errors which may have occurred.

National Library of Australia Cataloguing-in-Publication data:

Young, Nat, 1947–
    Nat's Nat, and that's that: an autobiography.

    ISBN 0 646 35778 6.
    ISBN 0 9585750 0 2 (pbk.)

    1. Young, Nat, 1947–. 2. Surfers – Australia – Biography. 3. Surfing – History. I. Title.

797.32092

Design and production by John Witzig, Mullumbimby, NSW 2482, Australia.
Editing by Frank Povah
Proofing by Anne Kern

Printed in Singapore by PH Productions Pte Ltd